What Whistle Would You Play at Your Mother's Funeral?

◆─────────────◆

L.E. McCullough's Writings on
Irish Traditional Music, 1974-2016

◆─────────────◆

Edited by L.E. McCullough

Volume I: Dissertation and Theses
Volume II: Everything Else

───────────────

Volume I: Dissertation and Theses

Published by Silver Spear Publications

P.O. Box 352, Woodbridge, New Jersey 07095

United States of America

www.SilverSpearPublications.com

This Edition © 2017 L.E. McCullough

First Printing: January, 2017

ISBN 978-0-9970371-4-2 (pdf)
ISBN 978-0-9970371-3-5 (softcover)

All Rights Reserved. This book may not be transmitted, reproduced or stored in part or in whole by any means without the express written consent of the publisher, except for brief quotations in articles and reviews.

Front & back cover design by David Simpson Design LLC
www.DavidSimpsonDesignLLC.com

~ <u>**DEDICATION**</u> ~

My sincerest thanks for —

    … having been given the gift of being able
       to be moved emotionally by Music;

                  … having been given the ability to learn how
                     to create Music that moves people emotionally;

… the knowledge and generosity of spirit I received
   from every single player I met while learning Music;

           … all the people who hear Music and appreciate
              its beauty and power in their heart.

L.E. McCullough

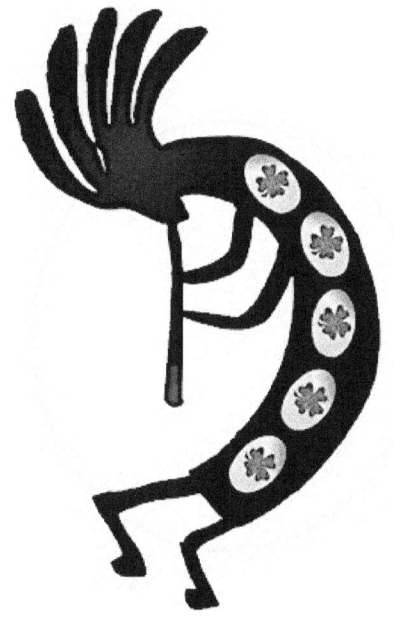

What Whistle Would You Play at Your Mother's Funeral?

L.E. McCullough's Writings on Irish Traditional Music, 1974-2016

Volume I: Dissertation and Theses ~ Volume II: Everything Else

~ CONTENTS, VOLUME I ~

Preface to Volume I	5
Farewell to Erin: An Ethnomusicological Study of Irish Music in the U.S. (Indiana University, B.A. thesis, 1974)	8
The Rose in the Heather: Irish Music in Its American Cultural Milieu (University of Pittsburgh, M.A. thesis, 1975)	71
Irish Music in Chicago: An Ethnomusicological Study (University of Pittsburgh, Ph.D. dissertation, 1978)	124
About the Author	284

~ PREFACE to VOLUME I ~

WELCOME TO THE two-volume anthology titled *What Whistle Would You Play at Your Mother's Funeral? L.E. McCullough's Writings on Irish Traditional Music, 1974-2016.*

It contains pretty much everything L.E. McCullough has written on Irish Traditional Music … and more.

This volume, Volume I, contains the three formal academic works he was required to write to earn a bachelor's degree, a master's degree and a doctoral degree:

- B.A. thesis — **Farewell to Erin: An Ethnomusicological Study of Irish Music in the U.S.**

- M.A. thesis – **The Rose in the Heather: Irish Music in Its American Cultural Milieu**

- Ph.D. dissertation — **Irish Music in Chicago: An Ethnomusicological Study**

The other volume, Volume II, is a collection of scholarly essays, book reviews, journal articles, concert reports, album notes, blog reflections, newspaper features, performer profiles, whistle-playing tips … and a screenplay.

With both volumes you have an assemblage of mostly every word Dr. McCullough has set down about Irish Traditional Music and related Irish cultural topics in just over four decades.

He's not done yet, of course. But let's take a moment to pause and smell the shamrocks.

And abruptly switch to First Person.

I wrote these three Volume I works in the mid-1970s, and I can state categorically that — up till then — Irish music, song and dance weren't getting much scholarly attention in the sphere of musicology/ethnomusicology, especially outside Ireland. The American offshoots of those idioms were getting even less.

That was about to change quite dramatically over the next few years.

Throughout North America and Europe during the 1960s and '70s, young people in their teens and twenties were discovering their cultural "roots" — older, folk-based forms of music, song, dance, art and language that had subsided beneath the waves of contemporary commercial culture trends but were now beginning to bob to the surface once more.

In North America this cultural re-acquaintance movement was termed The Folk Revival. After idioms like Blues, Bluegrass, Tex-Mex, Appalachian, French-Canadian, Cajun and Zydeco had their moment in the Revival spotlight, it was Irish music's turn. By the mid-1970s, young musicians spanning a diversity of ethnic and social backgrounds had started to show up at céilís in Boston, sessions in Chicago, feiseanna in New York — all eager to receive initiation into the venerable mysteries of *ceol traidisiúnta na hÉireann*.

Coming as they did between 1974-78, these three works were the distillation of the extant scholarship on Irish Traditional Music at the time.

Farewell to Erin (1974) gave an overview of the music's history in Ireland and the U.S., an inventory of instruments, styles and performance settings along with sociological observations; ***The Rose in the Heather*** (1975) focused on the music in its American context, past and present; ***Irish Music in Chicago: An Ethnomusicological Study*** (1978) was an in-depth analysis of the unique Irish Traditional Music milieu that existed in one specific locale.

In effect, they served as a museum-like cataloguing of what appeared to be, in the 1970s, an endangered ethnic idiom isolated on the periphery of the musical mainstream.

So if the authorial tone occasionally conveys a slight wisp of pessimism about the future of Irish music, song and dance in the U.S., you have to realize that 40-some years ago it wasn't certain these traditions were going to be passed on to very many young people at all — anywhere, even in Ireland.

Yet from today's vantage point, it is clear there were signs of imminent resurgence percolating in that placid Disco Decade — between 1975's **The Rose in the Heather** and 1978's **Irish Music in Chicago** a slew of new Irish Traditional Music recordings were issued by several new labels; an enthusiastic cadre of youthful musicians from outside the Irish-American community were taking up the music and spreading it at quantum rates among their cohorts; the audience base for Irish music, song and dance was expanding far beyond the ethnic enclave, helped considerably by increasing media attention and festivals like the full week devoted to Irish music and culture at the 1976 Smithsonian Festival of American Folklife.

And academic acolytes like yours truly were writing all kinds of stuff about it every chance we got.

Q. Is everything L.E. McCullough's ever written on Irish Traditional Music in these two volumes?

A. Not quite.

As of this writing, I've created 187 original Irish traditional musical compositions, of which about 70 have been formally published and/or recorded. The full catalog, plus a few theatre scores, will appear in a special volume of its own. Soon. Promise.

The commercial instruction books I wrote — *The Complete Irish Tinwhistle Tutor* (1976), *Favorite Irish Session Tunes* (1988), *St. Patrick Was a Cajun: 61 Traditional Irish Compositions by L.E. McCullough* (1998), *The Complete Irish Tinwhistle Tunebook* (2002), *Whistle Around the World* (2003) — those you can find for sale on the magical internets, though a few essay chapters from these works have been included in Volume II.

Q. So, why should anyone read this?

A. To share the Adventure!

Because that's what my decades pursuing the Irish Traditional Music grail have been. *What Whistle Would You Play at Your Mother's Funeral?* is an itinerary of the many unusual places I've visited on this vast musical map and a few various and sundry trail signs marking my passage.

Of course, in the first flush of my immersion, there was no imaginable thought that this cloistered, seemingly receding musical genre would someday occupy a globally acclaimed status and be performed by tens of thousands of musicians and enjoyed by tens of millions of listeners spanning every continent on Earth and thousands of videos on Youtube.

Irish Traditional Music's late 20th-century revival would be sparked by the emergence of innovative groups like the Chieftains and Bothy Band, the *Riverdance* phenomenon, as well as the relentless grass-roots promotional efforts performed by a worldwide legion of music and dance teachers, CCE branch leaders, feis, fleadh and festival organizers — the dedicated people who do most of the working and paying, living and dying, music-making and music-loving in our society.

But the main reason Irish Traditional Music flourishes today is because of ordinary folks — probably many of you reading this — who came to love this music so much that against all logic you kept learning, playing, studying, rapturously absorbing it into your emotional DNA till you couldn't live without it.

I managed to recognize some of you in these writings. Still, there are hundreds of other performers and scholars, session-attenders and concert-goers I've met along the way whose names won't appear.

Rest assured: everyone I've met on *an bóthar draíochta de cheol*, your voice is in the melodious mix every time I pick up that whistle and blow.

Very best wishes,

L.E. McCullough
Woodbridge, New Jersey
December, 2016

_____

NOTE RE: GRAPHICS

WARNING: Many of the graphic images (photos, musical notations, illustrations, tables) you are about to encounter in Volume I suffer from the extremely poor reproduction quality endemic to 1970s college copying machines.

Could have changed them out with newer, different, cleaner images — but decided to roll with historical fidelity (actually showing the original images that went with the original thesis or dissertation).

Sometimes when you dig up an old time capsule, you find a little dirt has seeped into the box. But the contents are just as precious.

✦ ✦ ✦

FAREWELL TO ERIN:
An Ethnomusicological Study of Traditional Irish Music in the U.S.

by

Lawrence E. McCullough

Senior Project for the
Independent Learning Program

April, 1974

CONTENTS

Acknowledgments	10
Preface	11
Introductory Note to Chapter I	13
Chapter I: An Historical Outline of Traditional Irish Music in the U.S.	14
Chapter II: The Musical Tradition	21
– Instruments	21
– Styles	34
– Repertoire	45
– Performance	55
Chapter III: Summary	60
Notes	62
References Cited	62
Appendix A: Musical Examples of Traditional Irish Musicians in the U.S.	65
Appendix B: Selected Discography of Traditional Irish Musicians in the U.S.	69
Appendix C: Pronunciation Key for Unfamiliar Terms in Irish	70

Cover Photo: The Irish Music Club, Chicago, c. 1909, from O'Neill's *Irish Minstrels & Musicians*, p. 479.

ACKNOWLEDGMENTS

I would first of all like to thank Dr. Charles Boilés, my academic adviser, ILP sponsor and ethnomusicology mentor, for the sagacity, patience and encouragement he has shown in his dealings with me.

This paper has also benefited from organizational and methodological advice given by Ann Christine Frankowski-Braganza, who also served as a tutorial sponsor, as did Dr. Jeffrey Huntsman and Dr. Henry Glassie.

One year ago the Independent Learning Program bestowed a grant upon me which aided immensely in covering the expenses of a summer's fieldwork which, in turn, made possible this paper. Thank you.

Incalculable thanks are extended to Breandán Breathnach, Tom Munnelly and Hugh Shields of Dublin, Ireland, all noted collectors and scholars in the field of Irish folk music, and to fiddler John Kelly and his family, also of Dublin, for the erudition and orientation they provided during my first encounters with traditional Irish music two years ago.

Special thanks must go to the innumerable performers of traditional Irish music, song and dance in the U.S. who gave most generously of their time, their hospitality, their knowledge and, most importantly, their artistry. Without their assistance and cooperation, this project could not have been undertaken.

Finally, my friend Miles Krassen must receive recognition for the contributions he has made through our numerous discussions on the subject of traditional Irish music.

                                                           L.E. McCullough
                                                           Bloomington, Ind.
                                                           April 1, 1974

PREFACE

THIS STUDY IS concerned exclusively with the instrumental music that is performed by Irish folk musicians and designated as "traditional Irish music" to distinguish it from other types of music commonly and indiscriminately labeled "Irish music" and "Irish folk music".

Traditional Irish music has received very little attention from music scholars in Ireland, where it is taken for granted, or from ethnomusicologists in the rest of the world, where it is unknown or else not considered exotic enough to merit serious ethnomusicological scrutiny.

If the reader is unfamiliar with this music, it might be helpful at this point to listen to the tape of musical examples that accompanies this paper, or, failing this, to find some recordings of authentic traditional Irish music, such as those included in Appendix B.

The use of the words "traditional" and "authentic" raise some interesting issues. There are a large number of Irish musicians in the U.S. who perform music that is oriented strictly toward Irish-American audiences. Much of this music, however, does not derive from Ireland at all but is of the pseudo-Irish or stage-Irish variety that has developed in the U.S. during the last century and a quarter. It does not fit the definition of traditional because it has been composed and, in many cases, copyrighted by known individuals who were not members of the community of traditional Irish musicians.

In addition, this music is not performed "authentically", i.e. as performed by traditional musicians, as judged by traditional musicians.

It becomes necessary to introduce two further distinctions: traditional Irish music is music that was originally developed by members of the community of native Irish musicians and is performed in accordance with standards set by this community.

This means that almost the entire range of "Irish entertainment" found at Irish-American weddings, Emerald Balls, St. Patrick's Day festivities and dances sponsored by Irish-American social organizations, as well as that heard in bars and on radio and records, must be excluded from this study.

Some examples of what is commonly believed to represent Irish music are:

- the sopranos, contraltos, tenors, baritones et, al. who warble and croon *Moore's Irish Melodies* in addition to other art music compositions that make use of Irish themes and settings, as well as popular songs native to Hollywood and Tin Pan Alley and its current equivalents;

- the pub balladeers and folk revival groups who, equipped with guitar, banjo and mandolin, are cut from exactly the same musical cloth as their counterparts in England, Europe and North America;

- the "Irish-American orchestras" whose repertoire consists overwhelmingly of foxtrots and waltzes;

- the "Irish cabaret" entertainers who appear in night clubs and bars from New York to Las Vegas with an occasional spot on a syndicated television program such as Merv Griffin, Mike Douglas, Ed Sullivan, etc., particularly around March 17 each year;

In order to begin to describe what traditional Irish music is, it has seemed advisable to first make clear what it is not, in the hope that confusion could be reduced. Having done so, some preliminary definitions can now be offered. These are merely a few general considerations concerning traditional Irish music, and each of them will be given a more comprehensive treatment in the main body of the paper.

Traditional Irish music in the U.S. is performed exclusively for Irish and Irish-American audiences, although some musicians have appeared at a few folk music and ethnic heritage festivals in recent years.

This dependence on the ethnic community for its sustenance has restricted the practice of the music to localities in which there are large concentrations of Irish and Irish-Americans — namely, the major urban population centers of the Northeastern, Middle Atlantic and Great Lakes states. In 1900 the states of Massachusetts, Connecticut, New York, New Jersey, Pennsylvania, Ohio and Illinois accounted for 75% of the Irish-born population in the U.S. (Schrier 1958:6), and, these proportions have not changed much since.

In the 19th century, the main parameters of traditional Irish music stretched south along the Eastern seaboard from Boston to Washington, D.C. and west along the lower Great Lakes from Buffalo to Milwaukee. These belts have diminished drastically in the 20th century. Currently, traditional Irish music exists primarily in Boston, New York City, Philadelphia, Cleveland and Chicago. A few musicians can still be found in other areas, including Washington, D.C., Pittsburgh, Detroit, St. Louis and Rochester, N.Y. West of St. Louis, only San Francisco and Vancouver, B.C. are known to contain active traditional Irish musicians.

Most U.S. traditional Irish musicians are either Irish emigrants or one generation removed from Ireland. The number of second-generation Irish-Americans involved in the music is slight; third-generation performers are extremely rare. The music flourished for well over a century by virtue of the steady stream of emigration which introduced new additions to the growing Irish-American musical community. With the substantial decrease in Irish emigration to America after 1930, the responsibility for preserving and perpetuating the tradition has fallen increasingly to traditional musicians of first and second-generation status.

The last five years have witnessed a revival of interest in traditional Irish music on the part of young Irish-Americans. Also, a significant number of individuals who possess no Irish antecedents whatsoever have become intensely interested in the idiom.

This phenomenon is regarded by veteran traditional Irish musicians with a good deal of wonder and surprisingly little suspicion. Of course, they are somewhat taken aback by this unexpected source of new recruits to the tradition, but they are glad of it, nonetheless, as it represents a vindication of their lifelong commitment to traditional Irish music and gives evidence that the music will continue to survive in America for at least another generation.

The primary purpose of this paper is to determine to what extent traditional Irish music has changed, evolved or developed since its transplantation to American soil. For information concerning the history and structure of the music, the reader should consult any of the two or three excellent works of a general, introductory nature that have been written on the subject. The entire area has long been neglected, and much work remains to be done.

Although the present study examines a specific branch of the tradition, the statements and conclusions offered herein are not intended to be taken as the final word on a subject that is only beginning to be analyzed in a detailed, systematic manner.

Rather, this study represents no more than a first attempt to break ground and make this fascinating and complex musical tradition more accessible for future ethnomusicological researchers.

◆_____◆

INTRODUCTORY NOTE to Chapter I

ANYONE WHO ATTEMPTS to chronicle the development of traditional Irish music in the United States is immediately confronted by a distressing paucity of sources on the subject, either reliable or unreliable, which might provide a logical starting point for a reconstruction of the music's history in America.

Before the 20th century, the references to the music appear infrequently and are scattered throughout a welter of printed media, primarily in the form of brief captions and announcements in Irish-American newspapers and journals, theatrical and vaudeville advertisements and random bits of biographia.

After the turn of the 20th century, the situation improves with the recording of Irish-American musicians on wax cylinders and discs. These were at first privately-recorded on a small-scale, often informal, basis; after c. 1915 they were manufactured by commercial phonograph companies for mass distribution. However, the number and depth of printed sources remains pitifully meager and diminishes considerably as the century progresses.

In addition, of the large corpus of private and public recordings — which might be expected to yield information regarding musical style, repertoire and instrumentation, as well as some insight into the impact of the recording process upon the subsequent development of the tradition — surviving copies in audible condition are scarce, and there has been to date no discographical study or attempted analysis of this rich, untapped lode of data.

In this reconstruction attempt, the reservoir of oral lore that exists among members of the Irish-American musical community has been utilized as the principal repository of information regarding the history of this musical tradition in the U.S. and has been supplemented by the judicious use and interpretation of the occasional references found in printed sources of the day.

It should be understood that the current living memory of informants extends no further than the first decade of the 20th century and is rather hazy beyond 1930. Also, the bulk of printed references are sketchy and infuriatingly vague as to details of musical style, repertoire and performance practice.

Nonetheless, in both the oral lore and the printed miscellanea, it is possible to catch a few fleeting and tantalizing glimpses of traditional Irish music in America as it existed in the full vigor of its most flourishing, halcyon epoch.

CHAPTER I: An Historical Outline of Traditional Irish Music in the U.S.

THE PRECISE ORIGINS of traditional Irish music in America are woefully obscure. Emigrants from Ireland to America before the 19th century were largely descended from the stock of the Presbyterian Scots who had been imported from Scotland and established in the northeastern section of Ireland to assist in the pacification and colonization that followed the final subjugation of the island by England in the 17th century.

When they arrived in the American colonies, these Ulster Scots still exhibited a strong cultural affinity with Scotland, despite their sojourn in Ireland, and the musical traditions which they brought to the New World were undoubtedly derivative of those of the non-Gaelic, Lowland Scots culture from which they were but three or four generations removed (O'Faolain 1972:86).

Although thousands of native, Catholic Irish were transplanted to the West Indies during the first years of the Cromwellian pacification program to serve as plantation slaves (Curtis 1952:251), there were relatively few Irish Catholics who emigrated freely to the North American colonies before the second quarter of the 19th century.

Those who did emigrate arrived individually or in very small groups and were quickly assimilated (Murphy and Mannion 1962:1). Also, the implacable anti-Catholic prejudice that was firmly entrenched among many colonial Americans served as an effective deterrent to "papists" contemplating settlement in Great Britain's American colonies. Many of the colonies enacted legislation which restricted Catholic Irish immigration specifically and deprived already-resident Catholics of all nationalities of various civil rights.

These legal strictures began to disappear after the institution of the American Republic in the 1780s, but discriminatory legislation against all "undesirable foreign elements", particularly those from poor, Catholic countries such as Ireland, continued throughout the Federalist period of the new nation and successfully obstructed the free flow of Irish Catholic immigration (Levine 1966:61).

It is difficult to state with certainty what sort of musical traditions were possessed by the native Irish who did settle in America before the 19th century. The numerous historical articles dealing with these early arrivals are almost exclusively concerned with listing how many individuals with Irish surnames settled in various parts of the country or were encamped with Washington at Valley Forge; they are devoid of any descriptions of the cultural activities of the early American Irish.

Similarly, the accounts of early American musical life center primarily on the musical occasions of the urban upper and middle classes or those of a few religious denominations, with occasional mention of the musical culture of the black slaves and no mention of the musical activities of lower-class urban or rural and frontier whites.

If there were not a similar dearth of detailed information on the state of instrumental folk music in Ireland at this time, it might be possible to gain some insight into the musical culture of those Irish who emigrated to America during the 17th and 18th centuries. Few particulars are known concerning matters such as repertoire, style and performance practices of Irish folk musicians, although travellers' accounts of the period (primarily English) often mention the instruments in use among the native Irish peasantry.

The current consensus of scholars in the field of Irish folk music is that the bulk of what is presently acknowledged as traditional Irish music was created by the musicians of the late 18th and early 19th centuries (Breathnach 1971:19).

Although a few remnants of the music of an earlier period still survive in the present repertoire in the form of instrumental airs derived from older song airs, the instrumental musical traditions of pre-conquest Ireland vanished during the period of cultural trauma that followed in the wake of the collapse of the Gaelic aristocracy and the accompanying social order.

The 18th century was a transitional and protean period in which the heretofore highly distinctive musical traditions of the aristocratic and peasant classes were merged. Though the harp still held high status and primacy of place in the households of many of the new Anglo-Irish, the harpers of the 18th century were "already archaic and somewhat anachronistic" (Rimmer 1969:66) and judged by some to represent a debased, degenerate form of the art.

By the second decade of the 19th century, the already-moribund harping tradition was effectively extinct (*ibid.*). In its place rose an instrumental tradition that had previously been confined to the lower orders of pre-conquest Gaelic society (Kuter 1973:8).

It is recorded in the memoirs of the Irish harper Arthur O'Neill that one of his 18th-century contemporaries, a blind harper named Owen Keenan, reportedly emigrated to America after eloping with his patron's French governess (O'Neill 1973b:65). However, it is more plausible that the first strains of traditional Irish music heard in the U.S. were sounded by either the uilleann pipes or the fiddle.

These two instruments of the Irish peasantry had risen to prominence in the wake of the demise of the aristocratic musical orders and effectively filled the vacuum in the native musical tradition caused by the disappearance of the harp. Most of the present traditional repertoire was composed by now-forgotten pipers and fiddlers of the late 18th and early 19th centuries (Breathnach 1971:61), and several of the basic stylistic techniques that have come to characterize traditional Irish music and are employed by all traditional Irish musicians are, to a large extent, modeled on techniques developed by early performers on the pipes and fiddle.

Irish emigration to the U.S. had begun to show a systematic increase throughout the 1830s and 1840s, and, although the specter of widespread famine had more than once menaced the precarious existence of the Irish peasantry, the severity of the potato blight of the late 1840s left tens of thousands of Irish with no choice but emigration. Upon their arrival in America, they clustered into the burgeoning Irish communities which began to appear in every major urban and industrial area of the U.S. Their recent disastrous experience with agriculture was impressed indelibly upon their collective consciousness, and, for this reason and others, the Irish experience in America became synonymous with the urban experience.

However, the entire previous history of the Irish had been largely oriented toward a non-urban life mode (O'Faolain 1972:60), and the culture they brought with them to the U.S. was a product of centuries of rural, peasant existence. The transition from countryside to shantytown was painfully abrupt, and much of the old Gaelic culture did not survive beyond the first generation of exposure to the new social environment.

The traditional music and dance, however, proved remarkably resistant to assimilative and acculturative pressures. Though both arts were strongly rooted in rural, folk society, they were adapted to an urban, non-traditional environment with little initial difficulty. Traditional Irish musicians and dancers moved smoothly into the popular American entertainment milieu of the time and were frequently employed as performers on riverboats and pleasure cruises, in hotels, saloons, dance halls and theaters.

The musicians often accompanied popular singers on nationwide concert tours and gained great public acclaim for their performances in travelling minstrel shows and vaudeville companies. Their activities in these troupes involved music, dance and comic monologues and sketches. The performances were usually delivered by pairs or trios but occasionally by one extremely versatile individual.

Some of the more talented and illustrious Irish musicians of the era maintained a substantial livelihood in this manner. Traditional Irish musicians of this period were also very active in the Irish-American communities and performed at various Hibernian social events such as picnics, house parties, balls, concerts and numerous other formal and informal musical occasions from Irish dance classes to neighborhood tavern sessions.

From all indications, the late 19th century was the most prosperous era for the Irish musician in America in terms of financial remuneration and high social status in the Irish-American community. This "golden age" was fittingly crowned by the erection in 1892 of Celtic Hall in New York City, which flourished as "the Mecca of the best class of Irish sociables and gatherings for many years" (O'Neill 1973b:320).

Like countless other immigrants, the traditional musicians of Ireland were undoubtedly attracted to the U.S. by the prospect of increased economic opportunity. Prior to the 1840s, a considerable number of itinerant musicians roamed the Irish countryside, plying their trade among the peasantry and the lower classes of the towns and cities. Most of these musicians were pipers or fiddle players, though other instrumentalists also occasionally took to the roads.

The status of these musicians was roughly equivalent to that of lower-class tradespeople who fulfilled a service function for the agricultural community, such as coopers, potters, tailors, basketmakers and wheelwrights. His occupational role necessitated that he be both a specialist and a professional. Admission to the itinerant ranks was attained through heredity as well as by choice; status within the musical profession was generally achieved, while in the larger society it was ascribed. It remains only to add that the itinerant musician was almost always male.

The extreme fondness — often a virtual mania — of the Irish peasantry for their traditional music and dance is well-attested by contemporary observers (Breathnach 1971:41, 42, 51; O'Keeffe and O'Brien 1954:16, 20). Together with the dancing master (another male itinerant specialist and professional accorded higher social status by the community in deference to his refinement, gentlemanly dress and decorum and role as an instructor), the itinerant musician figured prominently in the cultural life of pre-Famine Ireland.

Indeed, says a noted Irish cultural historian:

> "Pre-Famine peasant society, for all its poverty, had plenty of sport and gaiety about it. Music and song were woven into the very fabric of society, and the fiddler and uillean piper were kept busy at weddings and wakes, fairs and markets." (Ó Tuathaigh 1972:150)

The massive, social upheaval caused by the Famine was instrumental in hastening the demise of both the dancing masters and itinerant musicians. The immediate economic impact of the Famine was to effect the nearly complete impoverishment of the classes upon which the musicians and dancing masters depended for support.

Although the dire economic condition of the peasantry would improve after some decades — mainly due to the emigration of most of the surplus population — the severe psychological trauma engendered by the "Great Hunger" proved more difficult to assuage. The national psyche was afflicted by a particularly stultifying lethargy which often combined with clerical puritanism to produce a listless, apathetic attitude regarding the pursuit of community cultural activities such as music and dance. [1]

As the number of musical occasions and the functional value of the musical profession in community life continued to diminish, many musicians who had formerly maintained a livelihood as itinerant or semi-itinerant performers found themselves forced to abandon their occupation.

Those who were old, physically handicapped or vocationally unskilled were driven into the local poorhouse or workhouse. Those who were more mobile or vocationally versatile could either take up a new trade and attempt to settle down, take to the roads again and join the hordes of "travelling people" displaced by the Famine, [2] journey to another part of Ireland where the situation was probably no less bleak or leave the country altogether. It was during these chaotic post-Famine years that the U.S. received its first significant influx of traditional Irish musicians.

The traditional Irish musicians who arrived in America during this period were undoubtedly quite pleasantly surprised by both the expanded range of economic opportunities and the increased social status accorded them in the Irish-American communities. Not only was the Irish musician popular with the cosmopolitan American audiences who thronged the music halls and minstrel shows, he was also recognized — as were the priest, politician and publican in their respective domains — as playing an important role in the maintenance of Irish-American cultural solidarity while serving as a role model for young Irish-American males who aspired to achievement and public renown.

Upward social mobility was not beyond the grasp of many musicians who became professional performers or engaged in other commercial pursuits besides music. Celtic Hall in New York City, mentioned above, was constructed by an uilleann piper from County Leitrim named Patrick Fitzpatrick only eleven years after he arrived in America at the age of twenty-one, and there were several other instances of musicians who earned enough money to invest in saloons, dance halls and theaters (O'Neill 1973b:320). This sudden rise in the economic and social hierarchies would not have been possible in the tightly structured economic and social networks of Ireland at this time, in which accession to land or a business concern was regulated by marriage and kinship variables.

The repertoire of the professional Irish-American musician was based on the same body of music shared by other traditional musicians in Ireland and America. However, musicians who chose a professional career in the U.S. were often required by the circumstances of their employment to perform quadrilles, strathspeys, waltzes, barn dances, schottisches, show tunes and even light classical music in addition to selections from the traditional Irish repertoire.

To what extent the professional musicians can be considered as representative of the entire community of American Irish musicians is a matter of speculation. It seems, however, that, despite the potential for interchange between the musical cultures of Ireland and the U.S., the traditional Irish repertoire remained intact during this period of contact.

The non-Irish music adopted by the professional Irish-American musicians was not introduced (or if introduced, was not accepted) into the traditional repertoire at this time.

Full-scale acculturation in the Irish-American musical community came later, in the 20th century, as a result of a change in tastes and preferences of the American Irish audiences — indicative of their increased assimilation within mainstream American society — rather than from any development within the community of traditional musicians, creating the demand for musical entertainment that was neither traditional nor Irish.

The performance of several musicians in consort, except during informal sessions, does not seem to have occurred until the first decades of the 20th century. The tradition, except for occasional duets and trios, remained one of solo performance throughout the 19th century. The fiddle, pipes and transverse flute made up the first rank of instruments in use among American Irish musicians at this time. Although the tinwhistle was present, it does not seem to have been accorded much notice but functioned primarily as the instrument used by novices when first learning Irish music.

The melodeon and its successor, the two-row button accordion, came into fashion during the last three decades of the 19th century but did not attain a significant niche among Irish-American musicians until the 20th century. It was also in the last decade or so of the 19th century that the practice of harmonic accompaniment on piano or guitar became increasingly widespread among Irish musicians in America — possibly introduced via the professional musicians of music hall and vaudeville.

There is little information on the stylistic techniques employed by Irish-American musicians of this period. One piper was described as favoring "the free and rolling style with a liberal sprinkling of graces and trills" (O'Neill 1973b:310); another was criticized for having a "too open and flute-like tone" (*ibid.*:301); yet another piper's playing was characterized by "a choppy execution subversive of both rhythm and melody" (*ibid.*:263).

Fiddle styles of the day are also a matter of conjecture, with players being described as a "fine, free-hand performer" (*ibid.*:410), or the style displaying "the exuberance of graces skillfully interwoven into the texture of the theme" (*ibid.*:375).

It is likely that the first comment refers to the amount of free variation in the bowing style and the second might indicate a lively, strongly accented and profusely-ornamented style of playing, but one can only speculate.

What seems certain is that during this period the traditional Irish music found in the U. S. was marked by a wide diversity of stylistic traits that reflected the variety of provincial, regional and local styles which existed concurrently in Ireland.

Despite the phenomenon of musicians representing different sectional and stylistic backgrounds suddenly coming into close contact, no pan-American style of playing traditional Irish music emerged, although several Irish-Americans made significant stylistic contributions. Stylistic sovereignty was maintained, although some styles gained a large number of adherents for short periods of time.

However, it was primarily in regard to the exchange and dispersion of repertoire that the increased interaction among musicians in the Irish-American communities had the most significant consequences upon the subsequent development of the tradition.

Traditional Irish music continued to thrive throughout the 19th century and well into the 20th, eventually producing performers who were not only outstanding musicians but important contributors to the development of the tradition in Ireland as well as America. Few of their names have survived into the present, however, since those who maintain oral tradition are highly selective and often forgetful. [3]

With the advent of the recording process, it becomes possible to examine more closely the relationship of individual musicians to the evolution of the larger tradition.

The emergence of the commercial recording industry occurred as the "golden era" of traditional Irish music in America entered its final phase (c. 1920-1945). Along with the "race" or "hillbilly" series, the major labels also maintained a special "Irish" series that featured a variety of Irish-American performers and included several of the finest traditional instrumental musicians of the day.

The recordings made during this period reveal an interesting assortment of instrumental styles that reflect not only the older styles brought over from Ireland in the immediate post-Famine decade, but ones subsequently developed in the U.S., as well as others first introduced by the musicians who arrived in the last great wave of Irish emigration in the 1910s and '20s.

As with the recording of other American folk and ethnic musics of the period, such as blues, jazz and hillbilly music, the recording of traditional Irish music facilitated a wider dissemination and more extensive cross-fertilization of styles and repertoire formerly unknown outside a particular locality or circle of musicians.

Although syncretic processes had already taken place to a limited extent in the repertoire of American Irish musicians, the diffusion of style was a much slower process wholly dependent upon personal interaction among musicians. Recordings rendered this method of style transmission obsolete by providing access to style on a mass, impersonal level that made it no longer necessary to know personally or to have ever heard the musician whose style one wished to copy or incorporate.

This acceleration and extension of the process of style acquisition exerted a profound influence on the future development of the tradition. Despite the fact that many of the styles in circulation among present-day Irish-American musicians are reflections of those currently popular in Ireland, the influence of these early recordings in shaping the norms of modern style in both Ireland and America has been substantial.

Several of the players recorded in the 1920s and '30s are still revered as paragons of excellence by which the efforts of modern musicians are measured, and many of their tunes are played by present-day musicians in the same grouping, order, and setting as they were recorded forty and fifty years ago.

Other tunes and tune-settings recorded during this period have since attained the status of "classics" or "standards" in the traditional repertoire and serve as test pieces by which musicians aspiring to eminence are judged. These recordings have become increasingly important since World War II, helping to preserve a sense of continuity within the Irish-American musical community.

In view of the many musicians recorded and the large number of recordings produced between the two World Wars, it would appear that traditional Irish music still retained a secure place in the musical affections of the American Irish.

However, an examination of catalogues of the major recording companies from the late 1920s to the early 1940s reveals a steady decrease in both the number of Irish musicians recorded and the number of recordings produced, until by 1945 (in some cases much earlier), the "Irish" series had disappeared from active catalogue lists.

Although a half dozen of the best-selling traditional artists were retained on studio rosters until the end of the 1940s, the market for traditional Irish music had evaporated, and even reissued material sold poorly. A few small labels, most notably the Copley company of Boston, carried on into the '50s, but were inoperative by the end of the decade.

The Depression was partially responsible for the diminished recording activity, but other factors of greater irreversibility were more decisive in contributing to the demise of traditional Irish music in the U.S. The increasing structural assimilation of the Irish into mainstream American society and their entrance into the realms of the American middle class were accompanied by the adoption of the cultural values and lifestyle of that society and particular social stratum. In most cases this movement up the social ladder involved the discarding of cultural paraphernalia such as traditional music and dance, pastimes and customs — items viewed as expendable or of no value in a society obsessed with the melting pot syndrome (Kelleher 1961:39).

This vacuum created by the assimilation of first-, second- and third-generation Irish-Americans was not, as in previous times, filled by a new wave of immigration from Ireland. Although civil strife and an unpromising economic situation brought 220,591 Irish to the U. S. between 1921 and 1930, the next decade witnessed the arrival of a mere 13,167.

Only 1,059 Irish came to the U.S. between 1941 and 1945, but the post-war shortages of jobs and consumer goods in Ireland were responsible for 26,444 Irish arrivals from 1946 to 1950 (Census Bureau 1960:56). A brief flurry of immigration in the mid-1950s introduced some new additions to the Irish-American musical community, but the reduction of the once-steady stream of immigration to a mere dribble has robbed the Irish-American musical tradition of an important source of fresh input.

In recent years New York City has become the major focus for activity among traditional Irish musicians in the U.S. Its large Irish and Irish-American population — currently estimated at 315,000 (Census Bureau 1972:607-612) — has made possible the support of some forty to fifty schools of Irish dancing, a half dozen schools of Irish music, numerous musical occasions featuring traditional music of a high standard and a class of semi-professional traditional musicians who derive a substantial portion of their income from public performance and teaching.

Another factor contributing to New York's status is that, with only two recent exceptions, all of the traditional Irish musicians who have been commercially recorded in the U.S. in the last two decades either live or have resided for lengthy periods of time in New York. The great number of active musicians and the frequency of public and private musical occasions have given New York musicians the reputation of being the most polished and practiced players in the country.

Musical activity among Irish-Americans in other cities has stagnated, although a few cities can still boast of three or four players acknowledged by their peers as "first-rate". Chicago long ago surrendered the position of eminence in Irish-American musical affairs it maintained in the 19th and early 20th centuries, although there are a number of active musicians and musical occasions there. Unlike New York, Chicago receives virtually no new permanent immigrants and very few transient arrivals from Ireland.

The isolation of the Chicago musical community has been intensified by the severe lack of interest in traditional music exhibited by young Irish-Americans (although there are approximately a thousand or so students enrolled in schools of Irish dancing in the Chicago area). Efforts to organize the musical community along lines similar to those proven successful in New York have received minimal support from the larger community and have been marked by factionalism within the musical community itself.

Boston, Cleveland, Philadelphia and San Francisco were also distinguished centers of Irish music at one time but have declined drastically due to general apathy, the lack of fresh blood from Ireland and the inability of local musicians to replenish their rapidly-thinning ranks with young American recruits.

Although attempts have been made to encourage young people to participate in local Irish musical events, the musical communities in these cities still consist overwhelmingly of musicians forty years of age and over who will likely be inactive in twenty years.

Unless this "generation gap" can be filled to some extent, it is very possible that cities will eventually suffer the fate of Milwaukee, Baltimore, Detroit, Pittsburgh, Indianapolis, St. Paul and St. Louis — cities with sizeable Irish and Irish-American populations now conspicuously barren of interest in traditional Irish music.

Like some rare species of wildlife endangered by a sudden ecological shift, the traditional Irish musicians of the U.S. have become a breed threatened with imminent extinction.

However, any discussion of the present state of traditional Irish, music in America must be cognizant of the slow groundswell of renewed interest that has begun to appear in various parts of the country among individuals encompassing a variety of ethnic and musical backgrounds.

The last decade has witnessed the phenomenon or re-emerging ethnicity and a concern for various aspects of ethnic culture as many nationality and racial groups in the U.S. have begun to question the wisdom of effacing their ethnic and cultural identity to achieve the anonymity and cultural desolation offered as rewards for successful assimilation into mainstream American society.

The revival enjoyed by traditional music in Ireland in recent years has had a considerable psychological impact upon Irish musicians in the U. S., providing a model for a similar movement in this country as well as establishing a much-needed sense of solidarity with the Irish emigrants and descendants of emigrants who have preserved this aspect of their ethnic heritage often without benefit of nourishment from the tradition's source.

These and other occurrences, such as the more than one hundred American musicians who competed in the 1973 Fleadh Cheoil na hÉireann at Listowel, County Kerry, augur well for the future of Irish music in America.

In addition, Irish music has begun to attract the notice of the urban folk revival and its attendant media. Irish-American musicians have been injected into the established folk festival circuit, recorded by a label specializing in North American folk music, celebrated in folk music magazines and hired to play in Greenwich Village clubs and coffeehouses.

While traditional Irish music will not prove as marketable or as enduringly popular among folk music devotees as has bluegrass, Appalachian music and country blues, it cannot fail to benefit from the increased exposure; already, a noticeable change has occurred in the attitudes and performance of musicians who have been "discovered" in this manner.

Buoyed by this new-found and unexpected appreciation, their pride and confidence in their musical abilities has grown, while their newly-acquired status as important musical artists has increased their stature within their own communities and resulted in a greater recognition of the Irish musician as preservers and propagators of the Irish cultural heritage.

If this current wave of interest can be sustained over the next few years, there is every indication that traditional Irish music in the U.S. might well stave off its decline and enter into an epoch of vitality and prosperity unknown since the passing of its "golden age" in the early 20th century.

CHAPTER II: The Musical Tradition

(A) Instruments

THE INSTRUMENTS USED by traditional Irish musicians in the U.S. can be divided into two groups on the basis of their role as <u>solo</u> or <u>accompanying</u> instruments (see Figure 1).

Solo instruments are of two kinds, <u>primary</u> and <u>miscellaneous</u>. Primary instruments have been accorded full traditional status by members of the tradition, while miscellaneous instruments are not regarded as being fully traditional but are performed and tolerated, nonetheless.

The second category comprises two sub-types — the first made up of instruments used for harmonic support, the second consisting of instruments that provide percussive accompaniment.

In traditional Irish music, these defined instrumental roles are scrupulously observed; instances of solo instruments being employed in an accompanimental capacity or accompanying instruments playing the melody are rare.

Figure 1: Musical instruments used by traditional Irish musicians in the U.S.

<u>Solo Instruments – primary</u>	<u>Solo Instruments - miscellaneous</u>
uilleann pipes	banjo
fiddle	mandolin
flute	banjoline
tinwhistle	harmonica
accordion	piccolo
concertina	harp

<u>Accompanying Instruments – harmonic</u>	<u>Accompanying Instruments - percussive</u>
piano	bodhrán
guitar	bones
	spoons
	drums

Role deviation occurs most frequently in ensemble musical performances. The fiddle, for example, might perform a pizzicato counterpoint to the solo instrument, or drones might be played which provide a basic harmony. Only recently has the use of solo instruments in this fashion come into the tradition, and it is almost wholly confined to ensemble performances (c.f. Section D of this chapter). On a few occasions the piano is used as a solo instrument, but when playing with a solo instrument generally assumes a strictly accompanimental role.

Almost all of these instruments can be found in every community of traditional Irish musicians in the U.S. The purist should not take offense at the inclusion of instruments whose pedigrees are not, strictly speaking, fully traditional or, in some cases, even partially traditional. The instruments discussed here are those used by traditional musicians in the U.S. for the performance of Irish music and for this reason demand consideration.

Certain of these instruments, such as the uilleann pipes, concertina and bodhrán, have become exceedingly rare in recent years, while others, such as the fiddle, accordion and tinwhistle, have flourished. This fluctuation in instrument popularity has occurred on a nationwide scale and reflects the success each particular instrument has had in adapting to a new musical and cultural environment. It also indicates which instrumental traditions seem likely to play a significant role in the future development of traditional Irish music in America.

Solo Instruments — Primary

At the beginning of the 19th century, the uilleann pipes, fiddle and transverse flute were the instruments most commonly used by traditional Irish musicians in the U.S. It was through these three instruments that the bulk of the current traditional repertoire was created and transmitted. The "little flute", or the tinwhistle, has always been present in some form and, in recent years, has gained greater currency and prestige among traditional musicians in the U.S.

The latter half of the 19th century witnessed the emergence of the free reed family of instruments in Euro-American music. Two members of this family, the melodeon and the concertina, were taken up at this time by folk musicians in a number of countries including Ireland. The concertina has now virtually disappeared from traditional Irish music in the U.S., although it has survived to some extent in Ireland. The melodeon succumbed in the early 20th century to first the button and then the piano accordion.

The Uilleann Pipes (musical examples 1-5) *

* [This description of the uilleann pipes is taken from Baines 1957, Baines 1960 and Breathnach 1971. The reader is referred to these sources for more detailed discussion of this instrument.]

The uilleann pipes (also, perhaps more correctly, known as the "union pipes" (or, occasionally, the "Irish organ") represent one of the most complex technological developments of the bagpipe species. (see Figure 2). It was devised in Ireland sometime during the latter half of the 17th century but did not fully emerge until the opening decades of the 18th (Breathnach 1971:76). At this point in time, the instrument bore a closer resemblance to the Scottish Highland pipes of the period (also called "píob mór" or "war pipes" in Ireland at present), having a chanter and only two drones (Baines 1960:123).

A full set of uilleann pipes has three drones and three (occasionally four or five) regulators. The drones — tenor, baritone and bass — are tuned to the bottom note of the chanter, sounding d1, d and D on a concert-pitch instrument (see Figure 3a). The regulators, shown in Figure 3b, are closed pipes with keys that sound individual notes when depressed. These keys lie just under the right hand of the performer and are arranged in rows so that chords can be sounded in accompaniment to the chanter by lowering the wrist. Regulators are also made in three tunings — tenor, baritone and bass. Unlike the drones, which are equipped with single reeds, the regulators are activated by a double reed.

The chanter possesses a range of two octaves and, when fitted with keys, can be made fully chromatic. The second octave is obtained by lowering the chanter against the knee and exerting a slight increase of pressure on the bag with the left arm. The sound of the uilleann pipe-chanter is much sweeter, mellower and considerably less penetrating than that of the Highland pipe chanter. The uilleann pipe chanter has a double reed and can be made to sound in concert pitch or a whole tone or more below modern concert pitch. Today, chanters in concert pitch are more or less standard, reflecting the higher pitch and brighter, sharper sound now preferred by most traditional Irish musicians (Breathnach 1971:79).

Unlike the Highland bagpipes, the uilleann pipes are yoked around the player's waist and are inflated by a bellows tied to the player's arm. The bellows is pumped with the right elbow, while the left arm controls the air pressure in the bag. The piper is seated when playing, the drones and the regulators joined in a stock that is placed across his lap, with the chanter held above the right knee in a diagonal slant (see Fig. 4).

There were a number of uilleann pipe makers in the U.S. during the latter half of the 19th century, the most famous being the Taylor brothers Charles and William, natives of County Louth, who emigrated to New York around 1872. They moved to Philadelphia within a year or so after their arrival in America, and it was in this city that their reputation as pipemakers *par excellence* was established (O'Neill 1973b:160-161).

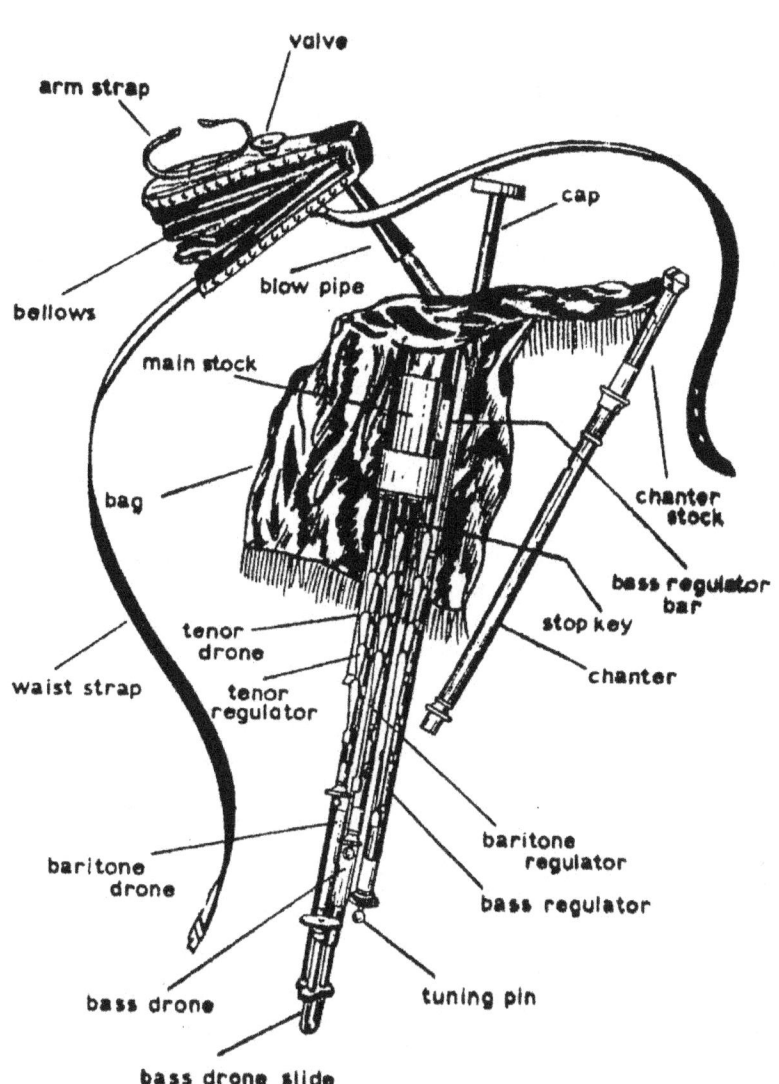

Figure 2: A modern set of uilleann pipes (from Breathnach 1971:77)

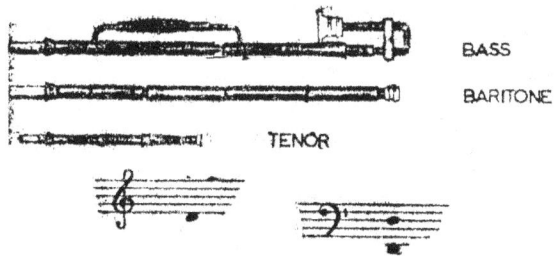

Figure 3a: The regulators of the uilleann pipes (from Breathnach 1971:80)

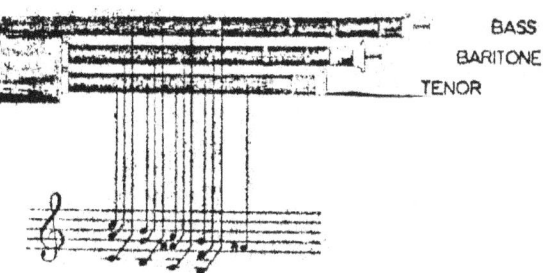

Figure 3b: The regulators of the uilleann pipes (from Breathnach 1971:80)

In addition to maintaining a standard of superb craftsmanship, the Taylors introduced several innovations into the construction of the pipes which virtually revolutionized the conceptions of pipemaking then current in the U.S.

Their brief experience in America had made it clear that some adjustments were necessary if the uilleann pipes were to survive in the new, urban climate of music hall and vaudeville.

After much experimentation, the Taylors began producing sets of pipes which they felt were better suited to the demands of American entertainment occasions, as well as the extremely variable American climate.

This new design possessed a more solid, streamlined, and compact body, with greater volume, often one or two double-bass regulators for extra power, and a much more ornate and formidable external appearance. Minute but highly significant changes in the internal dimensions of the instrument, particularly the chanter bore and the regulator pipes, were also introduced (O'Neill 1973b:vii). Figures 5 and 6 show the Taylor style in two sets of pipes, one massive and squat (Figure 5) with the other lighter and more condensed (Figure 6)

Presently, there is only one maker of uilleann pipes in the U.S., Patrick Hennelly of Chicago, whose work owes much to inspiration received from the Taylor style of pipemaking.

Figure 4: An Irish uilleann piper (from O'Neill 1973b:318)

The disappearance of American pipemakers has coincided with the sharp reduction in the ranks of American uilleann pipers, of which fewer than a dozen active players remain. Although one or two individuals in the U.S. have made pipe chanters, the focus of pipemaking activity has shifted to Ireland in the 20th century.

American pipers are a highly individualistic breed, occasionally exhibiting tendencies toward reclusiveness and mild xenophobia. Most pipers have been isolated not only from recent developments that have occurred in Ireland but have lost contact with pipers and other musicians in America.

The inability of the American pipers of the 1920s and '30s to ensure the continuance of their art in the succeeding generation of Irish-Americans has been largely responsible for the decline of uilleann piping in the U.S.

Those pipers who remain exist only as preservers of the tradition; they have yielded their former role as leaders and innovators in the traditional community to fiddlers and accordion players.

Interest in the uilleann pipes is beginning to be aroused in a few young (under age thirty) Americans, but the commitment of these individuals is often ephemeral. Although the pipes will very likely survive at least through the next two decades, the future of this instrument in traditional Irish music in America does not appear promising at the present time.

The Fiddle (musical examples 6-25)

Along with the uilleann pipes, the fiddle played the most significant role in the initial evolution of the traditional Irish repertoire. After two centuries, the fiddle and its performers still figure prominently in the development of the tradition. In America, fiddle players have continued to perfect their art and have maintained high standards of performance in spite of the overall malaise that has afflicted Irish music in this country.

Figure 5: A set of Taylor pipes (from O'Neill 1971 3b:280)

Figure 6: A set of Taylor pipes (from O'Neill 1971 3b:264)

In the 20th century particularly, Irish-American fiddlers have been primarily responsible for the innovations in style and repertoire that have had such a widespread impact on the entire tradition in Ireland as well as America.

All makes of violins, from the cheap, shoddy, pawn-shop variety to instruments exhibiting high-quality craftsmanship, may be found in the hands of Irish-American fiddlers. However, due to the rather sophisticated and complex technique demanded of a traditional Irish fiddle player, as well as desire for a full, rich tone, most fiddlers endeavor to obtain an instrument of at least average quality.

Many Irish-American fiddle players have increasingly resorted to the use of amplifying devices — pickups or microphone systems — during public performances, such as dances, feiseanna and tavern gigs, where the fiddle needs to be heard over a noisy crowd. This is an example of how a folk instrumental tradition has had to make use of modern technology and incorporate elements from outside the tradition in order to make a successful transition to the changing cultural contexts of the traditional musical occasion.

Fiddlers using these devices are aware of the compromise they are making in sacrificing traditional tone for increased volume, and the pickups and p.a. systems are discarded when the occasion permits. As of yet, the sound of an amplified fiddle has not been accorded any place in the traditional Irish fiddling aesthetic.

The Flute (musical examples 26-30)

The transverse flute has been used in traditional Irish music since the early 18th century (Breathnach 1971:85). It is often referred to by traditional players as the "big flute" or the "concert flute" in order to distinguish it from the tinwhistle, which has had the title "little flute" appended to it.

A wide variety of flutes are used by Irish musicians, but wooden flutes possessing conical bores, "simple" fingering systems and pre-Boehm, open-hole key mechanisms are most commonly found.

Currently, there is a controversy among flute players in the U.S. regarding the use of metal vs. wooden flutes. The dissension centers primarily on the tonal qualities of each instrument and on the advantages and disadvantages of complex vs. simple fingering systems.

Advocates of the wooden flute maintain that the sound of the metal instrument is not appropriate to traditional Irish music. Its "metallic" tone, they feel, does not do justice to the music and represents an intrusion of modern, alien influences similar to the cultivation of classical violin sound and technique among erstwhile fiddlers.

Players of the metal flute assert that the sound produced by most wooden flutes is weak, indistinct and uneven in the upper and lower registers. The Boehm flute, they claim, is easier to blow, thereby minimizing faulty intonation and ragged phrasing caused by a strained embouchure and an insufficient air supply. Most importantly, its greater clarity and increased volume enables it to compete with louder instruments, particularly accordions, on more equal terms.

Hybrid instruments are sometimes found, such as those with a modern, metal head joint attached to an open-hole, simple-system, cone-shaped body.

There are a few cylindrical wooden flutes with cylindrical wooden head joints and simple-system fingering methods such as the Rudall Carte 1867 model, the Radcliff 1870 model, the Pratten model and other miscellaneous and sometimes unique systems invented and made popular in England in the wake of the Boehm revolution. These combinations are rare, but those who possess such flutes claim that they have the advantages of both the wooden and metal instruments without the disadvantages of either.

Most wooden flutes used by Irish musicians are completely open-holed and unencumbered by key ring mechanisms. Many flute players whose wooden instruments do possess keys refrain from using them or else employ them only in rare instances. This is largely a matter of personal preference and is not a stylistic trait.

The key ring mechanism of the Boehm flute, however, makes it difficult to slide into a note from the one below it. This method of approaching a pitch from anywhere to a quarter or less to a whole tone beneath it is considered by traditional musicians as a most expressive and essential element of traditional playing. Even the French model Boehm flute with its perforated keys is not able to fully overcome the hindrance of the key ring mechanism in this respect. Boehm-system flutes, however, possess the advantage of being fully chromatic and are not limited, as are most wooden flutes, to playing in only a few keys.

The difference in fingering systems, particularly the position of the F# on the Boehm flute, has also contributed to the reluctance of wooden flute players to adopt the new instrument. For players who have used one system of fingering throughout their playing lives, it is no easy task to readjust their thinking and motor patterns to cope with the Boehm system used on metal flutes. Such a transition entails the re-learning of virtually one's entire repertoire.

The controversy also involves disagreement about the basic conception of the role of the flute in traditional Irish music. Metal flute players tend to look upon players who persist in clinging to the wooden flute and simple fingering system as primitive, unprogressive, musically inferior and unsophisticated. They consider themselves, on the other hand, as innovators within the tradition and believe that the adoption of the metal flute and the Boehm system represents a higher, more advanced plane of development in traditional Irish flute playing.

Wooden flute players quite naturally resent these pretensions and view the crusade to raise the standards of traditional flute playing as a blatant attempt to introduce alien influences into the traditional idiom.

A number of older players have switched over to the metal flute in the last few years, and almost all young musicians taking up the flute in the U.S. begin with the metal, Boehm instrument. Due to the scarcity in this country of good-quality wooden flutes in playable condition, the modern instrument seems likely to gain favor among traditional players in the next few decades despite its drawbacks. Neither instrument, however, has won a secure place with young Irish-American musicians, who have confined their collective attention almost exclusively to the accordion and fiddle.

The Tinwhistle (musical examples 31-33)

This instrument is known by a variety of names — "tin flute", "little flute", "flageolet" and "the whistle". Although it is not considered to have been of major importance in the development of traditional Irish music, it is acknowledged as a bonafide solo instrument and has received much greater recognition from traditional players in the last few years.

It is quite often played as a secondary instrument by pipers, flute players and even a few fiddlers and accordionists. There are also a number of musicians who have devoted their efforts to the tinwhistle exclusively, in an attempt to develop its previously unexplored expressive capabilities to the fullest extent.

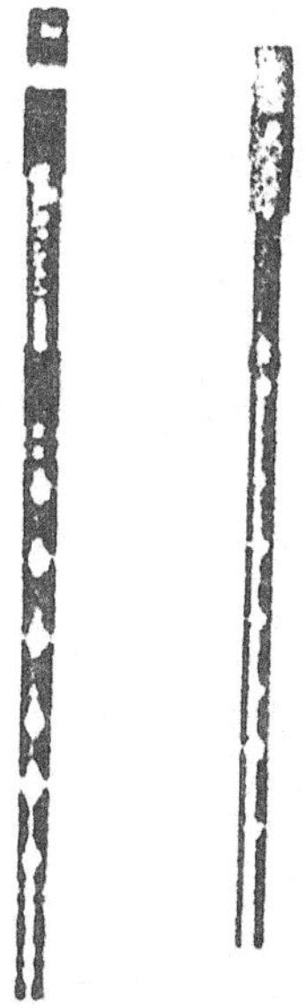

Currently, two types of tinwhistles are used by Irish musicians in the U.S., the Clarke and the Generation brands (see Figure 7).

The Clarke is a six-hole flageolet of the basic fipple-mouthpiece variety, with a small block of wood placed under the lip of the top of the instrument. It is made of tin and comes in the key of C major (though actually pitched a whole tone flat).

It is easily distinguished from the other kind by its conical shape and soft, flute-like tone. The Clarke tinwhistle is now used mostly by older players or when playing with pipers whose pipes have flat-pitch chanters.

The Generation model, like the Clarke, has a two-octave, diatonic range, chromatic notes being obtained by utilizing cross-fingering, fork-fingering or half-holing techniques. However, it has a plastic mouthpiece affixed to the top of a cylindrical body of brass or nickel-coated alloy.

Figure 7: Tinwhistles – Clarke (left), Generation (right). Photo: M.B. Wallace.

The Generation is available in six keys — G, F, Eb, D, C, Bb — with D being most commonly used, particularly when playing with other concert-pitch instruments. The tone of the Generation tinwhistle is much sharper and more piercing than the Clarke, and it is ubiquitous among all ages of traditional Irish musicians in the U.S.

The Accordion (musical examples 34-36)

A relatively recent (20th-century) addition to the family of traditional Irish instruments, the accordion is currently the most popular instrument among Irish-American musicians. Its acceptance into the tradition came at a time when the other instrumental traditions were entering a period of decline, and, in several cities, the accordion exists as the sole survivor of a once flourishing legacy of traditional Irish music.

Both button and piano accordions are used by Irish-American musicians. The button accordion — often referred to as the "Irish accordion", the "chromatic accordion" or, simply, the "box" — is a development of the single-row melodeon that was common in the 19th century and in the early part of the 20th. The new instrument had two rows and was pitched in various keys, C#/D being one of the favorites (see Figure 8).

In the last two decades the C/D button accordion model has been almost completely superseded by the two-row accordion pitched in B/C. The older kind can still be seen in the hands of a few players who learned the instrument in the 1920s, '30s and '40s, but only the B/C variety is now being taken up by young accordionists.

The recordings made by the Irish accordion player Paddy O'Brien during the early 1950s marked the beginning of the switch to the B/C accordion, a change which also heralded the emergence of a new style of Irish accordion playing. The proponents of the B/C instrument maintain that, although it is initially more difficult to manipulate, it offers a much greater range of technical possibilities than the older models, particularly in respect to the ease with which certain embellishments such as triplets of the form g/f#/g can be played.

B/C accordions, most of them of the Paolo Soprani model, also have more keys, thus more notes, than the older models. Octave couplers and extra bass notes are also available on the B/C accordion; these are used to achieve a variety of rhythmic, harmonic and dynamic effects, (see Figure 9 and compare with Figure 8).

The piano accordion has recently come into prominence in traditional Irish music, although it is most often found at Irish-American musical occasions in which traditional elements are noticeably absent — cabaret and nightclub entertainment, weddings, the majority of dances sponsored by Irish-American social organizations and so forth. Its autonomy has been firmly established in Ireland, however, and in the U.S. it has been given its own separate category in traditional Irish music competitions. Its currency among young musicians has been greatly stimulated by its inclusion in the schools of Irish music found in the U.S.

The popularity of the piano accordion among all ages of musicians seems to be due in large measure to the fact that it can be used to play other types of music which are more financially remunerative than traditional Irish music. In fact, it is not uncommon in the U.S. to find instances of fiddlers, pipers, flute and tinwhistle players who have taken up the piano accordion in order to increase the scope of their commercial music career.

Figure 8: C#/D button accordion (photo courtesy of Mr. Thomas Senier, Boston)

Figure 9: B/C button accordion (photo courtesy of *Treoir* magazine)

However, the instrument has yet to make any significant contributions in style or repertoire to either the tradition of Irish accordion playing or the larger tradition of Irish music, but has to date remained in the shadow of the button accordion.

The accordion has assumed an increasingly large role in the maintenance of traditional Irish music in the U.S. and, indeed, to many it is the first instrument that comes to mind when Irish music is mentioned. The accordion has not been harmed by technological advances in its basic construction, but has, on the contrary, profited enormously from such innovations. At the same time, its performers have discovered and applied new techniques of playing the instrument that have elevated the accordion to a status equivalent to that enjoyed by the pipes and fiddle.

The Concertina

The concertina is rarely heard at a public traditional Irish musical occasion in the U.S., though there are a few Irish-Americans who possess the instrument and play it privately. There is no indication that the concertina was ever widely used by Irish musicians in this country.

At least one record of a concertina player — Columbia 33086-F — is known to have been produced in the 1920s (Columbia 1927:216). However, the paucity of recordings by traditional Irish concertina players in the U.S. is so acute that no musical example could be obtained for this thesis.

Although the first concertina invented by Sir Charles Wheatstone in 1844 was octagonally-shaped (Howarth 1971:322), the modern instrument is hexagonal with keys on both sides of the bellows for playing the melody. The two makes most commonly used by Irish musicians are the German and the Anglo-German, which is also known as the Celtic or the Anglo-Celtic (Ó Duibhir 1972:19).

The German model has single action, like the button accordion, and two rows of keys on either side of the bellows. With a single-action instrument, two different notes can be obtained from a single key depending on whether the bellows are pressed in or drawn out. A double-action key gives the same note whether the bellows is pressed or drawn (*ibid.*:16).)

The single-action, two or three-row Anglo-German concertina was derived by combining features of the German type with the double action and three rows of keys of the English Wheatstone. The addition of the third row increased the number of keys in which a full diatonic scale is available (*ibid.*:17).

The concertina as used by traditional Irish musicians is capable of a surprising amount of rhythmic and melodic subtlety that is often lacking from performances on other free reed instruments. Its rather puny sound, when compared to the accordion, is undoubtedly a major factor that has prevented the concertina from being used at public musical occasions where loudness is a prerequisite for performance. In Ireland, the concertina has recently to enjoy a slight revival but can be said to flourish only in the County Clare and in the bordering districts of Counties Limerick and Tipperary.

Solo Instruments — Miscellaneous

A number of miscellaneous instruments have been taken up by traditional musicians, almost always as secondary instruments.

These instruments have not figured significantly in the tradition's development, nor are they considered of more than slight importance by the majority of traditional Irish musicians. Indeed, there are many who would deny that these instruments deserve any place in traditional Irish music at all.

Despite their lack of proper accreditation in traditional circles, these miscellaneous instruments appear at a number of formal and informal, public and private Irish-American musical occasions, and, on these grounds, must receive some consideration in this discussion of the material musical culture of traditional Irish music in the U.S.

More than anything else, the use of these instruments in performing traditional Irish music indicates the existence of the diverse musical influences currently impinging upon the tradition. It should be remembered, too, that at one time, such foreign imports as the accordion, the concertina, the flute and even the fiddle were doubtlessly regarded with similar suspicion in certain quarters.

Whether any of the current group of miscellaneous instruments will ever attain the position of a front-ranking instrument in the tradition remains to be seen.

The Banjo (musical example 37)

The banjo used by Irish musicians is the four-string banjo. It is played with a plectrum and is tuned in standard fiddle tuning (GDAE). With this tuning, the skilled banjoist can duplicate much of the ornamentation employed by fiddlers; even the rapid bowing-out of triplets in the form of a shake can be simulated on the banjo by adroit manipulation of the plectrum.

Banjos appeared in the tradition in the late 19th century, and a number occur on some of the recordings of the 1920s and '30s, generally as members of duets, trios and céilí bands (music examples 50, 53, 54).

Although the popularity of the banjo among Irish-American musicians was undoubtedly increased by its currency in music hall and vaudeville entertainment, the influence of popular plectrum banjo styles on the style of traditional Irish banjo playing, such as those found in early ragtime and jazz, has been negligible.

The Mandolin and Banjoline

The mandolin and banjoline (a hybrid with a mandolin fingerboard and tuning attached to a banjo frame) were both introduced very recently into Irish musical occasions via the urban folk revival that took place in the British Isles as well as America during the 1960s and '70s. They are played with a plectrum and make use of the same tuning and technique as the four-string banjo. The status of these instruments in traditional Irish music, however, remains extremely marginal.

The Harmonica (musical example 40)

The harmonica, or mouth organ, was another free-reed instrument introduced into Ireland in the mid-19th century. Simple dance tunes and airs constitute the bulk of the mouth organ player's repertoire. Various types of harmonies are used; the chromatic Hohner models are most favored because of their greater range and versatility in regard to key.

Ornamentation on the harmonica is limited to triplets and single grace notes, though with the chromatic models double grace notes and rolls can be obtained by a virtuosically dextrous use of the slider bar by which accidentals are achieved. The technique of many Irish mouth organ players includes the use of chords to support the melody in a manner reminiscent of the accordionist's use of chords and bass notes in the left hand to fill out the melodic framework.

It remains to add that the harmonica is not a commonly-found instrument in traditional Irish musical communities in America. From numerous remarks made by American Irish musicians, as well as from personal observation, it seems that the harmonica is an instrument played mostly by young children when other instruments are unavailable or unsuitable; the adult population of orgán béil players in the U.S. is extremely slight.

The Piccolo

The piccolo occasionally appears as a substitute for the transverse flute or as an added dimension of tonal coloring in a céilí band. No logical reason for its rarity can be given other than that its high pitch (generally an octave above the other traditional instruments) does not yield a sound considered satisfying to the traditionally-oriented ear. The expense of a piccolo, either old or new, is also a likely deterrent.

The Harp

The harps used by Irish-Americans today are but distantly related to the instruments of the harpers who flourished in Ireland three centuries ago. The harps currently employed are modern pedal harps, and their antiquity in most cases extends no further than the late 19th century.

There are also a number of so-called "Irish harps" modeled either after the Queen Mary Harp of the Scottish Clarsach Society or the harps made in the latter half of the 19th century in Ireland ostensibly based on 18th-century patterns but actually derived from the harps of the Continental European variety (Warren 1971:18).

The replica of the 14th-century, wire-strung "Brian Boru" harp built three years ago by Christopher Warren of Kerry has not appeared in the U.S. as of yet.

The harp appears mostly in competitions for musicians and never at any other traditional Irish musical occasions in the U.S. Only young persons enter the harp events at feiseanna and fleadhanna, and they are required to perform pieces from the repertoire of Western art music with perhaps a few of the 19th-century pseudo-Irish airs devised by popular tunesmiths and classical composers. Occasionally, one of the more Italianate compositions of the 18th-century Irish harper Turlough O'Carolan is placed on the program along with one or two "traditional airs" that have been transmogrified by art music arrangement and harmonization practices.

It is obvious that the harp events are meant only to test the mechanical skill of the competitors and are not intended to promote traditional Irish harp music.

A deeply rooted Irish harping tradition is non-existent in the U.S. Despite the oblique reference in the memoirs of Arthur O'Neill to the emigration of an Irish harper to the U.S. in the 18th century (O'Neill 1973b:65), it is exceedingly doubtful that it ever existed in this country, as it was completely moribund in Ireland by the second quarter of the 19th century (Rimmer 1969:66).

Accompanying Instruments — Harmonic

The practice of harmonic accompaniment was not introduced into the tradition until the late 19th century (excluding from consideration the drones and regulators of the uilleann pipes).

The origins of the practice are not known, but, as is evidenced by the early recordings of traditional Irish music, it was firmly entrenched by 1910. Whether the use of accompanying instruments received its genesis in the artificial environment of the recording studio and did not actually reflect the traditional performance practice of the period is a question that has not been completely resolved.

Recordings of the 1920s and '30s show that some form of accompaniment, either harmonic or percussive (or occasionally both) was standard recording practice. Even uilleann pipers, whose instruments possess their own elementary accompaniment in the form of drones and regulators, were frequently recorded with piano accompaniment.

The most important function of harmonic accompaniment in traditional Irish music is to maintain a consistent tempo. Accompanists are evaluated according to their ability to sustain a steady, unambiguous beat; the actual harmonic content of the accompaniment is of secondary importance. Not infrequently, it bears no more than a distant relationship to the underlying harmonic structure of the melody.

This rhythmic function, however, does not entail a percussive function. The distinction is perhaps somewhat vague, but it is considered important by traditional musicians, nonetheless. For example, the New York Céilí Band failed to win first prize in the céilí band competition at the 1960 Boyle Fleadh, despite a superior performance, because the judges felt their piano player was trying to "act like a drummer", i.e. was exceeding the limits of tasteful piano accompaniment.

Most traditional musicians in the U.S. regard some form of harmonic support as desirable, especially in formal musical occasions such as public solo performance or recording sessions. The opinion most frequently expressed is that accompaniment helps the soloist maintain proper tempo, lends color and contrast to the overall performance and provides the soloist with a framework around which melodic and rhythmic variations can be woven.

There are others, however, who believe that traditional Irish music is rendered best in the solo performance.

The Piano (musical examples 6, 8-9, 12-14, 16, 20, 24, 27-29, 31, 34-36, 38-39, 43, 47, 49-50, 53-55)

In traditional Irish music, the major role of the piano is to provide simple chord accompaniment for the solo instrument.

Although a few exceptionally able pianists have been able to give acceptable solo performances of traditional Irish music (musical examples 38-39), such performances are regarded as novelties and in no way alter the conventional accompanying role of the instrument in this idiom.

The usual method of piano accompaniment to Irish dance music is known as "vamping" (see other musical examples). This consists of a constant succession of single notes in the bass by the left hand alternating with block chords in the treble by the right.

Both single notes and chords occur precisely on the beat; there is no syncopation, except possibly at the final cadence of an eight-bar section (musical example 16). In duple meter (2/4 and 4/4) the single notes generally occur on the strong accents, the block chords on the weak ones.

In triple meter tunes (6/8, 9/8 and 12/8) either single notes or chords are used on the first note of each group of three eighth notes, so that a measure of 6/8 would have two chords or single notes, a measure of 9/8 would have three and a measure of 12/8 would have four.

Slow airs are often provided with an arpeggiated-chord accompaniment that attempts to simulate harp accompaniment.

There is a certain amount of surface variation in piano accompaniment in respect to the texture and spacing of the left and right-hand voices, the linear sequence of the chord progressions (which nominally correspond to the harmonic structure of the tune) and the single-note accompaniment pattern which might take several forms: a broken-chord figure such as a modified Alberti bass or a simple ostinato pattern, a wide-ranging, arpeggiated outlining of the chord or a pedal point pattern.

This variation is dependent on the harmonic structure of the tune, the meter of the tune and the sensitivity and ingenuity of the accompanist. An exceptionally daring accompanist might occasionally play a few bars of the melody in the treble while continuing some ostinato or pedal point pattern in the bass. Except for the one case noted above, variation in the basic rhythmic pulse of the tune is not the prerogative of the accompanist.

The Guitar (musical examples 10-11, 15)

The guitar has only recently become popular as an accompanying instrument in traditional Irish music. It appears less frequently in this context than does the piano and is more often found at informal sessions in taverns and clubs than at formal public performances or on recordings. Acoustic six-string guitars are the standard, although in crowded, noisy musical environments, the electrically-amplified instrument is used.

Chord-strumming is the most common method of guitar accompaniment, but single-string and finger-picking styles are not unknown. As with piano accompaniment, guitar accompaniment in Irish dance music follows the harmonic and accentual patterns of the tune.

Accompanying Instruments — Percussive

Percussive accompaniment occurs in both formal and informal musical contexts. It is used primarily by ensembles such as céilí bands (a unit functionally equivalent to a dance band, c.f. Section D of this chapter) in order to provide a constant, unambiguous rhythmic pulse for the musicians and a lively, danceable beat for listeners and dancers.

Informal musical occasions such as impromptu sessions are often enlivened by the appearance of a dextrous spoons player, and it is not uncommon, if the proper pair of culinary utensils cannot be procured, for coins, sticks, shoes, rings and other objects to be used to beat out an accompanying rhythm.

The Bodhrán (musical examples 26-27, 52)

The bodhrán is best visualized as a large tambourine without jangles (see Figure 10). More specifically, it is a drum covered on one side with skin that is tacked, tied or sewn onto a wooden hoop approximately two feet in diameter.

Figure 10: A bodhrán (right). Photo courtesy of *Treoir* magazine.

This serves as a frame for the skin; two perpendicularly crossed pieces of wood are attached to the other side of this frame. Goat, sheep, calf and pig skins have been used, and hardwoods are most commonly used in the construction of the frame.

In performance, the bodhrán is held by the cross-pieces while the head is struck with a small wooden stick eight to twelve inches in length that is knobbed on both ends. Both ends of the stick are used in beating the skin; the frame as well as the skin is also frequently part of the playing surface.

The technique of skilled bodhrán playing lies in the ability of the performer to provide an accompaniment that is steady and strongly-accented yet, at the same time, inventive and varied.

The accomplished bodhrán player, like any other first-rate accompanist, is able to enhance the solo performance by responding to the changes in melodic phrasing and rhythm.

Although percussive accompaniment in Irish dance music serves primarily to define the basic rhythmic pulse of the tune — one beat per each eighth note — a great deal of rhythmic variation is possible on the part of the percussive accompanist.

In Ireland, the bodhrán has always held a secure place in the pockets of tradition that have been relatively uninfluenced by modern trends, but it has been thoroughly displaced in the U.S. by the modern drum set, an innovation thrust into prominence by the céilí band explosion of the 1920s and '30s.

The bodhrán is beginning to reappear in isolated places around the U.S. due to the recent revival of interest in the instrument that has occurred in Ireland, but the tradition of bodhrán playing is not presently a flourishing one in America.

The Drums (musical examples 53, 55)

The modern drum set was introduced into traditional Irish music via the céilí bands, and it is in this context that it is almost exclusively found.

Drum sets of this nature are comprised of one bass drum, one or two snare drums, one or two standing cymbals, with perhaps a high-hat cymbal. Woodblocks are an essential piece of equipment and play an important role as signaling devices. Two sharp raps on the woodblock, for instance, cue the other instrumentalists either to prepare to change into a new tune or to stop playing at the end of the phrase. The use of wooden drumsticks is universal, and drummers often use the snare rim, woodblock and cymbal(s) to achieve various timbrel effects.

Drum accompaniment is less subtle and more emphatically straightforward than is bodhrán accompaniment. In its most overbearing form, drum accompaniment reduces reels to marches and jigs to military two-steps (Meek 1972:7); when played with a modicum of taste and restraint, however, the drums can contribute a good deal of liveliness and vigor to an otherwise plodding ensemble performance. Like the bodhrán, the drums are but rarely used to accompany solo performers on records.

The Spoons (musical examples 45-48)

Probably the most ubiquitous percussive device employed by traditional Irish musicians in the U.S. are the spoons. They are the lineal descendants of pairs of polished animal bones, some of which are still used in Ireland. In the U.S., ordinary kitchen spoons are used, though it is claimed by some that spoons of pure silver possess the most desirable tonal qualities. They appear most often at informal sessions in taverns, clubs, and homes, but are occasionally used to enliven a recording.

(B) Styles

"Style" in traditional Irish music denotes the composite form of the distinctive features that identify an individual's musical performance. The elements of style can be translated into the following variables:

- ornamentation: type and frequency of embellishments and the rules governing their usage within the environments of various melodic structures

- variation in melodic and rhythmic patterns: type and frequency of variation and the rules governing its occurrence in a particular environment

- melodic phrasing: length of phrase units and the consistency with which standard units of length are maintained

- tone: quality of sound or of tone color as perceived and expressed in affective, connotative terms such as mellow, harsh, sweet, brilliant, etc.

- articulation: enunciation of individual notes along a legato to non-legato continuum and the general pattern of articulation in regard to melodic phrasing

- stress: the accentuation and emphasis of defined rhythmic groupings

These variables can be viewed as stylistic universals for this idiom in that their occurrence or non-occurrence comprises the distinctive features that characterize every performance and figure most prominently in the evaluation of an individual's performance by other traditional musicians.

In addition, each instrument has its own extra variables peculiar to itself; these variables also exist as criteria for defining and assessing style.

For example, the direction, strength, duration and frequency of bow strokes, the amount and area of bow employed and the use of double stops or open strings as drones are additional features which contribute to the identity of fiddle styles.

In piping, the use or non-use of the regulators is a distinguishing stylistic trait as is the method of fingering and manipulating the chanter to produce the desired articulatory pattern and changes in the tone color of individual notes.

The styles of traditional Irish music have coalesced from a number of diverse sources. Some styles are representative of a particular locality, region or province; others are associated with individual musicians whose playing greatly influenced their contemporaries and left a substantial imprint on the tradition's subsequent development.

Some styles have adapted techniques used in the sean-nós ("old custom") style of Gaelic singing, while a few have borrowed heavily from other instrumental traditions. Still others have been generated by the development of technical features peculiar to a particular instrument.

The evolution of a style is a cumulative process. A style is essentially a conglomeration of elements absorbed or appropriated outright from other styles and then reshaped and refined into a "new" style that is distinct yet never entirely divorced from its predecessors or contemporaries. This process is not exclusively eclectic, for elements derived from the personal creativity of individual musicians frequently form the basis of a new style.

However, these innovations are always conceived and channelled within an established, accepted framework such that even the most seemingly idiosyncratic stylistic traits will, upon closer inspection, be seen to reflect the shaping influence of the stylistic norms characteristic of the larger tradition. Viewed from this perspective, stylistic evolution is primarily a matter of the re-interpretation of existing material rather than the innovation of new material from outside the tradition.

Though guided by certain conventions, style in traditional Irish music is not perceived by its practitioners as a rigid, static set of rules that must be dogmatically or slavishly followed. It is, instead, a flexible, context-sensitive medium through which an individual's musical expression can be given a form and substance that will invest his performance with communicative value.

Instrumental Styles in the U.S.

To date, there has emerged no distinctively Irish-American style of performing traditional Irish music that has become a pan-Irish-American style. Although there have been several Irish musicians in the U.S. who have made extensive contributions to the current stylistic corpus, the great bulk of Irish musicians who arrive in America do not jettison their stylistic habits when exposed to different styles but tend initially to retain a tenacious hold on their own style. Musicians might occasionally adapt certain characteristics of another style, but this occurs mostly with younger musicians who have not yet settled upon an established personal style.

However, despite the increased interaction among musicians of different styles that has taken place in the U.S., communities of traditional Irish musicians exhibit great heterogeneity in style.

Occasionally, a certain style might be designated as an ideal — such as the Coleman style of fiddling or the Tuohey style of piping — from which fiddlers and pipers claim to draw inspiration and to base their musical style. In most cases, the homage is merely token. The stylistic ideal which they are striving to emulate exists as a rather vague conception that is defined differently by each performer according to his taste and judgment.

For example, the uilleann pipers who believe that they are imitating Patsy Tuohey's style range along such a broad continuum of style that one marvels at how the same source can be perceived in so many drastically different ways.

American-born musicians who were learning the music during the 1920s, '30s and '40s received their stylistic input from two sources — the musicians of the preceding generation with whom they had personal contact and the records of Irish-American musicians that were produced in the period between the two World Wars. In some cases, these sources overlapped, as several of the musicians who made recordings also taught young musicians on both formal and informal bases.

The decades since the Second World War have witnessed a reversal of the direction of stylistic influence. The post-war generation of upcoming Irish-American musicians has not been able to rely upon personal instruction from the preceding generation — which has declined considerably in number and accessibility — nor upon inspiration from Irish-American records of that period, which are almost non-existent.

In terms of style, musicians in the U.S. have come to regard Ireland as the major source of direction. Young musicians, especially, are apt to have a very strong orientation toward Ireland and are generally unaware of or unreceptive to the older styles manifested by several American players. Records exist as the primary means of style transmission for the present generation of musicians learning Irish music, but it is Irish instead of Irish-American musicians who serve as stylistic models.

A trend toward stylistic consolidation has also become noticeable in the last few decades, largely as a result of the crystallization of style and repertoire promoted by radio and records. In recent years, too, Irish-American musicians have become increasingly dependent upon Ireland as a source of new developments in style and repertoire. Nevertheless, the diversity of style currently displayed by traditional Irish musicians in the U.S. serves as proof that the tradition is still vital and evolving.

The Uilleann Pipes (musical examples 1-5)

Uilleann piping styles are distinguished primarily on the basis of the method of fingering the chanter and by the type of articulation that is thereby produced. Two styles, "open" and "close", are presently recognized. In the open or loose style, the melody is uttered in a very legato manner, with little or no distinct articulation of individual notes. This fluidity is achieved by employing a method of fingering in which "only those fingers necessary to sound the note correctly are left on the chanter" (Breathnach 1971:95).

In the close or tight style of piping, however, "the only fingers taken off the chanter are those which must be taken off if the note is to sound correctly" (*ibid*.). This results in "an instant of silence between notes" (*ibid*.) and produces a sound that is markedly non-legato. At its best, close piping can be tremendously dynamic and zestful, but in its extreme form can degenerate into an excessively-staccato and choppy delivery in which melody, rhythm and phrasing are obfuscated.

Pipers generally maintain strict adherence to one style, although a few have managed to reach a medium that includes elements of both styles. Many pipers believe that the two types of playing are so fundamentally opposed as to be virtually irreconcilable.

Largely due to the influence of the recordings of Irish-American piper Patsy Tuohey and Irish piper Leo Rowsome, the continuous use of the regulators in dance music has become associated with open piping. Open players regard the regulators as an integral and important element of piping, while close players use them more sparingly to achieve the maximum dramatic effect. The constant use of the regulators is often looked upon with contempt and disdain by close pipers as an attention-catching device of street players.

Historically, the styles had a regional basis, with open fingering found throughout areas in the province of Leinster and in east Munster, and close piping cultivated in Connacht and in other areas on the west coast. In the 20th century, piping styles have ceased to be determined by strictly geographical factors, as radio and recordings have promoted a wider dissemination of styles formerly restricted in currency to their immediate area of provenance. Today, the style chosen by aspiring pipers is either that of their teacher or that of a piper whose playing has made a substantial impact upon them (*ibid.*).

There is impressionistic evidence that a number of styles that incorporated elements of both open and close piping were developed by American Irish pipers in the 19th century. Almost all of them have vanished, but vestiges of one still survive.

This has been termed the Tuohey style of piping after Patrick J. Tuohey (1865-1923), a professional musician who was hailed by his contemporaries as having "no equal anywhere" (O'Neill 1973b:313). Although it is doubtful that Tuohey originated the style, his role in developing and popularizing it through public performance and recordings cannot be overestimated.

It has been suggested (*ibid.*:vii) that this style may have been formulated by John Egan (died c. 1897), an Irish-American with whom Tuohey "took what may be regarded as a post-graduate course" in piping (*ibid.*:313), or by William Taylor (d. 1892), the Philadelphia piper and pipemaker whose influence among his contemporaries was extensive.

In attempting to explain the growth of this style, one commentator has hypothesized that the abrupt transplantation of a music of rural, peasant origins to an urban, multi-cultural sphere gave impetus to the development of a repertoire and style of performance that "evolved for use on the stage of the variety hall and in vaudeville, and was designed to catch the attention of listeners of any ethnic origin, not relax them in an entertainment lasting for hours" (*ibid.*:vii).

To be sure, Tuohey's ability to arouse audiences to fever pitch is legend, and it is highly probable that this dynamic new style of piping appealed to Irish-American audiences as well as audiences of mixed nationality. What is of even greater interest is the capability of a traditional art to maintain its integrity while successfully adapting to a non-traditional performance situation.

This style of piping was characterized by innovations in the treatment of the melodic line and rhythmic structure of Irish dance tunes, particularly reels. A profusion of embellishments — primarily rolls, crans, triplets, single and double grace notes — were used to create a fluid, varied melodic line in which there was a minimum of vacant space. The shortening of the duration of the final note of a note grouping consisting of an underlying pattern of four eighths in duple meter, three eighths in triple meter) was a favorite device that hastened the entrance of the first note of the following note group and imparted a sense of continuous forward thrust (musical examples 1, 2).

In addition, the regulators were employed more extensively and more ingeniously than had previously been common. Originally intended as a means of simple harmonic accompaniment, the regulators were used by Tuohey to fulfill a percussive function. In some instances, they were made to produce an accompaniment that amounted to rudimentary harmonic counterpoint (musical example 2).

This style has not been transmitted without interruption to the present. While it may be possible to detect evidence of the existence of what has been called a "distinctive American style" of piping in the recordings made by Irish-American pipers of forty and fifty years ago (*ibid.*), the majority of present-day American pipers exhibit only a tenuous relation to this stylistic legacy.

Contemporary American pipers have been greatly influenced by the traditional open and close styles of piping as rendered by Leo Rowsome, Willie Clancy, Seamus Ennis, Felix and Johnny Doran and other Irish pipers who have flourished in the post-World War II period and have made numerous recordings.

That a break in the continuity of the transmission of the American piping traditions of the late 19th and early 20th century had occurred sometime in the 1930s and '40s became apparent in the 1950s and '60s when U.S. pipers found themselves dwindling in number and almost wholly dependent upon Irish pipers for inspiration and guidance in style.

This dependence on Ireland is most clearly observed in the American pipers under age thirty who acquire the bulk of their stylistic traits and repertoire from pipers in Ireland, though they might consult a piper in the U.S. about matters of basic technique involved in the first stages of learning the instrument.

Many have heard of Patsy Tuohey and perhaps even heard one of the four recordings he made for Victor in 1923, but Tuohey's piping exists as a pinnacle upon which one may gaze with admiration yet never fully attain.

The lesser-known giants of Irish-American piping who were recorded along with Tuohey — Tom Ennis, Liam Walsh, Michael Gallagher, Bernard Delaney, Michael Carney, Patrick Stack — are names now familiar only to a small coterie of record collectors and to the few remaining pipers who represent the last link with the American pipers and piping traditions of the pre-World War II generation.

The Fiddle (musical examples 6-25)

Although a variety of styles can still be heard in America, the style that has dominated Irish-American fiddling for the last half century is known as the "Sligo style".

This is a broadly descriptive generic term used to describe a style which embraced several variants or related sub-styles within its boundaries. It serves, however, to identify a style of fiddling that had been up to the 1920s largely restricted to the area of southern County Sligo, particularly the district of Killavil.

Oral lore attributes the development of this style to an itinerant fiddle master, Cipín (Stick) Scanlon, so named for his prodigious facility with the bow. Scanlon flourished in the late 19th century and is said to have had a profound influence on the succeeding generation of Sligo fiddle players, many of whom emigrated to the U.S. in the early 20th century.

In America, the Sligo style as expounded by Scanlon underwent an extensive amount of refashioning and refinement. Although the style's roots were clearly and recently based in Ireland, the tumultuous sensation caused in that country by the early recordings of American Sligo-style fiddlers indicates that the style had been considerably transformed during its brief sojourn in the U.S.

The Sligo style was well represented on the commercial recordings of the period. In fact, recordings by Sligo-style fiddlers dominated the field, especially from the late 1920s onward. Although several fiddlers espousing different styles derived from other sources were recorded in the early part of the decade, their impact on the tradition was negligible, and their styles did not survive their lifetime (musical examples 12-13).

The large contingent of Sligo fiddlers in the U.S. at that time and the extraordinary quantity of their recordings can only partially account for this phenomenon. More than either of these factors, the rapid spread of the Sligo style was due to its utilization and extension of instrumental techniques and stylistic possibilities that already existed in the idiom but had not been fully developed. The Sligo style presented a synthesis that was novel yet wholly rooted in tradition.

In the 1920s and '30s, New York (particularly Brooklyn and the Bronx) boasted a large and thriving population of traditional Irish musicians. Included in this hosting were numerous "first-rate players" such as Lad O'Beirne, Paul Ryan, Tommy Cawley, Packie Dolan, Paddy Sweeny, Ed Reavy, Hugh Gillespie and Larry Redican, to name but a few.

There were three fiddlers, however, whose playing was acknowledged as supreme and whose careers dominated the New York Irish music community of the period. These three — Michael Coleman, James Morrison and Patrick Killoran — were all natives of County Sligo. They were natural heirs to the Sligo style (indeed, Coleman received extensive tutelage in his youth from Cipín Scanlon) and played the greatest roles in popularizing it in the U.S.

Through the records, public performances and teaching of these three fiddlers, the Sligo style was firmly established in New York and widely disseminated throughout the larger Irish-American musical community within a decade after its initial appearance on record.

As previously stated, the Sligo style is simply a convenient label to attach to what is actually a set of closely-related yet distinct sub-styles of fiddling that are today found throughout Ireland and America. An examination of the corpus of recordings by Coleman, Morrison and Killoran (who may be considered to represent the three most seminal figures in the style's evolution in America) reveals that the most distinctive feature of Sligo-style fiddling is the highly-ornamented and highly-developed melodic line marked by considerable melodic and rhythmic variation.

Much of this variation is achieved by subtle changes in the sequential and rhythmic patterns of the ornaments as well as by changes in articulation and phrasing produced by skillful and varied use of the bow. Drones and double stops are absent from this style, for they would interfere with the development and decoration of the melody. A variety of embellishments are employed — single and double grace notes, triplets achieved by fingering and by bowing, an abundance of quick, crisp rolls — to attain fluency and cohesion in the statement of the melodic line.

Differences in style are evident in the performances of each individual. Michael Coleman's remarkably innovative tune settings and astounding capacity for introducing a seemingly endless number of spontaneous variations in the melody, rhythm and phrasing of a tune have given him an exalted status among Irish fiddlers.

His superb fingering and brilliant usage of ornamentation enabled him to weave an intricate tapestry from the melodic substance of even the most simple, ordinary tunes (musical examples 6-7).

Many fiddlers, though they hold Coleman in great reverence, prefer the style of James Morrison (musical examples 8-9). This style is more accessible to most fiddlers than the protean and intensely personal style of Coleman which occasionally borders on the idiosyncratic. Morrison is most admired for his strong, vigorous rhythm and his exuberantly expressive renditions. Although his playing was not as sensational or as adventurous as that of Coleman, Morrison's technique was highly developed, nonetheless.

Paddy Killoran (musical examples 10-11) entered onto the U.S. scene in the early 1930s, a decade or so later than Coleman and Morrison, and it is said that he listened closely to Morrison's records. Certainly, his treatment of the melodic line also tended to be less innovative than Coleman's; unlike Morrison, Killoran had a smooth, polished delivery highlighted by vividly-delineated phrasing. Killoran is best remembered for the many unusual and exquisite tunes he brought to wider public attention.

Today, the Sligo style as defined by Coleman, Morrison and Killoran is present in various forms among Irish-American fiddlers (musical examples 16-24). Although fiddle styles associated with Donegal, Kerry and West Clare have been gaining widespread notice in Ireland recently, the Sligo style and its progeny remain predominant in the U.S.

In the last two decades, however, a sub-style has emerged which might be termed the modern New York style, although it is not restricted to New York musicians but has its greatest number of adherents in that locality. This is a derivative of Sligo-style fiddling and is, in fact, very similar in its approach to the melodic line, use of ornamentation, rhythm and melodic phrasing. The modern New York style aims for a tone quality that is refined, smooth and closer to the tone of a classically-trained violinist.

It is marked by an emphasis on a display of impressive technique that is frequently felt to be lacking in expression. The modern New York style possesses little of the rhythmic drive of Morrison, nor does it exhibit any tendency toward the spontaneity of Coleman (musical example 24).

In a sense, the modern New York style represents a hybrid style created by the imposition of classical violin technique upon traditional fiddling styles. The influence of the classical violin aesthetic has become more pronounced in a number of Irish-American fiddle players in the last few years. Such players emphasize the attainment of a brilliant, vibrato-full tone and cultivate unusual bowing techniques borrowed from violinists.

The introduction of classical tone and technique into traditional Irish fiddling has resulted in a dilution rather than an improvement of the traditional idiom as its advocates have sought. It exists as an artificial sweetening that in many cases serves only to draw attention from playing that is expressionless and deficient by traditional standards.

The majority of young fiddlers under age 25 have had training in classical music. While this enables them to cope more easily with the technical demands of Irish music, it has made the achievement of authentic, acceptable traditional fiddling more challenging. With very few exceptions, young Irish-American fiddlers have turned to Ireland for stylistic guidance and are unaware of the American Irish fiddle styles that flourished only a generation ago.

The deaths of Coleman in 1945 and Morrison in 1947 can be seen as signaling the end of one of the most prolific eras in American Irish music. Other excellent fiddlers remained, notably Killoran and Lad O'Beirne, but they labored under the shadow of the two deceased giants. The 1960s brought the death of Killoran and the retirement of O'Beirne and several others from the active musical community.

The links to the styles of Coleman and Morrison have been weakening in recent years, and, presently, these traditions are maintained with full fidelity by only a handful of active fiddlers, notably Paddy Cronin of Boston, Andy McGann, Paddy Reynolds and Johnny Cronin of New York, John Vesey and Ed Reavy of Philadelphia and John McGreevy of Chicago. Although Coleman, Morrison and Killoran currently exist as distinct legendary figures, their evaporation into shadowy, purely mythological realms appears inevitable and is perhaps no more than a generation distant.

The Flute and The Tinwhistle (musical examples 26-33)

The distinction between the different styles of playing these instruments is largely a matter of articulation, phrasing, and frequency of ornamentation. One style of flute and whistle playing is characterized by staccato articulation of individual notes and phrases. Phrase boundaries are often determined by the length of the breath span. This type of playing is strongly accented and achieves its maximum effect by the use of rhythmic variation (Breathnach 1971:96-97).

Contrasted with this is a type of playing articulated in a legato fashion with tonguing of the notes rarely occurring. This style makes greater use of melodic embellishment. Phrasing is occasionally obscured by a tendency toward over-ornamentation and indistinct articulation. This is, however, a fluid and highly-decorated style of playing which bears a close resemblance to the Sligo style of fiddling in the use of ornamentation and in its treatment of the melodic line.

The two most renowned Irish-American flute players who recorded in the 1920s and '30s were John McKenna and Tom Morrison, originally from Counties Leitrim and Sligo respectively. If their recorded performances can be taken as representative of the style of flute playing then in vogue among Irish-American flutists, it appears likely that the legato, heavily-embellished style currently favored is of comparatively recent introduction to this country or else was simply not prominent nor prestigious enough to be recorded during this period. These recordings also indicate that the tempo of traditional flute playing has quickened considerably over the last thirty years (musical examples 26-30).

The surviving corpus of recordings by tinwhistle players of that era is too minute to permit meaningful, detailed analysis. However, it can be stated with some certainty that a shift to a more legato, profusely-ornamented, faster style of playing seems to have taken place in this instrumental idiom also (musical examples 31-33).

It will be noticed that the two main styles of flute and tinwhistle playing correspond roughly to lithe close and open styles of the uilleann pipes. Much of the ornamentation used by flute and whistle players is similar to and often identical with that used by pipers; this is due to the fact that both the flute and the tinwhistle are taken up as secondary instruments by many pipers (*ibid*.:97). The current leadership of Irish flute and whistle players in the area of style seems to have always been recognized by Irish-American players who do not appear to have developed any separate, indigenous style but have modified the existing ones.

The Accordion (musical examples 34-36)

When mentioned in print or public announcement, the name of Paddy O'Brien of Nenagh, County Tipperary, is inevitably followed by a statement that further identifies him as "the man who revolutionized accordion playing". Certainly, O'Brien is largely responsible for initiating the style of accordion playing which has become nearly universal among Irish box players in the last two decades. His recordings in the early 1950s first brought this new style to public attention, and his eight-year residence in New York from 1954 to 1962 firmly established it among players in the U.S.

As mentioned in the previous section on instruments, this new style also established the supremacy of the accordion pitched in B/C, generally the Italian-made Paolo Soprani model, which ousted both the older C#/D instrument and the style that went with it.

The basic principle upon which the new style is founded is so simple and so seemingly obvious that one wonders why it remained undiscovered and unused before O'Brien's time. The older style of accordion playing (musical examples 34-35) was adopted from the method of playing the melodeon. Although the button accordion had two rows instead of one, "players trained on the melodeon used the first or outer row of the accordion as they had used the single row of the older instrument, resorting only to the inner row to obtain a note not otherwise available. In this way the traditional style and technique of playing associated with the melodeon was retained almost intact" (*ibid*.).

This style employed a limited amount of ornamentation, primarily single and double grace notes ("splitting the note") and occasional triplets. The melodic phrasing and rhythmic groupings were clearly and emphatically defined (*ibid*.). This style was dominant in the U.S. until the middle 1950s and can still be found in the playing of accordionists who reached their stylistic maturity in the 1920as and '30s.

The new style utilized the full technical possibilities offered by the development of the heretofore neglected inner row of buttons. With the inner row functioning as the main one, the outer row was relegated to a subsidiary role and was used strictly for embellishment purposes. This reversal made possible new forms of ornamentation which in turn transformed the accordionist's treatment of the melodic line (*ibid*.).

O'Brien once stated in an interview that "I try to achieve the same variations on the accordion as are possible on the fiddle" (Finian 1970:10). Herein lies the truly revolutionary aspect of O'Brien's contribution to the idiom.

With the new, fully chromatic fingering system of the B/C accordion, a box player can simulate quite closely the ornamentation used by fiddlers; the far-reaching consequence of this development has been to elevate the status of accordion playing to an art form comparable to that of piping and fiddling.

However, the strongly-accented rhythmic pulse and the precise, articulate phrasing that were characteristic of the older style are often absent in new-style accordion playing. Unlike the fiddler, the accordion has no extraneous implement such as a bow with which to obtain varied articulation patterns, and the bellows cannot fully compensate for this inherent structural shortcoming.

Furthermore, the use of the inner row as the primary one has enabled triplets of the g/f#/g variety to be sounded with incredible ease and speed, with no changes necessary in the direction of bellows movement. In some cases, this form of embellishment is relied on excessively, and the melody is overwhelmed and obscured by an unarticulated torrent of non-stop triplets (*ibid.*:98).

Irish-American accordion players do not accord any of their peers on this side of the Atlantic the same admiration or status as is given to Irish accordionists, especially Paddy O'Brien and Joe Burke (who has also spent a considerable amount of time in the U.S.). In terms of style, American box players presently derive their inspiration from Irish sources. The once-renowned accordion players who set the stylistic norms in the 1920s, '30s and '40s are all but completely forgotten now.

Joe Cooley (Clare, Chicago and San Francisco), who died in December, 1973, was one of the last representatives of the breed of accordionists who served as transitional figures between the old and new styles. His style was a personal synthesis of the best elements of both styles, and his influence among younger players is said to have been considerable. By his death, the traditional Irish accordion community has been deprived of a valuable source of stylistic diversity.

Aesthetic Evaluation of Traditional Irish Music

The problems involved in the cross-cultural aesthetic analysis of musical performance have been thrashed out at length by Merriam (1964:259-276). As used in this paper, the term "aesthetic" designates the idealized set of concepts and criteria by which performances of traditional Irish music are evaluated by members of the traditional musical community (which includes non-performers knowledgeable in the idiom as well as performers).

"Expression" is perhaps the most important concept used in the aesthetic evaluation of this music. Expression is never explicitly defined by traditional musicians, but its presence or absence in a particular performance is duly noted. As used in traditional Irish music, expression refers to the emotion, the feeling, the spirit which a musician instills into his playing.

These terms are admittedly subjective, but they are meaningful, nevertheless. Players judged to be "expressionless" — no matter how technically impressive their performance, no matter how well they have mastered the technical demands of the idiom — are regarded with much less approbation than performers whose playing contains flaws in execution but is judged to be full of "expression".

An examination of the techniques by which expression is obtained might result in a more satisfactory comprehension of the concept. It should be remembered that traditional Irish music is essentially a solo performance tradition in which a piece of music is subjected to reinterpretation by each performer. Subtle variations in the melody, rhythm, ornamentation, articulation and phrasing of a tune are the means by which a player infuses his performance with expression.

Expression is achieved by redefining and reinterpreting the tune's basic melodic material and rhythmic structure in such a manner that the tune is, in effect, recreated with each performance. However, the player is concerned with nuances and finely-shaded points of contrast; the variations employed are minute and often imperceptible to those unfamiliar with the idiom.

Figure 11 contains numerous examples of expressive techniques commonly used by traditional musicians. Notes can be emphasized by sustaining their length longer than usual, as in measure 50. In that same measure, another expressive element appears when the g2 note is approached by sliding up from below. In several places (measures 3, 4, 6, 7, 20, 22, 23) principal notes are approached from above by a grace note a half or whole tone distant. This lends a certain sharpness, or bite, to the assertion of the first note of a note group. It also separates two consecutive notes of the same pitch and adds variety and fluidity to the melodic line.

Figure 11: "The Wicklow Hornpipe", John McGreevy, fiddle. Recorded Chicago, Ill. September 29, 1973. (see musical example 19)

Double grace notes (measures 2, 8, 10, 16, 24) and rolls (measures 4, 6, 17, 18, 19, 22) are also used in this manner. The stress pattern of this piece is such that the first and third beats of each bar are heavily accented. Variations in this pattern occur when the main pulse is momentarily obscured by an ornamented figure, as in measure 4 on the third beat and in measures 6, 14, 22, 30 on the first beat.

Other techniques include melodic variation (compare the melodic material of measure 1 as it reoccurs in measures 5, 9, 13, 21, 29, 33, 37, 41, 45, 53, 62 and contrast measure 4 with 12, 36, 44), rhythmic variation (compare measures 1 and 9, 2 and 6, 18 and 50, 19 and 51) and varied ornamentation patterns such as the insertion of a short or long roll at the end of a phrase (measures 2, 4, 6, 12, 18, 22, 26, 30, etc.).

This example is a simple piece, and the variations that occur are not particularly brilliant or perhaps even original. However, this rendition is considered to be expressive; it is one individual's interpretation of a tune that has been played by thousands of musicians thousands of times, yet, by redefining the tune to agree with and express his stylistic intuitions, McGreevy has succeeded in permeating the tune with his unique musical personality.

The concept of expression is inextricably entwined with the notion of individuality. The traditional Irish musician draws his repertoire and style from a variety of sources, personal and impersonal, aural and written.

Although learned by direct imitation, these new acquisitions are rarely absorbed intact but are subjected to a process of selective assimilation in which certain elements are incorporated by the musician, others are modified in varying degrees and some are not incorporated at all.

When a player hears a new tune, a certain variation, or a stylistic trait that pleases him, he proceeds to appropriate it immediately without the slightest compunction. Once he has done so, however, he brings the borrowed item within the compass of his own stylistic system.

He does not reproduce the tune verbatim but makes use of the expressive techniques mentioned above to give his particular rendition of the tune a distinctive and individual flavor. Likewise, when a variation or stylistic trait is adopted, the player varies the contexts in which they are employed so that a sense of individuality is maintained.

Although some musicians have developed styles of performance that are more individual than others, most performers seriously committed to the music attempt to instill their playing with a certain amount of individuality. This part of the aesthetic is best expressed by the epithet "a second-hand player always remains a second-rate player" (Breathnach 1971:129).

For to say that a particular musician is a "second-hand player" or a "bookplayer" is to say that his settings are stereotyped, unexciting and unimaginative, as if copied directly from a version of the tune in print.

These terms are consciously derogatory and are pronounced with an air of disdain by those who make the judgment. It is not enough to simply duplicate what others have previously done; instead, one must seek to establish oneself as a contributor to the development of the tradition.

Innovation is a corollary of the concept of individuality. As discussed at the beginning of section B, innovation within the confines of the traditional musical structure is highly valued by traditional musicians. The performances of innovative musicians are distinguished by unpredictability and inventiveness.

The innovative player is a "brave" player, an adventuresome player who is not afraid to "take chances", i.e. to attempt to introduce innovation into his playing through spontaneous variations in the melody, rhythm, ornamentation, phrasing and articulation. Though all good players employ variations, most have prepared them beforehand and simply insert them into the appropriate places at the appropriate times.

Only a few, however, possess the capacity for creating such variations on the spur-of-the-moment during performance. As one commentator has stated, "the ability to vary in this manner is a gift which, when combined with superior powers of execution, makes the supreme player, the virtuoso" (*ibid.*:103).

Another, more mundane level of evaluative criteria also exists. This has to do with keeping one's instrument in tune during performance; with the ability to execute difficult passages or tunes with flawless perfection; with showing taste and restraint in one's performance; with achieving innovation without depending upon gimmicks or devices alien to the tradition.

These criteria are considered important by traditional musicians, yet, if a performance is neither expressive nor individual, compliance with the more routine, perfunctory norms does not count for much.

Finally, the use of the term "aesthetic" can also be extended to include the affective, emotion-evoking properties of traditional Irish music.

Members of the traditional musical community frequently speak of a tune as being "lovely", "sweet", "grand", "fine", "slashing" or "lonesome". No particular classification or genre is associated with any particular affective state; thus, a good many dance tunes are "lonesome", while a large number of airs are far from lamenting or mournful.

Although the performer has a significant role in interpreting the tune, the particular affective quality attached to the tune is considered to lie in the melodic and rhythmic structure of the piece. It is rarely defined by an extraneous factor such as the context of performance or the instrument used in performance.

It would be possible but rather pointless to make the generalization that tunes in major and minor keys produce opposite affects, i.e. the light vs. somber, happy vs. sad dichotomy, for there are numerous exceptions to this maxim; furthermore, traditional Irish music is constructed on an underlying modal foundation — the major-minor key concept has come to be used simply for the sake of convenience when describing the surface characteristics of a tune.

(C) Repertoire

In the area of repertoire, traditional Irish music in the U.S. has remained distinct from other native and imported American musical traditions; Anglo-American instrumental music (commonly known as old-time, Southern mountain or Appalachian music) is the only tradition with which traditional Irish music has interacted and exchanged repertoire.

This exchange appears to have been largely unilateral, with numerous tunes of identifiable Irish origin — primarily reels, jigs, and hornpipes — being incorporated into the traditional Anglo-American repertoire, but relatively few Anglo-American tunes being adapted by traditional Irish musicians.

A possible explanation for this is that the nucleus of the traditional Irish repertoire had crystallized by the middle of the 19th century when most of the interaction between the idioms appears to have taken place. The Anglo-American repertoire, on the other hand, was still in a formative stage and relied on input from other musical traditions that were to some extent similar in structure and tonality.

The phenomenon might also be seen as a demonstration of the strength of the processes by which innovation introduced from outside the tradition is reworked into a form that is in accordance with the tradition's standards.

It is possible that the filtering processes of traditional Irish music during this period of musical and cultural contact were so powerful that whatever tunes were borrowed from the Anglo-American tradition were refashioned to the extent that their distinctive Anglo-American features were obliterated and the tunes transformed beyond recognition.

It is much more likely, however, that the music of the rural hills and hollows rarely, if ever, reached the ears of the Irish musicians of the Bronx, Boston, Philadelphia, Chicago and the other northern and midwestern urban Irish communities during the 19th century. There is also no evidence that if such music was heard, it would be appreciated or emulated.

A brief taxonomy of the current traditional Irish repertoire performed in the U.S. might be helpful at this point — see Figure 12.

The two major divisions are <u>dance music</u> (*ceol éasca*; "nimble music") and <u>airs</u> (*ceol mall*; "slow music"). Dance music is subdivided according to the type of dance it accompanies. Most of the dance music currently performed was created in the late 18th and early 19th centuries by folk musicians to accompany the solo dances or step dances devised by itinerant dancing masters of the Irish countryside (Breathnach 1971:61).

Some tunes, such as reels, were borrowed from the 18th-century repertoire of Lowland Scots fiddle player-composers such as Daniel Dow, William Marshall and Niel Gow and his sons. Although the hornpipe, jig and slip jig have parallels in the dance forms of England and Scotland, most of the music for these dances originated in Ireland with only a few appropriated from English and Scottish traditions.

DANCE MUSIC (Ceol Éasca)	AIRS (Ceol Mall)

<u>accompaniment for solo dances</u>
• reels
• jigs:
  - single (slides)
  - double
• hornpipes
• slip or hop jigs
• set or figure dances
 	
<u>accompaniment for ensemble dances</u>
• sets, half-sets
• céilí dances:
  - 3-4-8-12-16-hand reels and jigs
  - long and country dances
• barn dances
• polkas
• highland flings
• schottisches
• waltzes
• choreographic compositions
	• slow airs
	• airs
	• harp tunes
	• marches
	• pieces
	• descriptive pieces

Figure 12: Current repertoire of traditional Irish musicians in the U.S.

Irish folk music scholars of the past have frequently maintained that many jigs were adapted from older clan marches, song airs or pre-18th-century dance tunes, but, aside from some of the more venerable pieces, it seems more plausible that they were brought into existence simultaneously with the development of the solo jig dance in the late 18th century (*ibid.*:60).

The musical accompaniment for ensemble dances is adapted from the already extant reservoir of dance tunes for solo dances. Céilí dances, such as the 3-4-6-8-12-16-hand reels and jigs, are danced to reel and jig tunes that also accompany solo reels and jigs.

Music for sets and half-sets (French quadrille figures introduced in the early 19th century and refitted by Irish dancing masters with steps and music from the existing Irish solo dance tradition) was created by annexing tunes in duple and triple meter or by refashioning new pieces from old ones (*ibid.*:64). The accompaniments to long dances were similarly derived.

Although barn dances, polkas, highland flings, schottisches and waltzes have only a peripheral status among musicians, they were tremendously popular among dancers in Ireland during the late 19th and early 20th centuries before the impact of the Gaelic Revival had fully affected Irish dancing in the countryside. These dances are still very popular among Irish-Americans and have supplanted other forms of traditional Irish dancing among most Irish-American social dance events.

The music for these dances has been subjected to the filtering process whereby "foreign" elements are transmuted into a form compatible with the native idiom. However, elements of the original form have not always been thoroughly blended or submerged, although waltzes, polkas, barn dances, etc. have been made to conform to the eight-bar, two-part structure characteristic of most traditional Irish dance music.

In the last decade at *feiseanna* (traditional Irish dance competitions) in Ireland and the U.S., a new event, the teachers' choreography competition, has appeared. This is a choreographed dance composition invented by a teacher and involving from six to sixteen male and female dancers.

Traditional solo dance steps and ensemble dance figures are blended and juxtaposed to form a series of consecutive, interlocking patterns that are intended to embody and communicate some theme, event or concept of Irish or Irish-American culture history such as "The Meeting of the Waters", "The Irish Dancing Teacher", "The Gates of Erin", "The Men behind the Wire", "A Nation Once Again", "The Fox Chase" and "The Mullingar Races".

The musical accompaniment is generally performed by a solo musician and is designed by this musician to fit the meter of each section of the dance composition. Tunes from the existing stock of dance music are used and organized into a medley that parallels the various changes in the course of the dance.

The other major classification, airs, encompasses a number of musical forms diverse in genre and origin. Chief among these are the slow airs, many of which are derived directly from the laments and love songs of the Irish-Gaelic folksong tradition, while others have been taken from Scottish sources. Often, only the tune has survived, the words having been forgotten. Pieces of music designated simply as "airs" are drawn from Irish-Gaelic, Anglo-Irish and Scottish folksong. They include instrumental airs which were used for a variety of purposes-lullabies, milking or ploughing songs, humorous, satirical, and drinking songs.

Very little of the music of the Irish harpers of pre-conquest Ireland has survived; most of the airs attributed to Irish harpers were composed in the 17th and early 18th centuries. The itinerant harper Turlough O'Carolan (1670-1738) was perhaps the most renowned and prolific of these post-conquest harpers, close to two hundred of his compositions having come down to the present, largely through printed sources.

Scholars have hotly disputed whether or not O'Carolan's compositions can be considered to belong to the native Irish tradition since many of them were created in expressed imitation of Corelli, Vivaldi, Gemimiani and other Italian composers of the Baroque period. O'Carolan's works are also denied admittance to full traditional status on the basis of the non-oral means of transmission through which his music has been perpetuated.

However, the music of O'Carolan and his harping contemporaries is currently enjoying a renaissance in Ireland and America. If not granted a complete traditional pedigree, the music must be recognized as being present in the repertoire of a large number of today's traditional musicians.

There are only a few clan marches that have survived intact, although scarcely more than half a dozen are commonly known and performed. There are numerous other marches dating from the 19th and 20th centuries that are usually associated with patriotic or nationalistic "rebel" songs of the Anglo-Irish tradition. These marches have little affinity, musically speaking, with the older Gaelic clan marches but derive instead from the idiom of modern European martial music.

A number of tunes known as "pieces" still exist. "These pieces were devised simply by filling, in intervals in the original tunes single and double jigs with elaborate runs and embellishments. They were played rather deliberately, somewhat at waltz tempo, for which dance, in fact, they could quite easily be adapted" (Breathnach 1971:35).

There are also a few descriptive pieces of music such as "The Battle of Aughrim", "The Old Man Rocking the Cradle", "The Fox Chase" and "Máirseáil Alasdruim" (Allisdrum's March), in which the sounds of battles, rocking of a cradle and a fox hunt are imitated (*ibid.*).

Surprisingly, the decline of traditional dancing as a community-wide social activity in Ireland did not also entail the demise of the dance music. Instead, the playing of Irish dance music has become an art form in its own right and is generally not performed as accompaniment to dancing. Similarly, the separation of instrumental airs from their lyrics has resulted in the loss of the lyrics rather than the airs.

Traditional Irish musicians in America favor playing dance music in preference to playing airs, and, of the dance music, it is the reel that is paramount. Airs are very seldom played; those that are performed represent only a very small portion of the total corpus of airs in the tradition.

Of the dance music, double jigs run a poor second to reels; hornpipes place barely ahead of slip jigs, single jigs, and set dances. In fact, it is not uncommon for musicians participating in an informal session to play reel after reel, one tune generating another, in succession for an hour or longer. At some point, however, someone usually realizes what has been happening, and the group will proceed to play a few token double jigs or even a hornpipe or two before resuming with another onslaught of reels. Sessions are often even described and evaluated in terms of the quantity and quality of reels performed.

This situation is in part due to the emergence or dance music as an autonomous musical system. As the performance of dance music became a self-fulfilling activity for performer and audience both, a reorientation of evaluative standards regarding the musical performance occurred. Aesthetic criteria which formerly granted high status to a musician who excelled in accompanying dancers now yielded to a set of values that emphasized the musician's mastery of his instrument and the musical idiom.

The development of instrumental technique assumed a new importance as it became the major means of evaluating a musical performance. The statement of an early 19th-century piper, Ned Gaynor, that "my music isn't for the feet or the floor, but for the ear and the heart" (O'Neill 1973b:202) aptly expresses this concept.

Reel-playing functions as a sort of *rite de passage* among traditional Irish musicians in Ireland and the U.S. It is one of the chief criteria by which a musician aspiring to full acceptance within the tradition is judged. Some hornpipes have also become recognized as "show pieces" specially suited for the exhibition of skill, and, in theory, any genre of Irish instrumental music, dance tune or air, is capable of fulfilling this function. However, it is the reel which has evolved as the focal point of the tradition.

When asked why they prefer playing reels over other types of dance music, traditional Irish musicians invariably make a reply to the effect that a reel offers more of a challenge to one's musicianship by providing increased opportunity for displaying finesse and ingenuity within the structural confines of the idiom.

It is felt that a reel is more malleable in form, and, therefore, better suited to serve as a vehicle for personal interpretation and expression.

Audience preference has also been responsible to some extent for the change in repertoire emphasis. Musical occasions, such as concerts, radio and television broadcasts, sessions in private homes or bars, that are not connected with dance events are attended by audiences whose ostensible, primary intention is to listen to the musical performance.

In those situations where the performance is directed toward creating and sustaining audience interest, the reel has become omnipotent. In listening to tapes or recordings of traditional Irish musicians performing in a live audience context, one is struck by the considerable amount of immediate vocal response the first few bars a "slashing" reel elicit from the listeners as compared to the relative indifference which greets the opening strains of an air or other dance tune genres.

The repertoire of traditional Irish music is not stagnant, but is constantly being revitalized by the rediscovery and recirculation of old or little-known tunes within the traditional community. In addition, newly-composed tunes are receiving immediate and widespread notice via the media of radio, television and recordings.

In regard to the acquisition of new repertoire, most musicians admit to having ceased to make a serious effort to add to their stock of tunes shortly after they arrived in the U.S. Similarly, many American-born musicians also state that they have become less inclined to learn new tunes once they have learned their basic core of tunes.

Musicians who have not been to Ireland in many years or have not heard recent tapes or records of Irish musicians are quite noticeably dated and alienated from current developments in the repertoire. The Irish-American musician who wishes to keep abreast of new tunes circulating in Ireland faces obstacles that are not insurmountable but quite formidable, nonetheless.

The number of Irish emigrants to the U.S. in the last decade has been reduced to miniscule proportions, and very few traditional musicians are among the new arrivals. Two or three times during the year, groups of traditional Irish musicians tour the major Eastern and Midwestern cities. Usually these groups are sponsored by an Irish or Irish-American cultural organization.

Visits by individual musicians occur also, as improvements in travel modes have made possible annual and even semi-annual trips between Ireland and America. These constitute the channels of personal interaction through which new repertoire has been introduced to American Irish musicians in the last few years.

Although many new tunes are received from contact with live performers, a considerable amount of new material is also introduced via the commercial records of Irish musicians. There is a substantial lag, however (often more than a year), between the time of the record's issue in Ireland and its arrival in the U.S. Though most records can be ordered directly from Ireland, Irish-American import stores are the chief sources for these records in America, and their stock is not always up-to-date.

It is difficult to ascertain the impact of new records of Irish artists on the repertoire of Irish-American musicians. Musicians who ceased learning tunes years ago are obviously not affected by developments in Ireland, but among younger players, as well many elder ones, new releases from Ireland receive careful attention, since they are often one of the main sources of new repertoire.

The isolation of Irish musicians in the U.S, has been greatly alleviated in recent years by the widespread use of the portable cassette tape recorder. This device has become the primary agent of repertoire transmission between the countries and among musicians separated by great distance in the U.S. Whenever an Irish-American musician goes to Ireland, or an Irish musician or group visits the U.S., the cassette recorder is certain to be present.

New records of traditional musicians are now being made in either Ireland or America, but the number of cassette tapes of private and public, solo and ensemble performances of traditional Irish music is inestimable. This is a rare instance in which a product of modern technology has proven immeasurably helpful to the preservation and perpetuation of a folk music tradition among its active practitioners.

It should not be concluded from the foregoing that innovation in repertoire has been completely the prerogative of musicians in Ireland. Although the roots of the tradition are much stronger in Ireland, American musicians have been able to make meaningful contributions to the total traditional repertoire.

In 1971 the collected compositions of fiddle player Edward V. Reavy (a County Cavan native, now resident in Philadelphia) were published in a work entitled *Where the Shannon Rises*. This consisted of 78 tunes composed by Reavy over a period of nearly a half century and included 45 reels, 18 hornpipes, 9 double jigs, 4 highland flings, 1 barn dance and 1 air (the fact that reels comprise 59% of the total, or three tunes in every five, is in agreement with the norm in current Irish-American repertoire preference).

Although the traditional Irish music repertoire is continually augmented by tunes newly-composed or refashioned, the publication of an entire book of new pieces by a single musician is unprecedented in modern times. [4]

Previous to the book's publication, several of Reavy's tunes were already in circulation among traditional players — mostly in America, but, to a lesser extent, in Ireland and Britain as well. Since the book's issuance three years ago, many more of his compositions have gained wide currency among Irish musicians in the U.S. and elsewhere. Among traditional musicians in America, opinion varies as to the merits of Reavy's compositional skill. Some consider his work superfluous, artificial and utterly devoid of spirit and expression, while others regard his compositions as having "arisen from hidden recesses, places sacred to the folk mind and unmistakably Irish in flavor" (Reavy 1971:iii).

Most musicians simply feel that some of his tunes are acceptable, others are less so, and, consequently, they learn the acceptable ones and ignore the others.

Despite divergence in opinion among the traditional musical community, it has become apparent that several of Reavy's compositions have survived the communal process of selection and rejection and have entered into the repertoire of musicians in the U.S. and Ireland. The 1971 Fiddler of Dooney fiddle contest was won by Padraig Ó Glacain with a Reavy tune, "The Highest Hill in Sligo".

Aside from enriching the already extant corpus of traditional music, [5] the publication of Reavy's book has stimulated the creative muse of several other American Irish musicians. A direct cause and effect relationship between the appearance of *Where the Shannon Rises* and the recent emergence of other Irish-American composers is not being proposed, but the coincidence of these phenomena points to the existence of a new development of more than passing significance.

None of the other composers have yet been as prolific as Reavy, but their tunes are beginning to achieve wider circulation among traditional musicians, a few of them having been printed in *Treoir*, the monthly magazine of traditional Irish musical arts.

Reels continue to monopolize the efforts of new composers, as they find that form most conducive to personal expression. They have also composed in other forms, including jigs, hornpipes, set dances and airs. It is significant that these composers are, with but one or two exceptions, fiddle players, for it is this instrumental tradition which has had the most influence on the repertoire and style of 20th-century American Irish musicians.

It is said that the best of Ed Reavy's tunes can be identified as his compositions simply by hearing them played. It is also maintained that the popularity of some of his pieces is due to the fact that they are technically challenging and contain unusual, unexpected twists and turns in melody and rhythm which prevent them from becoming monotonous or stereotyped (though critics might maintain that these twists and turns follow a monotonously predictable pattern that soon becomes clichéd).

Underlying statements such as these is the implicit assumption that these compositions represent a departure from the existing stock of traditional music, a departure that derives from distinct and perceptible differences in melody, rhythm and harmonic structure.

While new compositions of Irish-American fiddlers manifest the individual musical personalities of their composers, they also exhibit some similar tendencies in external form.

One of the most apparent is the extension of the pitch compass in these tunes down to the G string of the fiddle, below the "traditional" limits of d1 of concert-pitched flutes, tinwhistles and uilleann pipes. Although it is perhaps a natural desire on the part of fiddle players to exploit the full range of their instrument's technical capabilities, the use of the notes from g to c#1 has, in many cases, resulted in creating compositions that are idiomatic to the fiddle (and accordion) and less suited for performance on the pipes, flute or tinwhistle.

Since the fiddler-composer is not limited by his instrument to certain keys or modes, he can make full use of the chromatic capacity of his instrument. Recent compositions have shown a marked proclivity toward the use of keys that are extremely uncommon in traditional Irish music, such as C major, E major, G minor, D minor. They are difficult if not impossible to obtain on key of C diatonic instruments, such as the uilleann pipes, most non-Boehm flutes and the tinwhistle, except by awkward cross- and fork-fingering techniques or by covering half of the hole.

In defense of this practice, fiddler-composers generally state something to the effect that they "like to compose in the key of G minor", and that they find these uncommon keys challenging, interesting or highly expressive. Another viewpoint is that of a flute player (Boehm system) who remarked prophetically and somewhat ominously: "Irish music isn't always going to remain diatonic."

Many of the new pieces also make extensive use of chromaticism. Chromaticism is certainly not unknown in traditional Irish music, but its occurrence in recent compositions is much more frequent. In accented position, the presence of a chromatic note or accidental interjects minor tonality into a major key.

For instance, in the environment of the opening measures of the second eight-bar section of a major-key tune, the introduction of a flattened seventh degree of the major scale would yield the I-VII-I harmonic sequence of the natural minor scale instead of the I-V-I progression characteristically used in this position (see Figure 13).

Figure 13a: "The Céilíer", composed by Ed Reavy (Reavy 1971: 18)

Figure 13b: "The Wild Swans at Coole", composed by Ed Reavy (*ibid.*:31)

Figure 14 shows another use of chromaticism in an accented position. Here, the harmonic progression is not actually altered but merely diverted for an instant by the introduction of a feeling of minor-ness.

Figure 14a: "The Shoemaker's Daughter", composed by Ed Reavy (*ibid*.:39).

Figure 14b: "The Lone Bush", composed by Ed Reavy (*ibid*.:59).

Chromatic notes also occur in non-chord tones; this is a stratagem intended to create a sense of variation in the melodic line where none exists by means of raising an unaccented lower neighbor tone by a semi-tone and restoring it to normal pitch the next time it occurs (see Figure 15).

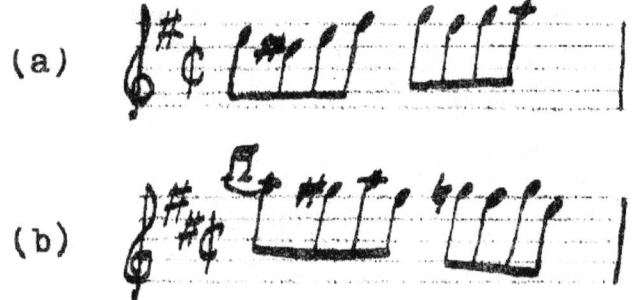

Figure 15a: "The Man from Barnagrove", composed by Ed Reavy (*ibid*.:57).

Figure 15b: "The Time We Had In Bansha", composed by Ed Reavy (*ibid*.:30).

Chromaticism is also employed to achieve a similar end in passing tones (See Figure 16) •

Figure 16a: "Tara Hill", composed by Ed Reavy (*ibid*.:63).

Figure 16b: "Hughie's Cap", composed by Ed Reavy (*ibid*.:27).

Modulation is another device occasionally used by current Irish-American composers (see Figure 17). Usually the modulation is only fleeting, but sometimes it is sustained for as much as three-quarters of an eight-bar section.

Figure 17a: "Riding Around With Carroll", composed by Larry Redican (*Treoir*,1972:#5).

Figure 17b: "O'Brien's Trip to America", composed by Larry Redican (*Treoir* 1970:11).

Figure 17c: "The House of Hammil", Ed Reavy (Reavy 1971:42-43).

This does not exhaust the possible uses of chromaticism that are available to the composer of traditional Irish music but only focuses on some of the more common ones. The use of accidentals and non-diatonic pitches is not alien to traditional practice, but it has rarely been employed in the past to the extent that it is appearing in many of the current compositions of Irish-American composers. Chromaticism is one of the chief methods by which one can endow one's tunes with individuality while staying within the boundaries of the traditional idiom (albeit expanding those boundaries somewhat).

Most of these compositions make use of the vast stock of melodic formulae out of which traditional Irish tunes are constructed. A considerable number, however, are formed around arpeggiated chord outlines with scarcely any independent melodic development. In others, the melody is spun out in sections of two or three bars in length which are awkwardly juxtaposed and linked in such a manner that failure to play the piece exactly as written would result in a serious loss of overall structural and melodic cohesion.

The basic immutability of such tunes renders them poor vehicles for the exercise of personal interpretation through variation, an element that is an essential aspect of traditional Irish musical performance. These tunes, however, do not usually enter the mainstream of the living tradition but remain entombed in printed collections.

This sudden renaissance of composers of traditional Irish music in the U.S. can be viewed as an attempt on the part of these musicians to expand their role as preservers and transmitters of the tradition to include that of contributors to the future development of the tradition.

By their efforts to define the shape and content of the traditional repertoire, they have sought to demonstrate that it is possible to participate fully in the growth of a tradition regardless of one's distance from that tradition's source.

Any discussion of the repertoire of traditional Irish musicians in the U.S. would be incomplete without reference to the work of Captain Francis O'Neill. A native of County Cork, O'Neill settled in Chicago around 1870 just as he entered his twenties. He began collecting tunes and airs from the members of Chicago's community of Irish musicians, which was at that time quite sizeable.

Originally, he considered the undertaking no more than a mere hobby, but, within a few years, his manuscript collection of Irish music comprised over two thousand traditional dance tunes and airs; consequently, wrote O'Neill, "there developed a general desire to have them printed" (O'Neill 1973a:54).

The first work, O'Neill's *Music of Ireland*, was published in 1903 and contained 1,850 airs and dance tunes culled largely from the Irish musicians who had resided in or passed through Chicago during the last three decades of the 19th century. So stunningly successful was this work that, in O'Neill's peerless prose, "letters of approval came pouring in, many suggesting the issuance of a smaller and less expensive volume devoted to dance music exclusively" (*ibid.*:62).

Four years later, in 1907, *The Dance Music of Ireland: 1001 Gems* appeared and was greeted with even more acclaim than its predecessor. O'Neill issued five more collections of Irish music in the next fifteen years, but the first two works are the ones by which this avid collector is chiefly remembered.

The first two collections are also the ones which have made the most significant and indelible impression upon the living tradition of Irish music both in Ireland and the U.S. Though the collection was initially undertaken solely in the hope of preserving from oblivion the music of O'Neill's Irish childhood, these works are of much different importance than most collections by 19th-century folklore and folkmusic antiquarians in that they were intended to be used primarily by the members of the folk tradition and only secondarily by nonmembers. They have served as a major source of repertoire for many traditional musicians since their appearance seven decades ago.

These books, however, are used by most musicians as a supplement for aural methods of repertoire acquisition. The tune versions contained within these books are not played note-for-note. Instead, they have in most cases undergone considerable alteration at the hands of the traditional musical community. Most of the settings in these collections are merely skeletal; ornamentation, phrasing, articulation and variations must be provided by the player.

Nevertheless, "the book" or "O'Neill's", as these works, especially *The Dance Music of Ireland*, are commonly designated, are ubiquitous among traditional Irish and American Irish musicians, and their role within the musical tradition as an agent of standardization and crystallization is much greater than current performance practice might indicate.

The impact of recordings on traditional styles was paralleled and prefigured by the effect of the O'Neill collections on the traditional repertoire. Until the appearance of these works, the transmission of repertoire was almost exclusively aural, with the exception of a number of private manuscript collections similar to the tunebooks of 18th- and 19th-century Scottish fiddlers. However, these collections were small and sporadically published, and tunes were primarily circulated via individuals.

It was not uncommon for the bulk of one small community's repertoire to be unknown outside of the locality, in spite of the numerous itinerant musicians of the period.

The O'Neill collections made available on a massive scale tunes which were previously restricted to provinces, counties, parishes and even individuals. The immediate effect of promoting great numbers of tunes into general circulation was to increase the size of the traditional repertoire held in common.

Another effect that became apparent later was the elevation of certain tunes to the status of "standards" because of their inclusion in the collections. The appearance of a particular setting of a tune in print established the concept of a correct version vs. variations. Although still subject to the process of communal refashioning in the area of style, the versions printed in O'Neill's publications naturally proliferated due to the increased exposure, while other settings came to be regarded as deviants or "non-standard".

O'Neill himself presided over the reconstruction of tune fragments, the selection of certain variant settings and the exclusion of those which were "least desirable" (O'Neill 1973a:55). An "Inquest Committee" consisting of several local Irish musicians and his chief aide in the work, Officer James O'Neill, also supervised the editorial proceedings. The reconstruction process was described in a *Chicago Tribune* article of March 2, 1902 (*ibid*.:viii):

> A striking example of this the reconstruction process is in the air "The Woods of Kilmurry". This was one of the old elusive and ever fugitive airs which Captain O'Neill had tried to call back from the time when, at the spinning wheel, his mother wound up the old song with the words "the flourishing state of Kilmurry". Only the last bars to which these words were sung were remembered sufficiently to recall. Officer O'Neill put these bars on paper and then went to work to write backwards to a logical Irish beginning. This he has done and the Chief (Captain O'Neill) and Inquest Committee are satisfied that the world's judges of Irish music will find it so.

This is a far cry from the usual selection process by which traditional Irish music has been winnowed and threshed throughout the centuries. One wonders how many tunes were similarly provided with "logical Irish beginnings", middle parts or endings by O'Neill and his associates.

The same method was practiced upon tunes found in other printed sources, particularly those which had been subjected to the effacement of an arrangement or harmonization intended to please polite, drawing-room tastes. It was declared that "the music as sung or whistled by Patrolman O'Neill has been pronounced by the Committee as better Irish and better music than were embodied in the print (*ibid*.:ix).

The merits of the standardization induced by Francis O'Neill's works is not at issue here. O'Neill's enterprise was motivated solely by genuine love of his native music and the all-consuming desire to have as much of that music as possible preserved and made accessible on a wide scale.

Nevertheless, it must be recognized that the translation of an aural tradition into written notation had a profound influence on the subsequent development of that tradition in Ireland as well as the U. S. The crystallization of a core repertoire did not, however, stop the machinations of the process of communal re-creation but endowed it with new vigor by providing an increased but more concentrated and sharply-defined areas of operation.

(D) Performance

Traditional Irish music is essentially a tradition of solo performance. Its repertoire and styles were evolved neither by nor for ensembles, and a performance by a single musician is regarded as a musical entity complete in itself. Neither does the instrumentalist sing songs or snatches of lyrics while playing, as do many American folk musicians. Harmonic accompaniment is a recent (late 19th-early 20th century) phenomenon; the tradition of percussive accompaniment appears to be somewhat older, however.

Duets and trios of traditional musicians are quite common in public and private performance occasions in the U.S. and Ireland. Compatible combinations of instruments that complement each other in timbre are used: fiddle and flute, fiddle and pipes, fiddle and accordion, fiddle and tinwhistle, accordion and banjo. A pair of fiddles or two flutes or accordions together are found less often. The possible instrumentation of trios is similarly varied; occasionally a piano is added as the third member (see musical examples 41-50).

In public performance, duets and trios are often characterized by a considerable degree of stylistic diversity and spontaneity, the idea being to complement rather than duplicate each other. Lead and second parts or melodic or harmonic counterpoint are not found, although perhaps, when two fiddlers are playing, one might play the melody an octave lower or possibly provide an elementary open-string drone accompaniment. Accordion players often throw in chords in the bass for emphasizing particular points of a tune. Although some duets and trios are highly-polished and professional, most are not but are formed largely on the basis of personal and musical affinity between or among the members.

There are three types of ensemble contexts in which traditional Irish music is performed: the session, the céilí band and the consort.

The first of these is an informal gathering of musicians in which the number of musicians and the type of instruments are unspecified variables. Participation is generally fluid and open to those who wish to join and who are accepted by the other musical participants. This musical occasion is known as "a session" and is ostensibly acephalous and spontaneous, although, like most public gatherings of human beings, there are certain minor rituals and rules which are observed.

Sessions take place in private and public sites, but their content and structure are determined by the participating musicians; the audience and external environment exercise no direct control over the course of a session. During a really exciting and intense session, the music pours forth in an unrestricted flow, tune after tune, as long as the musicians can muster enough energy to continue.

Largely because of the informal setting and the spontaneous nature of the occasion, the music heard at sessions is often considered to be of high quality, as each musician is free to fully express himself (see musical examples 51, 52).

The céilí band is a dance band. Its repertoire consists entirely of dance music, and its function is to provide musical accompaniment for dancers at a céilí. It is a professional or semi-professional troupe that consists of from four to twelve musicians and generally follows a local performance circuit. A variety of instruments are employed; in recent years, the fiddle and accordion have formed the nucleus of most céilí bands in the U.S., with flutes and banjo used frequently, tinwhistle and uilleann pipes used rarely. Céilí bands also maintain a rhythm section consisting of piano and drums.

The efforts of individual musicians in the band are oriented toward the achievement of a musical performance that is rhythmically regular and melodically uniform. The professional character of the céilí band dictates that the repertoire be prearranged and carefully rehearsed for performance.

In common parlance, *céilí* denotes "an evening visit, a friendly call" (Dinneen 1970:184) or a social gathering of neighbors. Only in this century has the word acquired the meaning of an occasion of traditional music and dance. The first céilí was a production of the Gaelic Revival and was held in London in 1891 under the auspices of the Gaelic League (Breathnach 1971:50).

Céilí dances were primarily designed to further the spread of national ensemble dances and provide a focus for the emerging Irish national consciousness of the period. These dance events were attended by large numbers of dancers and were frequently convened in large halls. This necessitated the use of louder instruments and/or a greater number of instruments, thus paving the way for the emergence of the accordion and the céilí band.

The first professional céilí band is believed to be one that was formed in Dublin in 1926 to perform on Radio Éireann (Acton 1967:119). However, other ensembles had existed in the countryside on a more informal basis before this time (Linnane 1973:5). Through the medium of radio and, later, through recordings, céilí bands proliferated in Ireland, England and the U.S., where they were commonly known as "Irish orchestras" or "céilídhe orchestras" through the 1920s, '30s and '40s (see musical examples 53-55).

While the céilí band in Ireland has retained close contacts with its traditional roots, the American Irish céilí bands have merged into the popular mainstream of pseudo-Irish musical entertainment. The term orchestra is still affixed to the name of the group, but the repertoire, style and instrumentation of these ensembles is not in any sense traditional.

One or two traditionally-based céilí bands have been formed in the last decade, but they have been short-lived. The New York Céilí Band of the late 1950s and early '60s was the most notable and included an all-star cast of musicians: Andy McGann, Paddy Reynolds, Larry Redican, fiddles; Paddy O'Brien, Mike Dorney, accordions; Jack Coen, flute; Jerry Wallace, piccolo; Felix Dolan, piano.

The band came in second in the 1960 céilí band competition at the Fleadh Cheoil na hÉireann in Boyle, Roscommon. In New York, however, jobs were scarce, and the band was forced to dissolve through lack of public engagements. Traditional Irish music is not a commodity that is highly valued in the U.S., even in New York, and Irish-American audiences overwhelmingly prefer American popular music flavored with just a touch of the shamrock for their dances.

The consort is a term used by this writer to describe the new type of ensemble which has appeared on the traditional Irish music scene in the last decade. Like the céilí band, the consort is professional, well-organized and meticulously rehearsed.

The consort, however, is not a dance band, though it often plays dance music. A consort performance, like that of any group of chamber musicians, requires a discerning, attentive audience. The concert hall (or the coffeehouse stage) is the natural habitat of the consort; it is not typically found at dances, weddings or other musical occasions where the musical performance is of secondary importance to other activities.

The instrumentation of the consort is carefully selected. Only instruments considered to be fully traditional or capable of expressing the traditional sound (as perceived by the members of the consort) are used. For this reason, banjos, guitars, pianos, drums and, frequently, even accordions are excluded. The uilleann pipes, fiddle, flute and tinwhistle are the main solo instruments, while the button accordion, concertina and harp are also employed on occasion. Only percussive accompaniment is used, and this is always by the bodhrán or bones.

Consort repertoire encompasses dance music, airs (especially slow airs), clan marches, descriptive pieces and tunes composed by O'Carolan and other 17th- and 18th-century harpers. Depending upon the particular emphasis of each consort, dance music may make up from fifty to seventy-five per cent of the total repertoire, while airs may account for fifteen to twenty-five per cent of the total.

The effort to achieve diversity and novelty in repertoire has resulted in the re-discovery of dance tunes and airs that were either unknown outside of a limited venue or were seldom played anymore, having dropped out of general circulation. In addition, several airs and harp tunes have been resurrected from obscure manuscript collections dating back to the 18th century in an attempt to bring these older representatives of the tradition to the attention of modern musicians.

The most distinctive feature of a consort is its arrangement and presentation of the musical material. Unlike the céilí band, the members of a consort do not always play together in unison. The instruments of the consort are carefully orchestrated so that different instruments are blended in a number of different combinations designed to achieve various textural and timbrel effects. Instruments appear, vanish and reappear throughout the course of a tune in an attempt to heighten interest and dramatic impact.

Consorts are organized along the lines of instrumental sections such that the two or three fiddles may comprise one section, the flute and tinwhistles another, with the pipes and accordion acting as free agents that may align themselves with either section at certain times. The basic dichotomous structure of most Irish dance tunes (two eight-bar parts each of which can be subdivided into four and two-bar phrase units) serves as a perfect ground for creating a musical dialogue in which successive parts or phrase units are alternately stated by opposing instruments or sections in a manner strongly reminiscent of one of the favorite techniques of much Baroque chamber music.

Melodic, harmonic and rhythmic counterpoint are an essential element of the consort approach to traditional Irish music. Sometimes the two parts of a tune are played against one another, or perhaps two close variants of the same tune might be juxtaposed.

Increasingly, however, consorts are beginning to devise original contrapuntal figures, usually nothing more than short ostinato patterns or simple countermelodies that supplement or embellish the main melody. Occasionally, the counterpoint can become quite elaborate with as many as four separate lines of more or less equal interest present at once. A controlled, abbreviated form of improvisation also occurs in some consort arrangements, generally in a context in which some form of counterpoint is also used.

This change in the presentation and structure of traditional Irish music has caused an alteration in the previously-defined concepts of certain instrumental roles. Solo instruments with capacities for harmonic accompaniment (such as fiddles, accordions, concertinas, uilleann pipes) are often used to provide harmonic support, while all instruments (including bodhrán and bones) can be employed to establish a contrapuntal background for the main melody. This is an inevitable result of the implementation of orchestration techniques to realize the concept of varied presentation, texture and tone-color.

The consort was introduced into traditional Irish music in the early 1960s by Seán Ó Riada, a successful composer of modern classical music who had become jaded with the contemporary European avant-garde. He began to delve into his native Gaelic heritage for inspiration and organized a group of traditional Irish musicians, subsequently called Ceoltóirí Chualann, which he hoped would bring his ideal of a new musical synthesis to fruition.

The ensemble consisted of uilleann pipes, flute, tinwhistle, three fiddles, button accordion, bodhrán and harpsichord, which he played himself (Acton 1967:119). In addition, the flute player could perform capably on concertina and tinwhistle, and the piper could also double on the whistle.

With this versatility, Ó Riada was able to produce a number of instrumental combinations that yielded a great variety of textures, tone-colorings and moods. The instrumentation of Ceoltóirí Chualann provided the basic organizational model for future consorts. It also established the primacy of what became known as the "Ó Riada treatment" of traditional Irish music, i.e. the use of variety and novelty in the arrangement and presentation of the music applying the techniques described above.

Ó Riada's experience as a classical composer, his genius as a writer and arranger of film music and his understanding of the traditional idiom enabled him to achieve a synthesis that was certainly unique, if not as profoundly significant as he might have hoped. In an interview two months after he had disbanded Ceoltóirí Chualann (and just a few months before his untimely death in October, 1971), Ó Riada stated that "I founded them originally with the intention of giving an example. There are now so many other groups imitating that kind of thing that I feel the job is done" (Acton 1971:108).

Ó Riada's example has already had a prodigious effect on many young musicians in Ireland and has stimulated the rise of an entire new genre of traditional Irish ensemble performance. It is still too early, however, to determine to what extent the consort is going to change the future course of the tradition.

The three or four Irish consorts that tour the U.S. once or twice a year are generally well-received by the Irish-American musical community, although they are more popular with younger people than with older persons who often tend to view the Ó Riada treatment as unnecessary and superficial gloss.

There are at the present time no consorts in the U.S. Few American Irish musicians are interested in undertaking such a venture which would require a considerable amount of time and energy. Also, there is no indication that such an ensemble would be able to be financially self-supporting in this country even if the necessary time and energy were duly invested.

Despite the recent developments in Ireland in the last half century, traditional Irish music in America remains primarily a tradition of solo performance. The only non-solo contexts in which it is currently regularly performed are those which permit a maximum of individualistic participation.

This situation is in part due to the lack of support shown by the Irish-American community for professional traditional performers, but it is also an indication of the preference for non-restricted solo performance held by the majority of traditional Irish musicians in the U.S. today.

CHAPTER III: Summary

NETTL (1962:59) postulates three avenues of possible development for European folk music traditions once they arrive in the U.S.

The first is that full-scale acculturation may occur, in which the stylistic elements, instrumental traditions, and repertoire of the folk tradition are merged with an American tradition (or traditions) to form a new synthesis.

A second possibility is that of selective or partial acculturation, in which the European folk tradition remains distinct yet manifests evidence of considerable borrowing from other traditions.

Finally, it might happen that the traditional music is not influenced at all and no acculturation takes place; the traditional music remains autonomous and sovereign as well as distinct and exhibits a continued close relationship to its Old Country source.

Traditional Irish music in the U.S. has staunchly resisted acculturative pressures, and the fundamental core of the music has remained virtually intact after more than a century of residence in this country. That is, the structural and metrical forms of the dance music and airs have not deviated from already established patterns.

The underlying modal basis of the music has also persevered, although new compositions by Irish-American musicians often exhibit innovation in the surface structure, such as an increase in the use of chromaticism, unusual key signatures and an extended pitch compass. However, these changes have been initiated from within the traditional community and reflect no discernible borrowing from other musical traditions present in the U.S.

The sound of the music continues to evolve as metal flutes begin to replace wooden ones, as piano accordions with octave couplers and often as many as 120 bass buttons become ever more popular, as fiddle players electrify their instruments for public performance and cultivate classical violin tone and technique and as the concept of standard pitch rises closer to conformity with the current standard of Western orchestral pitch.

The relative ease with which technological refinements or innovations have entered the tradition in the last century are a reminder of the eclecticism that marked the first emergence of the idiom in the 18th century. Traditional Irish music has never been static in this regard, yet, until the last few decades, changes have been less rapid and more diffuse and random in their spread.

The relative popularity of various instruments has been characterized by a great deal of fluctuation. One hundred years ago, the uilleann pipes and the fiddle dominated traditional Irish music in the U.S.; today, the pipes have declined to the verge of near extinction and even the fiddle has yielded primacy of place to the ubiquitous accordion.

The pipes and the fiddle still maintain a vague sort of "spiritual" leadership as the revered progenitors of the tradition, yet it is highly probable that in the decades to come, accordion players will exercise more initiative in matters such as composition, repertoire and perhaps even style.

Since World War II, traditional Irish musicians in the U.S. have become more dependent upon musicians in Ireland for leadership in style and repertoire. Consequently, stylistic heterogeneity among musicians in the U.S. has decreased somewhat (except for a few "marginal survivals" who have been too isolated to be affected by new trends), and additions to the repertoire have been imported also. This imbalance has recently begun to be redressed, at least in the area of repertoire, as a number of musicians in the U.S. have taken to composing new tunes, many of which have already entered the traditional repertoire.

The long-term effect of this activity on the tradition in America or Ireland is difficult to predict, but it cannot help but serve as a stimulus to the tradition in the U.S.

Despite a brief flourish of céilí bands in the 1930s and '40s, traditional Irish music in the U.S. has remained primarily a tradition of solo performance. The consorts that are so tremendously popular in Ireland are greeted by Irish-American audiences with more nostalgia than actual enthusiasm, and no American musicians have attempted to organize an ensemble of this nature.

Moynihan (1963:98) has isolated three factors which he believes are responsible for "a weakening of Irish identity in America: the decline of immigration, the fading of Irish nationalism, and the relative absence of Irish cultural influence from abroad on the majority of American Irish."

As the ethnic consciousness of the Irish has declined, certain aspects of their cultural heritage, such as traditional music, have become meaningless and irrelevant when transferred from their native physical environment and cultural context.

While it is true that traditional Irish music in the U.S. has been seriously stunted by the lack of new arrivals from Ireland and by the ensuing isolation from the source of the tradition and the culture that generated it, continuity has been successfully maintained for the most part, and links with the tradition in Ireland are beginning to be re-established to ensure that the tradition in America will not succumb from lack of nourishment from the source.

However, traditional Irish music in America has never been totally separated from the tradition in Ireland. Changes that have occurred in Ireland have been paralleled in America, and vice versa. No separate tradition has evolved in the U.S.; deviation has consisted merely of differences and developments in the area of style, while the instruments and repertoire have remained essentially similar to what is found in Ireland.

Had the tradition in Ireland declined to a similar extent, the connection might have been permanently severed, and an even more complex chain of developments would have been set in motion resulting in a substantial alteration of the present form of traditional Irish music in the U.S.

✦_____✦

NOTES

1. The cultural torpor of the post-Famine Irish countryside was the subject of frequent comment by contemporary novelists, journalists and chroniclers. The following eloquent and impassioned appeal for rejuvenation was issued by traditional dance instructors in the first decade of the 20th century:

   > If we are to have a revival of things Irish we cannot in reason pass by the dances. This, however, is only the academic view of the question. The study of Irish dances can well afford to be put on a higher plane of consideration. No one who has given any thought to our town, and village, and, above all, to our rural life, can deny that it is sadly lacking in the most elementary resources of pleasure. This dullness, this death in life, has often been advanced, and surely with justice, as one of the main reasons for the terrible drain of emigration from our country. Everywhere people tell you that beyond the daily round of labour there is nothing to look forward to in Irish provincial life. Can it, therefore, be a matter for surprise that, the noisy streets and music halts of foreign cities allure our people? It was not so at any time, so far as we are aware, in Irish history down to the end of the eighteenth century. Town and country life in Ireland, for many centuries within the ken of observant travellers, appears to have resounded with music of the pipes and the accompanying movements of the dancers. We would desire to see once more the village cross-roads peopled with merry groups of dancers, to hear the music of the pipes borne down the lanes between the white-thorn trees in the interval between the long day of labour, and the night of rest (O'Keeffe and O'Brien, "*A Handbook of Irish Dances*, pp. 29-30).

2. "The travelling people" is the sympathetic term used for the small nomadic communities also known as "gypsies", "tinkers" and, in official government parlance, "itinerants". These were, and still are, groups of individuals and families who travel throughout Ireland living off the countryside and plying various skilled and semi-skilled trades, many of which have now become obsolete in modern Irish society. The genesis of these groups occurred in the wake of the Famine when thousands of farmers and their families were evicted from their holdings and given no alternative but to take to the roads. They were joined by tradespeople dislocated by the general social turmoil, migrant labourers and — not infrequently — formerly itinerant musicians who could no longer rely on their home community for support and were compelled to join a travelling group for reasons of survival.

3. Most of those which have been preserved are to be found in *Irish Minstrels and Musicians* by Francis O'Neill, first published in 1913. It is a splendid volume of anecdotes, historical essays and biographical accounts of over 250 Irish musicians, including many Irish-Americans of the 19th and 20th centuries. Though heavily weighted toward uilleann pipers, it is the best contemporary source for information on traditional Irish music in the U.S. from 1875-1915.

4. A book of tunes by Walter "Piper" Jackson entitled *Celebrated Irish Tunes* was issued in 1774 by Edmund Lee of Dublin (O'Neill 1973a:238). Pieces by O'Carolan appeared in three works during his lifetime: in an untitled work published by John and William Neale of Dublin, c. 1721; in *A Collection of the Most Celebrated Irish Tunes* published by the Neales of Dublin, c. 1726; in *Aria Di Camera* published by Daniel Wright of London, c. 1730 (O'Sullivan 1958:125-126).

5. Breathnach (1971:58) asserts that the traditional repertoire contains "at a conservative estimate, over 6,000 individual pieces". If memory does not fail, I recall him expressing in a personal communication a number closer to 15,000.

6. See MacColla (1972:6) for an interesting and incisive assessment of Irish-American social organizations and traditional Irish dancing.

REFERENCES CITED

Acton, Charles. "Seán Ó Riada: The Next Phase," *Eire-Ireland* 2(4):113-122, 1967.

Acton, Charles. "Interview with Seán Ó Riada," *Eire-Ireland* 6(1):106-115, 1971.

Baines, Anthony. *Woodwind Instruments and Their History.* London: Faber and Faber, 1957.

Baines, Anthony. *Bagpipes.* Oxford: Pitt Rivers Museum, Occasional Papers on Technology, No. 9, 1960.

Breathnach, Breandán. *Folkmusic and Dances of Ireland.* Dublin: Talbot Press, 1971.

Census Bureau. *Historical Statistics of the United States.* Wash, D.C.: U.S. Bureau of the Census, 1960.

Census Bureau. *Census of Population (1970): General Social and Economic Characteristics — New York.* Wash., D.C.: U.S. Bureau of the Census, 1972.

Columbia Phonograph Company. *Columbia Record Catalogue, 1927.* New York: Columbia Phonograph Co., 1927.

Curtis, Edmund. *History of Ireland.* London: Methuen and Co., 1952.

Dinneen, Patrick S. *An Irish-English Dictionary.* 8th edition. Dublin: Educational Company of Ireland, 1970.

Finian. "The Legend of Paddy O'Brien", *Treoir* 2(4):10.

Howarth, James. "Free Reed Instruments", in Baines, Anthony, ed., *Musical Instruments through the Ages.* Harmondsworth, Middlesex, U.K.: Penguin Books. Pp. 318-326, 1971.

Kelleher, John V. Kelleher. "Irishness in America", *Atlantic*, 208 (July, 1961).

Kuter, Lois. *The Musician in Irish Society and Folklore.* Oberlin University: unpublished B.A. thesis, Anthropology, 1973.

Levine, Edward. *The Irish and Irish Politicians.* Notre Dame, Ind.: Notre Dame University Press, 1966.

Linnane, Kitty. "Kilfenora Céilí Band," *Treoir* 5(1):5, 1973.

MacColla, Eoin. "Céilí Dancing in Chicago", *Treoir* 4(4):6, 1972.

Meek, Bill. "Thumps in the Night", 1972, *Treoir* 4(6):7, 1972.

Merriam, Alan P. *The Anthropology of Music.* Evanston: Northwestern University Press, 1964.

Moynihan, Daniel. "The Irish of New York," *Commentary* (36)8:93-107, 1963.

Murphy, Richard C. and Lawrence J. Mannion. *The History of the Society of the Friendly Sons of St. Patrick in the City of New York, 1784 to 1955.* New York: J.C. Dillon, 1962.

Nettl, Bruno. *An Introduction to Folk Music in the United States.* Detroit: Wayne State University Press, 1962.

Ó Duibhir, Seán. "The Concertina," *Treoir* 4(4):16-19, 1972.

O'Faolain, Seán. *The Irish.* Harmondsworth, Middlesex, U.K.: Penguin Books, 1972.

O'Keeffe, J.G. and Art O'Brien. *A Handbook of Irish Dances.* 7th edition. Dublin: Gill and MacMillan, 1954.

O'Neill, Francis. *Irish Folk Music.* Reprinted. Yorkshire, U.K.: EP Publishing, Ltd., 1973a.

O'Neill, Francis. *Irish Minstrels and Musicians.* Reprinted. Darby, Pa.: Norwood Editions., 1973b.

O'Sullivan, Donal. *Carolan: The Life, Times, and Music of an Irish Harper, Vol. I.* London: Routledge and Kegan Paul, 1958.

Ó Tuathaigh, Gearóid. *Ireland before the Famine, 1798-1848.* Dublin: Gill and MacMillan, 1972.

Reavy, Edward V. *Where the Shannon Rises: Selected Compositions of Ed Reavy.* Philadelphia: privately printed, 1971.

Rimmer, Joan. *The Irish Harp.* Cork: Mercier Press, 1969.

Schrier, Arnold. *Ireland and the American Emigration, 1850-1900.* Minneapolis: University of Minnesota Press, 1958.

Warren, Rev. C.B. "What Kind of Harp?" *Treoir* 3(6):18, 1971.

APPENDIX A: Musical Examples of Traditional Irish Musicians in the U.S. *

* I would like to thank the many individuals who provided these recordings; special thanks must go to the Archives of Traditional Music, Indiana University. Bloomington. Ind., for the use of archive materials.

#	performer(s)	selection	recording data
1	Patsy Tuohey-pipes	reels: Drowsy Maggie-Scottish Mary-The Flogging Reel	Victor, 1923
2	Patsy Tuohey-pipes	reels: The Steampacket-The Morning Star-Miss McLeod's	Victor, 1923
3	Michael Gallagher-pipes	reels: The Collier's-The Salamanca Reel	no data
4	Liam Walsh-pipes	reel: The Portlaw Reel-The Chicago Reel	Victor 79059, c. 1927
5	Tom Ennis-pipes	reels: The Maid That Left the Country-Drowsy Maggie-Around the World for Sport	Victor 18366, c. 1921
6	Michael Coleman-fiddle w/pno.	reels: Lord McDonald's	Columbia 33237, c. 1928
7	Michael Coleman-fiddle	jig: The Girls of Bainbridge	recorded Wurlitzer's Music Store, New York, NY, 1940
8	James Morrison-fiddle w/pno.	reels: Rakish Paddy-The Wheels of the World	Columbia 33422, c. 1928
9	James Morrison-fiddle w/pno.	jigs: Apples in Winter-The Frieze Breeches	Gennett 5304-B
10	Paddy Killoran-fiddle w/gtr.	reels: The Jolly Tinker-The Pretty Girls of Mayo	Decca 12081, c. 1934
11	Paddy Killoran-fiddle w/gtr.	jigs: The Luckpenny-The Coach Road to Sligo	Decca 12081, c. 1934
12	Michael Hanafin-fiddle w/Dan Sullivan-pno.	reels: Miss McLeod's-The Greenfields of Rossbeigh	Columbia 33115, c. 1927
13	Packy Dolan-fiddle w/pno.	reel: Mullin's Fancy	Victor 21484, c. 1928
14	Edward V. Reavy-fiddle w/pno.	reels: The Boys at the Lough-Tom Clark's Fancy (The Greenfields of Rossbeigh)	Victor 21593, c. 1928
15	Hugh Gillespie-fiddle w/Mick Callahan-gtr.	hornpipes: McCormick's	Decca 12112

#	performer(s)	selection	recording data
16	Paddy Cronin-fiddle w/Tom McSharry-pno.	reels: The Mountain Top-The Galtee Mountains	Copley 9-114-A, c. 1950
17	Paddy Cronin-fiddle	hornpipe: The Liverpool Hornpipe	recorded by author in Boston, MA, 6-3-73
18	John McGreevy-fiddle	reel: John McGreevy's	recorded by author in Chicago, IL, 9-29-73
19	John McGreevy-fiddle	hornpipe: The Wicklow Hornpipe	recorded by author in Chicago, IL, 9-29-73
20	Andy McGann-fiddle w/Ed Cruz-pno.	reels: Tom Ward's Downfall-The Reel of Mullinavat	recorded by author in Bronx, NY, 6-26-73
21	John Vesey-fiddle	jig: Joe O'Dowd's	recorded by author in Philadelphia, PA, 12-26-73
22	John Vesey-fiddle	reel: The Tramp (The Reel of Bogie)	recorded by author in Philadelphia, PA, 12-26-73
23	Larry Redican-fiddle	reel: The Reel of Bogie (The Tramp)	recorded by author in Philadelphia, PA, 6-21-73
24	Paddy Reynolds-fiddle w/Felix Dolan-pno., Tom O'Neill-bass	reels: The Providence-The Dudeen	from *Sweet and Traditional Music of Ireland*, Rego Irish 1000
25	Breandán Mulvihill-fiddle	reel: The Maids of Mitchelstown	recorded by author in Bronx, NY, 6-18-73
26	Tom Morrison-flute w/John Reynolds-bodhrán	reels: Dunmore Lassies-The Manchester Reel-The Castlebar Traveler	Columbia 33210
27	Tom Morrison-flute w/John Reynolds-bodhrán, Ed Gagan, pno.	hornpipes: The London Clog-The Rights of Man	Columbia 33210
28	John McKenna-flute, lilting w/pno.	reel: The Sailor on the Rock	no data
29	John McKenna-flute, lilting w/pno.	reels: The Woman of the House- ?	no data
30	Seamus Cooley-flute	reels: Seán sa Ceo-Mike Preston's	recorded by Philo Records, N. Ferrisburg, VT, 1-20-74

#	performer(s)	selection	recording data
31	Myles O'Malley-tinwhistle w/pno.	hornpipes: The Quarrelsome Piper-The Harvest Home	Decca
32	Liz Carroll-tinwhistle	reel: Paddy Taylor's	recorded by author in Chicago, IL, 5-19-73
33	Larry McCullough-tinwhistle	reels: The Rainy Day-Killavil Fancy	recorded by author in Bloomington, IN, 3-1-74
34	Peter J. Conlon-accordion w/pno/	reel: Paddy on the Turnpike	Lyric 4806
35	John J. Kimmel-accordion w/Joe Linder-pno.	hornpipes: Bryant's Favorite-Birds in the Tree	Columbia A2951, c. 1920
36	James Keane-accordion w/Felix Dolan-pno., Tom O'Neill-bass	reel: The Morning Mist (Roland's Favorite)	from *Sweet and Traditional Music of Ireland*, Rego Irish 1000
37	Larry Redican-banjo	reel: The Pigeon on the Gate	recorded by author in Queens, NY, 6-21-73
38	Eleanor Kane Neary-piano	reel: Roland's Favorite (The Morning Mist)	recorded by John Maguire in Chicago, IL, 1962
39	Nancy Harling-piano	reel: The Boys at the Lough	recorded by author in Chicago, IL, 5-18-73
40	Sean McDonnell-harmonica	jig: The Blackthorn Stick	recorded by author in Chicago, IL, 5-20-73
41	Edward Mullaney-pipes/ Patrick Stack-fiddle	reel: The Maid in the Cherry Tree	Victor 79003, 1927
42	James Morrison-fiddle/ Michael Carney-pipes	hornpipes: Poll Ha-penny-Fisher's	Columbia 33350
43	Michael Coleman-fiddle, Tom Morrison-flute w/pno.	reel: The Humours of Ballyconnell	Columbia 33069
44	John McGreevy-fiddle/ Seamus Cooley-flute	reels: Tim Maloney's-Cooley's- ?	recorded by author in Chicago, IL, 9-29-73
45	Packy Dolan & His Melody Boys (fiddle, tinwhistle, piano)	highland fling: The Lasses of Donnybrook	Victor 21484, c. 1928
46	John McGreevy-fiddle/ Larry McCullough-tinwhistle	jig: Saddle the Pony	recorded by author in Chicago, IL, 9-29-73

#	performer(s)	selection	recording data
47	John McKenna-flute/ Eddie Meehan-flute	reels: Bridie Morley's-The Hunter's Purse	no data
48	John McGreevy-fiddle/ Miles Krassen-fiddle, w/spoons	reel: Farewell to Ireland	recorded by author in Chicago, IL, 9-29-73
49	Peter J. Conlon-accordion/ James Morrison-fiddle, w/pno.	reels: The Taproom-The Moving Bog	Columbia 33318
50	John McKenna-flute/ Michael Gaffney-banjo	reels: Miss Lyon's Fancy-Scottish Mary	Columbia (?)
51	Padraig Ó Glacain-fiddle/ Paddy Ryan-fiddle/ John McGreevy-fiddle/ Antoin MacGabhann-fiddle/ Patsy Hanly-flute/Noel Rice-flute	reels: The Boys of Ballysodare-The Five-Mile Chase	recorded by author in Chicago, IL, 10-18-73
52	John McGreevy-fiddle/ Miles Krassen-fiddle/ Jimmy Considine-accordion/ Seamus Cooley-flute/ Malachy Towey-bodhrán	reel: The Woman of the House	recorded by author in Chicago, IL, 10-18-73
53	Tom Senier Céilídhe Orchestra (fiddles, accordions, banjo, piano)	reel: Johnny in the Glen	Folk-Dancer 1074-A
54	Irish All-Star Orchestra (2 accordions, banjo, piano)	reel: Miss McLeod's	Copley 9-170-B
55	Traditional Irish Musicians Association (7 accordions, 6 fiddles, 1 flute and tinwhistle, piano, guitar, drums)	reels: Green Mountain-The Bucks of Oranmore	*From Ireland in America*, Avoca 33-ST-166

APPENDIX B: Selected Discography of Traditional Irish Musicians in the U.S.

As this appendix indicates, traditional Irish musicians in the U.S. have not been extensively recorded in the last few years. These records are all long-playing albums that have been recorded within the last decade by private individuals or small, independent companies, generally of the "one-shot" variety. Only currently available items are given.

Within the next year, however, two more records of traditional musicians in the U.S. will be on the market: a second Paddy Cronin LP and an album from Philo Records, N. Ferrisburg, Vermont, featuring two Chicago musicians, John McGreevy (fiddle) and Seamus Cooley (flute).

Coleman, Michael-fiddle (with piano accompaniment). *The Musical Glory of Old Sligo.* New York: IRC Records. 12 selections: 5 reels, 3 jigs, 3 hornpipes, 1 schottische. A reissue of original recordings made between 1921 and c. 1930.

Coleman, Michael-fiddle (with piano accompaniment). *The Heyday of Michael Coleman.* New York: Intrepid Records. 12 selections: 6 reels, 3 jigs, 1 hornpipe, 1 slip jig, 1 set dance. A second reissue of original recordings made between 1921 and c. 1930.

Cronin, Paddy-fiddle and flute (with piano accompaniment). *The House in the Glen.* Boston: Talcon KG-240. 13 selections: 4 reels, 5 jigs, 2 hornpipes, 1 slide, 1 polka.

McGann, Andy-fiddle/Joe Burke-accordion/Felix Dolan-piano. *A Tribute to Michael Coleman.* New York: Shaskeen 08-360. 15 selections: 8 reels, 4 jigs, 2 hornpipes, 1 air and set dance. Solos and duets.

Reynolds, Paddy-fiddle/Charlie Mulvihill-accordion/James Keane-accordion and concertina/Felix Dolan-piano/Tom O'Neill-bass. *Sweet and Traditional Music of Ireland.* New York: Rego Irish 1000. 13 selections: 7 reels, 4 jigs, 1 hornpipe, 1 O'Carolan tune. Solos and duets.

Traditional Irish Musicians Association: 6 fiddles, 7 accordions, 1 flute and tinwhistle, guitar, piano, drums. *Ireland in America.* New York: Avoca Records 33-ST-166. 13 selections: 4 reels, 2 jigs, 3 hornpipes, 1 highland fling, 1 waltz, 1 march, 1 polka. Ensemble performance throughout.

APPENDIX C: Pronunciation Key for Unfamiliar Terms in Irish

This is meant to serve as a makeshift expedient which will enable the reader unfamiliar with the Irish language to cope with the various Irish terms that appear in this paper. Despite dialect differences and gaps in the author's rudimentary knowledge of Irish, the pronunciations given here are reasonably accurate.

bodhrán (bo-*rawn*)

céilí (*kay*-lee)

ceol éasca (kyol-*ias*-ca)

ceol mall (kyol mowl)

Ceoltóirí Chualann (Kyol-*tor*-ee *Koo*-e-lin)

feis (fesh)

feiseanna (fesh-*ahn*-a)

fleadh (flah)

Fleadh Cheoil na hÉireann (flah kyol nah *(h)a*-rin)

fleadhanna (flah-*han*-a)

Máirseáil Alasdruim (Mar-shayl *Al*-es-drim)

orgán béil (or-gawn *bel*)

píob mór (peeb *mor*)

sean-nós (shan-*nos*)

uilleann (*il*-in)

◆―――――――――◆

The Rose in the Heather:
Irish Music in Its American Cultural Milieu

By Lawrence E. McCullough
B.A. Indiana University, 1974

Submitted:

To the Graduate Faculty of the Department of Music
in the Faculty of Arts & Sciences
in Partial Fulfillment of the Requirements
for the Degree of Master of Arts
University of Pittsburgh
December, 1975

Dr. Carol E. Robertson-DeCarbo
Director of Thesis, Music

Dr. Nathan Davis, Music

Professor Colin Sterne, Music

Dr. Eileen Kane, Anthropology

~ CONTENTS ~

Acknowledgments	72
Preface	73
Chapter I: An Historical Outline of Traditional Irish Music in the U.S.	76
Chapter II: Musical Occasions	85
1) commercial entertainment	86
2) concerts	87
3) dances	88
4) dance classes	91
5) dance competitions	92
6) dance exhibitions	93
7) sessions	94
8) audience-performer interaction	96
Chapter III: Performers	97
1) general characteristics	97
2) specialists and professionals	98
3) interactional networks	101
4) status and role	103
Chapter IV: Institutions	108
1) musicians' associations	109
2) schools	111
3) media	113
4) institutions as agents of change	116
Chapter V: The Role of Traditional Irish Music in Contemporary Irish-American Culture	118
References Cited	122

Cover photo: The Irish Music Club, Chicago, c. 1909, from O'Neill's *Irish Minstrels and Musicians* (1913), p. 479.

~ ACKNOWLEDGMENTS ~

I would like to thank Dr. Carol Robertson-DeCarbo who has served as my academic adviser and thesis adviser; her helpful, incisive comments on a variety of ethnomusicological subjects have been greatly appreciated.

My grasp of the interrelationship of Irish music, history and culture was greatly enhanced by discussions and coursework with Dr. Eileen Kane of the Anthropology Department and Dr. Hugh Kearney of the History Department, who have both shown a keen interest in my work.

This paper is an outgrowth of an earlier thesis I wrote for my B.A. degree at Indiana University, Bloomington, Ind. in April, 1974. My adviser for that work was Dr. Charles Boilés, an eminent ethnomusicologist and theoretician who gave my ethnomusicological studies their original guidance and to whom I still owe a debt of thanks.

Special thanks are extended to Breandán Breathnach, Tom Munnelly and Hugh Shields of Dublin, Ireland, all noted collectors and scholars in the field of Irish folk music, and to fiddler John Kelly and his family, also of Dublin, for the erudition and orientation they provided during my first encounters with traditional Irish music four years ago.

Incalculable thanks must go to the innumerable performers of traditional Irish music, song and dance in the U.S. who gave most generously of their time, their hospitality, their knowledge and, most importantly, their artistry.

Without their assistance and cooperation this thesis could never have been undertaken. I hope this work compensates for the gifts of music and friendship they have freely bestowed upon me.

Seamus and Mary Cooley of Chicago have been exceptionally hospitable, and this thesis is especially dedicated to the memory of Seamus's brother, Joe Cooley, one of the most popular Irish musicians to have ever played in this country. Ar dheis Dé go raibh a anam uasal.

Finally, my friend, research colleague and fellow musicianer Miles Krassen must receive recognition for the contributions he has made through our numerous discussions on the subject of traditional Irish music.

L. E. McCullough
Pittsburgh, Pa.
December 1, 1975

◆――――――――◆

~ PREFACE ~

THIS IS A study of the cultural setting in which traditional Irish music has existed in the United States.

That is, it focuses on the social, psychological, political, economic and demographic factors that have influenced the development of the music during its sojourn in America, from the early 1800s up to and including the mid-1970s.

Traditional Irish music in America has undergone a number of significant changes in that time-span. While many of these changes were the result of innovations or developments stimulated by performers within the tradition, the extra-musical factors mentioned above have also played a decisive role in shaping the form of the music as it exists today.

To obtain a full comprehension of traditional Irish music in America, it is necessary to take into account such diverse though interrelated phenomena as:

- the ebb and flow of Irish emigration to America;
- the transition from rural to urban performance contexts;
- the changes in socio-economic levels of performers and patrons and the resulting revision of attitudes toward the musical tradition;
- the impact of technological developments leading to the emergence of new dissemination patterns and media;
- the increasing use of institutions to maintain, and transmit the tradition;
- the effect of the urban folk music revival;
- the resurgence of ethnic cultural consciousness among the American Irish.

Otherwise, it is not possible to genuinely understand the dynamics of the process by which musical traditions evolve, flourish or disintegrate.

The terms "traditional Irish music", "Irish music" and "Irish folk music" as used in this paper refer only to the idiom of instrumental music that was given definitive shape in the 18th century in Ireland. Folk song is not dealt with here; although the instrumental and vocal traditions are certainly related structurally and stylistically, Irish folk song is a separate development with its own repertoire, aesthetic standards and performance traditions.

Furthermore, both traditions are so extensive in scope and complex in character that it would be an act of folly and presumptuousness to attempt to treat both subjects within the confines of a master's thesis. Any consideration of the relationship between folk music and song in Ireland need also assess the entire range of performing arts traditions including dance, drama and recitation. Hopefully, this may be achieved in a later work.

The reader may also wonder why this work does not discuss, except in brief, rather uncomplimentary asides, the music one characteristically associates with Ireland, i.e. the music that one hears during St. Patrick's Day celebrations or in the soundtrack of the *Knute Rockne Story* or from the Irish comedians and singers that appear on the Mike Douglas show.

Aren't pieces like "Harrigan", "Maggie Murphy's Home", "When Irish Eyes Are Smiling", "Glocca Mora", "The Unicorn", "The Last Rose of Summer", "Killarney", "Danny Boy", "The Blarney Stone", "I'll Take You Home Again, Kathleen" and "That Old Irish Mother of Mine" considered to be "Irish music" by a large number of Irish-Americans?

Indeed, to many Americans of various nationalities, these items represent the sum of Irish musical accomplishment. In reality, however, the idiom the writer has characterized as "pseudo-Irish music" (in Ireland, it is rather sneeringly termed "emigrant" or "Irish-American") bears the same relationship to the music created by folk musicians in 18th-century rural Ireland as the 19th-century "coon songs" of the black-face minstrels bore to the musical traditions of the Afro-American.

In both instances, a new musical idiom was concocted by persons who were in nearly every case not members of the musical tradition they were adapting for the entertainment of persons also ignorant of the tradition; the new idiom, though superficially reminiscent of its model, represented no more than a condensation and refinement of the most exaggerated and, as is often the case, falsely-based stereotypes.

In addition, the borrowing process was not reciprocal; though composers of pseudo-Irish music might use the traditional 6/8 jig rhythm for a tune like "McNamara's Band", traditional Irish musicians did not begin composing reels based on the melodic or rhythmic characteristics of "The Notre Dame Victory March".

However, the idiom of pseudo-Irish — or to use a more neutral term, Irish-American music — is most definitely deserving of a complete study in its own right. Yet, the reader should be aware that clear distinctions between this music and traditional Irish music do exist, and that this present work is concerned with the latter.

Although numerous sources in anthropology, history and sociology were consulted in the preparation of this thesis, many of the facts presented here will not be found in print elsewhere. The subject of acculturation in the music of American emigrant groups has received scant attention from scholars, and the subject of this paper has never received any previous study.

Consequently, much of the data and conclusions presented here are the result of the writer's extensive involvement with traditional Irish music in America for the past four years. Two trips to Ireland have been supplemented by intensive fieldwork in seven U.S. cities from May through July, 1973, sporadic visits to Irish-American communities six or seven times a year and ongoing field and archive research in conjunction with a music-collecting project funded by a grant from the National Endowment for the Arts.

Personal observation, formal interviews, written correspondence, mailed survey questionnaires and informal conversations with hundreds of individuals — performers and non-performers alike — have served as the primary research techniques for gathering information.

Subjectivity inevitably creeps into even the most rigorously "scientific" analysis, but the interpretations and conclusions found in this paper are based on an attempt to present the subject not only as it appears to the writer but as it exists in the minds of those persons who are most intimately involved with it.

The writer's perspective is somewhat complicated by the fact that he is a performer of traditional Irish music and is deeply committed to the tradition. This may help to explain some passages in which a distinct and unabashed personal viewpoint emerges.

This admission of intimacy, however, should not be taken as a confession of guilt or as an apology, for this paper could never have been written without a commitment of this kind. While the merits of the participant-observation technique may be open to question, it is the writer's belief that being involved in the performance of the tradition served to enlarge the range of insight rather than limit or distort it.

It is hoped that the present study, which concentrates on a single musical tradition of a specific ethnic group in one multi-cultural nation, will provide something of value to other scholars examining the process of acculturation.

The statements and conclusions offered here are not intended to be taken as the final word on a subject that is only beginning to be analyzed in a detailed, systematic manner. Rather, this study represents nothing more than a first attempt to shed some light on a complex and fascinating musical tradition that has remained in the dark for too long simply because no one has bothered to look at it.

Chapter I: An Historical Outline of Traditional Irish Music in the U.S.

ANYONE WHO attempts to chronicle the development of traditional Irish music in the United States is immediately confronted by a distressing paucity of sources on the subject, either reliable or unreliable, which might provide a logical starting point for a reconstruction of the music's history in America.

Before the 20th century, references to the music appear infrequently and are scattered throughout a welter of printed media, primarily in the form of brief captions and announcements in Irish-American newspapers and journals, theatrical and vaudeville advertisements, and random bits of biographia.

After the turn of the 20th century, the situation improves with the recording of Irish-American musicians on wire cylinders and discs. These were at first privately recorded on a small-scale, often informal, basis; after c. 1915 they began to be manufactured by commercial phonograph companies for mass distribution.

However, the number and depth of printed sources remains pitifully meager and diminishes considerably as the century progresses. In addition, of the large corpus of private and public recordings — which might be expected to yield information regarding musical style, repertoire and instrumentation as well as some insight into the impact of the recording process upon the subsequent development of the tradition — surviving copies of audible condition are scarce, and there has been to date no discographical study or attempted analysis of this rich, untapped lode of data.

In this reconstruction attempt, the reservoir of oral lore that exists among members of the Irish-American musical community has been utilized as the principal repository of information regarding the history of this musical tradition in the U.S. and has been supplemented by the judicious use and interpretation of the occasional references found in printed sources of the day.

It should be understood that the current living memory of informants extends no further than the first decade of the 20th century and is rather hazy beyond 1930. Also, the bulk of printed references are sketchy and vague as to details of musical style, repertoire, and performance practice.

Nevertheless, in both the oral lore and the printed miscellanea, it is possible to catch a few fleeting glimpses of traditional Irish music in America as it existed in the full vigor of its most flourishing, halcyon epoch.

The precise origins of traditional Irish music in America are woefully obscure. Emigrants from Ireland to America before the 19th century were largely descended from the stock of the Presbyterian Scots who had been imported from Scotland and established in the northeastern section of Ireland to assist in the pacification and colonization that followed the final subjugation of the island by England in the 17th century.

When they arrived in the American colonies, these Ulster Scots still exhibited a strong cultural affinity with Scotland, despite their sojourn in Ireland, and the musical traditions which they brought to the New World were undoubtedly derivative of those of the non-Gaelic, Lowland Scots culture from which they were but three or four generations removed (O'Faolain 1972:86).

Although thousands of native, Catholic Irish were transplanted to the West Indies during the first years of the Cromwellian pacification program to serve as plantation slaves (Curtis 1952:251), there were relatively few Irish Catholics who emigrated freely to the North American colonies before the second quarter of the 19th century.

Those who did emigrate arrived individually or in very small groups and were quickly assimilated (Murphy and Mannion 1962:1). Also, the implacable anti-Catholic prejudice firmly entrenched among many colonial Americans served as an effective deterrent to "papists" who might be contemplating settlement in Great Britain's American colonies. Many of the colonies enacted legislation which restricted Catholic Irish immigration specifically and deprived already-resident Catholics of all nationalities of various civil rights.

These legal strictures began to disappear after the institution of the American Republic in the 1780s, but discriminatory legislation against all "undesirable foreign elements", particularly those from poor, Catholic countries such as Ireland, continued throughout the Federalist period of the new nation and successfully obstructed the free flow of Irish Catholic immigration (Levine 1966:61).

It is difficult to state with certainty what sort of musical traditions were possessed by the native Irish who did settle in America before the 19th century. The numerous historical articles dealing with these early arrivals are almost exclusively concerned with listing how many individuals with Irish surnames settled in various parts of the country or were encamped with Washington at Valley Forge; they are devoid of any descriptions of the cultural activities of the early American Irish.

Similarly, the accounts of early American musical life center primarily on the musical occasions of the urban upper and middle classes or those of a few religious denominations, with occasional mention of the musical culture of the black slaves and no mention of the musical activities of lower-class urban or rural and frontier whites.

If there were not a similar dearth of detailed information on the state of instrumental folk music in Ireland at this time, it might be possible to gain some insight into the musical culture of those Irish who emigrated to America during the 17th and 18th centuries. Few particulars are known concerning matters such as repertoire, style and performance practices of Irish folk musicians, although travellers' accounts of the period (primarily English) often mention the instruments in use among the native Irish peasantry.

The current consensus of scholars in the field of Irish folk music is that the bulk of what is presently acknowledged as traditional Irish music was created by the musicians of the late 18th and early 19th centuries (Breathnach 1971:19).

Although a few remnants of the music of an earlier period still survive in the present repertoire in the form of instrumental airs derived from older song airs, the instrumental musical traditions of pre-conquest Ireland vanished during the period of cultural trauma that followed in the wake of the collapse of the Gaelic aristocracy and the accompanying social order.

The 18th century was a transitional and protean period in which the heretofore highly distinctive musical traditions of the aristocratic and peasant classes were merged. Though the harp still held high status and primacy of place in the households of many of the new Anglo-Irish, the harpers of the 18th century were "already archaic and somewhat anachronistic" (Rimmer 1969:66) and judged by some to represent a debased, degenerate form of the art.

By the second decade of the 19th century, the already-moribund harping tradition was effectively extinct (*ibid.*). In its place rose an instrumental tradition that had previously been confined to the lower orders of pre-conquest Gaelic society (Kuter 1973:8).

It is recorded in the memoirs of the Irish harper Arthur O'Neill that one of his 18th-century contemporaries, a blind harper named Owen Keenan, reportedly emigrated to America after eloping with his patron's French governess (Fox 1912:127). However, it is more plausible that the first strains of traditional Irish music heard in the U.S. were sounded by either the uilleann pipes or the fiddle.

These two instruments of the Irish peasantry had risen to prominence in the wake of the demise of the aristocratic musical orders and effectively filled the vacuum in the native musical tradition caused by the disappearance of the harp. Most of the present traditional repertoire was composed by now-forgotten pipers and fiddlers of the late 18th and early 19th centuries (Breathnach 1971:61), and several of the basic stylistic techniques that have come to characterize traditional Irish music and are employed by all traditional Irish musicians are, to a large extent, modeled on techniques developed by early performers on the pipes and fiddle.

Irish emigration to the U.S. had begun to show a systematic increase throughout the 1830s and 1840s, and, although the specter of widespread famine had more than once menaced the precarious existence of the Irish peasantry, the severity of the potato blight of the late 1840s left tens of thousands of Irish with no choice but emigration. Upon their arrival in America, they clustered into the burgeoning Irish communities which began to appear in every major urban and industrial area of the U.S. Their recent disastrous experience with agriculture was impressed indelibly upon their collective consciousness; for this reason and others, the Irish experience in America became synonymous with the urban experience.

However, the entire previous history of the Irish had been largely oriented toward a non-urban life mode (O'Faolain 1972:60), and the culture that they brought with them to the U.S. was a product of centuries of rural, peasant existence. The transition from countryside to shantytown was painfully abrupt, and much of the old Gaelic culture did not survive beyond the first generation of exposure to the new social environment.

The traditional music and dance, however, proved remarkably resistant to assimilative and acculturative pressures. Though both arts were strongly rooted in rural, folk society, they were adapted to an urban, non-traditional environment with little initial difficulty. Traditional Irish musicians and dancers moved smoothly into the popular American entertainment milieu of the time and were frequently employed as performers on riverboats and pleasure cruises, in hotels, saloons, dance halls and theaters.

The musicians often accompanied popular singers on nationwide concert tours and gained great public acclaim for their performances in travelling minstrel shows and vaudeville companies. Their activities in these troupes involved music, dance and comic monologues and sketches. The performances were usually delivered by pairs or trios but occasionally by one extremely versatile individual.

Some of the more talented and illustrious Irish musicians of the era maintained a substantial livelihood in this manner. Traditional Irish musicians of this period were also very active in the Irish-American communities and performed at various Hibernian social events such as picnics, house parties, balls, concerts and numerous other formal and informal musical occasions ranging from Irish dance classes and to sessions at neighborhood taverns.

From all indications, the late 19th century was the most prosperous era for the Irish musician in America in terms of financial remuneration and high social status in the Irish-American community. This "golden age" was fittingly crowned by the erection in 1892 of Celtic Hall in New York City, which flourished as "the Mecca of the best class of Irish sociables and gatherings for many years" (O'Neill 1973b:320).

Like countless other immigrants, the traditional musicians of Ireland were undoubtedly attracted to the U.S. by the prospect of increased economic opportunity. Prior to the 1840s, a considerable number of itinerant musicians roamed the Irish countryside; plying their trade among the peasantry and the lower classes of the towns and cities. Most of these musicians were pipers or fiddle players, though other instrumentalists also occasionally took to the roads.

The status of these musicians was roughly equivalent to that of lower-class tradespeople who fulfilled a service function for the agricultural community, such as coopers, potters, tailors, basketmakers and wheelwrights. His occupational role necessitated that he be both a specialist and a professional. Admission to the itinerant ranks was attained through heredity as well as by choice, and status within the musical profession was generally achieved, while in the larger society it was ascribed. It remains only to add that the itinerant musician was almost always male.

The extreme fondness — often a virtual mania — of the Irish peasantry for their traditional music and dance is well-attested to by contemporary observers (Breathnach 1971:41, 42, 51; O'Keeffe and O'Brien 1954:16, 20).

Together with the dancing master (another male itinerant specialist and professional accorded higher social status by the community largely in deference to his refinement, gentlemanly dress and decorum and role as an instructor), the itinerant musician figured prominently in the cultural life of pre-Famine Ireland:

> Pre-Famine peasant society, for all its poverty, had plenty of sport and gaiety about it. Music and song were woven into the very fabric of society, and the fiddler and uillean piper were kept busy at weddings and wakes, fairs and markets. (Ó Tuathaigh 1972:150)

The massive, social upheaval caused by the Famine was instrumental in hastening the demise of both the dancing masters and itinerant musicians. The immediate economic impact of the Famine was to effect the nearly complete impoverishment of the classes upon which the musicians and dancing masters depended for support.

Although the dire economic condition of the peasantry would improve after some decades — mainly due to the emigration of most of the surplus population — the severe psychological trauma engendered by the "Great Hunger" proved more difficult to assuage. The national psyche was afflicted by a particularly stultifying lethargy which often combined with clerical puritanism to produce a listless, apathetic attitude regarding the pursuit of community cultural activities such as music and dance.

An elderly Donegal woman who had survived the Famine made this comment in the early 1880s:

> It didn't matter who was related to you, your friend was whoever would give you a bite to put in your mouth. Sport and pastimes disappeared. Poetry, music and dancing stopped. They lost and forgot them [the arts] all, and when the times improved in other respects, these things never returned as they had been … the Famine killed everything (Dunleavy 1974:55).

The cultural torpor of the post-Famine Irish countryside was the subject of frequent comment by contemporary novelists, journalists and chroniclers. The following eloquent and impassioned appeal for rejuvenation was issued by traditional dance instructors in the first decade of the 20th century:

> If we are to have a revival of things Irish we cannot in reason pass by the dances. This, however, is only the academic view of the question. The study of Irish dances can well afford to be put on a higher plane of consideration. No one who has given any thought to our town, and village, and, above all, to our rural life, can deny that it is sadly lacking in the most elementary resources of pleasure. This dullness, this death in life, has often been advanced, and surely with justice, as one of the main reasons for the terrible drain of emigration from our country. Everywhere people tell you that beyond the daily round of labour there is nothing to look forward to in Irish provincial life. Can it, therefore, be a matter for surprise that, the noisy streets and music halts of foreign cities allure our people? It was not so at any time, so far as we are aware, in Irish history down to the end of the eighteenth century. Town and country life in Ireland, for many centuries within the ken of observant travellers, appears to have resounded with music of the pipes and the accompanying movements of the dancers. We would desire to see once more the village cross-roads peopled with merry groups of dancers, to hear the music of the pipes borne down the lanes between the white-thorn trees in the interval between the long day of labour, and the night of rest (O'Keeffe and O'Brien, "*A Handbook of Irish Dances*, pp. 29-30).

As later events were to prove, it was not the rejuvenation of native culture that managed to slow down the emigration rate but, rather, a gradually-improving national economic life and social welfare schemes (Murphy 1975:154).

While the number of musical occasions and the functional value of the musical profession in community life continued to diminish, many musicians who had formerly maintained a livelihood as itinerant or semi-itinerant performers found themselves forced to abandon their occupation.

Those who were old, physically handicapped or vocationally unskilled were driven into the local poorhouse or workhouse. Those who were more mobile or vocationally versatile could either take up a new trade and attempt to settle down, take to the roads again and join the hordes of "travelling people" displaced by the Famine, journey to another part of Ireland where the situation was probably no less bleak or leave the country altogether. It was during these chaotic post-Famine years that the U.S. received its first significant influx of traditional Irish musicians.

The traditional Irish musicians who arrived in America during this period were undoubtedly quite pleasantly surprised by both the expanded range of economic opportunities and the increased social status accorded them in the Irish-American communities.

Not only was the Irish musician popular with the cosmopolitan American audiences who thronged the music halls and minstrel shows, he was also recognized, as were the priest, politician and publican in their respective domains, as playing an important role in the maintenance of Irish-American cultural solidarity while serving as a role model for young Irish-American males who aspired to achievement and public renown.

Upward social mobility was not beyond the grasp of many musicians who became professional performers or engaged in other commercial pursuits besides music.

Celtic Hall in New York City, mentioned above, was constructed by an uilleann piper from County Leitrim named Patrick Fitzpatrick only eleven years after he arrived in America at the age of twenty-one, and there were several other instances of musicians who earned enough money to invest in saloons, dance halls and theaters (O'Neill 1973b:320).

This sudden rise in the economic and social hierarchies would not have been possible in the tightly structured economic and social networks of Ireland at this time, in which accession to land or a business concern was regulated by marriage and kinship variables.

The repertoire of the professional Irish-American musician was based on the same body of music shared by other traditional musicians in Ireland and America. However, musicians who chose a professional career in the U.S. were often required by the circumstances of their employment to perform quadrilles, strathspeys, waltzes, barn dances, schottisches, show tunes and even light classical music in addition to selections from the traditional Irish repertoire.

To what extent the professional musicians can be considered as representative of the entire community of American Irish musicians is a matter of speculation. It seems, however, that, despite the potential for interchange between the musical cultures of Ireland and the U.S., the traditional Irish repertoire remained intact during this period of contact.

The non-Irish music adopted by the professional Irish-American musicians was not introduced (or if introduced, was not accepted) into the traditional repertoire at this time. Full-scale acculturation in the Irish-American musical community came later, in the 20th century as a result of a change in tastes and preferences of the American Irish audiences — indicative of their increased assimilation within mainstream American society — rather than from any development within the community of traditional musicians creating the demand for musical entertainment that was neither traditional nor Irish.

The performance of several musicians in consort, except during informal sessions, does not seem to have occurred until the first decades of the 20th century. The tradition, except for occasional duets and trios, remained one of solo performance throughout the 19th century. The fiddle, pipes and transverse flute made up the first rank of instruments in use among American Irish musicians at this time. Although the tinwhistle was present, it does not seem to have been accorded much notice but functioned primarily as the instrument used by novices when first learning Irish music.

The melodeon and its successor, the two-row button accordion, came into fashion during the last three decades of the 19th century but did not attain a significant niche among Irish-American musicians until the 20th century. It was also in the last decade or so of the 19th century that the practice of harmonic accompaniment on piano or guitar became increasingly widespread among Irish musicians in America — possibly introduced via the professional musicians of music hall and vaudeville.

There is little information on the stylistic techniques employed by Irish-American musicians of this period. One piper was described as favoring "the free and rolling style with a liberal sprinkling of graces and trills" (O'Neill 1973b:310); another was criticized for having a "too open and flute-like tone" (*ibid.*:301); yet another piper's playing was characterized by "a choppy execution subversive of both rhythm and melody" (*ibid.*:263).

Fiddle styles of the day are also a matter of conjecture, with players being described as a "fine, free-hand performer" (*ibid.*:410) or the style displaying "the exuberance of graces skillfully interwoven into the texture of the theme" (*ibid.*:375).

It is likely that the first comment refers to the amount of free variation in the bowing style and the second might indicate a lively, strongly accented and profusely-ornamented style of playing, but one can only speculate.

What seems certain is that during this period the traditional Irish music found in the U. S. was marked by a wide diversity of stylistic traits that reflected the variety of provincial, regional and local styles which existed concurrently in Ireland. Despite the phenomenon of musicians representing different sectional and stylistic backgrounds suddenly coming into close contact, no pan-American style of playing traditional Irish music emerged, although several Irish-Americans made significant stylistic contributions. Stylistic sovereignty was maintained, although some styles gained a large number of adherents for short periods of time.

However, it was primarily in regard to the exchange and dispersion of repertoire that the increased interaction among musicians in the Irish-American communities had the most significant consequences upon the subsequent development of the tradition.

Traditional Irish music continued to thrive throughout the 19th century and well into the 20th, eventually producing performers who were not only outstanding musicians but important contributors to the development of the tradition in Ireland as well as America. Few of their names have survived into the present, however, since those who maintain oral tradition are highly selective and often forgetful.

Most of those which have been preserved are to be found in *Irish Minstrels and Musicians* by Francis O'Neill, first published in 1913. It is a splendid volume of anecdotes, historical essays and biographical accounts of over 250 Irish musicians, including many Irish-Americans of the 19th and 20th centuries. Though heavily weighted toward uilleann pipers, it is the best contemporary source for information on traditional Irish music in the U.S. from 1875-1915.

With the advent of the recording process, it becomes possible to examine more closely the relationship of individual musicians to the evolution of the larger tradition. The emergence of the commercial recording industry occurred as the "golden era" of traditional Irish music in America entered its final phase (c. 1920-1945). Along with the "race" or "hillbilly" series, the major labels also maintained a special "Irish" series that featured a variety of Irish-American performers and included several of the finest traditional instrumental musicians of the day.

The recordings made during this period reveal an interesting assortment of instrumental styles that reflect not only the older styles brought over from Ireland in the immediate post-Famine decade, but ones subsequently developed in the U.S., as well as others first introduced by the musicians who arrived in the last great wave of Irish emigration in the 1910s and '20s.

As with the recording of other American folk and ethnic musics of the period, such as blues, jazz and hillbilly music, the recording of traditional Irish music facilitated a wider dissemination and more extensive cross-fertilization of styles and repertoire formerly unknown outside a particular locality or circle of musicians.

Although syncretic processes had already taken place to a limited extent in the repertoire of American Irish musicians, the diffusion of style was a much slower process wholly dependent upon personal interaction among musicians. Recordings rendered this method of style transmission obsolete by providing access to style on a mass, impersonal level that made it no longer necessary to know personally or to have ever heard the musician whose style one wished to copy or incorporate.

This acceleration and extension of the process of style acquisition exerted a profound influence on the future development of the tradition. Despite the fact that many of the styles in circulation among present-day Irish-American musicians are reflections of those currently popular in Ireland, the influence of these early recordings in shaping the norms of modern style in both Ireland and America has been substantial.

Several of the players recorded in the 1920s and '30s are still revered as paragons of excellence by which the efforts of modern musicians are measured, and many of their tunes are played by present-day musicians in the same grouping, order and setting as they were recorded forty and fifty years ago.

Other tunes and tune-settings recorded during this period have since attained the status of "classics" or "standards" in the traditional repertoire and serve as test pieces by which musicians aspiring to eminence are judged. These recordings have become increasingly important since World War II, helping to preserve a sense of continuity within the Irish-American musical community.

In view of the many musicians recorded and the large number of recordings produced between the two World Wars, it would appear that traditional Irish music still retained a secure place in the musical affections of the American Irish. However, an examination of catalogues of the major recording companies from the late 1920s to the early 1940s reveals a steady decrease in both the number of Irish musicians recorded and the number of recordings produced, until by 1945 (in some cases much earlier), the "Irish" series had disappeared from the active catalogue lists.

Although a half dozen of the best-selling traditional artists were retained on studio rosters until the end of the 1940s, the market for traditional Irish music had evaporated, and even reissued material sold poorly. A few small labels, most notably the Copley company of Boston, carried on into the '50s, but were inoperative by the end of the decade.

The Depression was partially responsible for the diminished recording activity, but other factors of greater irreversibility were more decisive in contributing to the demise of traditional Irish music in the U.S. The increasing structural assimilation of the Irish into mainstream American society and their entrance into the realms of the American middle class were accompanied by the adoption of the cultural, values and lifestyle of that society and particular social stratum.

In most cases this movement up the social ladder involved the discarding of cultural paraphernalia such as traditional music and dance, pastimes and customs — items viewed as expendable or of no value in a society obsessed with the melting pot syndrome (Kelleher 1961:39).

This vacuum created by the assimilation of first-, second- and third-generation Irish-Americans was not, as in previous times, filled by a new wave of immigration from Ireland. Although civil strife and an unpromising economic situation brought 220,591 Irish to the U. S. between 1921 and 1930, the next decade witnessed the arrival of a mere 13,167.

Only 1,059 Irish came to the U.S. between 1941 and 1945, but the post-war shortages of jobs and consumer goods in Ireland were responsible for 26,444 Irish arrivals from 1946 to 1950 (Census Bureau 1960:56). A brief flurry of immigration in the mid-1950s introduced some new additions to the Irish-American musical community, but the reduction of the once-steady stream of immigration to a mere dribble has robbed the Irish-American musical tradition of an important source of fresh input.

In recent years New York City has become the major focus for activity among traditional Irish musicians in the U.S. Its large Irish and Irish-American population — currently estimated at 315,000 (Census Bureau 1972:607-612) — has made possible the support of some forty to fifty schools of Irish dancing, a half dozen schools of Irish music, numerous musical occasions featuring traditional music of a high standard and a class of semi-professional traditional musicians who derive a substantial portion of their income from public performance and teaching.

Another factor contributing to New York's status is that, with only two recent exceptions, all of the traditional Irish musicians who have been commercially recorded in the U.S. in the last two decades either live or have resided for lengthy periods of time in New York. The great number of active musicians and the frequency of public and private musical occasions have given New York musicians the reputation of being the most polished and practiced players in the country.

Musical activity among Irish-Americans in other cities has stagnated, although a few cities can still boast of three or four players acknowledged by their peers as "first-rate". Chicago long ago surrendered the position of eminence in Irish-American musical affairs it maintained in the 19th and early 20th centuries, although there are a number of active musicians and musical occasions there. Unlike New York, Chicago receives virtually no new permanent immigrants and very few transient arrivals from Ireland.

The isolation of the Chicago musical community has been intensified by the severe lack of interest in traditional music exhibited by young Irish-Americans (although there are approximately a thousand or so students enrolled in schools of Irish dancing in the Chicago area). Efforts to organize the musical community along lines similar to those proven successful in New York have received minimal support from the larger community and have been marked by factionalism within the musical community itself.

Boston, Cleveland, Philadelphia and San Francisco were also distinguished centers of Irish music at one time but have declined drastically due to general apathy, the lack of fresh blood from Ireland and the inability of local musicians to replenish their rapidly-thinning ranks with young American recruits.

Although attempts have been made to encourage young people to participate in local Irish musical events, the musical communities in these cities still consist overwhelmingly of musicians forty years of age and over who will likely be inactive in twenty years.

Unless this "generation gap" can be filled to some extent, it is very possible that cities will eventually suffer the fate of Milwaukee, Baltimore, Detroit, Pittsburgh, Indianapolis, St. Paul and St. Louis — cities with sizeable Irish and Irish-American populations now conspicuously barren of interest in traditional Irish music.

Like some rare species of wildlife endangered by a sudden ecological shift, the traditional Irish musicians of the U.S. have become a breed threatened with imminent extinction.

However, any discussion of the present state of traditional Irish music in America must be cognizant of the slow groundswell of renewed interest that has begun to appear in various parts of the country among individuals encompassing a variety of ethnic and musical backgrounds.

The last decade has witnessed the phenomenon or re-emerging ethnicity and a concern for various aspects of ethnic culture, as many nationality and racial groups in the U.S. have begun to question the wisdom of effacing their ethnic and cultural identity to achieve the anonymity and cultural desolation offered as rewards for successful assimilation into mainstream American society.

The revival enjoyed by traditional music in Ireland in recent years has had a considerable psychological impact upon Irish musicians in the U. S., providing a model for a similar movement in this country as well as establishing a much-needed sense of solidarity with the Irish emigrants and descendants of emigrants who have preserved this aspect of their ethnic heritage often without benefit of nourishment from the tradition's source.

These and other occurrences, such as the more than one hundred American musicians who competed in the 1973 Fleadh Cheoil na hÉireann at Listowel, County Kerry, augur well for the future of Irish music in America.

In addition, Irish music has begun to attract the notice of the urban folk revival and its attendant media. Irish-American musicians have been injected into the established folk festival circuit, recorded by a label specializing in North American folk music, celebrated in folk music magazines and hired to play in Greenwich Village clubs and coffeehouses.

While traditional Irish music will not prove as marketable or as enduringly popular among folk music devotees as has bluegrass, Appalachian music and country blues, it cannot fail to benefit from the increased exposure; already, a noticeable change has occurred in the attitudes and performance of musicians who have been "discovered" in this manner.

Buoyed by this new-found and unexpected appreciation, their pride and confidence in their musical abilities has grown, while their newly-acquired status as important musical artists has increased their stature within their own communities and resulted in a greater recognition of the Irish musician as preservers and propagators of the Irish cultural heritage.

If this current wave of interest can be sustained over the next few years, there is every indication that traditional Irish music in the U.S. might well stave off its decline and enter into an epoch of vitality and prosperity unknown since the passing of its "golden age" in the early 20th century.

~ Chapter II: Musical Occasions ~

THE PREVIOUS CHAPTER mentioned a number of musical occasions at which traditional Irish music has been featured during its sojourn in the U.S., and this chapter examines several of them in detail. The performance occasions discussed here are those where traditional Irish music is found in this country in 1975.

The seven types of occasions are distinguished according to a number of interrelated criteria, and each type represents a certain kind of <u>performance domain</u>. The context of the occasion, the role of the performer and the orientation of the performance itself are factors that distinguish one domain from another.

For instance, the <u>domain of dance classes</u> consists of a number of individual occasions that all feature musicians performing for dancers receiving instruction in dance; the primary orientation of the musical performance is toward the dancers, and the musician's role is to provide a service, that of musical accompaniment, for persons involved in a learning situation.

The <u>domain of dance competitions</u>, on the other hand, is made up of occasions that feature musicians performing for dancers involved not in a learning situation but a competitive one; the context is different, as is the orientation of the performance, but the role of the musicians in providing dance accompaniment is the same. These, then, are two different but closely related domains of musical activity.

The <u>concert domain</u> is a set of musical occasions in which the musician orients his performance for an audience whose primary motivation (nominally, at least) is to listen to a prepared, formal musical presentation.

The <u>domain of commercial entertainment</u>, however, consists of occasions in which musical performance is secondary to other activities. The performer is oriented toward providing a set performance routine for the entertainment of an audience that is there for reasons other than hearing music; thus, within the domain of commercial entertainment, traditional Irish music may be found in several diverse contexts that are related by virtue of their use of musical performance. The performance of an Irish musician in a bar is similar in nature to Irish musicians playing at a suburban shopping mall during St. Patrick's week; in both instances, the musical performance is secondary to other activities — drinking, shopping, participation in raffles for trips to Ireland — that are part and parcel of innumerable St. Patrick's week events.

By contrast, <u>a session is a domain of musical occasions</u> that often shares the same environment as other occasions belonging to different domains. Although a session may occur in a bar, it does not belong to the domain of commercial entertainment since the orientation of the performance is not toward a general audience but to oneself and to one's fellow performers.

Session performers are not paid, their performance is not formal nor prepared in advance, nor must they shape their performance to the desires of any audience that is present. The context is the same as performances intended to serve as commercial entertainment, yet the orientation and motivation of the performance, as well as its format are different.

For a more detailed discussion of methods designed to analyze the contexts of performance occasions, the reader should consult Fishman (1970:37-56) in which the major concepts of micro- and macro-sociolinguistics are outlined.

These preliminary remarks on the nature of musical occasions are meant simply as an explanation for the format in which they are presented. There are undoubtedly instances where the data does not fit snugly within the rigorous categories that have been established for it; what, for instance, is the domain when a traditional Irish musician is playing at a formal concert that is broadcast over the radio and played in a bar where customers are dancing to the music? That is a particularly slippery Gordian Knot which the reader is invited to entangle at leisure.

Commercial Entertainment

Traditional Irish musicians were formerly very much in evidence as commercial entertainers in the U.S. and were employed by proprietors of hotels, taverns, restaurants and even the pleasure boats that plied the nation's waterways in the 19th century. The traditional Irish musician has vanished from most of these contexts as the tastes and preferences of American audiences have asserted themselves in other directions.

The only context in which traditional Irish musicians in America will currently be found as commercial entertainers is that of the Irish-owned or Irish-oriented bars, although sporadic appearances during St. Patrick's week in mid-March may take place in other commercial environments such as shopping centers or restaurants.

In the era when bars were known as saloons, traditional Irish musicians were frequently hired to entertain the patrons of such establishments. Some Irish musicians in 19th-century America owned or managed taverns, and many more found work in the numerous Irish-owned bars that flourished in urban centers — well over half of Boston's 1,200 drinking establishments surveyed in 1851 were controlled by Irishmen (Handlin 1970:121).

In the 20th century, Prohibition undoubtedly reduced the number of Irish musicians playing in bars, but of greater and more lasting significance were the changes that occurred in the musical entertainment tastes of taverngoers as the 20th century progressed. Irish-owned bars were also gradually losing their Irish clientele, and drastic changes in the popular music idiom eventually succeeded in forcing the traditional Irish musician from all but a few Irish-oriented taverns.

Presently, there are no more than a half dozen traditional Irish musicians in the U.S. hired on a consistent basis to provide entertainment in bars. Jukeboxes, muzak systems, radio and television have replaced much live music in taverns, and proprietors do not consider traditional Irish music to be a particularly "hot" commercial item. Even in bars that take immense pains to style themselves as genuine Irish pubs, traditional Irish music is only inadvertently heard.

Changes in the demographic composition of taverngoers is also a significant factor. Though many Irish-oriented bars have a regular clientele of largely-male persons over forty years of age who have fairly recent family ties with Ireland (and whose aesthetic tastes, nevertheless, often find their fullest expression in a Sinatra ballad rather than a jig, reel or hornpipe), there has been a much greater number of persons of both sexes and under thirty years of age entering these sanctums formerly inhabited only by "old-timers".

In bars such as these which still remain nominally Irish-oriented, one is likely to find virtually any type of American popular music of the last twenty years, from vintage Presley to modern country-western to current rock'n'roll numbers and disco hits. The new young and affluent customers require music that will enable them to "boogie" and "get down" more efficiently; tavern-owners are not slow to grasp that traditional Irish music does not, for most of these patrons, go far enough in meeting those requirements.

When traditional Irish musicians are hired to play in a bar, they must make innumerable musical compromises to satisfy, as one performer put it, "the lowest common denominator". The music they themselves want to play is usually barely tolerated, never encouraged and interrupted by incessant requests (more often expressed in the form of ultimatums) for renditions of the pseudo-Irish songs and tunes that many Irish-Americans (particularly those who frequent the Irish-oriented taverns that are literally reeking with nostalgia) have come to accept as their cherished musical heritage.

Poor sound systems, a noisy and indifferent audience, innumerable drunks of varying degrees of obnoxiousness, low pay ($50 a night is the top price paid for a traditional Irish musician to play for several hours a night in a bar, and that is an exception rather than the rule) and occasional brawls make a tavern gig more of a chore than a pleasure.

For those performers who can retain their composure and a modicum of sobriety, playing in a bar is not entirely a negative experience. Visiting musicians from other cities may drop in occasionally, and a lively session may result. The opportunity to perform in public and to receive some form of compensation — whether money, drinks or flattery — is another aspect of the situation to be considered. Low status is perhaps preferable to no status, and the disinclination of the traditional Irish musician to quietly abdicate from the tavern stage is indicative, perhaps, of a tenacity that refuses to yield any more ground to the cultural revolution that has already rendered him obsolete and curiously exotic in a context formerly indisputably his own.

Concerts

In the 19th and early 20th centuries, the traditional Irish musician in the U.S. was found on the program of concerts given by various Irish-American social organizations.

Changes in musical preferences were already detectable among the American Irish early in the 20th century, and it was not long before traditional Irish musicians were no longer seen on the concert platforms of the musical occasions sponsored and attended by their own ethnic community.

The following comment made by an Irish piper at the turn of the 20th century described a pattern that became universal within the next few decades:

> The great popularity Irish music has gained in Chicago is not to be attributed to any special efforts of the representative Irish organizations or the local Irish press. For some incomprehensible reason it is almost totally ignored by both. In some instances I have noticed Germans, Bohemians and Italians engaged by the managers of entertainments given under the auspices of the leading Irish organizations to play music. What a sad commentary on the Irish musical knowledge of the "committee on talent"! (Ennis 1902:37)

The concert concept itself increasingly lost favor with Irish-American social organizations who discovered that their members would rather attend a dance where they could be up on their feet dancing and socializing with other members and not be bound by the concert decorum of maintaining silence and motionlessness.

This general disinterest in the concert as a form of community entertainment also implied that there was nothing worth listening to, and traditional Irish music sank even deeper into the status of an oddity or, at best, an anachronism associated with the days of poverty and discrimination most upwardly-mobile Irish-Americans preferred to forget about.

When the traditional Irish musician began appearing as a featured concert performer in the late 1960s, it was outside the Irish community; the urban folk music revival of the '60s had uncovered a number of outstanding performers in various folk traditions languishing in obscurity for want of a sympathetic, appreciative audience. Bluesmen and hillbilly musicians who had spent the last thirty or forty years away from public performance were now rediscovered and elevated to a new status within the revivalists' community, if not always within their own.

By the 1970s, the momentum of the revival carried it into other traditions besides those of the Afro- and Anglo-American, and traditional Irish musicians started turning up at folk festivals, university concerts and coffeehouses and bars run by local folk music clubs. Articles on traditional Irish music and musicians occasionally graced the pages of general folk music magazines in addition to reviews of Irish records.

The result of this sudden focusing of attention on what had a decade before been a relatively unknown musical tradition was that traditional Irish music reasserted its claim to the concert venue, a claim denied for decades.

Other factors were influential in this situation. In Ireland, traditional Irish music in the early 1960s adapted to an ensemble concert format; traditional Irish music was now being listened to (in addition to being sung along with and danced to), with large halls and auditoriums, rather than small private clubs, serving as the venues.

Several of these ensembles toured the U.S. beginning around 1970 and appeared at Irish centres and other concerts sponsored by Irish-American social organizations.

In 1972, Dublin-based Comhaltas Ceoltóirí Éireann (Irish Musicians' Association) began conducting annual concert tours of fifteen to sixteen U.S. and Canadian cities with a troupe of traditional Irish musicians, singers and dancers. These concerts were also convened in halls and auditoriums, with male performers dressed in black-tie and tuxedo and ladies in formal evening gowns. Traditional Irish music was presented in a dignified, respectable manner (the $5 dollar and beyond ticket prices were another reminder that this music was not to be sneezed at).

For many Irish-Americans, the CCE concerts were the first real contact with traditional Irish music they had ever had, and the sober, professional concert presentation undoubtedly gave many persons in the Irish-American community cause to appraise their local traditional musicians with a bit more esteem. The CCE concerts also stressed the importance of traditional Irish music as part of the Irish cultural heritage, and this message was a major part of its appeal to Irish-Americans for support in the organization's efforts to raise money for an Irish cultural center in Dublin.

By 1973, local traditional Irish musicians' associations were putting on benefit concerts to obtain funds for carrying out their own programs of furthering the tradition. Other events that brought traditional Irish musicians to American concert stages in the early 1970s were money-raising activities sponsored by groups providing aid to persons in strife-torn Northern Ireland.

Increasingly, traditional Irish musicians were regaining their place as concert artists, and, in September, 1975, the first Philadelphia Traditional Irish Music Festival was held at Lansdale, Pennsylvania, just north of Philadelphia. This event consisted of workshops, sessions, a céilí dance and an evening concert, drawing a crowd of nearly three hundred.

It was a program designed to promote the maximum amount of participation by the two dozen musicians from New York, Philadelphia and Pittsburgh who attended. An important element of the festival was the series of workshops in which musicians discussed aspects of their music to an attentive, highly interested audience.

Not since the Irish music conventions of the early 1960s had there been an entire day-long gathering devoted specifically to traditional Irish music in the U.S., and many performers were understandably excited by the prospect that the music was beginning to invoke a new level of serious appreciation.

Most traditional Irish music activity in America still takes place away from the concert stage, and the halcyon days of the 19th century are not due to return again in the near future. However, in looking back on the first three-quarters of the 20th century, one notes an intensification of the trend remarked upon by John Ennis in 1902.

Yet, it is also possible to discern within the events of the last few years, the seeds of a possible renaissance heralded by the emergence of traditional Irish music from the confines of its sequestration within the musty back shelves of Irish-American cultural consciousness.

Dances

The role of the traditional Irish musician in providing accompaniment for the dances held by members of his ethnic community has decreased steadily throughout the 20th century. The reason for this phenomenon is not to be found solely in the adoption of alien dances by the Irish in America, for many of the "traditional" dances of Ireland, including those of early 19th-century origin, were first fashioned from dance forms introduced from Europe and Britain (Breathnach 1970:117).

Those imported dances, though, were not merely adopted; they were completely reshaped in accordance with the already-established steps and meters so that they became, in effect, fully nationalized Irish dances.

Later in the 19th century, however, a new wave of foreign dances flooded the country — the schottische, waltz, barn dance, varsovienne, mazurka, one-steps, two-steps and others. The Famine had wiped out the class of Irish dancing masters that flourished before the mid-19th century, and not all of these imports were successfully adapted to the Irish dancing idiom.

In America, the contact with other dance forms was much more frequent. However, there seemingly existed no filtering process as had previously operated in Ireland. Dances emanating from the mainstream of American popular culture were adopted in whole, and the result was not a blend or a syncretism of two different dance traditions but a complete supplanting of one tradition by another.

The distinction is best comprehended by the realization that, in the past, the dancing performed at a mid-19th century Irish crossroads dance in the countryside would not have been referred to by its participants as "Irish-French dancing" or "Irish-Bohemian dancing" or "Irish-Spanish dancing", despite the fact that many of these dances being performed were originally inspired by dance forms popular in France, Spain, and Central Europe, i.e. quadrilles and polkas; yet, the dancing that takes place at the vast majority of Irish dances in the U.S. are invariably described in preliminary advertisements and by dancers themselves as "Irish-American".

The widespread use of this term, particularly in contrast to what is referred to as "Irish" dancing, indicates that a process of annihilation rather than acculturation has occurred.

When discussing the subject of Irish dancing in America with persons involved in the promotion of Irish culture, it becomes quickly apparent that Irish-American dancing is much more American in character than Irish. An Irish-language instructor commented that at Irish-American dances, the participants begin with a traditional Irish ensemble dance "to establish nationality; then they start jitterbugging."

A former leader of a New York-based Irish cultural revival group stated that "there are numerous Irish organizations in the New York area which have sponsored public dances. While they call their dances Irish, it's a rare occasion that they may dance a Walls of Limerick or Siege of Ennis, which are rather simple folk dances."

An examination of the program of dances at the Annual Reunion and Ball of the Irish Music Club of Greater Boston in 1938 suggests that Irish-American dancing had firmly taken root by this time in Boston. Seven of the sixteen dances scheduled were waltzes, and of the remaining selections, there were only two (both hornpipes) that were distinctly Irish in character (Irish Music Club 1938:centerfold). An announcement of an "Irish Day" in Pittsburgh, Pennsylvania, that appeared in a 1914 issue of the *Gaelic American* found it necessary to add, after mentioning the presence of Irish step-dancing, that "American dancing will begin at the same time" (Anonymous 1914:5).

In a 1917 issue of the same paper, it was stated that the Philadelphia Gaelic League held classes twice a week, with "Irish and American dancing Saturdays" (Anonymous 1917:7). The distinction between two different dancing traditions was being made perhaps even earlier; it was closer to mid-century that the two traditions spawned a hyphenated offspring.

The musical ensembles that play for Irish-American dances are essentially pop groups with a sparse flavoring of pseudo-Irish tunes performed "to establish nationality". The staple instrument is an 80- or 120-bass piano accordion, particularly one with a wide range of stops so that it can be made to sound like several other instruments. A full set of drums with snares, bass and cymbals is added, and there may also be a guitar, string or electric bass, tenor saxophone, organ and, in rare instances, a violin. All the instruments are electrically amplified, with the exception of the drums, and there is also a vocalist who sings the pop hits of the day as well as the older pseudo-Irish favorites. The overall effect is perhaps best described as "Lawrence Welk with a brogue".

Had the dances adopted by the Irish in America been subjected to the filtering process and transmuted into the native Irish patterns, it is very likely that the music that accompanied them could have been altered to fit traditional Irish musical structures as had been successfully accomplished in the past. There are hundreds of polkas in the traditional Irish repertoire, but few of them bear the slightest surface resemblance to the tunes one hears from an average American polka band.

Similarly, the music used to accompany the sets and half-sets fabricated in the early 19th century from imported quadrilles was fashioned from already existing tunes in the traditional Irish repertoire, with very few foreign tunes entering the active tradition (Breathnach 1971:64).

In light of these past precedents, it is conceivable that the fox-trot, the waltz, even the Big Apple and the Charleston might have been integrated into the indigenous dance tradition of the Irish, though, admittedly, a considerable amount of revamping would have been necessary in some cases. However, one can only speculate and take notice of the fact that, though the traditional dance music of Ireland numbers thousand of individual tunes in its stock, one will be fortunate to hear even a half-dozen of them at an average Irish-American dance.

Céilí dancing, Irish dancing or Rincí Gaelacha, is a form of ensemble dancing developed around the turn of the 20th century. It corresponds to the general concept of "folk dancing" as presently practiced in the U.S., and it is this type of dancing that American folk dance groups perform when they turn to the folk dances of Ireland. Céilí dancing in its present form was shaped by persons involved in the Gaelic League revival of Irish culture.

The term *céilí* is a Gaelic word that denotes in common parlance "an evening visit, a friendly call" (Dinneen 1970:184) or simply an informal social gathering of neighbors in rural Ireland. It was not until the 20th century that céilí came to signify an occasion of traditional Irish music and dance. This newly-attached meaning resulted from the efforts of the London branch of the Gaelic League that held the first céilí at Bloomsbury Hall in London on October 30, 1897.

The occasion consisted of an evening of Irish folk music, song and solo and ensemble dancing and was intended to provide an informal, sociable atmosphere of Irishness for Irish emigrants in London. By calling the event a céilí, the organizers hoped to convey a general feeling of neighborliness and nostalgia reminiscent of the nocturnal assemblies in Irish country houses (Breathnach 1971:50).

Today, the céilí has become the refuge for those who have become irritated by the absence of traditional Irish music and dance at most Irish-American dances; the céilí also serves as a focal point for the scattered remnants of the Irish communities and is a major means of fostering Irish cultural activity in the U.S. (McCullough, forthcoming).

Céilí dances such as the Walls of Limerick, Bridge of Athlone, Siege of Ennis, Haste to the Wedding and Paudeen O'Rafferty were the result of the Gaelic League's unceasing efforts to create an "Irish Ireland". In the area of dance, this entailed the purging of "foreign" dances from the ballroom, and new dances believed to be truly Gaelic and Irish in origin were devised.

The efforts of the revivalists, though inspired by laudable intentions, seem to have actually done more harm than good, for they succeeded in banning a considerable number of excellent and unique Irish dances, replacing them with dances that, ironically, were based on adaptations of foreign quadrilles created early in the 19th century (Breathnach 1971:49).

In any event, many connoisseurs of traditional Irish dancing believed that "these simple contra dances proved inadequate as substitutes for all those that had been prohibited" (Roche 1927:v).

Inadequate or not, céilí dancing continued to thrive, and the céilí is one of the only public musical occasions where the balanced, reciprocal relationship between traditional Irish music and dance is still in evidence. Céilí dances are danced to traditional Irish tunes, and these tunes are supplied by as many musicians as are able to attend the event.

In the 1930s, '40s and '50s, a number of céilí bands formed specifically to accompany dancers at a céilí existed in various parts of the U.S.; as the years progressed, the lack of céilís eventually forced them to disband. A few céilí bands of former days still get together for a reunion occasionally, but a professional American céilí band is not currently a viable economic possibility. Most of the music at céilís is, therefore, provided by whatever local or visiting musicians turn up.

Céilís are often sponsored by Irish-language revival groups such as the Gaelic League of New York or the Irish Language Association of Chicago, or by a group formed for the specific purpose of promoting céilí dancing such as the Philadelphia Céilí Society and similar groups in Baltimore and Washington, D.C. Admission is charged to help put funds in the group's coffers and defray the expenses of refreshments and hall rental. The atmosphere is one of informality, and musicians, dancers and spectators mingle freely.

The format of the céilí is never precisely organized, but there is always a director who organizes dances, acts as liaison between the musicians and dancers, makes necessary general announcements and serves as the master of ceremonies. Céilís are often preceded by a good deal of music-making by performers, and, between dances, musicians are apt to start up a brief, impromptu session and play a few tunes of their own choosing until they are asked to provide the accompaniment to the next dance. Occasionally, musicians are called out for solos, and other participants are often called on to sing a song or to do a solo step dance.

Leadership among the musicians is provided by one or two musicians who are usually experienced céilí performers and high in seniority; there is no formal acknowledgment of their leadership role at this event, but they are inevitably the final arbiters in deciding what tunes to play for the dances, what the initial pace should be and when to go from one tune into another during a medley.

Céilís draw a crowd varying widely in age and distributed almost evenly between males and females. University students, teenagers, families with small children and single adults of all ages are present. Though attended primarily by persons of Irish family background, céilís are often frequented by persons who are not Irish or of Irish ancestry but who come to hear Irish music and dance Irish folk dances and who may well become "more Irish than the Irish themselves" through this initial contact with living Irish culture.

The céilí has been a safe haven for the traditional Irish musician in America. As his services were rejected with increasing frequency by the sponsors and participants of dances held under the auspices of Irish-American social organizations, it became clear that only a group that insisted on Irish dancing and Irish music at a dance event could stem the tide of changing tastes.

It is doubtful whether the traditional Irish musician will actively participate in Irish-American dances to the same degree as a century or even a half century ago. The turnover in dance traditions has been too complete, and while the majority of adult Irish-Americans do not seem inclined to forsake the fox-trot and waltz for the Stack of Barley and the High Caul Cap, it is even more unlikely that very many of their children will exchange the dances of the disco for those of the céilí.

Dance Classes

A half century ago, it was not uncommon to find a teacher of Irish step-dancing who was a musician as well. Those teachers who did not play traditional Irish music engaged the services of an individual who did, as the technological processes that made it possible for pre-recorded music to be played in any situation had not yet been refined. Lacking the presence of a musician, the teacher could always lilt the tune; yet, as his pupils progressed to more intricate dances and steps, musical accompaniment became imperative.

Currently, traditional Irish musicians do not play for Irish step-dance classes except when rehearsing an especially elaborate choreography piece that changes meter, tempo and tune. Otherwise, dance teachers (who are almost all non-musicians) find it much cheaper and easier to teach their pupils by means of a few records and cassette tapes.

Although technological improvements rendered the musician obsolete in this performance domain, dance teachers are quick to point out that pre-recorded music is more efficient for their purposes since, barring battery failure or surges in the line current, a record or tape is always the same every time it is played.

That this dependence on automated musical performance creates an expectation in the pupil's mind that live musical performance should be equally unvarying with each rendition and that the carefully-balanced, symbiotic relationship of the two art forms of music and dance has been estranged by the establishment of the pre-recorded performance as the "correct" performance in the pupil's consciousness are two points that have often been overlooked by dance teachers who have decided to dispense with live performers when giving instruction in Irish step-dancing.

Dance Competitions

The Gaelic word *feis* (pl. *feiseanna*), means a "feast, festival; a parliament, session, convention" (Dinneen 1970:445). In 1897, the Gaelic League inaugurated an annual gathering of musicians, singers and poets in the spirit of the thrice-yearly gatherings of the brehons, bards and poets convened during the pre-Christian period of Irish history when the kingdom of Tara was at its zenith.

The Gaelic League called its event a Feis Cheoil, or Music Convention, and held competitions in traditional music, song, and poetry in Irish in the hope of rejuvenating what was felt to be a moribund traditional culture. When competitions of Irish step-dancers were organized later, the general term, *feis*, was used to describe the event.

Before the early 1960s, there were no more than a handful of annual feiseanna in the U.S.; by 1970, the number of American feiseanna had risen to nearly forty. The rapid proliferation of these events resulted not only from a sharp increase in the number of dance schools and pupils interested in Irish step-dancing but from an expansion and growth in complexity of the institutional structure of the American Irish dancing community that made possible an entire network of feiseanna following similar formats and employing standardized regulatory procedures.

Paradoxically, it was a consolidation of a widely-dispersed network of schools and teachers within two or three key organizations that enabled the feis system to be successfully introduced into a number of areas — a centralization process breeding in its wake an enlargement of the original, decentralized network.

Although pre-recorded tapes have been used in exceptional circumstances, live musicians still accompany the competitors at feiseanna. Dancers are assigned to various stages where the adjudicator or panel of adjudicators judge their efforts in particular genres. Depending on the number of stages and the number of available musicians, there may be from one to three musicians performing at a stage.

The selections played by musicians are dependent upon the age and experience of the dancer; if a group of children under age seven is dancing reels, a simple, easy-to-follow polka or single reel will be played. As the competitors increase in age and skill, tunes that are more complex and more interesting to the musicians can be played. It is not an uncommon occurrence for a player stationed at a stage where dancers in the novice grades are competing to play the same tune for well over an hour.

Musicians are paid for performing at feiseanna; in some localities, musicians have to be brought in to compensate for the lack of musicians in the area. These performers usually receive a small travel stipend as well. The practice of using performers from outside the area is also resorted to by feis committees who have plenty of musicians in the area.

The reason for this is the belief that the hotly-contested championship events should have non-local performers as well as non-local adjudicators; this is done both for an attempt at preserving impartiality as well as for the safety of the musicians and adjudicators, who may well become the target of abuse from the more vehement and embittered losers.

The North American Feis Commission, the chief regulatory body of all North American feiseanna, has seriously considered the feasibility of using pre-recorded music at all feiseanna. The proponents of this plan claim that further standardization is necessary for all competitors to be judged on equal terms; also, they admonish, musicians at feiseanna occasionally forget to turn up at the right stage at the proper time, or they become too incapacitated by drink to perform competently; sitting out in the blazing summer sun or in a hot, humid gymnasium playing the same half dozen tunes for eight hours or more with but a short break or two is certainly no paradise for the musicians.

Whether the advocates of pre-recorded dance accompaniment will be able to implement their program remains to be seen, but a decision in this case may not be too far off in the future. As long as there are enough moderately competent musicians available, pre-recorded music will be used only in contingency situations, such as a championship competition in which the musician or musicians do not know the set dances required of the competitors.

Considerations of efficiency aside, it is not easy to imagine several hundred brightly costumed young dancers mounting a variety of stages for eight or more hours and stepping it out to a succession of two-minute tape loops emanating from a loudspeaker above them (or perhaps the tapes would be in stereo or even quad to create a more realistic impression of a live performer?).

Most musicians do not particularly relish playing for a feis, but they do so out of a sense of duty and are, in fact, somewhat pleased that their talents are sought. Though the working conditions and pay are far from ideal, the feis is an occasion at which the traditional Irish musician plays an indispensable role in the public manifestation of an important element of contemporary Irish-American culture.

The feis is a day-long pageant replete with the color, excitement and communality that vividly recall the rollicking fairs, pattern days and other large-scale social gatherings that have held a vital place in Irish society since its earliest, pre-Christian beginnings. Were the traditional Irish musician to vanish from this domain, something more than a musical tradition would have passed from the scene.

Dance Exhibitions

Occasionally, teachers of Irish step-dancing schools are invited to have their pupils, or select group of their pupils, give a performance for an institution or institutionally-sponsored event. Dance exhibitions of this kind take place throughout the year (but especially around the middle of March) at old age homes, Rotary Club luncheons, church festivals, Irish Centres, television studios and local, national and international folk festivals.

Teachers regard these performances as an important means of not only advertising their own teaching operation but as a means of creating a greater awareness of the art of traditional Irish dancing to which they have devoted an enormous amount of their lives.

Exhibitions are also seen as a way, in addition to competitions, of eliciting approval for the pupils by securing public recognition for the skills they have painstakingly acquired.

The musician's role in all of this is comparatively minor, and he is engaged to provide exactly what is required of him, no more and no less. Exhibitions of this sort rarely exceed a half an hour, and the musicians need only play a few simple reels, jigs, hornpipes and other miscellaneous dance tunes while the dancers go through their paces.

Most of these can be chosen on the spur-of-the-moment, though for some of the more complicated choreography pieces, advance rehearsal is necessary. Still, the musician may share a portion of the acclaim which the dancers and their teacher are accorded. Failing that, he will at least have the satisfaction of receiving a few dollars for his troubles.

Sessions

The six performance domains discussed above all have one element in common: they are musical occasions at which the performer directs his performance to an audience made up largely of non-musicians.

The session, however, is an occasion where the musician plays primarily to satisfy himself while in the company of fellow musicians. The musicians playing in a session are not attempting to entertain, although there may be a number of bystanders who are thoroughly entertained by the performance; the chief motivation of a performer in a session is to express his musical individuality by engaging in a communal performance event with other musicians, and his performance priorities are: (1) himself, (2) his fellow performers, (3) the audience.

The session is an informal gathering of musicians in which the number of musicians and the type of instruments are unspecified. Participation is casual and open to those who wish to join and are accepted by the other musicians. Sessions are found in a number of public and private venues, including homes, clubs, bars, dances, subways and open-air festivals. Certain of these, such as homes, clubs or bars, may develop a reputation as a place where a good session can be regularly found.

Although participants in a session are not compensated with anything other than food or drink provided by listeners or a generous barman, they are often encouraged to perform in taverns by publicans because of the extra business they attract.

The absence of a monetary arrangement leaves the musicians free to perform what they wish; though they may acquiesce and play a tune requested by a listener, they are not bound to do so and may just as likely ignore the request if it does not meet with their liking. This emphasis on individual autonomy is the most valued aspect of the session, as it allows each musician the opportunity to express himself as freely as possible within an ensemble context. Each performer in a session is a soloist in his own right and pursues an independent course, concentrating on presenting his own interpretation of the music.

Sessions are loosely organized and usually acephalous and democratic, depending upon the personalities of the performers. Some sessions are strongly dominated by an aggressive player who attempts to set the pace of the session and select the tunes that will be played, but such behavior is not looked upon favorably by the majority of musicians.

Sessions are spontaneous in format and repertoire, and virtually any tune in the traditional Irish repertoire may be performed. Dance music predominates in sessions, and most of the dance tunes are reels. Sometimes a slow air or a song is heard if specially requested. During a really exciting, fast-paced session, the music pours forth in an unrestricted flow, each tune suggesting another, as long as the musicians can muster enough energy and enough new tunes to continue.

Although the session has a fluid organizational structure, there are unwritten and largely unspoken points of etiquette that participants in a session observe. Obnoxious behavior is not tolerated, nor is the performer who deliberately insists on playing too fast or too loudly.

An important part of the session code of conduct is concerned with the selection of which tunes to play. Visitors or young musicians are often invited to select a few tunes for the group. Often a musician will "suggest" a tune by playing a few bars of it; if no one responds, he will cease and either attempt another tune the others might know or allow someone else to make a choice. If the performer's suggestion is taken up by the other players, there is a sense of satisfaction that, despite whatever differences might exist among them, they are on the same wave length in at least some respects.

Although the session is an occasion where an individual can be free of the restraints that bind him in other domains, there is also a strong desire to achieve a measure of solidarity with other persons who possess the same commitment to an esoteric, specialized body of knowledge.

In explaining the dynamics of the session, one immediately thinks of the jam-sessions of jazz musicians, and comparisons between the two idioms is not without interest. Cameron's definition of a jazz session as "an informal but traditionally-structured association of a small number of self-selected musicians who come together for the primary purpose of playing music which they choose purely in accordance with their own esthetic standards" (1954:177) is an adequate encapsulation of the points discussed above with regard to traditional Irish music sessions.

However, the xenophobia that many observers of jazz sessions believe is endemic to the jazz community does not exist to the same degree with traditional Irish musicians in a session context. Irish musicians, while they do not like to be incessantly harassed by bystanders devoid of intelligent interest in the music, do not make a concerted effort to hold their sessions in obscure, out-of-the-way places.

Some environments are more conducive to a good session than others, and the primary considerations in selecting a public session venue are the good will of the management and a relaxed atmosphere. Public attendance is welcomed, as it is felt to make the session more lively, and except in rare instances, admission to sessions held outside of private homes is never exclusive.

The Irish music session also functions, like its jazz counterpart, as a means of enculturating the novice (Becker 1951:136). Aspiring musicians are exposed to the lore of the idiom as well as the aesthetic attitudes of other performers. They also learn a good deal about the technical performance of the music by watching mature musicians and, above all, by listening to them.

While one might agree that the Irish music session, like the jazz session, is "a proving ground for upwardly mobile individuals" within the musical community (Stebbins 1968:322), there is not the same degree of tension or conflict that many commentators have attributed to the jazz session. The Irish music session is not a "cutting session" in which the newcomer must challenge and conquer the established performers or be himself demolished and humiliated.

Possibly because the Irish music session has a flexible structure that allows performers to play all the time if they wish without deferring to others and because Irish musicians are not competing with each other for jobs, the tension and conflict that might be present in a situation where musicians in the same economic market might be required to "prove themselves" are not present.

Performers do not come to an Irish music session to demonstrate superiority or to elevate their status at the expense of others, although one must not lose sight of the fact that the ego involvement of musicians with their music is high.

The Irish music session does offer a young player to display his command of the idiom and his ability to perform competently and in an acceptable traditional style. Strangers at an Irish music session are not "viewed, if at all, with critical reserve and condescension", as frequently occurs in a jazz context (Cameron 1954:178); they are, instead, viewed with interest until their abilities can be judged, and, if they are still in the learning stages, they receive encouragement and supportive comments with some occasional mildly expressed constructive criticism.

If the newcomer is a fully accomplished performer, he may expect to be asked to play a solo or two that will listened to with great interest, and he will be eagerly plied for new and unusual tunes the others may not have heard. In any event, as long as the stranger is not personally offensive, he is not regarded as a threat or as an interloper but as a welcome member of the musical community.

In assessing the importance of the session in the musical culture of traditional Irish musicians in the U.S., it should be realized that the session is the one musical occasion that has remained firmly within the control of the musicians themselves. It is the nucleus of the tradition and is the chief means of transmitting the values and knowledge possessed by the experienced elders of the idiom.

The session serves as a forum for the exchange of new ideas and new repertoire and is, at the same time, a solid reaffirmation of the existing musical order, as the old tunes are resurrected and given another airing. It is cathartic and thoroughly revitalizing.

The session has been the chief vehicle for keeping the tradition alive during the excessively lean years suffered during the last half century; though traditional Irish music vanished from the mainstream American popular entertainment world and even receded into the backwaters of its own ethnic community, it continued to thrive in sessions in private homes and small taverns among musicians and aficionados fired by an insatiable enthusiasm for a "good crack".

The last decade may have witnessed an increase in céilís, feiseanna and concerts featuring traditional Irish music, but, without the existence of the session, it is difficult to see how the revival of the last few years could ever have been possible.

Audience-Performer Interaction

A discussion of musical occasions would be incomplete without some mention of the interaction between performer and audience. One might start by observing that a great deal of interaction does take place, even in concert situations, and that it is both verbal and physical. Although the musicians may perform on a stage or platform or in a remote corner, the physical separation is never a barrier to audience involvement that may take the form of greeting the players, requesting tunes, shouting encouragement, conversing with the players or simply emitting loud, sharp whoops.

Except at formal concerts, the audience is continually active, and a hum of innumerable conversations provides a steady drone accompaniment to the music. There are, of course, persons who listen quite attentively to the music, and who spend much time in the immediate performance area talking to the performers, buying them drinks, encouraging them and often asking for favorite tunes.

It is this hard-core group of devotees who are the last ones to leave a session or a céilí, and who may, in fact, do their utmost to prolong a good session by supplying drinks or prompting the performers to keep playing. In the absence of regular patronage, the occasional beneficence of these individuals is greatly appreciated by performers.

While traditional Irish musicians do not have any exaggerated respect for the musical knowledge and perception of the majority of their audiences, neither do they express any overt hostility with regard to those who attend the musical occasions at which they play.

They may subscribe to the feelings of one fiddle player who stated that, in general, "the American Irish have no more respect for tradition than a dead dog", but they are not specifically critical of the persons who surround them at céilís, feiseanna, concerts or sessions, unless there is noticeable apathy or antagonism on the part of the audience.

Otherwise, the traditional Irish musician continues to coexist with his audience in a state of amicable detente.

Chapter III: Performers

WHEN CONSIDERED AS a group, performers of traditional Irish music in America exhibit a great deal of heterogeneity, defying the analyst who would rashly attempt to draw a clear composite portrait of the "typical" representative of this population.

Indeed, it is this tremendous variation in musical and demographic features that renders the traditional Irish musician in America such an absorbing subject of study.

It is possible, however, to obtain a general view of the persons involved in the performance of traditional Irish music in the U.S. and of the personal and musical relationships that exist among them. In addition, this chapter discusses the relationship of the musician to the non-musical community and examines the importance of the musician within the changing value system of the Irish-American community.

General Characteristics

As far as national origin, the majority of performers of traditional Irish music in America are natives of Ireland. First-generation Irish-Americans whose parents came from Ireland make up most of the American-born musicians. Second-generation performers are rare, and it is only within the last decade that persons who are three generations removed from Irish forebears have become involved with the music.

Continuity of the tradition seems limited to only two generations; that is, second-generation performers did not have parents who played the music, nor do first-generation performers whose parents played succeed in transmitting the tradition to their offspring. The last decade has also seen the hitherto nearly unknown phenomenon of persons with no Irish ancestry whatsoever taking up performance of traditional Irish music in sizeable numbers.

Still, traditional Irish music in the U.S. remains an activity predominantly performed by Irish emigrants or by persons with very immediate familial connections with Ireland. This close relationship with the tradition's source has pertained throughout the history of the music in America and has undoubtedly contributed to the preservation of the idiom in this country in the same form as it exists in Ireland.

If one were to chart an age profile of traditional Irish musicians in America, one could not help but notice the preponderance of performers born before 1925 and the comparatively miniscule number of active performers born between 1925 and 1950. The reasons for this disparity were discussed in Chapter I and can be seen as an indication of the breakdown in the continuity of the transmission process that began in the 1930s and continued through the 1950s.

Coupled with the marked decline in Irish emigration to America after 1930, the inability to pass the music on to the generation of Irish-Americans growing up in the 1930s, '40s and '50s has had serious effects on the general strength of the tradition.

Within the last ten years, however, many performers have been drawn from the generation born after 1950, and the continuity of transmission has, to some extent, been partially restored. This resurgence of interest following a lapse of one generation can best be explained by the increased public accessibility of the music that has been paralleled and, in some cases, inspired by the growth of festivals, musicians' associations and schools offering instruction in traditional Irish music (see Chapter IV).

The increased participation of musicians born after 1950 has occurred alongside a growth in the number of female performers of traditional Irish music. Although males make up the majority of active performers, the proportional gap between male-to-female performers is substantially lower in the under-25 age bracket than in the 25-to-50 group or among musicians over 50 years of age.

Participation by females is not limited to any particular instrument, nor are there separate male-female categories in instrumental competitions. However, the greater activity of women in traditional Irish music has not been responsible for any changes within the tradition as far as musical performance is concerned; that is, an identifiable "feminine dimension" has not emerged in the performance of traditional Irish music.

Most performers of traditional Irish music are of the Roman Catholic faith or are from Roman Catholic backgrounds. Of the comparatively smaller number of non-Catholic Irish emigrants to the U.S. in the last century, few have associated themselves with the mainly Catholic Irish-American community and its related cultural pursuits. In Ireland, traditional Irish music has always been most prolific in predominantly Catholic areas, and the scarcity of non-Catholic performers of traditional Irish music seems to result from lack of exposure to the music arising from cultural or social class differences rather than from any blatant policy of sectarian abstention.

In terms of socio-economic traits, most Irish musicians in America belong to the various sub-categories ranked under the heading of "middle-class". In this they reflect the socio-economic experience of the American Irish in general (Greeley 1972:185). Occupations of performers are widely varied, encompassing blue-collar jobs (maintenance employees, telephone repairmen, workers in the building trades, policemen, firemen, electricians, butchers, factory workers) and white-collar positions (civil servants, teachers, salesmen, employment service contractors and even one active priest).

Residency patterns are equally diverse, with performers spread throughout the city limits and suburbs of large metropolitan areas, living in one- and two-bedroom apartments and small duplexes in the city as well as spacious split-level and two-story homes in the suburbs.

Despite the high regard for education that exists among the American Irish, most traditional Irish musicians have achieved their present station without recourse to post-secondary level education.

It was noted in Chapter I that the American Irish have tended to lose their cultural distinctiveness as they have risen in the American socio-economic pyramid, casting off old traditions and attitudes like worn, out-of-fashion clothes. Though the "lace curtain"/"shanty" Irish dichotomy is less acute now than it was a few decades ago, it becomes quickly apparent to any observer of Irish-American social functions featuring traditional Irish music that the "lace curtain element" (i.e., those of the upper class or aspiring to upper-class status) is noticeably absent at these occasions.

Despite the improvement in socio-economic status achieved by many performers of traditional Irish music — both emigrants and American-born — there is a strong feeling among them that traditional Irish music in America is a "grass-roots" music that has been in the past, is presently, and will be in the future supported primarily by persons of non-elite backgrounds.

The Irish-American social clubs and social occasions attended primarily by American-born lawyers, doctors, high-level corporation executives, university professors and administrators, politicians and wealthy businessmen rarely prove to be any more supportive of traditional Irish music than the members of a Masonic Lodge, a B'nai B'rith Society or a Bulgarian-Macedonian Beneficial Association.

Specialists and Professionals

Among the larger community of traditional Irish musicians, there exist sub-groups of musicians delineated according to the degree of specialization and professionalism that characterizes their performances. These two terms have been discussed in detail by other authors, most notably by Alan Merriam, who has set forth the basic definitions that will used in this discussion (1964:124-125).

A specialist is an individual who performs a particular service utilizing a set of skills of body of knowledge that is not possessed by all members of the society; a professional is a specialist who receives some form of economic compensation for performance of his specialized activity.

By these definitions, all performers of traditional Irish music in the U.S. are specialists in that they have acquired a unique set of musical skills and possess a restricted body of musical knowledge; however, as will be seen, some performers are more specialized than others. Similarly, most traditional Irish musicians have been the recipients of some kind of economic compensation, ranging from free food or drink to actual monetary payment.

The degree of professionalism, however, varies considerably among musicians. Very few performers of traditional Irish music in the U.S. are fully professional, i.e. able to live entirely by their earnings from musical performance or music teaching. This was not always the case, as has been mentioned previously, but the current value of traditional Irish music as a commodity in the entertainment market of the Irish-American and mainstream American communities is low.

A great deal of respect is given to professionals by their non-professional colleagues, as it is generally held that professional performers are able to practice music intensively and perfect their technique and their command of the idiom by frequent public performance. However, since the professional musician is most often hired to play in bars, his reputation not uncommonly becomes tinged with the unsavouriness generally attached, to persons working regularly in a tavern environment. Thus, while his status as a musician is high, his status as an individual in the society-at-large is often considerably lower.

Traditional Irish musicians have often been the chief musical specialists in their communities, but specialization within the musical community itself has also been known. Many musicians who performed with vaudeville companies during the last century oriented their repertoire and performance style for a specific, stage performance situation.

It was not uncommon for such performers to limit their repertoire to a few tunes that were carefully selected and rehearsed for frequent public performance; some performers, in fact, possessed only a small repertoire of tunes — mostly popular song airs and simple dance tunes — but played for audiences generally unacquainted with the tradition who would not be too critical concerning this point.

Also, since comedy monologues and sketches, songs and dances were also combined in many stage acts of these musicians, a small stock of tunes was all that was necessary. O'Neill relates one amusing incident illustrating this type of musical specialist:

> A very capable performer on the Union pipes of the few tunes comprising his theatrical repertory, was "Charley" McNurney, the musical member of the "Callahan and Mack" vaudeville combination, which toured Australia very early in the twentieth century.
>
> Some four of five days after their first performance at Sydney, Mack was approached on the street by a man whom he recognized as the occupant of a seat in the front row at every performance.
>
> "Excuse me, Sir," said the man, "but would you mind telling what might be the tail of your name."
>
> "The tail of my name! What do you mean?" answered the piper, in surprise.
>
> "Oh, I mane no offense at all, sir; only surely there must be something afther Mack."
>
> "So there is, indeed," replied the man of music, goodnaturedly. "My name is NcNurney."
>
> "For God's sake, Mr. McNorney," exclaimed the fascinated exile, "is there only three 'chunes' in the pipes? Night afther night I've been going to hear you play, but never a 'chune' comes out of your chanter but the same three."
>
> Of course the disappointed lover of the music of his motherland was not aware that "Charley" McNurney was but following the custom of musicians and vocalists in the theatrical profession, who seldom vary the favorite numbers in their program (1973b:344).

Most non-professional performers, on the other hand, play at a variety of musical occasions and, consequently, have developed a diverse repertoire to meet the various demands placed upon them at these occasions. Many musicians, however, concentrate in certain areas of the tradition in consonance with their own personal preferences and capabilities. Some play only dance music and have but one or two airs; others know mostly song airs and only a few dance tunes besides a plethora of waltzes; fewer musicians have an evenly-balanced repertoire encompassing the full spectrum of the tradition.

In the last decade, a new class of specialists has come into being whose repertoire is tailored especially for accompanying Irish dance competitions. Along with the increase in dance schools, pupils and dance competitions came an entirely new style of solo dancing introduced into the U.S. by teachers who had been visiting Ireland for several years and began returning with new steps based on changing aesthetic conceptions of traditional Irish solo dancing.

The new dancing style is marked by a growth in complexity of step patterns, and the relationship between the steps and the musical accompaniment has in many cases been drastically altered, most noticeably in the matter of tempo. Reels are danced to extremely rapid accompaniment, while the increased complexity of step patterns for hornpipes and figure dances has necessitated a great decrease in the tempo of the accompaniment to these dances; the treble jig, a new genre fashioned from already extant dances, requires the playing of a double jig slowed down to less than half the normal speed.

It is a common complaint of many musicians that dancers are now trained in such a way that they are unable to dance to music as it is normally played outside of dance contexts (Breathnach 1965:3 and 1970: 118; McCullough 1975). These criticisms ignore the fact that traditional Irish dance music and traditional Irish solo dancing have long been separate artistic entities that have developed in isolation from each other, though they originally were inextricably intertwined and are still often performed together. Nevertheless, the revolution in dancing that took place in Irish-American dance circles during the 1960s required a revised approach to dance music accompaniment.

There were several records issued in the 1940s and '50s by American céilí bands produced specifically to provide accompaniment for céilí or ensemble dances. It was not until the 1960s, however, that music for solo as well as ensemble dances was subjected to a rigorous performance concept known as "strict-tempo".

Strict-tempo accompaniment is performed precisely according to the requirements of the dancers. Although the term specifically denotes only a regulation of tempo, as a general approach to performing dance music for dancers trained in the new style, strict-tempo has other implications. Strict-tempo music is quintessentially accompaniment that is entirely subservient to dancing and should in no way interfere with the comprehension of the music by the dancer.

Dance tunes are played in simple, skeletal versions, barren of ornamentation that might clutter up the tune and confuse the dancer. Rhythmic and melodic variations are eschewed, and changes in phrasing and articulation are likewise avoided, as it is felt they would also distract the dancer. Strict-tempo music represents, in effect, a complete inversion of the aesthetic values regarding the performance of dance music in non-competitive dance contexts.

However, strict-tempo recordings are universally used by teachers of Irish step-dancing in the U.S., and they are highly valued for the fact that they are predictable, repetitive and simple for pupils to follow. That they may also be musically vapid and bereft of interest for the musician is irrelevant to those who use them for pedagogical purposes, as witness this comment in a record review that appeared in a newspaper devoted to Irish step-dancing:

> … both of these last albums are their best yet in the field of Irish music recorded in strict dance tempo. It is not surprising to learn that the Shandonairs' recordings are now being used by many Irish dancers and Irish dance schools throughout North America and around the world (Anonymous 1971b:7).

The musicians who make these recordings and who are, understandably, in great demand at feiseanna to play for dancers weaned on strict-tempo recordings, form a new breed of musical specialists within the larger community of traditional Irish musicians. Their repertoire and performance style are oriented exclusively toward performing for dancers trained to dance competitively. Tunes are learned not so much for their musical interest but for their suitability for dancers or because dancers demand that the musicians know them.

One musician whose performances have been wholly geared to playing for competitive and exhibition dance events commented, when asked if he knew a particular tune, that since the tune had six parts it would not be welcomed by dancers; subsequently, he had "no call to learn it".

Thus, the worth of the tune is no longer intrinsically inherent in its musical characteristics or in the personal satisfaction obtained from its performance; its value rests in its usefulness to competitive dancers who judge it according to a different set of standards.

The musicians who have absorbed this value system have different priorities in terms of repertoire and in performance style. Set or figure dances are extremely important in the competitive dancing hierarchy, as they are used to determine "champions" of various age groups and represent the most rigorous test of a dancer's skill. They are not generally played by most musicians, since few set dances are regarded as particularly interesting as musical compositions. However, musicians playing for the championship events must know the specific set dance tune that accompanies each of the thirty-odd set dances, as a competitor may request anyone he or she desires, and certain dances may be required for a championship.

It is not necessary to know a great number of tunes in other dance genres such as the jig, reel or hornpipe, since any tune in that genre will suffice, and dancers tend to feel more comfortable with tunes they have heard often; consequently, only a few simple tunes need be learned. Performance style is similarly adjusted: ornamentation and variation in rhythm, melody, phrasing or articulation are liabilities and not assets to the musician orienting his performance for competitive and exhibition dancing.

A few of these specialists are fully professional. Along with a handful of musicians who play in bars and another few who operate schools of traditional Irish music, these are the only professionals that currently exist in traditional Irish music in the U.S. Most of them have been able to attain professional status only in the last few years, as new opportunities have arisen for the traditional Irish musician in America stemming from recent revivals in Irish music and dance.

Although it might be possible to gauge a tradition's health according to the number of professional performers and instructors it can support, it should be remembered that the bedrock of traditional Irish music in America has always been its non-professional performers who play solely for "the crack"; professional performers may provide an ideal role model and have an effect on the surface consciousness of their non-professional colleagues and audiences, but it has been the largely unpaid and publicly unrecognized amateur performers who have maintained the tradition through both fat and lean periods and made the most lasting impression on its form and character.

Interactional Networks

The model giving the clearest insight into the patterns of interaction among performers of traditional Irish music in the U.S. is that of a large constellation of small clusters comprised of individuals sharing a number of personal and musical affinities.

These clusters are not based on a hierarchy of musical competence, as their members span a number of ability levels. Instead, extramusical factors are the chief determinants of the composition of these small groups, with individual performers, geographic areas, and aesthetic attitudes toward traditional Irish music serving as the main organizational foci. While some clusters are almost wholly isolated and self-contained, most are linked with other groups by musicians whose activities are not restricted to one group.

Interactional patterns are to some extent shaped by the frequency of an individual's participation in public musical performance. Some players are almost total recluses, having retired from active musical life years previously. Others may shun public performance but may perform occasionally in the company of a few select friends who are also musicians. Among musicians who perform in public regularly and mix freely with other musicians at public events, there are still numerous cliques of performers who feel musical or personal affinities with each other and who, at a céilí or a session, will be seen performing together most of the time.

Parochialism and intense loyalty to factions or cliques have been the subject of frequent remark by many observers of Irish and Irish-American social and political patterns, and these tendencies have also appeared in the interactional patterns of Irish musicians.

Factional strife and personal rivalries appear occasionally, and instances of a particular musician refusing to attend or participate in a musical occasion where he knows a rival performer will be present are not unknown. An event such as a céilí or concert sponsored by one group may be boycotted by musicians belonging to a rival organization in the aftermath of some kind of dispute.

These differences stem from personal disagreements and personality conflicts and are generally concealed under a veneer of cool formality. Individual musicians sometimes complain of receiving the "cold shoulder" from musicians in another clique, but such incidents are reportedly less common now than in former years.

Traditional Irish musicians in America do not think of themselves as a class or as a national body. Their loyalties are strongly localized, and a musician in Chicago, for instance, forms his identity in terms of his immediate environment. He considers himself a Chicago musician and also, perhaps, a Southside Chicago musician. He may also have had a close musical relationship with other musicians in a céilí band or during regular sessions at a certain venue and may still feel a special tie to this group.

Similarly, members of the Traditional Irish Musicians Association in New York, though they belong to the main umbrella organization, are attached to local music clubs in their part of the metropolitan New York area and define themselves as a member of the Patsy Tuohey Branch or the Michael Coleman Branch.

Since the early 1960s, there have been no national conventions or national organizations that draw together dispersed groups of musicians, and there is very little contact among musicians living in different cities, aside from occasional visits by individuals.

Even the two regional fleadhanna cheoil in New York and Chicago are attended almost exclusively by performers from the local metropolitan area. Communication between musicians in different cities is, understandably, by personal means — via letter, telephone and personal visits; no national communication network or channel exists among performers of traditional Irish music in America.

This fragmentation of the musical community has had deleterious consequences for the tradition, as the decline in interaction among performers has led to a weakening of the process by which new members are initiated into the tradition. The reduced accessibility and visibility of traditional Irish music in the U.S., as it retreated into private homes and private gatherings, has made it difficult to attract new performers.

The disappearance of musical occasions has in many areas brought about a diminishing of performance standards. Performers who were once highly accomplished have, through lack of performance opportunities with other musicians on a regular basis, lost a considerable amount of interest, technique, and repertoire.

Initiation into the idiom is not difficult to achieve once the novice has become proficient in performance. Until recently, most performers were introduced to the music through a member of the family or by a neighbor or family friend who played. This pattern still holds for the most part, but increasing numbers of new musicians have entered the tradition after hearing traditional Irish music on records or in concert rather than by experiencing it from a member of their family or local community.

No special ceremonies or elaborate, formal rites of passage regulate or confirm the novice's musical maturity; graduation into the ranks of the fully-initiated is conferred by a hearty handshake, a few concise words of sincere praise, and some simple acts of hospitality.

It would seem that a process of entropy is steadily atomizing the interactional networks of traditional Irish musicians in America.

Many musicians are aware of this trend, and, as will be seen in the next chapter, are taking active steps to reverse it. It is interesting to note that in the case of a rural music like traditional Irish music, the transition to an urban environment in the U.S. did not uproot its basic interactional patterns but, if anything, intensified them.

Whereas in a desolate country parish in Ireland with a low population density, there might be very few musicians and even fewer musical occasions, a thriving Irish community in a major American city of the latter half of the 19th century could boast a flourishing musical culture stimulated and shaped by performers from all areas of Ireland, their former local loyalties transferred intact to another highly localized situation in the Irishtowns of 19th-century America.

Suburbanization, rather than urbanization, is the cause behind the dissolution of the community of Irish musicians in the U.S. The diaspora to the far-flung suburban areas of major metropolitan areas that marked the rise of the American Irish to unprecedented heights (for them) on the socio-economic ladder has engendered in its wake the dispersion and isolation of traditional Irish musicians into small clusters of musicians tenuously bound in a steadily-contracting network of vastly reduced interaction.

Status and Role

This discussion centers around two types of status distinctions: musical and personal status. Any attempt to characterize the status of musicians must inevitably view the performer from the perspective of both his performing peers and the larger community of which he is a part. To put it another way, one can define the status of a musician in terms of his musical traits and in terms of the personal traits that derive or are believed to derive from the fact of his being a musician.

Within the community of traditional Irish musicians and knowledgeable aficionados, a performer's musical status is dependent upon a number of variables. Technical excellence is an obvious criterion for high musical status, and virtuosity is recognized and enthusiastically commended. Although there are no vote polls like those conducted in the jazz and pop idioms, the relative strengths and weaknesses of outstanding performers of the past and present constitute a frequent topic of discussion among Irish musicians. Professionalism is a related status determinant, as professional players are often judged to be highly polished, "gold-medal" performers, although this is not always borne out by reality.

Many musicians who are not exceptionally talented in the technical execution of the music often achieve a high status by virtue of their inventiveness and ability to instill a large amount of individuality and distinctiveness into their playing. Stability and dependability are other traits that draw praise; musicians often state that a certain player is "solid" or "steady", meaning that the performer maintains a competent level of musicianship and is not subject to erratic spells or loss of control. "Steady" players are especially valued for céilí bands or dance accompaniment because of their consistent, predictable level of performance.

The ability to adapt to an unfamiliar style or tune setting is another praiseworthy characteristic that implies a sensitivity to other musicians. Having a large or unusual repertoire also increases an individual's musical status, and if a musician does not possess any of the above-mentioned attributes but has lived long enough, he may attain some measure of status by virtue of his seniority.

Musical status is generally achieved, although the offspring of a distinguished performer often absorbs some of the high status reflected from the parent. However, the son or daughter of a famous musician must eventually prove the legitimacy of his or her own claim to high musical status on the basis of musical performance.

Dynasties of traditional musicians, with performers occurring in three or more generations into the past, are not uncommon in Ireland. There are, in fact, popular sayings in Irish that indicate the respect given to those whose musical abilities can be traced through their forebears and are rooted in a family heritage — *Ní ón ngaoth a thóg sé é … It wasn't from the wind that he got it* — the "it" referring to the individual's musical skills.

Status ranking among traditional Irish musicians is fluid, and status hierarchies fluctuate according to the relative strength with which the determining factors are held by individual musicians. A performer might have a high musical status due to brilliant technical ability, but this might be offset by arrogance and insensitivity to other players. Conversely, mediocre performers might have a high status among their colleagues as a result of their seniority, occupying a revered position as an "old-timer".

Stability and consistency of performance, technical ability and seniority are the most significant traits that define a performer's leadership role in a session or at a céilí. These are the factors that command the most amount of respect among musicians, and they are the ones most frequently mentioned by musicians when evaluating their peers.

The status of musicians in the eyes of non-musicians in the larger community is shaped by a different set of standards. Musical status among persons outside the musical tradition is the result of the performer's visibility in the public eye. Performers who have been commercially recorded or who play often in public are the first mentioned by persons whose knowledge of the music is minimal and superficial or whose contact with the music is infrequent. Occasionally, the opinions of other musicians may help mold the status hierarchy of a non-performer.

A performer who is accorded a high musical status may frequently not be the recipient of an equivalently exalted personal status. To some extent, the musical occasion has a certain effect on determining personal status in the eyes of the larger society; a musician who performs habitually in bars would be accorded a lower status than a musician who plays only at dances sponsored by social or cultural groups and attended by families.

The professional musician also suffers from this ambience; he is respected for the musical proficiency that enables him to make a living from his talents, yet he is simultaneously denigrated because — if he entertains in bars — his work environment is often populated by persons of ill repute, or — if he operates a school — his profession is considered to be nothing more than a hobby of slight value.

The fundamental determinant, however, is that the traditional Irish musician in America is not viewed as being indispensable nor as possessing a unique body of knowledge and skills. His role in most of the musical occasions in which he participates is that of an adjunct; he provides a service — musical entertainment or accompaniment to dancing — for which he may or may not receive some form of compensation.

The necessity for his service is decreasing, however; Irish dance classes use records and tapes in the strict-tempo mode, and Irish-oriented bars use any type of musical entertainment that will bring in a crowd, sell a large amount of drink and be satisfied with minimum payment. Curiously, the only occasions where a traditional Irish musician receives recognition and status as an artist rather than a hireling are at concerts of festivals outside the Irish community attended predominantly by persons who have in many cases never before heard traditional Irish music.

Persons who regularly attend musical occasions sponsored by Irish cultural revival organizations, such as Irish-language instruction groups, are generally more aware of the musician as a preserver of an important aspect of the Irish cultural heritage.

Although harpers were patronized by the Gaelic elite and, along with uilleann pipers, were often subsidized by some of the Anglo-Irish Ascendancy in the 18th and early 19th centuries, they did not achieve a status or importance beyond that of a for-hire entertainer. More often, they were itinerant and dependent upon the support of the more humble orders of society. As the 19th century progressed, professional Irish musicians found it more difficult to eke out a living from public performance in Ireland.

The segment of society that had provided them with their living had been economically and psychologically ravaged by the Great Famine; an all-consuming land hunger and the onset of a severely puritanical worldview encouraged and enforced by stringent clerical authority reduced the performer of traditional Irish music to a level of insignificance never before encountered and sounded the death knell for the class of professional folk musicians of Ireland.

As mentioned in Chapter I, the Irish musician was greeted by a much greater range of opportunities in 19th-century America. However, by 1900, changes in the tastes of popular entertainment audiences had forced a number of Irish musicians to abandon an entertainment medium that no longer had use for their talents. Other musicians, who had comedy routines in their acts, were harassed into an early retirement by zealous protectors of Irish national honor who asserted that the comedy sketches of many Irish vaudeville performers represented scandalous calumnies upon the Irish character.

In addition, the irreversible workings of the American assimilation process was undermining the position of the traditional Irish musician within his own ethnic enclave. Writing in 1913, Francis O'Neill, the chief chronicler of traditional Irish music in 19th- and early 20th-century America discussed the reasons behind the decline of the traditional musician in the Irish-American community:

> A score of years ago pipers, fiddlers, and singers, filled a large part of every Irish programme, and they were invariably treated with due consideration; and it is more than likely they would be at least as much in evidence on Irish platforms in more recent times were they satisfied with conventional compliments for their services. Irish music has come to be regarded as merely an accessory to the success of some money-making entertainment, independent of all consideration of its ethical value.
>
> In new and growing communities, church extension absorbs not a little of the energies of the Irish race, and the majority of their organizations also have religious affiliations. Consequently their entertainments, with few exceptions, are gotten up in the interest of charity or church building, hence paid talent is not in favor. Pleasure clubs engage bands or orchestras to play at their halls because nothing but the latest in steps and music will satisfy the members, and if an Irish tune is played at all, it is a hackneyed one included in a set of quadrilles.
>
> Where then is the Irish musician to obtain patronage? If neglected by our own people, what can we reasonably expect from others?
>
> The most accomplished Irish music an must inevitably drop out of sight, unless willing to respond to calls in any part of the city to "play a few tunes" without expectation of fee or reward, other than applause and good wishes.
>
> Under such circumstances, of which we have many instances in mind, what motive except pure love of it can those musically inclined have, to spend time and money in learning to play Irish music from which they can seldom hope to derive any pecuniary advantage.
>
> Commercialism of the day has apparently stunted the nobler impulses of our natures, as far as music is concerned. Instead of securing the best talent available for Irish gatherings, committees on entertainments not infrequently engage the lowest bidder (which of course means the poorest performer) if free service can not be obtained. Quite obviously the result is not calculated to advance the interests of Irish music.
>
> If Irish music is to regain its lost prestige — and its fruition is not beyond the range of possibilities — the attitude of chronic apathy must come speedily to an end. Difficulties will disappear, and the problem will solve itself when we make the study of Irish music worth while, and that will be when we show our appreciation by paying for it liberally on all occasions. The demand will create the supply as with other commodities (1973b:480, 482).

Unfortunately, the dynamic of demand-and-supply advocated by O'Neill was overwhelmed by the competing dynamic of acculturation already making substantial inroads into the cultural life of the American Irish. O'Neill's assessment of the social factors contributing to the decline of traditional Irish music in the U.S. was incisive and, six decades later, remains an accurate description of the music's current status.

O'Neill perceived the root of the problem in fundamentally economic terms. The traditional Irish musician was a skilled craftsman who deserved to be paid according to his level of technical accomplishment, his store of unique knowledge and his role as a cultural conservator.

Above all, the Irish musician was to be treated with the dignity accruing to his singular role. However, the profession of a musician, or any artist, is not ranked highly by Irish-Americans (Greeley 1972:199), probably because of the taint of social irresponsibility and lack of respectability that the average non-artist tends to associate with artists and their lifestyles.

A low status for musical specialists is found in many cultures throughout the world, yet, in many of these cultures, the musician, despite his social ignominy, is recognized as an essential member of the society who performs a role that is important, even crucial. The importance of traditional Irish music in America, however, is open to serious speculation, and the role of the musician is no longer clearly defined even, in many cases, to himself.

Desirable role models have also changed; it is no longer necessary for an Irish-American youth to rise in the socio-economic ranks by becoming a boxer, stage artist, priest, politician, policeman, gangster or musician. Other avenues are open, and young Irish-Americans, who might a half century or more ago have sought admission to the occupation of entertainers, may now enter virtually any profession or career.

The intensity of musical involvement is another decisive factor in the formulation of the personal status of a traditional Irish musician by his non-musical peers. Overindulgence in or excessive seriousness about musical activity contributes to a lowering of status in the eyes of those who are not "addicted" to such a pastime. Performers who are zealous enthusiasts of traditional Irish music are held to be "mad for the music" or "cracked about music altogether".

These terms, though often delivered good-naturedly, imply a lack of control on the part of the "cracked" performer when in the presence of music; he is rendered helpless by his inability to contain his fondness for music to the extent of becoming so involved that he loses track of time, forgets or ignores necessary obligations and generally relinquishes contact with the reality of the non-musical world.

With a popular mythology of this kind widespread among the people O'Neill hoped would undertake a cultural renaissance, it is not difficult to understand why a performer of traditional Irish music is not viewed as a valuable repository of a unique tradition but simply as someone who can liven up a social gathering with an "old tune" or two.

Irish musicians may count themselves lucky, however, that they have escaped the yoke of social deviancy that has been placed upon musicians in other American idioms, such as rock, jazz, blues and country-western, and in several other societies throughout the world (c.f. Merriam 1964:123-144 for a number of studies relating to the status and role of musical specialists).

Traditional Irish musicians are not considered to be degenerate or reprehensible, nor are they shunned or ostracized; they are simply not accorded the high degree of personal status that one might expect a performer of a venerable, complex musical tradition to receive from the community that gave birth to that tradition and nourished it to maturity.

Unlike American jazz and rock musicians, who have often been at serious ideological and aesthetic loggerheads with their audiences and with the mainstream society in general, traditional Irish musicians have not had to maintain a special role-distance by cultivating special role-behavior patterns, argot or gestures (Coffman 1971:20-32; Stebbins 1969:406-415). Performers of traditional Irish music in the U.S. live conventional, "normal" lives.

They hold steady jobs, dress and groom conservatively, raise typical nuclear families and are not noticeably in the vanguard of movements agitating for social, economic or political change.

It is this unrelenting diet of normalcy, however, that might perhaps offer the best explanation as to why these people continue to spend inordinate amounts of their leisure time playing a music that pathetically few other people are interested in hearing.

When a bricklayer, janitor, warehouse worker or office employee has emerged from the nether regions of the blue-or-white-collar workaday world they inhabit forty or more hours a week, the search for a means of unlocking the door to the part of oneself that lies fitfully sublimated beneath the outward semblance of orthodoxy becomes paramount and urgent.

For most people, that door is never unlocked, and the years are spent in attempting to forget it ever existed at all.

For a few fortunate ones, however, that barrier is dissolved in the heat of the sublime passion fired by a "great rake of reels".

Chapter IV: Institutions

ONE COMMENTATOR has stated that most European emigrant groups in the U.S. possess "semi-official organizations which try to insure the preservation of the folk music heritage" (Nettl 1962:66). These institutions have come into existence since the group "does not usually trust to the usual channels of oral tradition to assure the survival of the songs" (*ibid*.: 64).

This chapter examines the phenomenon of institutionalization as it has developed within traditional Irish music in the U.S. Institutionalization as used in this context refers to the creation of formally-constituted organizations (institutions) that assume responsibility for the preservation and propagation of the musical tradition.

The institutions discussed here are all revitalistic in nature and origin (c.f. Linton 1943:230-240; Wallace 1956:268-275); that is, they came into being well after the musical tradition was established, and they were organized for the specific purpose of strengthening the tradition and preventing an actual or anticipated decline in the quality and quantity of its exponents.

The 20th century has witnessed a remarkable growth in the number, scope, and complexity of institutions concerned with the fortunes of traditional Irish music. Even more significant is the concurrent increase in the influence of these institutions in shaping the development of the musical tradition itself. Institutions have become steadily more concerned with not merely stimulating the tradition but regulating it, and the reliance of the tradition upon such institutions is another result of this trend.

The first institutional activity undertaken in support of Irish music occurred during the period from roughly 1780 through 1815 and was centered primarily in Belfast and Dublin. Festivals in which the last few performers of the old style of Irish harping assembled and competed for prizes were held in Granard, County Longford from 1781-1785 and in Belfast in 1792.

These were sponsored by wealthy, nationalistically-minded patrons (O'Sullivan 1958:162, 174) whose other cultural revival projects during this period involved the collection and publication of melodies representing the remnants of the Irish harping tradition, the operation of a school where poor blind boys would be taught the harp and thus continue the tradition, and the payment of pensions to distinguished, elderly, indigent harpers (*ibid*.:177; Rimmer 1969:66). These activities had to cease within a few years after their inauguration due to the lack of public support and the exhaustion of the liberality of their original patrons.

Though the harp was occasionally the subject of brief periods of interest among upper-class parlor society in the first four decades of the 19th century, the launching of numerous harp societies was unable to revive the now completely moribund tradition (Flood 1913:322).

Societies to raise funds for the publication of Irish music collected by the 19th-century antiquarians Edward Bunting (1773-1843), George Petrie (1789-1866) and Patrick Joyce (1827-1914) were started but were able to achieve very little as far as helping the living tradition to flourish (Breathnach 1971:116).

It was not until the last decade of the 19th century that the emergence of several institutions designed to actively promote the performance of traditional Irish music on a wide scale began to take place. Again arising from nationalistic impulses, these activities were viewed as an essential element of the cultural revival program of the Gaelic League, which was prominent in sponsoring annual public events such as the Oireachtas and Feis Cheoil in Dublin that attracted performers from all over the country.

Similar events occurred in other parts of Ireland, and institutionally-organized events like the céilí were designed to stimulate performance of traditional Irish music on a local level. Pipers' Clubs in Cork and Dublin were also organized and held concerts, competitions and meetings of their own (O'Neill 1973b:329-330, 344-346). Most importantly, steps were taken to record many outstanding musicians who possessed unique tunes and styles.

The Gaelic Revival lost much of its potency after 1916, when the nation was embroiled in a decade of civil strife. It was not until the early 1950s that a new surge of institutional activity dedicated to the revival of traditional Irish music in Ireland took place.

National organizations such as Gael-Linn and Comhaltas Ceoltóirí Éireann were among the most wide-ranging institutions that undertook campaigns to stimulate a renewed interest in Irish music among the Irish public. More specialized groups such as Na Píobairí Uilleann and the Cork and Armagh Pipers' Clubs also contributed significantly to the revival that has continued through the 1960s and into the 1970s.

The institutions involved in the preservation of traditional Irish music in the U.S. have taken two forms: (1) musicians' associations and (2) schools offering instruction in Irish music.

Though these forms have occasionally been combined, as in the case of musicians' associations that sponsor musical instruction programs, they are, in most cases, quite separate in their genesis and in the nature of their activities.

In appraising the impact of institutionalization on traditional Irish music in the U.S., it is necessary to examine the role of the mass communications media (recordings, radio, television, publications), since the various channels of the media have contributed significantly to the development of traditional Irish music in the U.S. The media represent a collective institutional network that is outside of the tradition yet intimately connected with its dissemination.

Musicians' Associations

Musicians' associations were first organized by traditional Irish musicians in America at the turn of the 20th century. They were outgrowths of informal gatherings and sessions that took place in private homes and were originally begun with the intention of transferring the sessions from a private to a public venue so that greater participation would be possible. The rise and fall of one such association, the Irish Music Club of Chicago, was chronicled by one of its founders, Francis O'Neill, and some excerpts from his account of the club have particular relevance to present-day musicians' associations.

Writing in 1910, he stated, "In an evil moment an aggressive enthusiast conceived the idea of forming a permanent (?) organization, with monthly meetings in a rented hall, etc. Picnics and balls were to vary the anticipated pleasures and provide a revenue which was to be disbursed among the musicians" (O'Neill 1973a:58).

The organization nearly foundered when the election of officers sparked off latent rivalries, but this initial crisis passed without seriously endangering the club. "Many citizens with Irish sympathies, though not of Irish ancestry, attended the monthly meetings and the free midsummer picnics at 'Leafy Grove', and everything went along swimmingly for a time" (*ibid.*:58-59).

However, disputes arose concerning the distribution of the proceeds from the club's grand ball, and other personality clashes festered in the wake of this incident. Wrote O'Neill:

> The musicians began to drop away from that forth. A few excellent ones maintained their membership with great pertinacity for a year or two, but there came a time when tactless and undiplomatic outbursts could no longer be endured, and the "Irish Music Club" was left without musicians worthy of the name. After less than eight years of inharmonious existence, the most enjoyable, companionable, and representative association of Irish musicians, singers, and dancers ever organized in America degenerated into a mere shadow of its former prominence, until its disruption in 1909, following a clash of mercenary interests (*ibid.*:59).

Still, the dissolution of the club did not effect the practice of traditional Irish music in Chicago, and musical occasions featuring Irish music continued to take place. The formation of the Irish Music Club had been an experiment, an attempt to extend the conviviality of a private session to a larger performance context. Although there were hopes that money could be raised by such a venture, there was no imperative need for its organization, nor was there any great hardship wrought upon the tradition by its demise.

The musicians' associations that were launched in the 1950s and '60s, however, were formed in response to a vastly different situation than what had existed a half century or more earlier. The impulse to organize a formal association was no longer felt to be the result of capriciousness or mercenary or grandiose schemes; instead, the formation of strong musicians' associations was viewed as a necessary measure to insure the continued survival of traditional Irish music in America.

The musicians' associations that had developed by the mid-1950s had done so independently of each other. However, an attempt was made to coordinate the activities of these groups under the guidance of a national organization. Annual conventions were held, with delegates being sent from the local associations, and such matters as a constitution, by-laws, election of officers and other items pertaining to the conduct of a national organization were discussed.

The conventions were held in a different city each year and served as opportunities for musicians who saw each other infrequently to meet and play music together. These Irish traditional music conventions of the late 1950s and early '60s are still fondly remembered by many musicians for the great sessions that took place.

As with the Chicago Irish Music Club of the early 1900s, factionalism and petty disputes over leadership, finances and the conduct of organizational business eventually caused the disintegration of the national association. The national conventions were discontinued, and several local associations collapsed or entered into a period of inactivity.

However, this failure to create a successful institutional framework to rejuvenate traditional Irish music in the U.S. only increased the sense of desperation and resolve felt by many individuals concerned with the retreat of the tradition into an ever-shrinking number of isolated circles of performers.

The success of Comhaltas Ceoltóirí Éireann in organizing local musicians' associations throughout Ireland served as the inspiration for musicians in several American cities to try once again to revive local associations. This new surge of organizational activity built upon the foundations of earlier associations, and, by 1975, had achieved some measure of success in stimulating new interest in traditional Irish music among the public.

Local independence and sovereignty are still maintained by these associations; some groups remain proudly unaffiliated with any other organization, while others are tenuously connected with CCE but reserve the right to resist any outside policy deemed incompatible with local needs and desires.

Perhaps as a result of the recent experiences of the early 1960s, no attempts have been made to fabricate a national institutional network, and the activities of local associations are not interrelated. The Traditional Irish Musicians Association of New York is a unique case, in that it consists of six individual branches scattered throughout the New York metropolitan area.

The activities of the associations vary with each group and include: organizing frequent public musical occasions such as sessions, dances or benefit concerts; teaching traditional Irish music to young people; offering scholarships for young performers to receive formal musical training or to compete in musical competitions in Ireland; arranging local musical competitions; supplying musicians for dancing competitions and other performance occasions which require traditional Irish music.

At least one musicians' association, the Irish Musicians' Union Local No. 1 of Philadelphia, has acted as a specialized union created to "mutually protect the members and promote their interests, to establish a minimum rate of charge for services which the members might render, and to enforce good faith, mutual friendship, and fair dealing among the members" (Irish Musicians' Union n.d.:1).

Musicians' associations have taken the leading role in fostering the revival of interest in traditional Irish music in the U.S. and have become a necessity rather than a superfluity. The capability of such associations to channel and utilize the available resources more efficiently and to undertake activities involving a high degree of coordination among different groups have given musicians' associations a prominent position in the community of traditional Irish musicians.

Associations have also been able to spark the growth of a latent spirit of unity and solidarity among musicians previously been isolated within a small, closed interactional circuit. The various separate networks of musicians dispersed throughout a large metropolitan area have been brought into more frequent contact with each other through participation in musical occasions organized under the auspices of a local musicians' association.

The increased visibility and accessibility of traditional Irish music brought about by these public occasions has not only stimulated the performers themselves but has aided greatly in the efforts to restore the continuity of the transmission process through the initiation of newcomers into the tradition. The mature exponents of the tradition are able to be seen and heard by young players, and an important element of the learning process is having the opportunity to observe the music in a live performance setting.

Furthermore, by performing in a public context among fellow musicians and a supportive audience, the connotations of inferiority, worthlessness and irrelevancy that have lain heavily upon traditional Irish musicians in the U.S. in recent years have been considerably dispelled.

The musicians' associations, by reintroducing traditional Irish music into the forefront of the Irish-American community's cultural consciousness, have done much to increase the status of the performer of traditional Irish music by bringing about a recognition of the performer as an active carrier of an important aspect of the Irish cultural heritage.

The attempts by musicians' associations to reintegrate traditional Irish music into the cultural life of the American Irish have had a noticeable psychological impact upon performers and audience alike.

Schools

With rare exceptions, formal schools with pupils and "professor" have not figured prominently in the transmission of traditional Irish music in the U.S.

The initiation of new performers and the acquisition of repertoire and performance technique by aspiring players has been primarily accomplished on an informal basis. The usual pattern is for an individual to become interested in the music after hearing it performed live or on a record; the next step is to seek a performer living in the area who can point out the musical fundamentals of the idiom and of the particular instrument the novice performs or is interested in performing.

At the same time, the individual attempts to locate other experienced performers and begins to attend musical occasions where the music is performed. Recordings and tapes are also utilized in an effort to increase repertoire and become familiar with the idiomatic features of the music. Any actual teaching that does take place generally occurs at the teacher's home.

The pedagogic methods employed in this situation are diverse and differ according to the amount of self-motivation possessed by the individual and the availability of learning resources. Contacts are always initiated and sustained by the learner, unless, perhaps, it is a parent or relative who is the instructor.

The learning process itself is informal and highly personalized; the frequency of learning sessions is variable, there is no set curriculum or schedule of events, nor are their generally more than one or two pupils involved at a time. What is actually transmitted depends upon the abilities of the pupil and the resources of the experienced performer. Though the student may later selectively absorb certain elements of what has been observed, the first level of the learning process consists of the pupil's direct imitation of the teacher's example.

Another feature of this personalized, individual method of transmission is that there is no monetary remuneration paid to the teacher. Many performers would refuse to accept such compensation, believing that their knowledge and skill should be passed on freely to others who are genuinely interested.

Although schools of traditional Irish music employing more formal methods of pedagogy had existed for brief periods of time in the U.S. (the most notable being that operated by the renowned Sligo-born fiddler, James Morrison, in New York during the 1920s, '30s and '40s), it was not until the mid-1960s that a discernible movement in this direction began. The opening of a school of Irish music by fiddler Peter Kelly, a native of Galway, in 1964 was the first attempt in two decades to conduct a formally-organized, commercial school of this kind in the New York area (McEvoy 1973:7). The success of this experiment was quickly realized, and schools of Irish music based along similar lines proliferated in the New York area over the next few years.

Presently, there are nearly a dozen such schools, the most popular with over one hundred pupils. New York is the only area that has so far been able to support schools of this magnitude; the large Irish and Irish-American population of the area is one important factor, as is the fact that a number of Irish music competitions are held within the area and provide public outlets for the demonstration of skills acquired in the school.

The contemporary schools of Irish music teach a variety of instruments, with most instructors being proficient at two or three. Violin and accordion (both button and piano) are most commonly taught, though the tinwhistle, flute, saxophone and piano are also taught. Pupils are instructed in groups and are given formal lessons lasting a specific length of time, thirty minutes or an hour. The instructor is paid a pre-arranged fee by each student per lesson, and the lesson is administered in a rented hall or studio.

The basic part of the curriculum consists of providing the student with fundamental elements of music theory and notation along with instruction in the operation of the instrument if needed. Once a student has acquired a rudimentary command of the instrument, simple Irish tunes are written out and subsequently memorized. Since these tunes are taught and performed in groups, efforts are made to present identical versions to all students.

This is especially important in that the more promising pupils in the school are organized by age into junior and senior ensembles that compete against other similarly organized ensembles and also perform at dances and fundraising concerts. Pedagogy in the schools is oriented toward ensemble performance of this kind, and standardized versions of tunes are learned for these occasions. A certain conformity is thereby encouraged and is, perhaps, inevitable in view of the group-approach to instruction and the reliance upon standardized printed materials as repertoire sources.

The chief purpose of these schools is to give students a basic acquaintance with the idiom of traditional Irish music. With one of the primary goals being to prepare students for cohesive ensemble performance, there is understandably less emphasis on imparting the more idiomatic elements and nuances of style. It is hoped by instructors that the more astute pupils will be able to develop an individual performance style of their own.

There has been a good deal of criticism, however, directed at the "products" turned out by the group-approach teaching utilized in the schools. While agreeing that traditional Irish music should be taught to young people on a wider scale, it is felt that those who have been taught the music by institutionalized pedagogical procedures acquire only a superficial understanding of the idiom and perform in an undistinguished, mediocre manner. The stress on uniformity and group performance, it is alleged, induces a reliance on non-individual and uncreative musical thinking and performance.

Though it is true that a larger quantity of musicians does not necessarily entail a rise in the quality of musical performance standards, the schools of Irish music have done much to disperse the tradition among a greater number of people than would have been possible if the individual, informal approach were exclusively followed.

One of the most critical problems the tradition has faced in the U.S. in the last few decades has been the drastic decline in the number of young performers arising to replenish the ranks thinned by the deaths or retirement from active performance of older players. The vast reduction in the numbers of emigrants from Ireland since World War II has made the recruitment of performers from the succeeding generation of young Irish-Americans even more crucial.

With the geographic fragmentation of the Irish-American communities continuing to accelerate, the task of maintaining an adequate number of competent performers to keep the tradition alive has been a formidable one that has had to make use of methods designed to cope with the exigencies of a changing social and cultural context.

The formation of musicians' associations has been one means of creating a greater enthusiasm for traditional Irish music within the Irish-American community; the organization of Irish music schools has been the chief method of recycling that enthusiasm back into a self-generating process of renewal.

Media

The mass communications medium that has had the most direct influence upon traditional Irish music in the U.S. has been that of the commercial recording. The emergence of the commercial recording industry and its relation to traditional Irish music in America was previously discussed in Chapter I; however, it would be appropriate to point out here that the major disseminating medium for traditional Irish music has been the commercial recording.

The formats used by the recording industry have changed as new technology has been developed (wire cylinders, 78 rpm discs, long-playing albums and cassette tapes have been the vehicles by which traditional Irish music has been circulated since the early 20th century), but the importance of the industry to traditional Irish music has not diminished over the years.

After World War II, the major commercial labels virtually ceased to issue new recordings by Irish musicians in the U.S. A few small, privately-owned, independent companies attempted to take up the slack, believing that a market for traditional Irish music still existed in the U.S., though it was not as large nor as lucrative as a decade or two before. Copley Records of Boston and Avoca Records of Westbury, N.Y. were among the most prolific and long-lasting of these ventures, and some notable recordings of Irish musicians in America were issued on those labels.

A number of other records have been put out by individual performers themselves, but these are limited in their area of distribution and are generally unavailable outside of the Irish-American import stores. Recently, a few small labels specializing in North American folk music have been recording traditional Irish music in Ireland and America, but these are also plagued by distribution problems. The major focus of recording activity has shifted from the U.S. to England and Ireland, and, consequently, fewer American Irish musicians are recorded.

Although new tunes are received from personal contacts with other performers, a considerable amount of new repertoire is introduced via the commercial recording. There is a substantial lag, however (often more than a year), between the time of a record's issue in Ireland or England and its arrival in the U.S. Although most new records can be ordered directly from overseas, Irish-American import stores are the chief sources for these records in America, and their stock is not always up-to-date. Nevertheless, the impact of new releases from across the Atlantic eventually becomes noticeable in the repertoire of American Irish musicians.

It is difficult to ascertain the total effect of new records of traditional Irish music on musicians in the U.S. Musicians who ceased learning tunes years ago are obviously not affected by new developments, but, among younger players — as well as many older ones interested in picking up a new tune or two — new releases of traditional Irish music receive careful attention, since they are often one of the main sources of repertoire.

It might be mentioned here that the portable cassette tape recorder has come to be the primary agent of repertoire transmission between musicians in Ireland and America and among musicians separated by great distance in the U.S. Whenever an Irish-American musician goes to Ireland, or an Irish musician or group visits the U.S., or a musician from one American city visits friends in another locality, the cassette recorder is certain to be present.

The isolation of many musicians in the U.S.. has been greatly alleviated in recent years by the widespread use of this device, and young musicians entering the tradition have also benefited vastly by having the chance to study experienced performers in the detail permitted by repeated listening to tape recordings. The deleterious effects of a decline in commercial recordings of traditional Irish music in the U.S. have, to a great extent, been offset by the emergence of the cassette tape as a means of disseminating repertoire and styles.

This is a notable instance in which a product of modern technology has proven immensely helpful to the preservation and perpetuation of a folk music tradition among its practitioners.

The broadcast media (radio and television) have exerted a less profound impact on the musical development of the tradition in America. Instead, they have functioned primarily as purveyors of aesthetic attitudes and musical entertainment preferences that have evolved among the American Irish in this century.

Of the two, radio is the most heavily involved with traditional Irish music; there are no regular television programs featuring traditional Irish music in the U.S., and the only time Irish musicians appear on America television is around St. Patrick's Day in March and, at that, only briefly as part of a dance troupe. Perhaps with the introduction of localized cable television systems, this situation will change to some extent.

Radio, however, is a more locally-oriented medium in many respects, and, currently, there are between fifteen to twenty radio programs specifically devoted to an Irish-American listening audience in the U.S. Irish music is also occasionally played on other programs in various cities that feature the music of the British Isles or present a variety of music from around the world.

[This discussion of Irish-American radio is based on data obtained from a survey questionnaire distributed by the author to Irish-American radio producers in the spring of 1973, personal interviews by the author with several producers and the author's frequent listening to innumerable hours of Irish Hours across the U.S. since 1972.]

The radio programs having the most relevance to performers of traditional Irish music are the "Irish Hours" that have a format of news from Ireland, announcements of local events of interest to the Irish community, advertisements for local Irish-owned or Irish-oriented businesses and pre-recorded musical selections. With but a very few exceptions, these Irish programs (lasting from a half an hour to as long as two hours) are aired over commercial stations on both AM and FM.

Due to the economic demands placed upon the producer of such a program, a large amount of the program time is taken up with commercials for the various sponsors, with the result that, in many instances, very little music is actually played. In some programs, the ratio of speech to music is as high as three-to-one, that is, three minutes of speech to one minute of music, with most of the speech not related to the particular musical selection.

Traditional Irish music is rarely played on Irish radio programs in the U.S. Instead, the preponderance of musical selections are drawn from the various hybrid, Irish-derived idioms that have arisen in response to the changing musical preferences of many Irish-Americans. When asked to discuss the basic criteria for choosing their musical selections, producers consistently state that their aim is to please the largest number of listeners. In doing so, they also assuage sponsors who lend their financial support to the program in anticipation that a large number of people will be listening.

Producers also solicit requests and dedications from listeners in an attempt to stimulate listener participation and to demonstrate to sponsors that people are actually listening. Due to the fact that a substantial number of Americans of Irish ancestry are unaware of the existence of traditional Irish music, program producers are not inclined to play recordings of a musical idiom that many listeners would quite possibly not even recognize as being Irish.

The amount of traditional Irish music played over the air is also determined by the attitudes of the producers themselves. With two or three exceptions, producers of Irish radio programs are not performers of traditional Irish music or dance, and their knowledge of the tradition is minimal. A few producers enjoy traditional Irish music and play it as often as they feel their largely uninitiated audience will tolerate; others are either apathetic toward the music or, in some cases, appear to be covertly hostile.

In the 1920s, '30s and '40s, Irish-American radio programs featured live performances of traditional Irish music to a much greater extent than is now the case. Many programs had regular performers who were renowned local exponents of Irish music and who would play listener requests as well as a set of pre-established tunes. Although live musicians have made occasional appearances on Irish radio programs in recent years, such an event is rare and reflects the decline in importance of the traditional Irish musician as an entertainer in the Irish-American community.

There is, however, one notable exception to this dominant pattern of pre-recorded, non-traditional music: an Irish program in Chicago broadcast live each Sunday evening from the basement lounge of Hibernian Hall (formerly broadcast from a now-defunct Irish tavern five blocks down the street).

The *Irish Hour* is sponsored by a travel agency specializing in flights to Ireland, but advertisements are brief and to-the-point. Local traditional musicians make up the "house band", and there is a good deal of traditional music performed during the half-hour, all-live program. Of the four Irish radio programs in Chicago, it is this one that receives the greatest attention from traditional musicians, who, in many cases, sit at home with their cassette tape recorder at the ready, waiting for a new tune or a new performer to arrive over the airwaves.

Though traditional Irish musicians in the U.S. may listen to their local Irish program for Irish news, upcoming local events, and information on charter flights to Ireland, the influence of radio as a medium capable of stimulating or disseminating new developments in the idiom of traditional Irish music has been nullified in the past few decades.

With one or two exceptions, Irish-American radio programs serve mainly to reinforce the existing status quo of musical tastes and aesthetic values of a listening audience that has been convinced of the worthlessness of its most distinctive musical tradition.

The printed media have never been as influential in contributing to the development of traditional Irish music in America as have the aural media. An obvious explanation lies in the fact that traditional Irish music is not a musical tradition that depends upon printed music notation for survival.

Aural methods of transmission are the chief means of perpetuating the tradition, although many musicians are musically literate and do not hesitate in picking up a tune from a printed source. The newly-acquired tune is then refashioned in consonance with the performer's own stylistic intuitions and may eventually assume a form radically different from the original printed version.

There is no printed publication in the U.S. that is concerned solely with traditional Irish music in this country. Comhaltas Ceoltóirí Éireann publishes a monthly magazine called *Treoir* (Direction) which is widely distributed in the U.S. Its chief value lies in its news items about performers, announcements of CCE-sponsored events and publishing versions of songs and tunes not frequently heard in current traditional repertoire.

Other than the communication of information, the magazine has little influence on the actual performance of music, and most American Irish musicians take only a passing interest in it. Two other journals, *Ceol* (Music) and *Éigse Cheol Tíre* (Irish Folk Music Studies), are published in Dublin and have almost no American circulation; they consist of scholarly investigations of certain aspects of Irish folk music and are much less "newsy" than *Treoir*.

Occasionally, a special-interest musicians' association puts out a newsletter. There are two newsletters concerned with uilleann piping, one published by Na Píobairí Uilleann in Dublin, the other by a group in North Carolina. A céilí group in Chicago also informs its members of upcoming events by means of a newsletter that contains in addition to news items an article or two of interest on Irish music or Irish history. The few Irish-American newspapers that still survive only infrequently contain any articles or information about traditional Irish music.

Though each of the publications discussed above possesses a definite and discernible viewpoint about traditional Irish music and its role in modern society, as well as opinions about innumerable aspects of current performance practices, they do not have the dynamic and immediate impact of recordings. Also, it is uncertain as to what extent their efforts in propounding aesthetic attitudes have been either noticed or accepted by musicians and translated into changes in performance.

Institutions as Agents of Change

In assessing the impact of institutions on the development of traditional Irish music in the U.S., it might be of interest to do so within a framework that is a revision of an outline devised by the German sociologist Honigsheim (1973:53-60) of the various components of a modern musical culture. These components are grouped into three areas: performance, transmission, dissemination.

In the area of performance, institutions such as musicians' associations have emerged to promote the public performance of traditional Irish music; the role of these associations in organizing and regulating public performance has increased in recent years as they have taken the initiative and assume the organizational responsibilities formerly exercised by other institutions within the Irish-American community.

In the area of transmission, a new system of instruction centered around a formal, commercial system of regular group classes has arisen to supplement the informal, non-commercial, one-to-one method of transmitting the tradition.

A marked increase in the use of music notation to transmit repertoire has also occurred along with the new instructional format. Within the area of dissemination, the gradual reorientation of media away from traditional Irish music has had a decisive role in relegating the tradition to a subterranean status within a specialized network of radio programs and record companies.

Musicians' associations have been a revitalizing force, but they have not been the cause of change within the tradition. They have not advocated new styles of performance, new instruments, new repertoire or any innovations relating to the music itself; instead, they have sought to arrest the decline of traditional Irish music in the U.S. by attempting to reassert the formerly prominent role of the Irish musician in Irish-American cultural life, while at the same time fostering a greater sense of solidarity and pride among performers.

Musicians' associations have arisen from a conservative impulse; the chief goal of the future is to restore many elements present in the past. When ideals of acceptable traditional performance are propounded by institutionally-sponsored activities, such as competitions, the net effect is that of attempting to control the change that is inevitable in a living musical tradition by insuring that the innovations are in accordance with the idiom's previously-established precepts and norms.

The schools of Irish music are, like the musicians' associations, "perpetuative" in nature (Linton 1943:231) and are engaged in preserving a particular aspect of the Irish cultural heritage from extinction.

The schools, however, are involved in the actual mechanics of the transmission process, and their capacity for introducing and disseminating change within the idiom is considerable. Instructors have a significant role in determining the playing technique, aesthetic attitudes, repertoire, stylistic traits and even the very instrument of the pupil. In addition, they have the power of peer group pressure to assist in the inculcation of their ideas about traditional Irish music and its performance.

It should not be taken from this, however, that instructors of Irish music are possessed of sinister Machiavellian intent, for such is hardly the case and would do great injustice to persons intensely dedicated to the cause of traditional Irish music; nevertheless, the possibility of instructors profoundly influencing the future character of traditional Irish music to a degree greater than ever before is definitely present due to the concentrated nature of the pedagogical process used in the schools.

The media have served traditional Irish music variously as agents for change, stabilization and stagnation. During the first four decades of the 20th century, commercial recordings and Irish-American radio programs were the channels by which new styles, new tunes, new performers and performance formats were introduced to traditional Irish musicians throughout the U.S. and across the Atlantic to Ireland.

Whatever importance printed works have had as sources of repertoire acquisition declined after the introduction of the aural media, particularly since the widespread adoption of the cassette tape format that made it possible for tunes and styles to be transmitted aurally with greater fidelity than is possible with print.

Commercial recordings and radio programs have ceased to be actively concerned with traditional Irish music in the U.S. and have relinquished the prominent role they once possessed as major innovative forces. Radio, particularly, has increasingly lost its usefulness as a medium involved in the dissemination of traditional Irish music in America, with the majority of "Irish Hours" pursuing a programming policy that appears to militate against the recognition of traditional Irish music as an important aspect of the Irish-American cultural heritage.

Chapter V: The Role of Traditional Irish Music in Contemporary Irish-American Culture

THE FIRST ISSUE that should be addressed here is that shadowy entity known as "contemporary Irish-American culture". Is there such an animal?

Several observers have claimed that the American Irish no longer have a distinctive culture — they are merely middle-class Catholic WASPs who have been extremely successful in assimilating into the socio-economic and cultural patterns of the American mainstream, or so the argument goes. Andrew Greeley, in his survey of the Irish in America, devotes a chapter entitled "Where Did the Past Go?" to the lack of a strong tradition of cultural identity among the American Irish.

> Seduced by the bright glitter of respectability and egged on by their mothers, the Irish have become just like everyone else, and the parades on St. Patrick's Day are monuments to lost possibilities, of which few people in the parades are aware (Greeley 1972:269).

Stephen Birmingham's account of the "First Irish Families", or "F.I.F.s", reveals how seductive and ultimately destructive the quest for approval from the established society can be. *Real Lace* describes the new Irish rich in their desperate, yet determined efforts to gain access to the most restricted social cliques of the wealthy Protestant elite. Pathetic in their attempts to mimic their chosen social models in every frivolous detail, the "Irishtocracy" quickly lost any vestiges of Irish culture they might have possessed in the frenzy of their continuous obsession with prestige and status within the elite social networks.

Unlike the newly-emerging Jewish elites of the 19th century, the new Irish rich did not manage to create a new culture that preserved elements of their past heritage; instead, they developed a parallel institutional structure that corresponded precisely to the institutional models of the "nice people" — an insular network of yacht clubs, exclusive resorts, prep schools and debutante balls. Even the cause of Irish independence, which captured the hearts and wallets of thousands of Irish-Americans, was ignored by the F.I.F.s, as their fortunes were used to make more money that could be used to buy their way into the ranks of the Protestant elite (Birmingham 1973:247).

Not only the Irish upper classes lost contact with their ethnic heritage, for the other Irish emigrants who were struggling slowly up the socio-economic rungs were also beginning to jettison aspects of their culture that were not considered respectable or as possessing value in the melting pot society. As one sociologist has observed, "The triumph of acculturation in America has been, if not complete, at least numerically and functionally overwhelming" (Gordon 1964:110).

What this meant for the bulk of the American Irish is described by Daniel Moynihan:

> Turning lower-middle class is a painful process for a group such as the Irish who, as stevedores and truck drivers, made such a grand thing of Saturday night. Most prize fighters and a good many saloon fighters die in the gutter — but they have moments of glory unknown to accountants. Most Irish labourers died penniless, but they had been rich one night a week much of their lives, whereas their white-collar children never know a moment of financial peace, much less affluence. A good deal of color goes out of life when a group begins to rise. A good deal of resentment enters (1963:101).

The complete rejection of all cultural traits identified with the emigrant's heritage need not necessarily occur, however. Acculturation is a process that divests the emigrant of his "extrinsic" cultural traits, such as language, dress and housing styles and behavioral stereotypes that are in conflict with the norms of the host culture.

Yet it does not necessarily reduce the reliance of an individual on the "intrinsic" cultural traits, such as oral history and folklore, folk music, song and dance. What happens, however, is that this distinction between extrinsic and intrinsic often becomes blurred; the emigrant attempting to adjust to the outward norms of American life is apt to begin discarding indiscriminately any of the traits he believes may impair his acceptance into the adopted society or that may conflict with the new self-image of a 100% American (Gordon 1964:113).

Or, as in the case of the American Irish, the individual comes to accept an artificially-fabricated pastiche of stereotypes as his own true cultural heritage, particularly if that pseudo-heritage is acceptable to the mainstream society; indeed, he may even come to prefer the ersatz heritage to the real one.

Although the following remarks refer specifically to the Irish in 19th-century England, they mirrored a similar situation in 19th-century America:

> The stage Irishman was at the height of his popularity at the end of the nineteenth century, and for all its ingratiating idiocy and bogus sentimentality, such folk hero status was welcomed by the mass of the Irish. In spite of the criticisms of later generations of immigrants in less dangerous times, their reasoning was sound: the caricature and ridicule meant that the English considered them harmless creatures. In the East End of the nineteenth century, regularly hovering on the brink of racial conflict, this refusal to take them seriously ensured their safety and marked the thin end of the wedge towards general acceptance (O'Connor 1974:27).

Moynihan (1963:98) has isolated three factors he believes are responsible for "a weakening of Irish identity in America: the decline of immigration, the fading of Irish nationalism, and the relative absence of Irish cultural influence from abroad on the majority of American Irish".

As the ethnic consciousness of the Irish has declined, certain aspects of their cultural heritage, such as traditional music, have become meaningless and irrelevant when transferred from their native physical and cultural contexts.

However, the Irish-American is no longer an inhabitant of a ghetto community; one may take part in activities that are a part of the Irish cultural heritage without abandoning the normal daily life routines followed in modern American society. Attending Irish-American musical occasions, playing traditional Irish music or taking lessons in Irish step-dancing are not in 1975 activities that mark one as unassimilated or un-American.

Thus, in speaking of contemporary Irish-American culture, one must recognize an implicit duality.

There is one type that is based on extrinsic cultural traits and only superficially different from mainstream American culture. It is represented by external symbols and symbolic behavior, such as Kiss-Me-I'm-Irish buttons, excessive indulgence in sentimentality and alcohol on March 17, fealty to "the Fighting Irish" of Notre Dame. It is, at root, a form of American mass consumer culture coated with a thin Irish veneer.

The other form of Irish-American culture is a manifestation of intrinsic cultural traits expressed by engaging in activities such as speaking Irish, playing traditional Irish music, dancing at céilís — activities not evocative of a vague sense of ill-defined ethnic chauvinism but an attempt to perpetuate ongoing cultural traditions intimately related to the social and cultural fabric of Ireland.

Cultural forms based on intrinsic traits are not substitutes or safe, acceptable, distilled versions of an alien heritage watered down for mass consumption; when a cultural form embodying intrinsic traits does make an appearance outside of its network of cultural institutions, it does so on its own terms without trying to accommodate itself to fit stereotypes of extrinsic cultural forms.

Traditional Irish music survives in the U.S. primarily among the community that created it. Its role within that community has undergone great change over the last century or more, yet it has not been wholly discarded; even a social organization that holds dances throughout the year at which the musical entertainment is emphatically pseudo-Irish will, at least once a year perhaps, decide to hold a special "Irish" dance with traditional Irish musicians providing the music.

The organizations in the Irish-American community that have made the most extensive use of traditional Irish music are the politically-based groups (such as NORAID) and cultural revival groups (such as the Gaelic League, the Irish Language Association and the American Irish Society).

Traditional Irish music is recognized for its value in assisting these groups with their programs to further the spread of Irish culture among Americans or to appeal for aid to victims of violence in Northern Ireland. Irish musicians become, in effect, cultural ambassadors, a role they have not been cast in before, but a role they certainly find agreeable.

In the midst of a revival in public demonstrations of ethnic self-consciousness among ethnic groups in the U.S, traditional Irish music rises to the status of a distinctive art form that embodies and communicates the genuine Irish heritage. If it is true that ethnic groups mobilize "their inherited lore as a means of security and self-identification" (Paredes 1968:79), then traditional Irish musicians are the vanguard unit in that mobilization effort.

Nettl (1962:59) postulates <u>three avenues of possible development</u> for European folk music traditions once they arrive in the U.S.

The first is that full-scale acculturation may occur, in which the stylistic elements, instrumental traditions and repertoire of the folk tradition are merged with an American tradition (or traditions) to form a new synthesis.

A second possibility is that of selective or partial acculturation, in which the European folk tradition remains distinct yet manifests evidence of considerable borrowing from other traditions.

Finally, it might happen that the traditional music is not influenced at all, and no acculturation takes place; the traditional idiom remains autonomous and sovereign, as well as distinct, and exhibits a continued close relationship to its Old Country source.

Traditional Irish music in the U.S has staunchly resisted acculturative pressures, and the fundamental core of the tradition has remained virtually intact after well over a century and a quarter of residence in this country. That is, the structural forms of the dance music and airs have not deviated from patterns that were established in Ireland during the 18th century.

There has also been a strong continuity in performance styles during this period, as well as repertoire. However, when considering the relationship of the musical idiom to its cultural milieu, certain changes become noticeable.

Again speaking of the traditional music of European ethnic groups in America, Nettl (*ibid.*:64) says that the group does not usually trust to the usual channels of oral tradition to assure the survival of the songs. Instead, it organizes singing groups and clubs, it sponsors professional entertainers, it develops specialists. Folk music becomes the concern of the intellectual leaders of the ethnic groups, "and it is changed under the pressure of Americanization and urbanization."

In applying this general developmental pattern to traditional Irish music in the U.S., some points of difference quickly emerge.

As was discussed in Chapter I, traditional Irish music was not initially affected by its transferral to an urban environment (rather, it is <u>suburbanization</u> that has actually been a significant factor in changing the patterns of musical performance), nor have Irish-American intellectuals over the last two centuries taken any particularly conspicuous interest in it.

There have been professionals and specialists among traditional Irish musicians since the idiom's genesis, and "oral tradition" has never been the exclusive means of transmitting the tradition. However, the chief legacy of the impact of the American cultural milieu on traditional Irish music has probably been the increasingly imperative need to organize a diminishing number of active performers into some kind of centralized activity, be it céilís, competitions or schools.

This is not, perhaps, evidence of Americanization, so much as it is the result of modernization, the attempt of an 18th-century tradition to adjust to the cultural context of the 20th century.

The concluding comments concerning the role of traditional Irish music in contemporary Irish-American culture were expressed in an article written by a member of the Traditional Irish Musicians Association of New York and entitled, "At a Music Club":

> What a wonderful study of Irish involvement, free of political inclinations, but instead a communal effort of participation and appreciation. If you ever wanted to play Irish music and wondered where you could make contact with an accomplished musician of the instrument of your choice, the place to go is to your local Irish Traditional Music Club where the musicians meet.
>
> In this day and age, where many parents worry about the companions their children associate with, the Traditional Irish Music Club will keep your child active and generated in the right direction gaining knowledge and at the same time being nurtured in the culture of his forbears. It is a family affair of togetherness where each member can participate — whether in music, singing, dancing, or just enjoying (Anonymous 1971a:4).

REFERENCES CITED

Anonymous. "Pittsburgh's Irish Day", *Gaelic American*, July 25, 1914:5.

Anonymous. Untitled article, *Gaelic American*, October 27, 1917:7.

Anonymous. "At a Music Club", *Feiseanna*, 1971, 2(3):4.

Anonymous. "Record Review", *Feiseanna*, 1971, 2(6):7.

Becker, Howard. "The Professional Dance Musician and His Audience", *American Journal of Sociology*, 1951, 57(2):136-144.

Birmingham, Stephen. *Real Lace: America's Irish Rich*. New York: Harper & Row, 1973.

Breathnach, Breandán. "As We See It", *Ceol*, 1965, 2(1):3-4.

Breathnach, Breandán. "The Dancing Master", *Ceol*, 1970, 3(4):116-118.

Breathnach, Breandán. *Folkmusic and Dances of Ireland*. Dublin: Talbot Press, 1971.

Cameron, W.B. "Sociological Notes on the Jam Session", *Social Forces*, 1954, 33(2):177-182.

Census Bureau. *Historical Statistics of the United States*. Washington, D.C.: U.S. Bureau of the Census, 1960.

Coffman, James T. "'Everybody Knows This Is Nowhere': Role Conflict and the Rock Musician", *Popular Music and Society*, 1971, 1(1):20-32.

Curtis, Edmund. *History of Ireland*. London: Methuen & Co., 1952.

Dinneen, Patrick S. *An Irish-English Dictionary*. 8th edition. Dublin: Educational Company of Ireland, 1970.

Dunleavy, Gareth W. *Douglas Hyde*. Cranbury, N.J.: Associated University Presses, Inc., 1974.

Ennis, John. "The Revival of Erin's Language and Music in Chicago", *The Gael*, February, 1902: 34-38.

Fishman, Joshua A. *Sociolinguistics: A Brief Introduction*. Rowley, Mass.: Newbury House, 1970.

Flood, W.R. Grattan. *A History of Irish Music*. Dublin: Browne, Nolan, 1913.

Fox, Charlotte Milligan. *Annals of the Irish Harpers*. New York: E.P. Dutton, 1912.

Gordon, Milton M. *Assimilation in American Life*. New York: Oxford University Press, 1964.

Greeley, Andrew M. *That Most Distressful Nation: The Taming of the American Irish*. Chicago: Quadrangle Books, 1972.

Handlin, Oscar. *Boston's Immigrants*. New York: Atheneum, 1970.

Honigsheim, Paul. *Music and Society*. Ed. by K. Peter Etzkorn. New York: John Wiley & Sons, 1973.

Irish Music Club of Greater Boston. *Annual Grand Reunion and Ball* (souvenir program). Boston, 1938.

Irish Musicians Union, Local No. 1. *Constitution and By-Laws*. Philadelphia, n.d.

Kelleher, John V. "Irishness in America," *Atlantic*, 1961, 208(July):38-41.

Kuter, Lois. *The Musician in Irish Society and Folklore*. Oberlin University: unpublished B.A. thesis (Anthropology), 1973.

Levine, Edward. *The Irish and Irish Politicians*. Notre Dame, Ind.: University of Notre Dame Press, 1966.

Linton, Ralph. "Nativistic Movements," *American Anthropologist*, 45(2): 230-240, 1943.

McCullough, Lawrence E. "Traditional Irish Music in the U.S. Today: Some Observations", *Ceol*, 1975, 4(3).

McCullough, Lawrence E. "The Role of Language, Music, and Dance in the Revival of Irish Culture in Chicago, Ill.", *Ethnicity*. Forthcoming.

McEvoy, Bill. "The Shannonaires", *Treoir* 5(5):7, 1973.

Merriam, Alan P. *The Anthropology of Music*. Evanston, Ill.: Northwestern University Press, 1964.

Moynihan, Daniel P. "The Irish of New York," *Commentary*, 1963, 36:93-107.

Murphy, John A. *Ireland in the Twentieth Century*. Dublin: Gill & MacMillan, 1975.

Murphy, Richard C. and Lawrence J. Mannion. *The History of the Society of the Friendly Sons of St. Patrick in the City of New York, 1784 to 1955*. New York: J.C. Dillon, 1962.

Nettl, Bruno. *An Introduction to Folk Music in the United States*. Detroit: Wayne State University Press, 1962.

O'Connor, Kevin. *The Irish in Britain*. Dublin: Gill & MacMillan, 1974.

O'Faolain, Seán. *The Irish*. Harmondsworth, Middlesex, U.K.: Penguin Books, 1972.

O'Keeffe, J.G. and Art O'Brien. *A Handbook of Irish Dances*. 7th edition. Dublin: Gill & MacMillan, 1954.

O'Neill, Francis. *Irish Folk Music: A Fascinating Hobby*. Reprinted. Yorkshire, U.K.: EP Publishing, 1973.

O'Neill, Francis. *Irish Minstrels and Musicians*. Reprinted. Darby, Pa.: Norwood Editions, 1973.

O'Sullivan, Donal. *Carolan: The Life, Times, and Music of an Irish Harper, Vol. II*. London: Routledge and Kegan Paul, 1958.

Ó Tuathaigh, Gearóid. *Ireland before the Famine, 1798-1848*. Dublin: Gill & MacMillan, 1972.

Paredes, Americo. "Tributaries to the Mainstream: The Ethnic Groups," in Coffin, Tristram P., ed., *Our Living Traditions: An Introduction to American Folklore*. New York: Basic Books, 1968.

Rimmer, Joan. *The Irish Harp*. Cork: Mercier Press, 1969.

Roche, Francis. "Note on Irish Dancing," in, *Collection of Irish Airs, Marches, and Dance Tunes*, Vol. 2. Dublin: Pigott & Co., 1927.

Stebbins, Robert A. "A Theory of the Jazz Community," *Sociological Quarterly*, 1968, 9(3):318-331; "Role Distance, Role Distance Behavior, and Jazz Musicians," *British Journal of Sociology*, 1969, 20(4):406-415.

Wallace, Anthony F.C. "Revitalization Movements," *American Anthropologist*, 1956, 58:264-281.

Irish Music in Chicago:
An Ethnomusicological Study

by

Lawrence E. McCullough

B.A. Indiana University, 1974
M.A. University of Pittsburgh, 1975

Submitted to the Faculty of Arts & Sciences
of the University of Pittsburgh
in Partial Fulfillment of the Requirements
for the Degree of Doctor of Philosophy
April, 1978

This dissertation was presented by Lawrence E. McCullough.
It was defended on April 18, 1978 and approved by:

Dr. Nathan Davis

Prof. Colin Sterne

Dr. Hugh Kearney

Dr. Robert Kauffman, Chairman

DEDICATED TO MY PARENTS:

*Who brought me into this chaos and then gave
me the tools to survive and overcome it.*

CONTENTS

Figures in the Text	127
Musical Examples on Accompanying Cassette	128
Acknowledgments	129
Foreword	130
Introduction: A Survey of Previous Research in Irish Folk Music	134
Chanter One: An Historical Survey of Irish Music in Chicago	139
Chapter Two: Instruments and Performance Practice	159
— instrumental traditions in Irish folk music	159
— instruments in use among Irish musicians in Chicago	162
- strings	163
- winds	164
- free reeds	167
- keyboards	168
- percussion	168
— performance practice	169
Chapter Three: Repertoire and Styles	174
— the Chicago repertoire	178
— composition of new tunes	179
— style in traditional Irish music	181
— Irish music styles in Chicago: the past	182
— Irish music styles in Chicago: the present	186
- uilleann pipes	186
- fiddle	188
- flute	194
- accordion	196
- other instrumental styles	200
Chapter Four: Song Repertoire and Vocal Styles	202
Chapter Five: Performance Occasions	207
— commercial entertainment	208
— non-commercial entertainment	209
— radio and television broadcasts	210
— concerts	211
— dances and céilís	213
— dance classes	216

— dance competitions	217
— dance exhibitions	218
— music competitions	218
— sessions	220
Chapter Six: Performers and Audiences	224
— general characteristics	224
— specialists and professionals	227
— interactional patterns	231
— status and role	233
— audiences	238
Chapter Seven: Performers' Associations	240
Chapter Eight: Methods of Transmission	245
— formal methods	246
— informal methods	249
Chanter Nine: The Tradition and the Media	251
— recordings	251
— radio and television	252
Chapter Ten: Continuity and Change: The Dynamics of Acculturation and Irish Music in Chicago	255
Appendix A: "Lines Written on the Most Dreadful Fire That Broke Out in Chicago in America"	260
Appendix B: Discography of Commercial Recordings Made by Chicago Irish Musicians	261
Appendix C: Minutes of the First Convention of the Irish Musicians' Association of America, Chicago, 1956	265
Appendix D: Maps Showing the Principal Venues for Irish Music in Chicago since the 1930s	269
Appendix E: Photographs of Various Chicago Irish Musicians	276
Appendix F: The Published Works of Francis O'Neill	277
References Cited in the Text	278

• FIGURES IN THE TEXT •

1	A complete set of uilleann pipes..	160
2	Tune genres in the Irish folk music repertoire..	175
3	Vocabulary of embellishments used by Irish musicians...	183
4	"The Broken Pledge" (reel) by Joe Shannon, uilleann pipes..	189
5	"The Widow's Daughter" (reel) by John McGreevy, fiddle..	192
6	"The Green Mountain" (reel) by Liz Carroll, fiddle...	193
7	An alternative, non-syncopated rendition of the opening figure in bars 1, 5 and 13 of "The Green Mountain"..	194
8	"The Flowers of Redhill" (reel) by Kevin Henry, flute...	195
9	"Michael Preston's" (reel) by Seamus Cooley, flute...	196
10	"Katie Scollard's" (slide) by Terry Teahan, accordion..	198
11	"The Green Fields of Kerry" (jig) by Jim Thornton, accordion...	199
12	"The Rocks of Bawn" (song) by James Keane, Sr..	203
13	"An Sceilpín Draighneach" (song) by Mary Cooley...	204

• MUSICAL EXAMPLES ON ACCOMPANYING CASSETTE •

1   "The Broken Pledge" (reel) by Joe Shannon, uilleann pipes. ¶

2   "The Widow's Daughter" (reel) by John McGreevy, fiddle. *

3   "The Green Mountain" (reel) by Liz Carroll, fiddle. ¶

4   "The Flowers of Redhill" (reel) by Kevin Henry, flute. *

5   "Michael Preston's" (reel) by Seamus Cooley, flute. From Philo 2005, Philo Records, 1974.

6   "Katie Scollard's" (slide) by Terry Teahan, accordion. +

7   "The Green Fields of Kerry" (jig) by Jim Thornton, accordion. +

8   "The Rocks of Bawn" (song) by James Keane, Sr. ¶

9   "An Sceilpín Draighneach" (song) by Mary Cooley. *

10 "Drowsy Maggie-Scotch Mary-Floggin Reel" (reels) by Patsy Tuohey, uilleann pipes.
    From Victor 18639, 1923.

11 "The Maid in the Cherry Tree" (reel) by Eddie Mullaney, uilleann pipes and Paddy Stack, fiddle.
    From Victor 79003, 1927.

12 "The Maid That Left the Country-Drowsy Maggie-Around the World for Sport" (reels)
    by Tom Ennis, uilleann pipes. From Victor 18366, 1923.

13 "The Drumshambo Jig" (jig) by Tom Cawley, fiddle; Paddy Doran, flute; Frances Malone, piano.
    From Columbia 33144, 1927.

14 "The Boys of Bluehill-The Stack of Wheat" (hornpipes) by Pat Roche's Harp and Shamrock
    Orchestra, fiddle, accordion, piano, drums, step-dancing. From Decca 12007, 1934.

+   field recording by L.E. McCullough

*   field recording by Miles Krassen

¶   field recording by L.E. McCullough and Miles Krassen

• ACKNOWLEDGMENTS •

I would like to thank my dissertation adviser, Dr. Robert Kauffman, for his helpful comments and assistance in this undertaking. My grasp of the interrelationship of Irish music, history and culture was greatly enhanced by discussions and coursework with Dr. Eileen Kane, formerly of the Department of Anthropology and now head of the Anthropology Department at University College Dublin, and Dr. Hugh Kearney of the History Department here at the University of Pittsburgh. Both Dr. Kane and Dr. Kearney have shown a keen interest in my work.

My original ethnomusicological studies as an undergraduate at Indiana University, Bloomington, Ind., received their impetus from Dr. Charles Boilés, to whom I still owe a debt of thanks. The opportunity to work for a few months as a graduate student here at the University of Pittsburgh Music Department with one of his pupils, Dr. Carol Robertson-DeCarbo, was also of significance in my academic evolution.

Special thanks are extended to Breandán Breathnach, Tom Munnelly and Hugh Shields of Dublin, Ireland, all noted collectors and scholars in the field of Irish folk music, and to fiddler John Kelly and his family, also of Dublin, for the erudition and orientation they provided during my first encounters with Irish music six years ago.

Barry O'Neill, Bill Healy, Richard Nevins, Mick Moloney and Miles Krassen provided useful data for the preparation of the discography in Appendix B.

Grants from the Independent Learning Program of Indiana University in 1973, and the National Endowment for the Arts and Illinois Arts Council in 1975 and 1976 were very important in the successful realization of the fieldwork necessary for this dissertation.

James Maguire, Frank Thornton, Terry Teahan, Noel Rice, Kevin Henry and James and Eleanor Neary of Chicago provided me with several important documents and photographs pertaining to the subject of this work. All of the above-mentioned, in addition to Joe Shannon, Pat Roche, Seamus and Mary Cooley, John McGreevy, Dick Cawley and Patrick Hennelly were invaluable sources of information concerning the earlier eras of Irish music in Chicago.

Incalculable thanks must go to the innumerable performers of Irish music in Chicago who gave most generously of their time, their hospitality, their knowledge and, most importantly, their artistry. Without their assistance and co-operation this dissertation could never have been accomplished. I sincerely hope this work compensates for the gifts of music and friendship they have freely bestowed upon me.

Finally, my friend, research colleague and fellow musicianer Miles Krassen must receive recognition for the contributions he has made through our numerous discussions on the subject of Irish music, particularly as it exists in Chicago.

To paraphrase the venerable Francis is O'Neill, the great collector and chronicler of Irish music in Chicago during the 19th century:

> "This work is respectfully dedicated to
> the multitude of musicians of
> all races all over the world
> who enjoy and cherish the
> Melodies of Ireland"

• FOREWORD •

THIS DISSERTATION IS the first attempt to examine in detail a local tradition of Irish music in the United States. It focuses on the social, psychological, political, economic, demographic and musical factors that have influenced the development of Irish music in Chicago from the 1870s up to 1978.

Of course, Irish music has undergone a number of significant changes during that time-span in Ireland as well as in America, and, while many of these changes were the result of innovations or developments stimulated by performers within the tradition, the extra-musical factors mentioned above have also played a decisive role in shaping the form of the music as it exists today.

To obtain a full comprehension of Irish music in Chicago, it is necessary to take into account such diverse though interrelated phenomena as the ebb and flow of Irish emigration to the city; the transition from rural to urban performance contexts; the changes in socio-economic levels of performers and patrons and the resulting revision of attitudes toward the musical tradition; the impact of technological developments leading to the emergence of new dissemination patterns and media; the increasing use of institutions to maintain and transmit the tradition; the effect of the urban folk music revival and the resurgence of ethnic cultural consciousness among the American Irish. Otherwise, it is not possible to genuinely understand the dynamics of the process by which musical traditions evolve, flourish, change and disintegrate.

In this dissertation the terms "Irish music", "Irish folk music", "Irish traditional music" and "traditional Irish music" are used interchangeably to refer to the idiom of instrumental music that coalesced in Ireland during the 18th century and has continued to exist in an unbroken tradition that has stayed remarkably close to its 18th-century form. Players of this music generally speak of the music as simply "Irish music", "Irish traditional music" or "traditional Irish music". "Irish folk music" is more often used by scholars of the idiom.

While all of these terms refer specifically to an idiom of instrumental music, they are also sometimes used in a broader sense to indicate vocal music forms. In this dissertation, however, these vocal forms will be brought under the rubric of "Irish folk song" or "traditional Irish song". Although the instrumental and vocal traditions are certainly related structurally and stylistically and have influenced each other over the last three centuries, each is a separate tradition with its own repertoire, aesthetic standards and performance traditions.

Irish folk song is traditionally sung unaccompanied; instrumental accompaniment is a modern development and does not alter the basic premise of the folk song idiom that an unaccompanied song is an entity complete in itself. Likewise, Irish instrumental music is not performed along with texts. Irish folk music contains many airs that are the vehicles for song texts, but these texts are not sung when a musician plays the air.

In only a few instances have dance tunes been fitted with words, unlike the idiom of Anglo-American instrumental music that derived much of its repertoire from Irish and Scottish dance tunes. Many Irish folk songs are sung to melodies that are in dance meters and have been shaped from dance tunes, but dancing is not performed while they are being sung, nor does the song receive instrumental accompaniment.

There is also the phenomenon of "lilting" or "diddling"; this is the vocalization of meaningless syllables in the performance of a dance tune. Musicians often lilt a tune to themselves when an instrument is not at hand; sometimes lilting is used by musicians to identify a tune when a title cannot be remembered. Although lilting is a vocal phenomenon, it is used exclusively in the performance of tunes from the instrumental idiom.

Irish folk song in Chicago has not adapted well to public performance, and, consequently, it is not possible to speak of it as a communally-performed tradition in the same vein as Irish folk music. In this dissertation, the two idioms have been dealt with separately, and Chapter Four has been devoted to a complete discussion of Irish folk song in Chicago. Of the two traditions, it is the idiom of instrumental music that has survived the most successfully in its transplanted American environment.

A few more distinctions in terminology should be made. When one speaks of "Irish music", one must always be aware that the words conjure up different images to different individuals. In fact, there are several musical idioms that have been derived from Irish folk music and song. There is what might be called "Irish art song", that is, the compositions by classically-trained musicians and singers who have taken Irish traditional airs and written new texts for them or have taken Irish folk song texts and composed new airs.

This practice began perhaps as early as Elizabethan times and was certainly in vogue in the 18th century. Beethoven was commissioned by the Scots publisher George Thomson in 1814 to arrange Scots and Irish airs for popular distribution, and the Irish composer and lyricist Thomas Moore wrote his own songs to airs taken from Edward Bunting's collections of tunes noted down from old Irish harpers at the Belfast Harp Festival of 1792.

These songs were intended for the urban upper classes who were musically literate, fond of polished poetry and enamored of harmonized airs from the peasantry. In performance today, these works are invariably performed by trained singers in the operatic style. In some cases, these songs and their airs have re-entered the folk tradition, though most never achieved any currency among Irish folk singers or instrumentalists, as they were meant for an entirely different type of audience possessing a radically different set of aesthetic standards.

Irish art song flourished up through the first decade or two of the 20th century. Throughout the 19th century, however, another derivative idiom had been evolving and gaining enormous popularity. This came to be known as the "stage-Irish" tradition since much of the repertoire was created for use on the vaudeville and musical theater stage. England and America had the greatest number of stage-Irish entertainers, although the idiom was popular for a time in Dublin.

Stage-Irish songs and music were originally drawn from the Irish folk song and folk music traditions and were essentially stereotyped replicas of the original material exaggerated for dramatic or comic effect. Soon, the stage-Irish idiom evolved into a tradition of its own, and the close ties that had once prevailed with the source traditions evaporated.

"Songsters" filled with stage-Irish songs from plays and comedy revues were enormously popular in 19th-century America, and it was this tradition that became widely disseminated when the sheet music industry was the primary means of song transmission among literate Americans. Many of the songs identified today in the popular mind as representing Irish music and song were, in fact, written and composed by Americans totally unfamiliar with Irish folk music and folk song.

When commercial recording companies sought out Irish entertainers, they naturally turned to those performers they believed would appeal to the widest possible audience, Irish and non-Irish alike. Thus, the stage-Irish tradition, augmented occasionally by operatic performers such as John McCormack, received a large share of attention from the companies. Irish folk music and folk song had by the early 20th century become displaced by the derivative idioms that sprang from them, and they remained very much a minority musical culture to many Irish-Americans who were so inundated with and conditioned by the derivative forms that the existence of the original idioms was rarely suspected.

This dissertation discusses these derivative, hybrid Irish music traditions several times in passing through the course of the work as they relate to the particular aspect of the traditional Irish music and song idiom under examination. Indeed, the development of these hybrid forms and their relationship to the folk tradition is deserving of a complete and separate study.

Anyone who attempts to chronicle the development of Irish folk music in an American city like Chicago is immediately confronted by a distressing paucity of sources on the subject that might provide a logical starting point for a reconstruction of the tradition's history. Irish folk music and song appear to have been beneath the notice of 19th-century Irish-American historians and journalists, with one or two exceptions. Or perhaps the traditions were so common that they seemed to need no special mention. Also, Irish-Americans of the time were concerned with more basic issues, such as freedom for Ireland and their own struggle for social and economic security in the U.S.

Irish music and song were also aurally-transmitted idioms that had never been a product of a print-oriented community of musicians or singers, nor had the performance occasions of these traditions been a part of the urban middle-class musical culture that received mention in contemporary newspapers, journals or books. In addition, those reports about Irish music and song that were made by contemporary 19th-century observers were in nearly every instance from the perspective of non-performers of the traditions.

Fortunately, there was one individual in Chicago during the late 1800s who was both a knowledgeable performer of Irish folk music as well as an incisive commentator upon the Irish folk music milieu in that city. Francis O'Neill, a native of Tralibane, County Cork, arrived in Chicago in 1871, joined the Chicago Police Force and eventually rose to the Chief Superintendency of that department.

He collected tunes from the city's Irish musicians and published several collections of his harvest. Even more importantly, O'Neill authored two books that detail the Irish musical community of Chicago during his era, that is, from 1871 until 1913. These works are first-hand accounts of musicians, musical occasions, and attitudes toward Irish music held by the Irish community of Chicago.

Aside from a few indirect references to the music in Irish-American newspapers and theatrical advertisements, the works of Francis O'Neill are the only true insight into the tradition that are available to the researcher hoping for information about this epoch in Chicago's Irish music history.

After the beginning of the 20th century, the situation improves somewhat with the recording of Chicago Irish musicians on wire cylinders and discs. These were at first privately recorded on a small scale, informal basis; starting in the 1920s, commercial record companies began to issue records by several Chicago Irish musicians. The number and depth of printed sources remains pitifully meager, however, and does not increase as the century progresses.

In this reconstruction attempt, the reservoir of oral lore that exists among the older Irish musicians and aficianados of Chicago have been utilized as the principal repository of information concerning the historical development of Irish music in the city.

Living memory among Chicago informants does not extend beyond 1920, and most of those individuals who recall that period were quite young at the time. Nevertheless, using the extant printed documents, oral histories, and the few copies of commercial and non-commercial recordings that have survived, it is possible to catch a few fleeting and tantalizing glimpses of Irish music in Chicago as it existed during the first several decades after its transplantation from rural Ireland to an urban American metropolis.

In addition to the surviving copies of Chicago Irish newspapers like *The Republic*, *The Chicago Citizen*, *The Irish News* and *The Irish-American News*, historical information about Irish music in Chicago has been gleaned from the varied holdings located in the Chicago Historical Society and Newberry Library of Chicago. Programs of musical occasions organized by 19th- and 20th-century Irish social and political groups and oral histories collected by survey teams interviewing Chicago residents over the years have also contained items of interest. Francis O'Neill's personal library is now held by the University of Notre Dame in South Bend, Indiana, and there are also several of his letters to individuals in Ireland discussing Irish music in Chicago.

However, what has contributed most significantly to the development of this dissertation has been my own five years of fieldwork among Irish musicians in Chicago that began on March 16, 1973, when I made the acquaintance of fiddler John McGreevy and flute player/piper Kevin Henry after their performance during a St. Patrick's Week exhibition at Ford City Shopping Mall on the city's Southwestside. I returned to Chicago two months later and established a pattern of field research that has continued to the present: tape recording, interviewing, performing and observing at musical occasions in the Irish community and searching for information in the city's libraries and municipal archives.

I have visited Chicago every two to four months over the last five years, spending a week or two in field and library research. During 1976, while engaged on a related project sponsored by grants from the National Endowment for the Arts and the Illinois Arts Council, I lived in Chicago for nine months and was able to become more completely involved in the city's Irish music community as a resident and not simply an outsider.

My role as a performer of Irish music has greatly facilitated the task of fieldwork, as it has helped minimize the barriers that exist between "informant" and "collector" in a field survey context. It will become apparent to the reader fairly quickly that the bulk of this dissertation derives from the fact of the writer's extensive personal involvement with the music as a performer in addition to an analyst and collector.

Chapter One provides some historical data about Irish music in Chicago from the mid-19th century to the present. With so many large gaps in the period due to a scarcity of adequate documentation, the task of drawing a historical portrait of Irish music in Chicago is not unlike attempting to put together a puzzle without having all the pieces or even having a positive notion of what the completed puzzle is supposed to look like.

In the years to come, more information about Irish music in 19th-century Chicago will be uncovered, and the picture may be more detailed. For the present, however, the historical survey that comprises the first chanter of this work is an attempt to discern trends and general features of the tradition throughout the last century.

Chapters Two and Three discuss the musical aspects of the tradition, examining instruments, performance practice, repertoire and styles. Chapter Four is devoted to the idiom of Irish folk song in Chicago, and Chapter Five begins to examine the tradition of Irish folk music in its Chicago cultural contexts. Chapter Six focuses on the performers of the tradition, their general characteristics as a group, their interactional patterns with each other and their status and role in their ethnic community and the larger non-Irish community.

Chapter Seven discusses performers' associations and their impact upon the tradition, and Chapter Eight takes a look at the methods by which the tradition is transmitted. Chapter Nine examines the relationship of Irish music in Chicago to the communications and entertainment media of the 20th century — recordings, radio and television. Chapter Ten concludes the work with some comments about the changes that have taken place in Irish music during its sojourn in Chicago.

The Appendices contain photographs of Chicago Irish music personalities over the last hundred years, maps showing the location of the primary musical occasions and major areas of Irish population, a discography of Chicago Irish musicians who have been commercially recorded and two items of important historical interest — an Irish broadside on the subject of the Chicago Fire of 1871 and the minutes of the first convention of the Irish Musicians' Association of America held in Chicago in August, 1956.

It is hoped that this dissertation — which concentrates on a single musical tradition of a specific ethnic group located in one metropolitan, multi-cultural area — will prove to be of value to other scholars studying the process of acculturation.

The statements and conclusions offered here are not intended to be taken as the absolute final word on a subject that is only beginning to be analyzed in a detailed, systematic manner. Rather, this study represents a first attempt to shed some light on a complex and fascinating musical tradition that has remained in the dark for too long simply because no one has bothered to take a look at it.

L.E. McCullough
Pittsburgh, PA
March 16, 1978

• INTRODUCTION •

A Survey of Previous Research in Irish Folk Music

THE SCHOLAR ENTERING the field of Irish folk music need not worry about finding an area of research that has not yet been explored. While innumerable collections of tunes and song texts have been made since the 18th century, the task of analyzing the harvested, archived material has been shrugged off for years by those persons most qualified to approach the work — the collectors and musicians.

Two contrasting viewpoints have played significant roles in this lack of analytical interest on the part of collectors and musicians. One is that the collectors felt that they were gathering the very last scraps of the musical tradition before it disappeared totally. Thus, they believed their function was simply to record and catalogue a rare species soon to become extinct.

The other viewpoint is that the music was so common and so much a part of the predominantly rural Irish society of the 18th, 19th and early 20th centuries that it was taken for granted and not deemed worthy of special consideration other than proving it existed. The result has been that not only have many important questions about the idiom been unanswered, they have not even been asked.

Irish tunes appeared in English collections of the 17th and early 18th centuries, such as *Playford's Dancing Master* and D'Urfrey's *Wit and Mirth, or Pills to Purge Melancholy* (O'Neill 1910:258). It was not until the 1720s, however, that Irish music collections published by Irish enterprises began to appear. John and William Neale of Christ Church Yard, Dublin, published a book of the Irish harper Turlough O'Carolan's compositions around 1721 (the title page and date of publication are missing from the only known copy). Approximately five years later, the Neales brought out *A Collection of the Most Celebrated Irish Tunes Proper for the Violin, German Flute or Hautboy* (O'Sullivan 1927:xxxi-xxxii).

From that point onwards, scores of tune books consisting of Irish tunes or Irish tunes mixed in with English and Scots tunes appeared throughout the British Isles with increasing frequency. These books, of course, simply gave a spare, basic, skeletal notation of the tune; no ornamentation or information about tune sources or the music's stylistic traits was included.

In 1786, Joseph Cooper Walker published his *Historical Memoirs of the Irish Bards interspersed with anecdotes of and occasional observations on the Music of Ireland; also an Historical and Descriptive Account of the Musical Instruments of the Ancient Irish, and an Appendix containing several Biographical and other papers, with the Select Irish Melodies*. This represented the first attempt to analyze the tradition in a scholarly manner.

Walker, however, was an antiquarian and viewed the music as a curious specimen. Typical of his orientation is his comment concerning the uilleann pipes: "it has ever been a favorite instrument of the vulgar" (Walker 1786:109). The work contained essays by two other Irish antiquarians: "Inquiries Concerning the Ancient Irish Harp" and "The Style of the Ancient Irish Music" by Reverend Francis Ledwich and "An Essay on the Poetical Accents of the Irish" and "An Essay on the Construction and Capability of the Irish Harp" by William Beauford.

These writings are valuable for an insight into the state of research in Irish music at that time. Reverend Ledwich published additional information about the ancient Irish bagpipes and the modern uilleann pipes in his *Antiquities of Ireland* (1804). Like the earlier essays in Walker's book, the conclusions reached by Ledwich were not based on documented facts but were more the result of conjecture.

The Belfast Harp Festival held in July, 1792, was the culmination of a decade of harp festivals held in other Irish cities. Ten Irish harpers, most of them over the age of seventy, had been invited to compete for cash prizes at the event organized by sympathizers with the United Irishmen, a revolutionary nationalist group that was to later spark the Insurrection of 1798.

Edward Bunting, an eighteen-year old organist, had been asked to notate the tunes played by the harpers. He did so and published in 1796 *A General Collection of the Ancient Irish Music* that included sixty-six tunes obtained from the harpers at the 1792 Festival. Bunting also annotated the tunes, discussed the instruments of the harpers, the tunings of the harps, terminology of musical terms in the Irish language and other matters pertaining to the event.

A General Collection of the Ancient Irish Music marked the first attempt to explain the music with examples collected first-hand from informants.

In 1802 Bunting hired an Irish-speaking schoolmaster, Patrick Lynch, to travel throughout the province of Connacht to collect songs in Irish. Bunting later joined Lynch and notated tunes. *A General Collection of the Ancient Music of Ireland* was published by Bunting in 1809.

Not until 1840, three years before his death, did Bunting publish his third volume of tunes collected by himself and by other collectors. This was *The Ancient Music of Ireland, Arranged for the Piano Forte, To which is prefixed a Dissertation on the Irish Harp and Harpers, Including an Account of the Old Melodies of Ireland.*

Although Bunting supplied a great deal of information about the practices and repertoire of the last few Irish harpers of the old style, his tunes are often set in fantastic keys that could not have been used by the harpers. Despite his love for the music, he came to the music as an outsider, and it is clear that his editorial alterations of the tunes to fit his ideas of correct harmony were entirely out of character with the musical idiom of the harpers.

As one commentator has stated, Bunting "had the curious belief that the more ancient the music, the easier it was to harmonize it, and ease of harmonization was, he declared, a certain indication of the purity of its structure" (Breathnach 1971:112). Nevertheless, the work of Edward Bunting proved to inspire others to follow after him.

Henry Hudson (1798-1889) was the musical editor of *The Citizen*, a Dublin monthly magazine. He collected tunes and accepted tunes for publication from correspondents throughout Ireland and, in addition, composed tunes of his own and passed them off as ancient folk tunes. Some of them were so finely molded in the shape of the originals that they were collected by other individuals and published by them as folk airs (O'Sullivan, 1952:16).

William Forde (1759-1850) and John Edward Pigot (1822-1871) collected tunes between the years 1840 and 1850. Their work was not published in their own lifetimes, but Patrick Weston Joyce (1827-1914) included much of their material in his collections published later in the century.

George Petrie (1789-1866) organized the Society for the Preservation and Publication of the Melodies of Ireland in 1851 to assist in the publication of his material collected from all parts of the country. 1855 saw the publication of Petrie's *Ancient Music of Ireland*; only one hundred and forty-seven airs were contained in this volume, and thirty-nine more airs were published as a supplement in 1882.

Petrie was more well-attuned to the real nature of Irish folk music and song than previous collectors, but he still believed in harmonizing the tunes to his own "correct" notions of harmony (Breathnach 1971:115). In many instances, of course, the airs were altered to adapt to the harmonies chosen by Petrie.

All the collectors mentioned so far were English-speaking Protestants from urban areas who had become aware of the music later in life. All approached the music from an antiquarian point of view and viewed much of what was vital and unique in the tradition as degenerate and corrupt. Patrick Weston Joyce (1827-1914) and Reverend James Goodman (1828-1896) were the first important exceptions to this pattern in that they were born in Irish-speaking, rural districts where the music was a thriving art form.

Goodman, though a Protestant clergyman, was an excellent performer on the uilleann pipes. Goodman's manuscript collections were never formally published but are archived in Trinity College Dublin. Due to his proficiency as a musician, there are many airs and dance tunes contained in the more than two thousand tunes he collected (O'Sullivan 1952:27).

Joyce published three works — *Ancient Irish Music* (1873), *Irish Music and Song* (1888), *Old Irish Folk Music and Songs* (1909) — and was busily engaged upon a fourth when he died at the age of eighty-seven. Although Joyce was the first collector of Irish folk music to refrain from revising the music played by his informants to suit the standards of another musical idiom, he was still at fault for altering the words of many texts that he found "too coarse for publication or unworthy of preservation" (Breathnach 1971:118) — hardly what one would expect of a man who had grown up in an Irish-speaking environment.

More material from the unpublished collections of George Petrie was published by Sir Charles Stanford in the years 1902-1905. But by far the most important collection of Irish music was brought out in Chicago in 1903 by Francis O'Neill, a native of County Cork who had risen to a position of Chief Superintendent on the Chicago Police Force.

O'Neill's *Music of Ireland* was the largest collection of Irish music yet published, containing 1,850 melodies. Eleven hundred of the tunes were dance tunes, an unprecedented feat, as previous collectors had ignored or been unable to obtain dance music in any important quantity. O'Neill was also a traditional flute player and an important fixture in the Chicago Irish music community; he understood the music from a performer's point of view, though he was also guilty of altering tunes that were incomplete or defective. As O'Neill stated, "Who, then, can lay claim to perfection; and why should palpably inferior versions or variants of traditional tunes be exempt from correction or alteration" (O'Neill 1910:53).

O'Neill might be excused in this instance on account of the fact that, as a performer of Irish music, he was more keenly aware than many previous editors of how to "improve" a melody without destroying the features that made it distinct from the music of other idioms.

1907 saw the publication by O'Neill of *The Dance Music of Ireland, 1001 Gems*. This was a revised work that deleted some dance tunes from *Music of Ireland* and added newer ones collected during the intervening years.

These two first works by O'Neill proved to be the most important of his output and had a tremendous effect upon the living tradition. They are still in use by performers of Irish folk music and have assumed a status of serving as the final arbiter in disputes concerning tune versions or titles. They were intended to be used primarily by the members of the tradition and only secondarily by antiquarians or other non-performers.

The impact of recordings on Irish music in the early 1900s was paralleled and prefigured by the impact of the O'Neill collections on the traditional repertoire. Until the appearance of *Music of Ireland* and *The Dance Music of Ireland, 1001 Gems*, the transmission of repertoire among performers was almost exclusively aural, with the exception of private manuscript collections possessed by a few musicians.

These collections, however, were small and sporadically located and were circulated chiefly via individuals. It was not uncommon for the bulk of one small community's repertoire to be unknown outside of the locality.

The O'Neill collections made available on a massive scale tunes previously restricted to provinces, counties, parishes, even individuals. The immediate effect of propelling great numbers of tunes into wider circulation was to increase the size of the traditional repertoire held in common.

Another effect that became apparent later was the elevation of certain tunes to the status of "standards" because of their inclusion in the collections. The appearance of a particular setting of a tune in print established the concept of a "correct version" versus variants or incorrect versions. Although still subject to the process of communal refashioning in the area of style, the versions printed in O'Neill's publications naturally proliferated due to the increased exposure, while other settings came to be regarded as deviant or non-standard.

Still, the crystallization of a core repertoire did not stop the machinations of the process of communal re-creation by Irish musicians but endowed it with new vigor by providing an increased but more concentrated and sharply-defined area of operation. O'Neill's first two works have been reprinted and revised by other publishers and continue to supply a major source of repertoire for aspiring Irish musicians.

Francis Roche of County Limerick brought out three volumes of dance music and airs in 1911 and 1927. These volumes contain the greatest diversity of repertoire of any collection of Irish instrumental music, consisting of airs, reels, double jigs, single jigs, slip jigs, highland flings, set dances, quadrilles, schottisches, two-steps, waltzes, polkas, barn dances, varsoviennes, old set tunes, country dances, hornpipe, marches and descriptive pieces.

While the Roche collections have not had the same substantial impact of the O'Neill collections upon the tradition, they remain of value to the scholar because of the variant settings and wide-ranging selection of tune genres.

It was not until 1963 that another collection of instrumental music would approach the importance of the O'Neill and Roche collections. This was *Ceol Rince na hÉireann (Dance Music of Ireland)* by Breandán Breathnach, an uilleann piper and collector employed by the Irish Department of Education. A second volume by the same title was brought out by Breathnach in 1976.

The first volume contained 214 reels, double jigs, single jigs, slip jigs and hornpipes, and the second work comprised 315 tunes in the above-mentioned genres, with some slides, polkas and set tunes in 2/4 meter included.

Breathnach included extensive notes on variant settings and titles of each tune when such information was available, and he also included the name of the musician and the instrument from which the particular setting published had been obtained. Thus, the ground for stylistic analysis exists. Furthermore, the tunes were recorded on tape, and their reliability as transcriptions is immeasurably increased by this fact of having the live performance as well as the notated version of it.

Since the 20th century began, collections of Irish music have been generally either instrumental music or vocal music with little mixture of the two, as was formerly the case in the preceding century. Numerous local and regional collections of Irish folk songs exist, and the Irish Folklore Commission made thousands of recordings during the 1930s and 1940s of singers and instrumentalists throughout Ireland.

Radio Éireann and the British Broadcasting Corporation also possess a great store of recorded material from Irish folk singers and musicians. Comhaltas Ceoltóirí Éireann, a Dublin-based organization dedicated to the promotion of Irish music, song and dance, also has been recording performers during the two-and-a-half decades of its existence.

However, despite this wealth of material, incisive analysis of Irish folk music and song has been lacking. Richard Henebry, a priest and university professor who died in 1916, wrote *A Handbook of Irish Music* that was published posthumously in 1928. Henebry was an early comparative musicologist whose knowledge and interests in music spanned the globe. His work was the first attempt to explain the structural and stylistic features of Irish folk music and song. He concentrated on discovering a system for a correct modal analysis of the airs and dance tunes and sought to comprehend the structure of the music by means of its stress patterns and intervallic construction. Much interesting information and speculation is contained in the work, but somehow Henebry never came to clear conclusions.

Oddly, Henebry used as data for his examination the Petrie Collection, a work that was loaded with inaccurate and altered transcriptions and only vaguely mirrored the living tradition. He also used a few phonograph records of contemporary musicians but only in order to support his theories based on Petrie's material. Henebry's contribution may not have been as comprehensive or precise as he had hoped for, but it did point out for future scholars potential paths for exploration.

Since Henebry, no general analytic works on Irish music's structural and stylistic features have appeared other than two wide-ranging surveys: Donal O'Sullivan's *Irish Folk Music, Song, and Dance* (1952) and Breandán Breathnach's *Folkmusic and Dances of Ireland* (1971).

O'Sullivan's work touches only a few points, primarily the important collections of Irish folk music and song, Irish folk song types, and Irish solo and ensemble dancing. The book was part of a 16-book series on Irish life and culture and was obviously not intended to examine the traditions in detail.

Breathnach's work is devoted mostly to the dances and the dance music, although there is valuable material on Irish folk song as well. Breathnach's chapter on instrumental styles in Irish music is particularly important and provides much-needed insight into the area of style in Irish instrumental music. While the book is limited by its survey approach, it remains the most extensive discussion of the idioms of Irish folk music, dance and song covering as it does a number of aspects of these art forms.

Joan Rimmer's *The Irish Harp* (1969) has been the only attempt to detail an instrumental tradition in Irish music. Donal O'Sullivan's *Carolan: The Life, Times, and Music of an Irish Harper* (1958) and Pat Mitchell's *The Dance Music of Willie Clancy* (1975) have been the only two books that explore individual performers.

Several historical and biographical works covering various phases of the tradition have appeared in the 20th century. These include *A History of Irish Music* (1905) by W.H. Grattan Flood, *Annals of the Irish Harpers* (1912) by Charlotte Milligan-Fox, *The Song Lore of Ireland* (1911) by Redfern Mason, *Irish Folk Music: A Fascinating Hobby* (1910) and *Irish Minstrels and Musicians* (1913) by Francis O'Neill, *Irish Songs of Resistance* (1962) by Patrick Galvin, *Songs of Irish Rebellion* (1967) by Georges-Denis Zimmerman, *Folk Songs Sung in Ulster* (1970) by Robin Morton, and *Irish Folk Song* (1976) by Seán Ó Baoill.

Two important studies of individual Irish folk singers are *Songs Ascribed to Raftery* (1903) by Douglas Hyde and *Come Day, Go Day, God Send Sunday* (1973) by Robin Morton. The first work examines the songs composed by the early 19th-century Irish singer, Anthony Raftery, and the second is an autobiographical account of a contemporary singer-farmer, John Maguire of Fermanagh, interspersed with songs from his repertoire.

However, the idioms of Irish folk music and song are far from being understood in their entirety. Aside from Henebry's work on modes and Breathnach's discussion of ornamentation, there has been no serious analytical work done that endeavors to show how Irish music and song operate, how the idioms are created and varied, or what elements are distinctive features of the traditions, aside from tentative journal articles that focus on narrow areas of the traditions. Neither have local or regional styles been adequately documented, although *Music from Sliabh Luachra* (1976) by Alan Ward in conjunction with a three-volume set of recordings by musicians from the Sliabh Luachra region of County Kerry has been the most ambitious attempt in this direction.

Discussion of Irish music and song in their cultural contexts has also been neglected, though both idioms are still flourishing traditions with an unbroken line of performance continuity that extends back three centuries.

This present dissertation is a study of how the traditions of Irish music and song exist in the cultural context of Chicago, Illinois. Instruments, repertoire, styles, performance practice, performers, audiences, musical occasions, methods of transmission, performers' associations and the media of dissemination are all explored in an effort to give as complete a picture as is possible of these traditions as they have fared in a transplanted setting.

No such work has been attempted with any other local tradition of Irish music and song, and it is hoped that this dissertation will prove to inspire other researchers in the field of Irish music to undertake a thorough documentation of local and regional traditions. There is plenty of musical and textual data available thanks to the efforts of collectors during the last three centuries. The opportunity to discover how the traditions of Irish music and song function in their human contexts, however, may not always be so readily accessible as it is at the present.

CHAPTER ONE: An Historical Survey of Irish Music in Chicago

BY 1850 Chicago's Irish-born residents formed over 20% of the city's population (Pierce 1937a:418).

The majority of these early Irish emigrants congregated along the south branch of the Chicago River in housing developments built up around the brickyards, slaughter houses, rolling mills, lumberyards, and other heavy industries that gave Chicago its reputation as Hog Butcher, Tool Maker, Stacker of Wheat, Etc. to the nation. Conley's Patch, Healy's Slough, Canalport, McFadden's Patch, Bridgeport, Brighton Park, Canaryville and the Back o' the Yards were strong Irish areas, and it was in these communities that Irish music, song and dance flourished most vigorously in the late 1800s.

Irish music was in great demand for both private and public meetings of organizations dedicated to the winning of Irish independence, of which there were more than fifty by the 1880s (Pierce 1937b:25). A humorous account of one such meeting appeared in the *Irish Republic* newspaper of May 4, 1867, signed by "Yoore rispicted frind, J. Delaney" and entitled "A Great Night for Ireland: Tim O'Kane's Headquarters, 8th Ward, April 16, 1867". It began:

> "Last night we held a slashing turnout at Tim O'Kane's sign of the Harp and Shamrock with a big puncheon at the door painted green to show where patriots should drink."

Political issues of the day were discussed, and then "the celebrated Limerick piper, Haybags from Ardagh" struck up a few tunes, including "Bony Crossing the Rhine" and "The Blackbird" in honor of two military leaders (Napoleon Bonaparte and the Stuart Pretender) dear to an Irish patriot's heart. Someone shouted for "Paddy O'Rafferty", and the meeting suffered an abrupt termination as half of the assemblage demanded "Paddy O'Rafferty the jig", while the rest insisted on "Paddy O'Rafferty the alderman".

Dances and parties held in private homes were a common form of entertainment among the Irish of Chicago during the late 19th century. One such party was particularly noteworthy, as it occurred at an historically significant juncture in the city's development.

On the night of October 8, 1871, fiddler Pat McLaughlin was providing the music for a house dance on the occasion of the arrival of his wife's cousin from Ireland. The McLaughlins' one-story wooden residence was located at 137 DeKoven Street on the city's near Southwestside. Another Irish family, the O'Learys, lived in an adjoining cottage at the back of McLaughlin's house.

Investigators have never been able to completely discern the facts, but at some point during the early evening fire broke out in the area immediately behind the O'Leary residence, and the welcome party for the newly-arrived Irish cousin was hastily removed to another venue as the Great Chicago Fire of 1871 began raging out of control (Sheahan and Upton 1871:424-425; McIlvaine 1915:xvii; Cromie 1958:26-27).

The fiery holocaust ravaged the homes of many Irish emigrants, causing loss of life and property to thousands and prompting a Dublin broadside publisher to issue a ballad on the event, the only contemporary song about the Fire in the Irish folk song tradition to have survived to the present (see Appendix A for the ballad text).

Finucane's Hall and Blossinger's Hall on Archer Avenue in the heavily-Irish Bridgeport section were often the sites of the more formal dances held by Irish social and political organizations like the Clan-na-Gael, the Fenian Brotherhood, the Ancient Order of Hibernians, the Catholic Order of Forresters, the Knights of St. Patrick, the Michael Davitt Land League, the Irish National League and the Irish-American Council.

Dances were also held at parish halls of the Catholic Churches, St. Bridget's on the Southside at Archer Avenue and Church Place being one of the most frequently mentioned by contemporary sources. There were impromptu occasions like the dances gotten up by neighbors in a butcher shop on the northwest corner of Bonfield and Archer during the 1890s (Chicago Historical Society 1930).

There were still more formal musical occasions held within the Chicago Irish community in the 19th century. These were concerts, balls and banquets hosted by the Irish-American elite. It is these occasions that have been most thoroughly documented during this era, yet it was these occasions that appear to have had considerably less Irish folk music and dance than their counterparts among the Chicago Irish on "the other side of the tracks".

The dance programs of two events in the second half of the 19th century give some indication of the trends current among the more formal dances sponsored by Irish-American social and political clubs of the day. The dance schedule of "The Second Banquet of the Knights of St. Patrick" held March 17, 1868, at the Maison Doree on Wabash Avenue commenced at 11 p.m. and included the following selections:

1	Quadrille	9	Quadrille
2	Schottische	10	Polka Redowa
3	Lancers	11	Lancers
4	Polka	12	Schottische
5	Virginia Reel	13	Eight-hand Reel
6	Quadrille	14	Polka
7	Waltz Montabello	15	Irish Jig
8	Monnie Musk	16	Quadrille Caledonia

The St. Patrick's Celebration of the Irish-American Club at the Palmer House Hotel in downtown Chicago on March 19, 1883, featured this program of dances:

1	Quadrille	8	Schottische
2	Waltz	9	Quadrille
3	Lanciers	10	Waltz
4	Galop	11	Prairie Queen
5	Quadrille	12	Galop
6	Polka and Newport	13	Lanciers
7	Waltz Quadrille	14	Waltz

There is, unfortunately, no report of what type of musical ensemble performed the accompaniment for either of these dance occasions, but it must certainly have included musicians who were well-versed in the European musical trends of the time.

The Quadrille, Schottische, Lancers (or Lanciers), Polka, Redowa, Galop, Waltz and Caledonia were all popular 19th-century ballroom dances among the aristocracy and upper and middle classes of Continental Europe and Britain (Richardson 1960). Quadrille steps had been reworked by dancing masters in Ireland during the early 1800s to conform to the native steps then current among the Irish peasantry (Breathnach 1971:48-49).

It is not certain in what manner the Quadrilles mentioned above were danced; they may have been in the form of the "Irishized" Quadrilles known as "sets" (Roche 1927:v), or they may well have been similar to the standard European and American ballroom Quadrilles.

It will be noticed that the 1883 event includes no specifically Irish dances, such as jig, reel, hornpipe, etc. The other two country dances — Monnie Musk and Virginia Reel — have also vanished in place of a format devoted entirely to ballroom dances.

To what extent these two programs are accurate indicators of other formal dances among the Irish of 19th-century Chicago still remain open to debate until more evidence is available. The following remarks made in 1902 by Chicago uilleann piper John Ennis offer some enlightenment in this respect:

> The great popularity Irish music has gained in Chicago is not to be attributed to any special efforts of the representative Irish organizations or the local Irish press. For some incomprehensible reason it is almost totally ignored by both. In some instances I have noticed Germans, Bohemians, and Italians engaged by the managers of entertainments given under the auspices of the leading Irish organizations to play Irish music. What a sad commentary on the Irish musical knowledge of the "committee on talent!" No matter what skill our Teutonic or Latin friends can display on their respective instruments they cannot play Irish music. None but an Irish musician properly schooled can give to it that tone color or "brogue", as it has been aptly called, without which it loses its chiefest charm (1902:37).

Though Ennis' comments might be construed as unduly chauvinistic, they do reflect a genuine concern that the musical tastes of the Chicago Irish were being affected by alien influences. What is not clear, however, is how the growing acceptance of non-Irish musical entertainment and dance forms among the Irish-American community came about during this period. Perhaps the assimilation processes long advocated and despaired of by Anglo-American social, educational and political leaders were finally starting to operate on the Irish in Chicago, at least in their public cultural sphere.

The subject of assimilation will be dealt with in more detail later in this work, but for now it is important to realize that as early as the late 1860s, certain segments of the Irish community in Chicago were expressing strong preferences for music and dance that was not even remotely Irish.

Traditional Irish music and dance in Chicago were far from extinct in the late 1800s. Irish musicians and dancers were prominently represented in the two Irish Villages at the 1893 Chicago World's Fair. Mrs. Alice Hart, founder of the Donegal Industrial Fund, organized an exhibit that recreated a County Donegal village and showed "a hive of busy, happy industry, a model village of Irish industrial life". It featured Celtic crosses, a ruined castle, wool-dyeing, wood-carving, glass-staining, marble-carving and the making of lace, tablecloths and handkerchiefs (*Chicago Citizen* 12/24/1892:5).

The Countess of Aberdeen's Irish Village was operated by the Irish Industrial Association and was originally the sole Irish exhibit planned (Corrigan 1977a:6).

The Donegal Village opened at 4 p.m. Friday, May 26, 1893, on the Midway Plaisance with uilleann piping by Donegal native Turlough MacSweeney and harping by Mrs. Clara Murray of Chicago (*Chicago Citizen* 5/20/1893:4 and 6/3/1893:5). Throughout the duration of the Fair there was Irish music on harp, fiddle, mandolin and uilleann pipes; the *Chicago Citizen* of July 8, 1893 reported on the Fourth of July festivities:

> The clog and jig dancing on the Village green was a never failing source of attraction, and the sound of the piper seemed to exercise a fascination which rooted some to their seats for hours and which drove others to their feet. Ballad singing and sweet playing of Irish melodies on the harp and mandolin alternated with the dancing.

Campbell's Illustrated History of the World's Columbian Exposition stated that: "Among the other entertaining features of the Village were many native bag pipers and jig dancers who gave exhibitions of their musical and terpsichorean abilities each day" (1894:624).

In addition, there was Miss O'Sullivan of Cahirciveen, Kerry, "with her famous harp" (*ibid.*). The Countess of Aberdeen's Blarney Castle exhibit on the Midway Plaisance at 60th Street advertised its attractions as "A bit of the Ould Counthry - Concerts of Irish Music during the day and evening; Irish Reels, Jigs, and Dances by the Villagers" for a 25-cent admission (*Chicago Citizen* 8/12/1893:8).

The two uilleann pipers are the only performers at either Irish Village about which much is known. Turlough MacSweeney was a Donegal-born piper of a family famed for its uilleann pipers. He was "a perfect type of the old Irish piper. He is a fine musician, and plays some grand old Irish pieces that are now almost obsolete. His rendering of the *Coolin* ... is indeed beautiful" (Ennis 1893:5).

Patrick Tuohey was hired to play inside the castle. Born in Loughrea, Galway, he came to Boston at the age of three and began to embark upon a career as a professional piper in vaudeville in the early 1890s. Ennis described him as "a close student of the old Irish music, and the beautiful old airs and the dance-provoking reels and jigs seem to take on a fresh charm every time they are played by the gifted Pat Tuohey" (Ennis 1893:5).

The two pipers provided an interesting contrast:

> While Turlough MacSweeney, the "Donegal piper", may have fittingly represented an antiquated and oppressed Ireland, playing his ancient instrument outside the entrance to Mrs. Hart's "Donegal Castle" at the World's Columbian Exposition at Chicago in 1893, the hopes and aspirations of a regenerated nation were pleasingly typified in "Patsy" Tuohey, the spruce young man in corduroy breeches and ribbed stockings, whose expert manipulation of a great set of Taylor pipes made him the centre of attraction within ... No two musicians on the Midway representing their respective countries, won more attention or elicited more praise than they (O'Neill 1913:313, 289).

The Irish activities at the Exposition culminated with "Irish Day" on September 30, 1893. This gala outpouring of national pride featured a parade, speeches by several religious and political dignitaries including the Lord Mayor of Dublin, Gaelic football games and musical presentations.

The Donegal Village program had songs by Miss Alice Smith, Mr. T.J. Darcy and Miss Ewing; harp solos, dancing, piping; and stereopticon views of Ireland by Mr. H.P. Grattan (*Chicago Citizen* 9/30/1893:4).

The afternoon concert in the Festival Hall featured a six hundred-voice choir (Corrigan 1977b:24), and the following items were interspersed among speeches:

- Miss Josephine Sullivan of Dublin playing a selection of Irish airs on the harp and, "being encored, gave "Tramp, Tramp, Tramp, the Boys Are Marching" and "The Wearing of the Green";

- C.P.S. Collins singing "The Minstrel Boy", "The Harp That Once", and "Let Erin Remember the Days of Old";

- Miss May Braddock singing "The Last Rose of Summer";

- W.P. Foran singing "Kathleen Mavourneen" and "The Girl I Left behind Me";

- Signorina Inez Carusi, "who captured the audience with her singing of three Irish ballads (*Chicago Citizen* 10/7/1893:1).

A steady downpour of rain lowered the attendance at Irish Day, and, when Turlough MacSweeney was asked his opinion on the occasion, he replied that "the next time there was an Irish Day, they ought to hold the parade the day before to fool the weatherman" (Corrigan 1977b:24).

This era might have faded into greater obscurity had it not been for the efforts of Francis J. O'Neill (1849-1936), Captain and later Chief of the Chicago Police Department.

A native of Tralibane, County Cork, O'Neill came from a family headed by a well-educated strong farmer. He taught school for a short while in his teen years and then signed on and sailed with several merchant ships for a few years until coming to America in 1871. He worked as a shepherd, a school teacher and a railway clerk before joining the Chicago Police Department in 1873. O'Neill won several citations and promotions for bravery in action and successfully quelled without violence a potentially dangerous labor strike at the Union Stockyards in July, 1894.

In 1901 he was appointed to the position of Superintendent of Police, a job that now corresponds to the Chief of Police. He served in this capacity until his retirement from the force in 1905 (French 1897:313,315; O'Neill 1973:v).

Wrote a biographer of prominent Chicago Irishmen in 1897:

> Captain O'Neill is in personal appearance a man of medium height and looks, as he assuredly is, every inch a soldier. Of robust constitution, great strength, and splendid endurance, he has never known what it means to have bad health. Never obtrusive with his own opinions, he is under all circumstances a courteous and obliging gentleman, tolerant of the prejudices of others. His student mind and delight in reading have found an outcome in a well-toned library, in which are quite five hundred volumes devoted to Ireland and Irish subjects, many of them being extremely rare and valuable editions (French 1897:314~315).

O'Neill's job on the police force gave him excellent opportunities to make the acquaintance of the city's Irish musicians. A flute player himself, O'Neill began taking an active interest in Chicago's Irish music scene almost immediately upon his arrival. As he noted:

> Many an impromptu concert in which the writer took part enlivened the old Deering Street Police Station about this time. An unique substitute for a drum was operated by Patrolman Michael Keating, who forcing a broom handle held rigidly against the marble floor at a certain angle, gave a passable imitation of a kettle drum. His ingenuity and execution never failed to evoke liberal applause (O'Neill 1910:19).

It is thus not too surprising to discover that during Francis O'Neill's period of service with the Chicago Police Department, there were several Irish musicians and Irish music enthusiasts, among them Patrolmen Patrick O'Mahony, Timothy Dillon, William Walsh, John P. Ryan, Barney Delaney, John Ennis, Inspectors John D. Shea and John McDonald, Sergeants James Kerwin, James Cahill, James Early, Michael Hartnett, Gerald Stark, Garrett Stack and James O'Neill.

As O'Neill began to attain positions of influence within the force, he made it a practice evidently to offer jobs in the department to any indigent Irish musician, local or itinerant, who felt inclined to forsake the free-and-easy (and often financially precarious) life for a career of relative ease, early retirement and much greater economic security.

Although the Chicago Police Department has since adopted other methods and criteria for hiring recruits, the force in O'Neill's day must certainly have been an entertaining environment in which to work.

O'Neill was an avid collector of Irish music in printed books and manuscripts, and he inspired his colleagues to pursue the same quarry. There was an enormous amount of music taken down from the playing of the many outstanding local musicians and from professional players like John Hicks, Patsy Tuohey, Eddie Joyce and John Moore (all pipers), who often travelled through Chicago. When over two thousand tunes had been amassed, "there developed a general desire to have them printed" (O'Neill 1910:54).

Sergeant James O'Neill of Belfast was Francis O'Neill's chief scribe and assistant in the preparation of a large collection. In 1903, the *Music of Ireland* was published at Francis O'Neill's expense. Representing the culmination of nearly three full decades of collection, the work contained 1,850 pieces of music spanning almost the whole spectrum of Irish folk music.

There were dance tunes (reels, hornpipes, double jigs, slip jigs, set dances), airs drawn from old and modern sources, marches, descriptive pieces, seventy-five compositions attributed to the harper Turlough O'Carolan (1670-1738) and a host of other miscellaneous tunes.

On the back page of O'Neill's *Irish Folk Music: A Fascinating Hobby* (1910), there were several accolades concerning the *Music of Ireland*. The *Dublin Weekly Freeman* stated that: "No one has ever done anything like this for Irish music". Said the *Chicago Examiner*: "There has been nothing more distinctive done in America by an Irishman than this".

John F. Finerty, editor of the weekly *Chicago Citizen*, proclaimed: "O'Neill deserves the gratitude of the Irish race and of all lovers of music for the labor of love which has embalmed the musical genius of the Irish people in this inestimable volume".

Fortunately, O'Neill's *Music of Ireland* was proof that Irish music in Chicago was not in a state of "embalmed" lethargy but was flourishing far from its source of origin. O'Neill remarked:

> The first tangible result of our many years of incessant effort, O'Neill's *Music of Ireland* includes over eleven hundred dance tunes classified for convenience, an amount many times more than were supposed to be in existence altogether. The appearance of this surprising aggregation aroused much latent enthusiasm in the ranks of a certain class of Irish musicians. Letters of approval came pouring in, many suggesting the issuance of a smaller or less expensive volume devoted to dance music entirely (1910:62).

The *Dance Music of Ireland, 1001 Gems* appeared in 1907. It was a revised edition of the dance tunes in *Music of Ireland* and included several new additions that had turned up in the years after *Music of Ireland* had been published. Both books have come to be regarded by traditional Irish musicians as the ultimate arbiter in disputes involving tune names and settings.

While the versions of most of the tunes have changed considerably in the living aural tradition since the books were first brought out, there remains an aura of special reverence for the O'Neill collections that no other collection of Irish folk music before or since has ever surpassed.

Following the publication of the *Dance Music of Ireland*, O'Neill realized that "a demand for an edition arranged and harmonized for the piano was being voiced insistently" (1910: 62), and to satisfy these requests, fiddler Selena O'Neill, a graduate of Chicago Musical College, arranged two hundred-fifty pieces from the earlier O'Neill collections for violin and piano. Four more editions of Irish music collections appeared under the aegis of Francis O'Neill up to 1922 (see Appendix F for a list of O'Neill's published work).

In addition to bringing a great deal of rare music to a vastly larger audience, O'Neill penned two biographical and historical works, *Irish Folk Music: A Fascinating Hobby* (1910) and *Irish Minstrels and Musicians* (1913). These two books have given future generations their only vivid insight into the personalities and events of Irish music in Chicago during the late 19th and early 20th centuries.

Both works contain historical chapters on various aspects of Irish music, song and dance as well as anecdotes and autobiographical experiences of O'Neill in his role as collector and promoter of Irish music. *Irish Minstrels and Musicians* includes biographical features on over three hundred Irish and Irish-American musicians of the past and present, and it is an invaluable compendium of information from the viewpoint of an individual who was intimately involved with the music.

A focal point for Irish musical activity around the turn of the 20th century was the Chicago Irish Music Club. This was an outgrowth of the frequent informal sessions held in the homes of O'Neill and his friends, and it included a vast array of outstanding performers. Pipers Barney Delaney, James Cahill, John Ennis, James Early, John Beatty, Adam Tobin, John Conners; fiddlers John McFadden, Edward Cronin, Timothy Dillon, James Kennedy, John McElligott, Abram Beamish, James O'Neill; flute players James Kerwin, Garrett Stack, Fr. Dollard, Fr. Fielding and Francis O'Neill himself were among the mainstays of the Club.

Internal disputes and personality clashes eventually caused the dissolution of the organization, and, in O'Neill's words, "the most enjoyable, companionable, and representative association of Irish musicians, singers, and dancers ever organized in America" dissolved (O'Neill 1910:59). A few wire cylinder recordings of McFadden, Early, Delaney and piper Billy McCormick still remain and indicate that O'Neill's assessment was not at all exaggerated.

Writing in 1909, O'Neill was quite confidently optimistic about the future of Irish music in Chicago: "Irish music, however, is neither dead nor dying in this great western Metropolis, for a young generation of Irish-American musicians bids fair to rival their progenitors in the divine art 'which gentler on the spirit lies, than tired eyelids upon tired eyes'" (1910:60).

Certainly, there were a number of young Chicagoans who were giving great promise of a distinguished future as adult Irish musicians. Pipers Eddie Mullaney, Tom Ennis and Hughie McCormick, fiddlers Selena O'Neill and Theresa Geary, and pianist Nellie Gillan did indeed prove to be competent and even outstanding performers in their maturity.

O'Neill was also encouraged at this time by the interest being shown in Irish music by groups of people who had never before been sympathetic to the tradition. "To believe that an Irish piper would be the chief attraction at entertainments given by the Chicago Athletic Association and by a Presbyterian congregation would severely tax our credulity a few years ago, yet such is the fact in this year of our Lord, nineteen hundred and nine" (O'Neill 1910:60).

Irish step dancing was also enjoying a renaissance in Chicago during the early 1900s. The Hennessy Brothers of Cork, John E. McNamara and James P. Coleman of Limerick and Dan and John Ryan of Tipperary were all excellent dancers schooled in the Munster tradition of step-dancing. (O'Neill 1910:306). It is believed that the province of Munster (and particularly the county of Kerry) was where modern Irish step-dancing received its basic form at the end of the 18th century (Breathnach 1970:118).

Yet, despite this flurry of activity, many members of the Irish community in Chicago were showing less and less of an interest in the traditional music of Ireland. Instead, the emigrants and their offspring who had managed to rise upward in the socio-economic scale in the United States turned toward the leisure pursuits of the mainstream Anglo-American middle class in their quest for respectability and integration within the majority society.

In the realm of music, this took the form of performing or listening to the popular music of urban America or the art music of European composers. Irish folk music and song came to be regarded as relics of a past best left forgotten; the older Irish music was intimately bound up with the history of an Ireland most emigrants wished to forget or alter.

Thus, the same year as an Irish uilleann piper played before the bastions of Anglo-American Protestant society in Chicago, the Chicago Athletic Association and a Presbyterian congregation, the Irish Choral Society of Chicago put on "King Conor: An Irish Cantata", with music by Joseph H. Adams and libretto by T.D. Sullivan. The Society had one hundred-four active members (listed in the program for the concert in Soprano, Contralto, Tenor, and Bass divisions) and over three hundred associate members.

The opening performance was held at Orchestra Hall on Michigan Avenue, April 20, 1909, with Thomas Taylor Brill directing forty members of the Theodore Thomas Orchestra. Sibyl Sammis-MacDermid (soprano), John A. Looby (tenor) and Frank J. Flood (baritone) were cast in the leading roles, with Kate Farrell-Reiplinger serving as accompanist.

Nearly three decades earlier, on February 15, 1882, the Palmer House Hotel in downtown Chicago had been the site of "The Celebration of the First Centennial of the Dungannon Convention and Declaration of Irish Independence", commemorating the establishment of a short-lived (1782-1800) independent Anglo-Irish Protestant parliament in Dublin.

"Irish music arranged specially for the occasion" was provided by W.W. Pound's Orchestra, and, following a series of speeches, eleven toasts were given, each one succeeded by musical selections. There exists no record of what kind of incidental music Pound's Orchestra may have played or what instruments made up the ensemble, but the program of musical toasts are of interest:

1. Medley of American and Irish Airs
2. The Meeting of the Waters
3. The Irish Volunteers
4. The Harp That Once
5. St. Patrick's Day
6. Let Erin Remember the Days of Old
7. The Minstrel Boy
8. The Bells of Shandon
9. The Song of Inisfail
10. The Wearing of the Green
11. The Girl I Left Behind Me

Eleven years later, on November 23, 1893, the Irish Nationalists of Chicago celebrated "The 25th Mortuary Anniversary of the Manchester Martyrs, Allen, Larkin, and O'Brien" in honor of the execution of three Irishmen involved in helping an Irish political prisoner escape from police custody in Manchester in 1867. An English policeman was killed in the scuffle; the capital punishment given Allen, Larkin and O'Brien helped them attain a martyrdom still strongly remembered today.

The program for this occasion, convened at Central Music Hall, included:

1. "The Memory of the Dead" by Mr. E.J. Quinlan
2. "Kathleen Mavourneen" by the Unity Male Quartette
3. "Come Back to Erin" by Miss Rosa Hiss
4. "Bagpipe solo" by Prof. B. Delaney
5. "Lament for the Irish Emigrant" by Mr. Charles Meeher
6. "Killarney" by Miss Nellie T. Cahill
7. "The Meeting of the Waters" by Mr. W.D. Haile
8. "God Save Ireland" by the Hon. M. McInerney
9. "Star-Spangled Banner" and "Columbia"

(*Chicago Citizen* 11/12/1892:8)

The *Chicago Citizen* (12/3/1892:5) reported that the concert had been well attended and that "the bagpipe solo by Prof. B. Delaney ... was rewarded by tumultuous applause." This is, no doubt, the same Barney Delaney, friend and informant of Francis O'Neill.

"The 31st Mortuary Anniversary of the Manchester Martyrs" was held at Central Music Hall on November 23, 1898 and featured the following program, with piano accompaniment:

1. "Medley of Irish Airs" by Prof. Thomas J. Purcell
2. "The Irish Exile's Return", soprano solo by Mollie Frawley
3. "Who Fears to Speak of '98?", baritone solo by John J. Phelan
4. "The Harp That Once", contralto solo by Eugenia Bayard
5. "Violin solo" by Frank F. Winter
6. "Believe Me If All Those Endearing Young Charms", tenor solo by William Barron
7. "God Save Ireland", closing ode by John J. Phelan

"The 121st Anniversary Celebration of the Birth of Robert Emmet", sponsored by the Irish Nationalists of Chicago, took place at Central Music Hall on March 4, 1899 with these musical and poetic selections (accompanied by Prof. Shaughnessy, organist):

1. "Rosy Darling", soprano solo by Mollie Frawley
2. "Believe Me If All Those Endearing Young Charms", tenor solo by William Barron
3. "Fontenoy", recitation by James Campbell
4. "Savourneen Deelish", soprano solo by Annie Harding
5. "Medley of Irish Airs by O'Carolan", instrumental duet on violin and piano by Thomas and Dan O'Malley
6. "Let Erin Remember the Days of Old", baritone solo by John J. Phelan
7. "Come Back to Erin, Mavourneen", Quartet by Annie Harding, Mrs. John J. Phelan, Mssrs. Phelan and Barron
8. "God Save Ireland", closing ode by John J. Phelan and Audience

From these few concert programs from the 1880s, 1890s and early 1900s, it is clear that Irish folk music as represented by Barney Delaney, Francis O'Neill and the Chicago Irish Music Club was becoming an insignificant part of the Irish community's formal musical life. Certainly, the traditional music and the newer favorites were able to co-exist for a time, but the handwriting on the wall, in retrospect, seems obvious.

While "the services of Prof. W.R. Murphy, the renowned Irish piper, and the no less renowned dancer, Mr. Fox Kenny" were secured for the benefit dance held for Mrs. Curley Homestead on February 8, 1893 (*Chicago Citizen* 1/21/1893:5), and W.R. Murphy was also engaged to perform at the Elliott Literary Club's Washington's Birthday Celebration on February 21, 1893 (*Chicago Citizen* 1/14/1893:5), traditional music was steadily losing ground in the Irish community of Chicago.

Of the thirty songs quoted in the programs above, only one was in Irish ("Savourneen Deelish"), and it was taken from an art music arrangement by Knight.

The overwhelming majority of songs were from the pens of 19th-century Anglo-Irish and English composers, particularly Tom Moore (1779-1852), "who compelled drawing-room dames to listen to the old-folk melodies of Ireland, as adapted to his own matchless lyrics" (Flood 1905:334).

Instrumental selections were also notably absent from these concerts, and the program classification of singers in terms of soprano, contralto, tenor, baritone and bass gives insight into the growing preference for operatic vocal performance.

The changing musical tastes of successful, respectable Irish-Americans in Chicago would become even more clearly merged with those of their Anglo-American social counterparts as the 20th century developed.

The St. Patrick's Day celebrations of the Irish Fellowship Club of Chicago between 1910 and 1919 included a mixture of Irish songs set to Irish airs arranged by art-music composers such as Herbert, Stanford Hughes, Moore, Balfe, works by Goddard, Serbais, Popper, Chopin, Bach-Gounod and "Dixie", "Suwanee River" and "Wacht um Rein" as performed by the Duke Smith Orchestra.

In 1928, the Club featured baritone Walter McNally backed by the Chicago Philharmonic Orchestra; in 1930, the St. Patrick's Festivities included Mischa Livschutz, the "celebrated Russian violin virtuoso".

By the 1950s, "The Ten White Guards", Lou Breese and His Musical Images and the Choral Club of the First National Bank of Chicago were providing the musical trimmings at the Club's Paddy's Day banquet.

The Irish Fellowship Club of Chicago is the most elite of the Irish organizations in terms of economic and political status in Chicago, and it is not surprising that it should have succumbed so readily to assimilative pressures in the musical entertainment realm. Throughout the 20th century, Irish songs manufactured by the American popular music industry and first sung by Hollywood and Broadway entertainers became commonplace items in the Club's musical programs.

It may be argued that these few examples are inconclusive as to the true extent to which Irish folk music was being replaced by other musical idioms, both foreign and derivative.

Granted, the paucity of documentation makes absolute judgments difficult to render, but what evidence is available strongly points to a gradual, steady reduction of interest in Irish folk music among the sections of the Chicago Irish community endowed with the greatest amount of influence in shaping musical ideals and aesthetic preferences (or, at least, the public image of those ideals and preferences) for the community.

It is possible, perhaps, that for every concert, banquet or dance sponsored by an Irish organization that contained a large proportion of music other than Irish folk music, there might have been many more informal, semi-private or private musical occasions held in taverns or kitchens (rather than the Central Music Hall or Palmer House Hotel) where Irish folk music, song and dance were present.

Clearly, these informal sessions were the preserve of ever-dwindling numbers of Irish emigrants and not Irish-Americans who were successfully assimilating within the mainstream American society.

Francis O'Neill himself soon became aware of the effects of the melting pot dynamic upon Irish culture in America. Writing in 1913, his concluding comments in *Irish Minstrels and Musicians* were far less sanguine about the future of Irish traditional music in Chicago than only four years previously. Indeed, the final pages of the work are beseeching, exhortative, admonishing and, paradoxically, curiously resigned. Contrast the following comments with those quoted on page 145 above:

> Among the children of the Gael the number seriously interested in the study of Irish music is insignificant. The Irish Music Club of Chicago, once so prosperous, is no longer in existence. A similar organization in Boston can scarcely be said to realize the expectations of its promoters, and a so-called Irish Pipers' Club of San Francisco was disbanded suddenly by the earthquake. Dissensions and jealousies are still doing their deadly work as of yore ... (O'Neill 1913:478).

> Aside from the few who love it instinctively and practice it for their own pleasure, there is all too little inducement to study Irish music ... We may as well be honest with ourselves and give up the delusion that much of value can be accomplished without united effort and personal sacrifice ... The attitude of chronic apathy must come speedily to an end. Something more effective than holiday oratory glorifying "our music, our language, and our literature" in set phrases and ready-made monotonous resolutions, is essential and imperative ... If the laborer is worthy of his hire, as the Scripture says, why make an exception of the Irish musician?

> When the Irish people, lay and clerical, abandon the conventional custom of imposing on the generosity of musicians of their race and creed, and treat them with the consideration and liberality of their ancestors, as recorded in history then, and not till then, will the long-hoped for Revival of Irish music become a living, lasting reality (O'Neill 1913:480, 482).

O'Neill viewed the lack of proper patronage, appreciation and respect for the Irish musician as the chief problems and held misdirected social reformers, over-zealous clergy and greedy entrepreneurs as the three groups mainly responsible for the debased state of musical and cultural sensibilities of the American Irish.

There were other significant factors at work, too. The decline of Irish emigration to Chicago (particularly after the turn of the 20th century), the geographical fragmentation of Irish neighborhoods and the dispersal of their inhabitants, the modification of cultural values and priorities that accompanies the emigrant's successful transition from "foreigner" to "native" and the chronic instability of American urban society in the Industrial Age. All of these contributed to the increased remoteness with which Irish folk music came to be regarded by many Irish-Americans.

Though Francis O'Neill lived until 1936, the halcyon epoch of which he was so distinguished a representative and spokesman can be said to have ended by the 1920s. The Irish and Irish-American population of Chicago had reached a peak of over 225,000 by 1900 (City of Chicago 1976a:24), yet even at this early date, Irish music was beginning to noticeably lose its appeal to a large segment of the Irish-American community.

Despite the admonitions of O'Neill and other perceptive cultural commentators, Irish music, song and dance would continue to recede into the backwaters of Irish-American cultural consciousness for the next half century.

The professional Irish-American musicians that had flourished as members of vaudeville troupes were among the first victims of changing musical tastes among the Irish-American communities.

The "stage-Irish" nature of the comedy routines and characterizations employed by many of these performers were found to be increasingly objectionable and repugnant to many American Irish, especially those who were trying to escape the very real bigotry and social stigmas that still afflicted Irish Catholics in the late 19th and early 20th centuries (c.f. Murphy 1893, Niehaus 1964, and Wittke 1962 for discussions of the stage-Irish character in 19th-century American entertainment).

Editors in the Irish-American press fulminated frequently against the distorted stage-Irish character actors. John F. Finerty of the *Chicago Citizen* offered a comment typical of the feelings of his colleagues when he said: "The traditional and conventional stage Irishman must be driven from the stage, if it takes murder to do it" (*Chicago Citizen* 3/8/1884:4).

By 1920, there were no more than a handful of professional Irish folk musicians working in American vaudeville troupes, the majority having been confronted with an early retirement caused by the opposition of influential Irish-Americans and by the changes in the musical entertainment tastes of Americans in general. The few Irish performers were gradually being ousted by Hawaiian steel guitarists, African-American blues singers and white southern string bands. The bleak economic situation of Irish music in America described by O'Neill would only intensify as the 20th century progressed.

Notwithstanding these ill omens, the period between the two World Wars saw a great deal of Irish musical activity in Chicago as several musicians made 78 rpm records for labels like Decca, Victor, Celtic, Gennett and Columbia. In the 1920s pipers Eddie Mullaney, Tom Ennis and Joe Sullivan, fiddlers Tom Cawley, Paddy Stack, Billy McCormick, Francis Cashin, Selena O'Neill and Michael Cashin, flute players Paddy Doran and Tom Doyle, and pianists Frances Malone and Kathleen Kearney appeared on commercial recordings.

While Chicago Irish musicians did not receive extensive attention from the record companies of the period that were mostly based in New York City, the sixty-odd sides featuring these performers provide an interesting assortment of styles and repertoires (see Appendix B for a discography).

The surviving 78 rpm records from this period reveal that reels and double jigs were the staple element of the traditional Irish repertoire in Chicago at the time, though hornpipes, polkas, slip jigs, set dances and airs were also recorded.

The fiddle, flute and uilleann pipes were the main instruments used by Irish musicians recorded in Chicago during the 1920s, although after 1925 harmonic accompaniment on piano and guitar became more prominent and more frequent. No accordion players appear on records made by Irish musicians in Chicago until the mid-1930s.

Bowen's Irish Orchestra consisted of Paddy Doran on flute, Joe Owens and Billy McCormick on fiddle, and Joe Sullivan and Denny Flynn on uilleann pipes. The group was named for the travel agency operated by John J. Bowen, a native of County Mayo. Bowen opened the agency in 1919 at 5548 S. Halsted and sold steamship tickets to Ireland, phonograph machines and 78 rpm records of Irish and Irish-American performers. The group never recorded under the name, but Doran, Owens and Flynn did make two sides for Columbia in the mid-1920s, as did Joe Sullivan and Billy McCormick.

Tom Ennis was the most renowned Chicago-born Irish musician of the early 20th century. His father, John, had come to Chicago from County Kildare and was a fine flute player and piper in addition to serving as a prime informant and sometime collector for Francis O'Neill. As a postscript to a biographical sketch of John Ennis, O'Neill commented: "His son Tom displays much musical talent and bids fair to rank high as an Irish piper" (O'Neill 1910:38).

After the death of Patsy Tuohey in 1923, Tom Ennis became the premier piper of the United States. He made at least forty commercial sides for several record companies and lived in New York City during the late 1910s. He gave up the music store he owned there in the early 1920s and took to travelling throughout the country accompanied by his wife, an actress of French extraction. They lived in Chicago from about 1929 until 1931 and used that city as their home base for travels around the Midwest.

Chicago uilleann pipe-maker Patrick Hennelly remembers Tom Ennis well. It was from John Ennis that Patrick learned a good deal of the finer points of reed-making when he came to Chicago from Philadelphia in 1928. In 1930, Tom Ennis asked Patrick to make him a new set of pipes. Tom and his wife lived with the Hennellys off and on, as the Depression was beginning to show its teeth and make life more and more uncertain for travelling entertainers like the Ennises. Tom spent many days and nights with Hennelly, watching the young pipe-maker create his pipes, exchanging lore of the pipe-making trade and chatting about the old-timers of O'Neill's day.

Hennelly finished the pipes in 1931, and Ennis was quite pleased with the handiwork. He had, however, only a short time to enjoy them, as he died in his sleep at a roadside inn near Jonesville, Michigan en route to an engagement in Detroit. The medical statement indicates only that "his heart stopped"; very likely, it was the pressures of the lifestyle of a professional entertainer that brought about his sudden demise. Hennelly never received payment for the pipes, as Ennis' widow disappeared immediately after his burial and allegedly took the newly-made, as yet unpaid-for pipes to her next destination. He does, however, still possess some parts of Ennis' old set of pipes made in the 1800s.

Fiddler James Neary remembers being at a party in 1931 with Tom Ennis the last time Ennis played in Chicago. Fifteenth Ward alderman Tommy Burns was hosting a gathering at his home at 6237 S. Washtenaw, less than a block from where James Neary and his wife, Eleanor, live today. Neary recalls that there were politicians and their attendant minions, priests from nearby St. Rita's parish, several Irish musicians and plenty of illicit moonshine and Canadian whiskey. That night was the first and last time Neary played in a session with Ennis, who, remembers Neary, played "awfully fast, but clean".

The only time piper Joe Shannon saw Tom Ennis was from afar at a Christmas party at Shannon's grade school in 1930. Ennis was playing onstage, and the eleven-year old Shannon had to be hoisted up onto an adult's shoulders to view the piper. Shannon was later told by Eddie Mullaney, who had spent some time with Ennis, that had Shannon been playing the pipes at the time, Ennis "would never have let him out of his sight". Indeed, Joe Shannon's piping style is highly reminiscent of Tom Ennis.

After Ennis' death, Eddie Mullaney replaced Ennis as the resident musician on Maurice Lynch's Irish radio program that aired every Sunday night on WCFL. Lynch was from near Listowel, Kerry; in the late 1920s he started the first program in Chicago oriented toward the Irish community. Mullaney's payment was a princely $10 per show, a not inconsiderable sum for the time.

Fiddler Tom Cawley (1905-1945) came to Chicago from County Sligo in 1925, joining his brother Richard who had arrived in Chicago in 1923. Tom Cawley worked in the daytime for United Cigar Company at 69th and Halsted but, during nights and weekends, played at dances, in taverns and for house parties throughout the city, often earning as much as $25 a night.

Cawley recorded six sides for Columbia with flute player Paddy Doran and pianist Frances Malone and four sides with fiddler Francis Cashin and a guitar player named Ford, also with Columbia. He moved to New York City in 1927 where he became a close compatriot of another great Sligo fiddler, Michael Coleman. Cawley died in New York in 1945 of leukemia.

There was less recording activity following the onset of the Depression in 1929, but those that were made in the 1930s continued to be of considerable interest.

In 1934 a recently-arrived Irish dancing teacher from County Clare named Pat Roche presented the Pat Roche Harp and Shamrock Orchestra at the Irish Village of the Century of Progress World's Fair. The band was one of the first American ensembles modeled on the newly-emerging Irish céilí band principle and, following a successful engagement at the Fair, the group made several records for Decca.

Included were fiddlers Jimmy Devine and John McGreevy, accordionists John Gaffney and Paddy Durkin, flute player Pat McGovern, uilleann piper Joe Shannon, pianist Eleanor Kane (later Neary), drummer Pat Richardson, and step-dancer Pat Roche.

Within this assemblage were three teenagers who would continue to provide the foundation for Irish music in Chicago for the next four decades: John McGreevy, Eleanor Kane Neary and Joe Shannon. Pat Roche, through his radio programs and organizational activities, has also played a significant role in the city's Irish music and dancing activities over the last forty years and more.

The Harp and Shamrock Orchestra played at the World's Fair seven days a week from June through September of 1934. Peter Bolton and Violet Danaher, two prize-winning step-dancers from Ireland, were also featured with Roche's band. Each player was paid $35 a week, a sum that Eleanor Kane Neary recalls as being considered extraordinarily bountiful.

The high point of the band's tenure at the Fair was the appearance one day of the venerable Francis O'Neill. Quite feeble at the age of eighty-five, "the Chief" presented an autographed copy of *Irish Minstrels and Musicians* to each of the performers in the band.

To piper Joe Shannon he dedicated an entire front page to "the best left-handed piper since Patsy Tuohey". Shannon remembers that, at the time, he had no idea of O'Neill's importance or the significance of the occasion. John McGreevy, who was working as a clerk in Lyon and Healy's music store on South Wabash Street when O'Neill died in 1936, recollects that all of O'Neill's hard-bound volumes were on "special clearance sale" for the price of five cents.

In 1938, Eleanor Kane, fiddler Jim Donnelly and accordionist Pakie Walsh recorded for Decca; the same year Eleanor and John McGreevy also made a few sides on the Decca label. These were to be the last commercial recordings of Chicago Irish musicians until John McGreevy and flute player Seamus Cooley were recorded by Philo Records of Vermont in January, 1974.

Yet there were still a number of places where Irish music could be heard in Chicago. Benefit dances for the Irish Independence movement in the early 1920s always accepted the donation of talent by Irish musicians, and some welcome income was earned by musicians during the Depression by playing for open-air dances or for public dance halls. Recalls Jimmy Neary: "At that time there wasn't a dollar in existence hardly. If you got three or four dollars for playing, it would do you the whole week."

Flute player Frank Thornton arrived in Chicago from County Kerry in 1929 at the beginning of the Depression and remembers times being so hard that "when you went to an Irish dance hall, the doorman asked you were you working or not. If so, you had to pay twenty-five cents; if not, you'd be allowed in free." At the Irish dance hall run by Martin Campbell at Madison and California on the Westside, it was common to find men who could not find or afford lodgings elsewhere sleeping overnight on the floor of the hall.

Some of the venues boasted specialized types of dancing, such as the hall at Madison and Sacramento that hosted Kerry Sets, the hall at Root and Wentworth that featured Clare Sets and the hall at Madison and California where the Mayo Set, or Plain Set, was danced to the music of Tom Lennon's Orchestra.

Gaelic Park at 47th and California was a large outdoor area that had different wooden platforms erected for Kerry, Clare, Mayo and American-style dancing. The Englewood Celtic Organization held weekly Sunday night dances at Celtic Field, 74th and Ashland.

Other dance halls that catered to Irish dancing were located at 69th and Wentworth and 69th and Emerald, both on the Southside. Mill Stadium on the Westside was another popular outdoor site for Irish dancing in the 1930s.

Accordionist Terry Teahan remembers that the Southside was the stronghold of the Clare Set, while devotees of the Kerry and Mayo Sets frequented dances on the Northside and Westside. Dances often became associated with their operators: Mrs. Feely's Grove at 51st and Halsted (as Oswald's Park in the 1880s it had been the site of many Irish gatherings), Tony Morrally's at 47th and Halsted, Margaret O'Malley's at 2409 N. Halsted, Flynn's Hall at 63rd and Kedzie, Tommy Ryan's Loft at Jackson and Cicero.

The dances continually shifted in their relative popularity with the Irish community, and Terry Teahan recalls how the charisma, competence and social contacts of the musicians often had a significant impact on the dancegoers:

> Tom Tracy left Flynn's Hall, and he went to play for Mrs. Feely. They had about twelve people in attendance. So she offered the open-air dancing to the Gaelic Athletic Club, and they didn't take it because it was outdoors and they figured, well, you know, they wouldn't make anything with it.
>
> So I said to Tracy, "Ask her for it." So he said, "No, no," he said, "I don't want to monkey around with it, because I'll play for her, and if the night is bad, whether it's bad or good I'll get a night's pay out of it."
>
> I went over and asked her for it anyway, and it was Tommy Sheahan and Maise Griffin (at the time, she's Mrs. Mitchell now), and she [Mrs. Feely] said to me, "Do you know of any reason why that I should give you this?" I said, "Yes, a pretty good one, I think; you'd only twelve people here last weekend." "Oh, you know already," she said. And I said, "Oh, yes, and I'm sure that we'll put a lot more into it."
>
> "Well," she said, "Let me hear you playing." I said, "What do you want to hear?" She said, "I want to hear 'O'Donnell Abu'." So, of course, I played it for her. And she said, "I want to hear 'The Wearing of the Green'."
>
> "Well, you're not going to draw much of a crowd with 'O'Donnell Abu' and 'The Wearing of the Green'," I said. "Don't you want to hear something else?" So she gave us the place, and, of course, she would have the bar. We'd have the admission, but it was only fifty cents.

I got the Sarsfield Limerick Club's mailing list, and we sat down and sent them out, and the first weekend we put over a hundred people into it. Do you know that we closed Flynn's Hall with the ten-piece band? She [Mrs. Feely] ran out of everything in the line of drink, only wine and whiskey. We ran it then for two nights, then finally we ran it for three nights a week, and do you know that we packed that place? One night we made a hundred dollars each, the four of us, with admission at fifty cents.

Irish music could be heard in taverns during the 1930s and '40s as well as at dance halls. John Breen's at 50th and Halsted, the Celtic Club at 76th and Halsted, Erin's Isle at 56th and Halsted, McGinty's Tavern at 7425 S. Cottage Grove, Naughton's Bar at Pulaski and Jackson, P.J. Concannon's at Cicero and Madison, Jack McDermott's at Fullerton and Lincoln and a tavern at 44th and Emerald were among the most memorable taprooms where Irish music was played.

These bars, of course, were not at all like the large, lavish, nostalgically-decorated Irish "pubs" that arose in the late 1960s and draw a clientele of "professional" Irishmen and seekers of an Irish atmosphere". Irish taverns of the 1930s and '40s were lacking in frills and were stocked only with the basic alcoholic necessities favored by their regular customers drawn from the Irish male working class.

Not infrequently, they were the scene of physical violence among intoxicated patrons. Even bartenders became excited, as was often the case with Jack McDermott, whose great delight with the music being played in his tavern was expressed by his flinging glasses on the floor at moments when his exuberance and joy could no longer be contained. Eleanor Neary, Tony Lowe, Joe Shanley, James Neary, John McGreevy and Joe Shannon often played at McDermott's, and they would receive a big steak dinner after the long night's work, compliments of the owner.

Five dollars a night was top pay for Irish musicians playing in the Irish bars of Chicago during this period, and the hours were from 8 p.m. to 2 or 3 a.m. Musicians were required to play more or less continuously with only an occasional short break. John McGreevy remembers arriving at a bar engagement twenty minutes late one night because of a sickness in his family and having the owner dock two dollars from his five-dollar wage.

Most musicians who recall the Depression, World War II and post-war period are not overly nostalgic in their reminiscences. Though there was plenty of music to he heard, Irish music in Chicago had fallen to perhaps its lowest ebb of esteem within the Irish-American community. Remuneration for performances was slight and infrequent when steady engagements were available at all. Few young Chicagoans had taken up the music, though those that did were certainly able to contribute significantly to the local music milieu. Increasingly, Irish music seemed to retreat within the narrowing community of newly-arrived emigrants.

The first Chicago Feis was held in August, 1945, in Pilsen Park at 26th and Albany. This event has been convened every year since, although the feis site was moved to Loyola University in the late 1950s and has been held at various locations during the 1960s and '70s, as the competitions have attracted ever-increasing crowds of dancers and onlookers.

Musical stalwarts of the 1930s and '40s included fiddlers Tom Fitzmaurice, Jimmy Neary, Jim Giblin, John McGreevy, P.J. Concannon, Jimmy Devine, Joe Shanley, Martin Wynne, Ann Cawley Scully, John McGinley, Jim McCarty, Anna McGoldrick, Dan Keogh, Tom Ryan, Theresa Geary; accordionists Tom Rush, Tony Lowe, Paddy Kenny, John Gaffney, Tim Gehene, Dan Shea, Willie Guerin, Jim Bresnahan, Tom Sheahan, Tom Tracy, Paddy Durkin, Pakie Walsh, Martin Hardiman, Tom Kerrigan, Mrs. McLaughlin, Nell O'Hara, John Scott, Terry Teahan; flute players Jim Rudden, Ed Noone, Paddy Doran, Pat McGovern, Frank Thornton; pipers Eddie Mullaney, Joe Shannon, Denny Flynn, Joe Sullivan, Mike Joyce, Mike Scanlon; pianist Eleanor Kane Neary; drummers Pat and Tom Richardson.

Other musicians participated in Chicago Irish musical affairs during these years and left their own legacy as well, though their names have in many cases not been remembered by those who have survived them.

The 1950s witnessed a new influx of musicians emigrating to Chicago from Ireland in a wave that lasted until the early 1960s.

Kerry fiddlers Paddy and John Cronin, Galway accordionist Kevin Keegan and the late Galway accordion player Joe Cooley and his brother Seamus (flute) were among the most widely acclaimed of the new arrivals. Though only Seamus Cooley would remain in Chicago permanently, each made a substantial impact on the city's Irish music community. Paddy Cronin moved to Boston after only a year or so in Chicago and made several 78 rpm records for Copley Records of Boston in the early 1950s. Johnny Cronin went to New York City around 1960 and has become a professional musician playing mainly in bars.

After the departure of the Cronins, the Cooleys and Kevin Keegan represented an important nucleus of Irish musical activities in Chicago. Seamus and Joe Cooley had been stalwarts of the famous, prize-winning Tulla Céilí Band in Ireland during the 1940s and 1950s (Ó hAllmhuráin 1974a:10-11), and Seamus had spent some years in London, England, playing with the outstanding musicians of that city. He had stayed in Chicago when the Tulla Céilí Band had made their American tour in 1958. Kevin Keegan also toured that year with the Aughrim Slopes Céilí Band of Galway, and he, too, stayed in Chicago.

The Cooleys and Keegan made up the resident band at the Keyman's Club at 4721 W. Madison during the four years that the Club existed, and they were also the fixtures at Jack Hanley's House of Happiness at 1423 W. 79th Street in the early 1960s. Hanley's was perhaps the most popular gathering spot for Irish music enthusiasts in the late 1950s and early '60s, although the bar frequently hired bands that played popular American music.

On Sunday nights, a live radio show would be broadcast from Hanley's, and a vast array of Chicago's Irish musical talent would perform. As one regular Sunday night patron expressed it: "Going to Hanley's on a Sunday evening was as important as going to Mass on a Sunday morning — and maybe more so even!"

The Irish dance halls of Chicago continued operations up to the mid-1960s. Popular spots in the 1950s and early 1960s included the Regent Tavern at 69th and Halsted run by Jim Glyman; the West End Ballroom at 121 N. Cicero; McEnery Hall at 4039 W. Madison; Connolly's Bar at Jackson and Cicero that featured the music of John Scott (accordion) and Pat Richardson (drums); the Keyman's Club at 4721 W. Madison owned by Bill Fuller and staffed by accordionists Joe Cooley, Kevin Keegan, Vince McAndrews, flute player Seamus Cooley and drummer Billy Soden; the Viking Ballroom North at 3257 N. Sheffield; the Viking Ballroom South at 6855 S. Emerald; the Blarney Club at 79th and Halsted; the Harp and Shamrock at 54th and Halsted; Flynn's Hall at 63rd and Kedzie; Tony Morrally's at 47th and Halsted; Margaret O'Malley's at 2409 N. Halsted; and Feely's Grove at 51st and Halsted.

Many of these venues were in large rooms of taverns, and temporary bars fully stocked with liquor and beer were set up at all the dances. Flute player/piper Kevin Henry made the rounds of all the Irish dances and music bars during this time and remembers that at the Harp and Shamrock, "They had two old-timers playing in the back on a Saturday night, and they used to dance the sets and the old-time waltzes and the Stack of Barleys in the old-fashioned ways. It was a great place for a session, and mostly all the guys at that particular time were coming in from Canada. Everybody loved the music because everybody had plenty of money at that time."

The 1950s also saw the rise of Comhaltas Ceoltóirí Éireann, a Dublin-based organization originally formed by Irish musicians to support Irish music by forming local branches throughout Ireland. CCE was initiated in 1951 and had achieved a fair amount of success by the mid-1950s. It was becoming apparent to many musicians that organizations, despite their inherent difficulties, were useful and even necessary for promoting greater interest in Irish music.

Accordingly, on August 19, 1956, at 4 p.m., the Irish Musicians' Association of America was founded by twenty-one musicians attending a meeting convened at the Midland Hotel in downtown Chicago. Frank Thornton had written letters to each of the convention delegates from New York, Philadelphia, Boston, Detroit, Cleveland, Houston and Kansas City, and the convention drew up a firm plan of action for combating the lethargy that had afflicted the Irish-American community in cultural matters (see Appendix C for the minutes of this historic meeting).

Thornton was elected the first president, and, by the first "Irish Musicians' Ball" held November 30, 1957 at McEnery Hall, sixty musicians had become active members of the Chicago branch. The national organization expanded to twenty-two branches within the next few years but dissolved around 1964 due to an inability in the Eastern cities to settle matters of organizational structure and procedure. However, the Chicago branch has completed over two full decades of continuous activity and is now aligned formally with Comhaltas Ceoltóirí Éireann.

Early in 1959, Frank Thornton conceived the idea of organizing a group of Irish musicians, singers and dancers from Chicago to tour Ireland. By doing so he hoped to show that Irish music and dance traditions had been successfully maintained in America. He also believed that a tour of this type would inspire the Irish community of Chicago to take a more active interest in promoting Irish music and dance in the city.

The group consisted of Jim Rudden, John McGreevy and Mary McDonagh (fiddles), John Lavelle (accordion), Michael Malone (piano), Patrick Gilhooly (drums), Joanne Hartnett and Beatrice Garrity (vocals), Margie Bartishell, Mary Campbell, Joan O'Connor, Michelle Johnston, Maureen Daly, Mary Lucid, John Woulfe and Dennis Dennehy (dancers). All were American-born, with the exception of Frank Thornton (flute), who acted as master of ceremonies during the concerts.

The group gave fund-raising concerts on June 12, 1959, at Calumet High School and on June 13, 1959, at Resurrection Auditorium. This would appear to be the only primarily traditional Irish musical event in Chicago from which a program of scheduled performances has survived.

There were some substitutions in personnel. For the concerts, Eleanor Neary played the piano, Jimmy Thornton was added on flute, Eileen Fitzgerald appeared playing the fiddle and Margie Friel replaced Joanne Hartnett as a vocalist.

"Chicago Gaelic Concert" — *June 12 and 13, 1959*

- American and Irish National Anthems
- Céilí Band Selection: "Preston's Jig" and "Cook in the Kitchen"
- Figure Dance: "Arches of Erin", a combined reel
- Song: "Let Him Go", by Margie Friel
- Piano Solo: Medley of Reels, by Eleanor Kane Neary
- Comedy Song: "Galway Bay", by Beatrice Garrity
- Set Dance: "St. Patrick's Day", by Margie Bartishell, Mary Jane Lucid, Patrick Gilhooly, Mary Campbell, John Woulfe, Maureen Daly
- Violin Solo: "Colonel Frazer" and "Miss Johnson's", by John McGreevy, reels
- Figure Dance: "Chicago Choice", a four-hand jig by Maureen Daly, Patrick Gilhooly, Michele Johnston, John Woulfe
- Solo: "The Bard of Armagh" and "The Coolin", by Eileen Fitzgerald
- Song: "Kerry Dances", by Margie Friel
- Set Dance: "King of the Fairies", by Michele Johnston, Dennis Dennehy, Joan O'Connor
- Céilí Band Selection: "Traveler's" and "Cooley's", reels
- Song: "The Moon Behind the Hill", by Beatrice Garrity Comedy
- Céilí Band Selection: "Woman of the House" and "Sally Gardens", reels

— *15 Minute Intermission* —

- Céilí Band Selection: "Harvest Home" and "Hennessy's", hornpipes
- Figure Dance: "The Ring of Kerry", a combined jig
- Song: "With My Shillelagh under My Arm", by Margie Friel
- Duet: "The Snowy-Breasted Pearl" and "Gentle Maiden", by Eleanor Kane on the piano and Eileen Fitzgerald on violin
- Dance: "The Fox Hunter", slip jig
- Solo: "Reavy's" and "Dublin", by John McGreevy, hornpipes
- Song: "Down by the Glenside", by Beatrice Garrity
- Figure Dance: "The Crossroads", a three-hand reel, by Margie Bartishell, Dennis Dennehy, Joan O'Connor
- Comedy Dance: "Ireland's Glory", a jig in couples, by Margie Bartishell and Dennis Dennehy
- Song: "The Hills of Glenswilly", by Margie Friel
- Solo: "Philadelphia Hornpipe", by Eleanor Kane Neary
- Song: "The Boys from the County Armagh", by Beatrice Garrity Comedy Songs: "The Whistling Gypsy" and "Danny Boy", by Margie Friel
- Dance: "Margie's Pride", a combined hornpipe
- Céilí Band Selection: Mayo and Kerry Polkas and "The Lakes of Sligo"
- Violin and Accordion Duet: "The Dawn Reel"

Comparison of this concert program with the concerts of Irish music listed on pages 140 and 146-47 reveals a great difference in character. First, the 1959 concert was able to integrate music, song and dance to a much greater degree; instrumental music is featured prominently along with solo and group dancing, whereas in earlier occasions they were very much in the minority if not absent altogether.

All of the instrumental selections for the 1959 concert, moreover, were traditional pieces drawn from the living tradition of contemporary Chicago Irish folk music. The songs also were more evidently products of the folk rather than the elite tradition of Irish folk song, although "Galway Bay", "Danny Boy", and "The Whistling Gypsy" were 20th-century "pop" hits that had become standard fare at Irish-American musical occasions.

Comedy was performed chiefly by John Lavelle, the accordion player, and was of the earthy, irreverent variety that had been banned from the stages of Irish-American concerts in the late 19th and early 20th centuries. On the eve of a Catholic Irishman's election to the White House, it is possible that the American Irish were able to afford a bit of self-criticism expressed through humor.

The chief determining factor in the concert's makeup, however, was that it was conceived and executed by Irish folk musicians, singers and dancers rather than by the "committees on talent" so common in the days of Francis O'Neill.

The tour gave twenty-two performances in Ireland, and each concert was a sellout. The Americans were, quite literally, a sensation, and the following review of a concert given in the small town of Drumshambo, Leitrim, is typical:

> Doherty's Hall, Drumshambo, was packed for the stage presentation by the Chicago Gaelic Concert Group, on Monday night week. In a very nicely arranged and balanced program, each of the Artistes distinguished him or her self in their own particular sphere of entertainment, while the

various exhibitions of Irish traditional Figure Dancing made a deep impression on the large audience. The vociferous applause and general manner in which the audience received the show, was, in itself, not alone, an indication and striking proof of the high standard of the presentation, which opened with the Irish National Anthem and closed with the American National Anthem. (McGivern 1959:2).

The Chicago Irish Musicians' Association sponsored the first Chicago Fleadh Cheoil in 1964 at the Keyman's Club Ballroom on W. Madison Street. The *fleadh cheoil* (literally, "feast of music") is a event comprising a series of competitions in Irish music and song. Comhaltas Ceoltóirí Éireann began the Fleadh Cheoil in modern times in 1951, though the Gaelic League had been sponsoring similar competitions under the title of Feis Cheoil from 1897 until the outbreak of World War I. Fleadhanna Cheoil were held in Chicago during 1965 and 1966, but the Association did not attempt to organize another Fleadh until 1974.

The disbanding of the Chicago Fleadh Cheoil in the 1960s was indicative of the low ebb at which Irish traditional music found itself in Chicago at this time. Few new emigrants from Ireland had arrived, there were no visible signs of any young Chicagoans becoming interested in the music, and the gradual disappearance of the Irish dance halls and music bars had accelerated. Each of these contributed to the stagnation that gripped the Chicago Irish music community.

Many of the musicians who arrived in Chicago during the 1950s and early 1960s are still actively performing, while some have returned to Ireland or moved to other American cities. Among the musicians active then were fiddlers Tom McMahon, Phil Durkin, Frank Burke, Pat Burke, Maida Sugrue, Ted Sullivan, Mike Boyle, Jack and Eileen Fitzgerald, Tom Cummane, Paddy and Johnny Cronin; flute players Noel Rice, Tom Masterson, Albert Neary, Bob Flately, Dan Lynch, Kevin Henry, Seamus Cooley; accordion players Pat Cloonan, Mike Madden, Vince McAndrews, Martin Byrne, Jim Coyle, Tim Clifford, Tom Maguire, Tom O'Malley, Des O'Grady, Jimmy Sullivan, Bill Hennelly, Con O'Sullivan, Pat Flannagan, Frank and Tom O'Malley, John Scott, Con Scannell, Joe Cooley, Kevin Keegan; tinwhistle players Mike Neary and William Mulvihill; piper Dave Page; banjo player Bertie McMahon; pianists Nancy Harling and Maise Griffith; drummers Billy Soden, James Sullivan, John McGrath and Johnny Smith.

Several Chicagoans also joined the Irish music ranks around this time, including fiddler Bob Murphy, fiddler/pianist Mary McDonagh, flute players John Murphy, Pat McPartland and Jimmy Thornton, accordion players John Murray and John Lavelle, pianist Michael Malone and drummers Pat Gilhooly and John Cooke. All of these players provided the backbone of the Chicago Irish music community of this period.

Ireland's 32, a tavern at Milwaukee and Montrose on the city's Northwestside, was an occasional meeting place for Irish musicians. Hoban's Tavern at 63rd and Kedzie was also a major spot for sessions in the early 1970s. However, Hoban's went out of business in 1975, and, presently, only the 6511 Club at 6511 S. Kedzie is a consistent meeting place for a handful of musicians on weekend nights. The weekly Sunday night Irish Hours hosted by Martin Fahey and broadcast live over radio station WOPA from the basement lounge of Hibernian Hall ceased in 1976 when the Hall was sold to new owners with radically different tastes and clientele.

In October, 1972, the Chicago Irish Musicians' Association brought in the Comhaltas Ceoltóirí Éireann North American Tour Group of musicians, singers and dancers from Ireland. If one event may be said to have started the rejuvenation process of Irish traditional music in Chicago in the 1970s, it is most certainly this first appearance of the CCE tour.

The groundwork for this concert had been laid in 1969 by Frank Thornton's organization of an American tour of eight cities for a group of Irish musicians that included Seán Ryan (fiddle), Peadar O'Loughlin (flute, uilleann pipes), Eibhlín Begley (vocals), Paddy O'Brien (accordion), Denis Gilroy (piano) and Thomas Quinlivan (vocals).

The proceeds of this tour went to the musicians and to the American Congress for Irish Freedom, a group created to raise funds for various political issues. In this instance the money was used for the relief of the destitute Catholic population in Northern Ireland. The group gave two concerts in Chicago and then had to give a third because of the public interest (Anonymous 1970:12-13).

CCE was inspired by the success of this brief tour and in 1972, using Thornton's methods as a model, brought over twenty musicians, singers, and dancers. The tour ended with a concert on the White House Lawn in Washington, D.C. and realized several thousand dollars to be used in constructing a cultural center in Dublin (De Brún 1973:1-4).

The CCE concerts have come at least once and sometimes twice a year to the U.S. since 1972, acting as a catalyst for the current revival of Irish traditional music in many areas besides Chicago. In Chicago at the present time, there are encouraging signs that this revival will not be short-lived, either. There are over thirty schools of Irish step-dancing in the Chicago area, and several of these frequently use Irish musicians for their public performances. The Chicago Gaelic Society has encouraged the revival of Irish music, song and dance by its monthly céilís and weekly Irish language classes.

The Francis O'Neill Music Club and the Emerald Music Club are two other organizations that sponsor Irish music and dance-events. The annual Chicago Feis is still operating, and the Chicago Fleadh Cheoil has since 1974 attracted musicians from all over the Midwest. Schools of Irish music instruction have increased in the last few years, and the emergence of several talented young musicians, such as Liz Carroll, James Keane, Jr., Michael Flatley, Marty Fahey, Johnny Harling and Tom Masterson, has ensured that Irish music will be heard in Chicago for at least another generation.

Four of Francis O'Neill's most important works have been reprinted and revised, and they are selling well at considerably higher prices than their 1936 level of five cents. Bloomington, Indiana, author/folklorist Miles Krassen brought fiddler John McGreevy and flute player Seamus Cooley to the recording studios of Philo Records in January, 1974; this was the first time Irish musicians from Chicago had been commercially recorded since the late 1930s. Following the Philo session, many of the city's musicians have been recorded by American and English companies, and the distinctive styles and repertoire of many Chicago musicians are now beginning to be recognized and appreciated by a much wider audience.

In addition, Chicago's Irish musicians are performing more often for non-Irish audiences at folk festivals, coffeehouses and college concerts, and it is perhaps a mild surprise to some that their music is so warmly welcomed by audiences who have heard little or no Irish music before.

Flute player/piper Kevin Henry was the first Irish folk musician to emerge from the Chicago Irish community in the 1960s and attempt to bring his music before non-Irish crowds at Chicago folk clubs like The Earl of Old Town, The Old Town School of Folk Music and The Quiet Knight. Now, Irish musicians are regular performers at these venues, and the number of persons from outside the Irish community attending Irish cultural events in Chicago sponsored by Irish social and political organizations has also risen appreciably in the last few years.

The situation is reminiscent of the popularity enjoyed by Irish musicians around the middle of the 19th century, when Irish traditional musicians were among the foremost popular entertainers of the day. It is the ability to attract new blood that characterizes a healthy musical tradition, and the increasing number of aspiring players of Irish music who have journeyed to Chicago to seek the advice, expertise and inspiration of many of the city's Irish musicians is an indication of the current growth of the tradition in Chicago.

There is no way of knowing how long this renaissance will last. Momentum in the Irish music community of Chicago appears currently to be building, and if the music clubs can remain stable and active, if young performers can be nurtured in the tradition and remain interested into adulthood and if the public performance of Irish music continues to be economically remunerative and more frequently encountered in the mass communications media of radio, records and television, it is very possible that the 1980s could represent a new golden age of Irish music in Chicago even greater than the epoch chronicled by Francis O'Neill.

CHAPTER TWO: Instruments and Performance Practice

- **Instrumental Traditions in Irish Folk Music**

AS THE 17TH century ended, Ireland was already deep into a transitional period during which the social, political, economic and musical structures that had existed since the early Middle Ages were undergoing drastic transformation.

The Treaty of Limerick in 1691 formally terminated the ruling authority of the established native Catholic aristocracy and invested the powers of state in a recently arrived Protestant Ascendancy that served as a colonial extension of the English Crown.

"When the 18th century dawned, the great majority of the former leaders of the people were either sunk in abject poverty or scattered as exiles over Europe" (Lecky 1972:36); indeed, the social upheaval had been so complete that, without exaggeration, "Irish Ireland had, by the 18th century, become purely a peasant nation" (Corkery 1970:23).

The effects of this change in the society were strikingly evident in the artistic sphere as well. The pre-conquest Irish nobility had supported through extensive patronage a sophisticated and thriving musical culture of poets and musicians. Aristocratic poetry of this sort was composed by the *file* (poet) in syllabic verse according to a system of metres reinforced by a rigid adherence to the bardic tradition. The *reacaire* (reciter) then performed the compositions at public occasions; quite possibly the airs wedded to the poems derived from ecclesiastical chant, since the poetic metres themselves were believed to have been strongly influenced by the Latin hymns of the early Irish church (Breathnach 1971:21). Although a great deal of bardic verse remains, no examples of the music to which it was sung have survived.

The chief instrument in use among Irish aristocratic circles since before pre-Christian times had been the **harp** (Ross 1970:102-104). The 17th century witnessed several changes in the instrument's construction, and still more evolution occurred in the 18th century (Rimmer 1969:2).

Very little of the music played by the Irish harpers before 1700 has been retained either in manuscripts or aural tradition, as the disintegration of the aristocratic order that made possible the development and practice of the harping tradition resulted in a wholesale change in the dynamics of musical supply and demand. The new nobility of English and Scots planters and the emerging urban middle classes of 18th-century Ireland possessed a radically different set of musical tastes, and those harpers who survived the fierce persecutions of the 16th and 17th centuries (c.f. Flood 1905) either adjusted accordingly to the new fashions or vanished altogether.

The picture of harping in 18th-century Ireland given by contemporary sources is that of the mere vestiges of a once-renowned instrumental tradition, a shell without foundation, essence, vitality, or *raison d'etre*.

The memoirs of harper Arthur O'Neill (Fox 1911:141-200), who lived from 1734 to 1818, vividly recount the lives and times of many of his 18th-century comrades, and Walker (1786), Bunting (1796, 1809, 1840) and O'Sullivan (1952, 1958) have also supplied documentation concerning this epoch. Scots, English and continental European influences became manifest in the harpers' repertoire during the 1700s, as they struggled to please their new patrons.

The harper Turlough O'Carolan (1670-1738) was perhaps the most notable example of an Irish harper who composed airs in conscious emulation of Baroque figures, such as Corelli, Vivaldi and Gemimiani. Bunting's analysis (1796) of the harpers who performed at the Belfast Harp Festival of 1792 revealed that changes in technique and performance style had also occurred throughout the preceding century.

The 18th-century harper, formerly a figure of permanence and importance in the retinue of a Gaelic chieftain or earl, now travelled throughout the country as an itinerant, often blind, lame, or otherwise infirm. While welcome at a number of Ascendancy Big Houses, the harper played more frequently now in the muddy villages of the peasantry. "Already archaic and somewhat anachronistic" in the rapidly-changing world of the burgeoning Industrial Age (Rimmer 1969:66), the tradition disappeared by the early 19th century as the musical sensibilities of the Anglo-Irish upper classes came to be shaped more completely by modern trends in England and on the Continent.

As the aristocratic art of the harpers declined, the poetic metres fostered by the bardic orders also merged with popular, non-elite types of stressed, heavily alliterative metres called *amhrán* (Byrne 1969:29). Like the harping tradition, the bardic poetry "was so closely woven into the fabric of political Gaeldom that without it that society could not continue to exist unless by changing its very essence" (Carney 1967:5) — and vice versa.

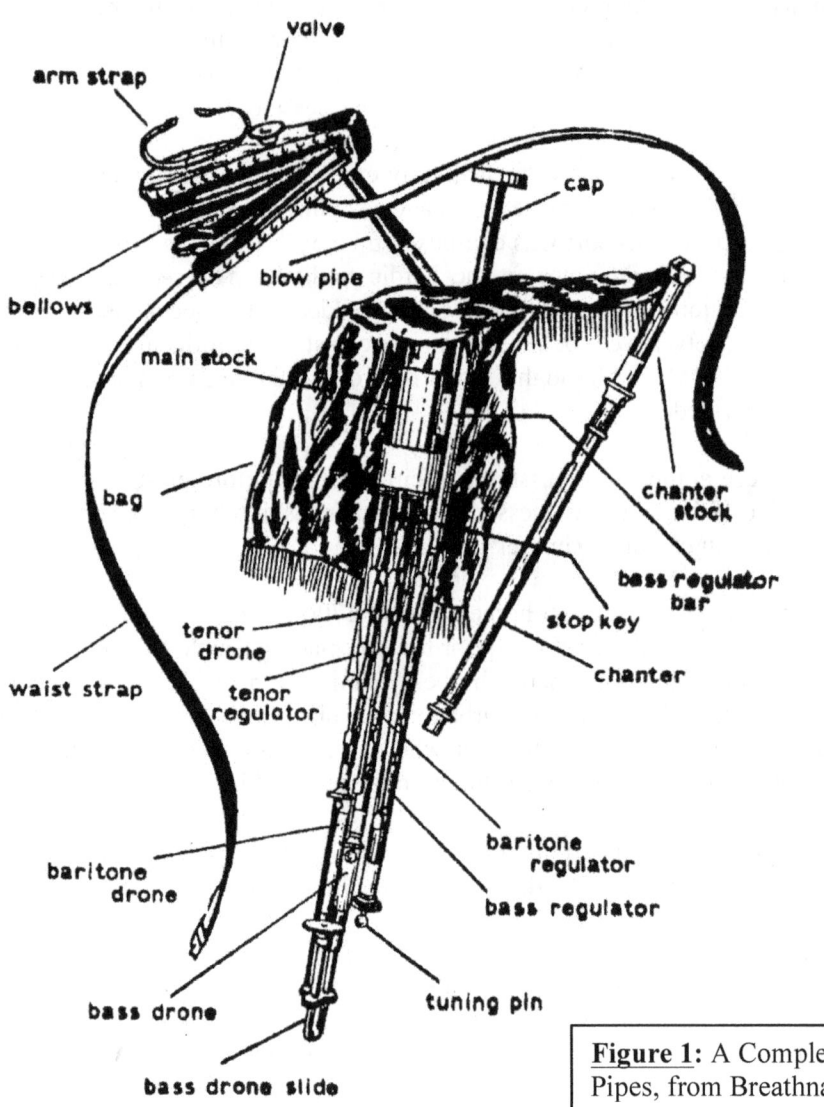

Figure 1: A Complete Set of Uilleann Pipes, from Breathnach 1971:77.

The 18th century saw the emergence into the Irish cultural milieu of poetic and musical traditions that had been beneath the notice of official chroniclers (both native and foreign) of pre-conquest Ireland (Ó Ceallaigh 1963:11-12). "Pipes, fiddles, gleemen, bones-players, and bagpipers; a crowd hideous, noisy, profane — shriekers and shouters" was the contemptuous assessment by an 11th-century Irish poet of aristocratic mien in discussing the common types of non-elite musicians at the great Fair of Carman in Wexford (O'Daly 1969:67).

Yet, it was this popular tradition of music and song that arose to fill the vacuum in Irish national musical life left by the dissolution of the harping and bardic traditions.

A new idiom of dance music was synthesized from diverse native Irish, Scottish and English sources to accompany newly-created solo and ensemble dances inspired by dances of Britain and France. Also emerging at this time were new songs and song structures that reflected the growing influence of the English language and a new set of political and economic realities and priorities in daily life.

The fiddle (violin), uilleann bagpipes and various transverse flutes, fifes and flageolets were the chief representatives of this newly-developing instrumental music tradition. The **fiddle** had been present in Ireland in medieval times in the form of a rebec; by the 18th century, however, the instrument in its present form was in use throughout Ireland and was found highly suitable for the new dance music (Breathnach 1971:84).

The **uilleann pipes** is a bellows-blown instrument that shares several features with the Northumbrian small-pipes and the Lowland Scottish bagpipe. The uilleann pipes evolved during the late 17th century, possibly in conjunction with the Northumbrian and Lowland Scottish varieties; the French musette and Italian surdelina, already in a developed form at the beginning of the 17th century, are other bellows-blown bagpipes that may have served as models. A mouth-blown bagpipe called the *píob mór* was in use among the Irish at a very early period (Fleischmann 1952:1) but fell into disuse sometime late in the 17th century (Breathnach 1971:83).

The uilleann pipes came into prominence at this time and became, along with the fiddle, the staple instrument of the professional Irish folk musician of the 18th and early 19th centuries. A complete set of uilleann bagpipes (see Figure 1) consists of a chanter with a range of two diatonic octaves (often fitted with keys for chromatic notes), three drones and three (sometimes four or five) regulators — pipes with four or five closed keys to provide harmony to the chanter melody. The instrument had achieved its present form by the end of the 18th century.

The **transverse flute**, known as the German flute in the 18th and early 19th centuries in Ireland, was obviously an import during the 1700s and quite possibly reached the Irish country musicians by way of the urban upper classes and wealthy rural landowners. In any case, the flute, along with military **fifes** and simple **flageolets**, was a common instrument in use among amateur musicians in Ireland during the 1700s and 1800s.

Representatives of the free-reed family of instruments began to appear in the idiom of Irish folk music after the middle of the 19th century. These were chiefly the **mouth organ, concertina** and **accordion**.

The latter part of the 19th century is also the period when the practice of harmonic accompaniment is believed to have started gaining favor among Irish folk musicians, first with the **piano** and later with the guitar and other plectrum instruments. The preference for harmonic accompaniment may well have originated in America, where Irish musicians were a staple element of minstrelsy, vaudeville and the musical theater during the 1800s.

Certainly, by the second decade of the 20th century, when Irish musicians were first being issued on 78 rpm records, piano accompaniment appears to have become commonplace, particularly for such formal performances as recording. Though plectrum instruments such as the **guitar**, **tenor banjo** and **mandolin** were being played by Irish musicians in the late 19th century, it is only in the 1960s that they have truly attained prominence in the idiom of Irish folk music.

Irish music is fundamentally a tradition of solo performance in which the melodic line is of paramount importance. Though Irish music is now often performed by more than one instrument and is frequently provided with harmonic and percussive accompaniment, a performance of a tune by a single musician is an entity complete in itself.

The development of organized ensembles of Irish folk musicians seems to have first developed in the late 19th century, possibly as early as the 1860s. Several rural localities had flute-and drum bands used primarily for political rallies (O'Sullivan 1976:5), Ó hEidhin 1977: 25), and it is possible that the urban brass bands which began to make their appearance in the 1840s also had an influence to some degree. By the end of the first decade of the 20th century, the prototype of what were later to be known as céilí bands were being organized in various parts of the country (Linnane 1973:5, MacMathúna 1974:12-13, Landers 1974:21).

These were ensembles designed for performing for large-scale public dance events. By 1940, after the emergence of radio and commercial recording in Ireland, scores of céilí bands had been formed and remained the most common kind of ensemble in Irish traditional music until the 1960s (for information about the development of several céilí bands during the first three decades of the 20th century, c.f. Jeffries 1973, Cotter 1973, Bray 1973, Ó hAllmhuráin 1974a, 1974b, Ryan 1975, Ui Sheathruin 1976, Anonymous 1976, Mills 1976, Ó Murchu 1976).

Céilí bands incorporated a variety of instruments, generally fiddles, accordions (first one- and two-row button accordions, then piano accordions) and flutes, but also included concertinas, saxophones, tinwhistles, piccolos, uilleann pipes and tenor banjos. Drums and piano provided the rhythmic and harmonic foundations, with sometimes a double bass or guitar.

In the 1960s ensembles of Irish folk musicians oriented more toward concert performances than dance halls started to appear with growing frequency. Much more emphasis was placed by these groups on arranging the material in novel ways by orchestrating instruments in combinations previously unknown to the idiom. There was also a greater exploration of the possibilities of harmony, counterpoint, and polyrhythm.

Eclecticism of instrumentation was also a distinctive feature of these new ensembles, with instruments such as the Greek bouzouki (both flat-backed and bowl-shaped types), French hurdy-gurdy, mandola, portative organ, clavinet, harpsichord, synthesizer and oboe coming into use.

The timpán (psaltery), the bodhrán (one-sided frame drum) and the bones were three ancient Irish instruments revived by these ensembles after having been heard rarely or not at all for many years.

- **Instruments in Use among Irish Musicians in Chicago**

Irish folk musicians began coming to the United States in larger numbers after the Great Famine of 1845-1849. The massive social upheaval caused by the Famine hastened the demise of the professional musicians from the Irish countryside. The severe psychological trauma engendered by the "great hunger" proved difficult to assuage. The national psyche of Ireland was afflicted by a stultifying lethargy in regard to cultural pursuits; as the number of musical occasions and the functional value of the musical profession in community life continued to diminish, many musicians who had formerly maintained a livelihood as itinerant or semi-itinerant musicians emigrated to America.

The instruments used by Irish musicians in America have been the same as those used by their counterparts in Ireland. There has been so much close contact between American and Irish players of Irish folk music over the last century that no separate instrumental traditions have developed. Chicago has been typical of other American cities in this respect.

A glance at the photograph taken of the Irish Music Club of Chicago around 1903 (see photo 3, Appendix E) reveals that, of the twenty-six musicians shown, eleven have uilleann pipes resting across their laps, nine are holding fiddles and six are equipped with concert flutes. From all indications this accurately reflects not only the chief types of instruments used by Irish musicians in Chicago during this period but their relative popularity as well. There is likewise every reason to believe that the situation was the same in Ireland at this time, particularly since almost all of the musicians in the Chicago Irish Music Club were Irish emigrants.

O'Neill (1913:478) mentions that "light-fingered pianists" also enlivened the sessions at the Club, although he mentions only one pianist by name. The fact that O'Neill felt compelled to bring out revised editions of his music collections arranged for piano (*O'Neill's Irish Music, 250 Choice Selections for Piano or Violin*, 1908; *O'Neill's Irish Music, 400 Choice Selections for Piano or Violin*, 1915) also suggests that the instrument was being used to play Irish music in Chicago around the turn of the 20th century.

Flageolets and tinwhistles were also present, though they seem to have been so taken for granted as an ephemeral, inconsequential type of instrument that they are but rarely mentioned. They appear to have functioned as a beginner's instrument or as a parlor instrument played for one's own amusement and with no serious intent.

As to the types of flageolets available, the 1902 edition of the Sears, Roebuck and Company Catalogue offered "Nightingale Flageolets" in six keys, and the accompanying illustration shows them to be almost precisely the same as the "Generation" brand of tinwhistles now used by Irish musicians (Sears, Roebuck and Company 1969:212). The possibility also exists that such a simple instrument may have been occasionally home-made.

In a biographical sketch in *Irish Minstrels and Musicians*, O'Neill takes note of a Thomas Kiley who played "'The Connemara Fiddle', as we facetiously termed the mandolin" (1913:394). Although tenor banjo and mandolin ensembles were tremendously popular in the U.S. around the turn of the 20th century, it does not appear that either instrument was in great favor among Chicago's Irish musicians.

Formal stage concerts seem to have been the most likely place to have heard the mandolin, perhaps in duet with a harp. The harp (now a "neo-Irish harp" in a revived and reconstructed form very different from the 18th-century type) and the mandolin in these contexts performed "polite" music, i.e. *Moore's Melodies* and even European classical airs; except in rare instances, such as Thomas Kiley noted above, Irish dance music was not heard often on these instruments in Chicago, as they were still too closely associated with contemporary Euro-American art music.

The **melodeon** was the name by which the one-row accordion was (and still often is) known by Irish folk musicians. It had ten melody buttons and two to four bass buttons on the other side of the instrument. The melody row was arranged diatonically and was limited to just a few keys. Though not often mentioned in sources of the late 19th and early 20th centuries, it was steadily gaining ground and was as common as the fiddle and flute in Chicago's Irish music community by the 1930s. After World War II, the two-row chromatic accordions replaced the one-row models, though a few older players retained the one-row type.

The material musical culture of Irish folk music in Chicago has not changed too drastically since the early 1900s in regard to the type of instruments found, but the proportional representation of the instruments has been altered considerably. The uilleann bagpipes that were the most numerous in the early 1900s are currently very scarce. The accordion, formerly disparaged as an instrument for those not skilled enough to master the pipes, fiddle or flute, is now the most common and, to much of the general public, typifies Irish music.

Although Irish musicians in Chicago are aware of the new instrumentation employed by ensembles in Ireland, there has to date been no frenzied rush on the part of those musicians to obtain bouzoukis, synthesizers, timpáns and the like. If any new instruments come into general use among the Irish music community in Chicago, it is probable that they will first find favor with young American-born players, and that two musical sub-cultures characterized by the use of either standard or more eclectic forms of instrumentation will inevitably result. Currently, no such movement is discernible, as the instrumental traditions of the last half century continue to hold sway.

- **Strings**

The fiddle is the most commonly found string instrument in Chicago and is likely to remain popular due to its pre-eminence as the only string instrument taught in the schools of Irish music in Chicago. Along with the accordion, the fiddle is the chief instrument used to provide accompaniment for step-dancing at competitions and exhibitions.

The fiddle is the only member of the violin family that has taken hold in Irish folk music, though occasionally one may see a classically-trained violist who has added two or three Irish tunes to his or her classical repertoire.

Plectrum instruments are represented by the mandolin, tenor banjo (four strings), banjo-mandolin and guitar. They are enjoying an increase in popularity at present, though they are not as yet a vital, indispensable element of the tradition as is the fiddle. The tenor banjo, mandolin and banjo-mandolin are usually tuned by Irish musicians like a fiddle (GDAE); this renders the fingering positions in the same sequence as on the fiddle, and many fiddlers play one or two plectrum instruments.

The guitar was formerly used almost exclusively as harmonic and rhythmic accompaniment, but some guitarists are beginning now to explore the instrument's capacity for playing the melody of Irish tunes.

The harp in use today, as mentioned in Chapter One, is quite different than the Irish harp of earlier centuries and derives its basic form from the modern pedal harp. Irish harp playing in Chicago is not heard in sessions or even in concerts but only in exhibition contexts where a great deal of the audience is not familiar with Irish folk music. It is not part of the main tradition of Irish traditional dance music but exists on the periphery.

There has been a revival of harp playing in Ireland during the last decade, however, and these harpers have gone to great lengths to recreate the sound, style and repertoire of the 17th- and 18th-century harpers in an effort to reintegrate the harp with the mainstream tradition of Irish folk music and expunge the aura of effeteness and maudlin sentiment that has tainted its image in recent times.

- **Winds**

There are only two active performers of the uilleann pipes in Chicago at present, though there are another half dozen persons under age thirty learning the instrument. The complexity of the instrument's construction and the scarcity of experienced pipe-makers have been major obstacles that have discouraged prospective performers.

The instrument's limited crossover potential for use in other types of music has also worked against its acceptance by more individuals, while instruments like the fiddle, accordion and flute have often been chosen by beginners because of their adaptability to other musical idioms. A revival of interest in the pipes over the last five years has increased the number of young players learning the instrument; as the availability of instruments grows, the uilleann pipes will continue to be heard in Chicago for at least another generation.

Two types of uilleann pipes are found in Chicago. One is the design style associated with pipe-making in Ireland that retains visible links to the 18th century (see photo 9, Appendix E). These pipes are what might be called the "classical" form of the instrument and were small, delicate, light in weight and soft and mellow in tone. They were also very often below concert pitch and were known as "flat" sets. Their keys were like those on the transverse flutes of the 18th century, usually fiddle-shaped or hour-glass touchpieces and flat rectangular coverplates. Keys were mounted by means of the shank being inserted in a slot cut in a small lump of wood left standing on the outside surface. A metal axle pin was driven through the wood and the shank to hold the key in place. The chanter was narrow and conical.

A flat set of uilleann pipes made by Michael Egan, a master mid-19th century maker, is owned by one piper in Chicago, and other examples of the classical Irish pipe-making style as exhibited in the work of Matthew Kiernan, William and Leo Rowsome (Dublin) and Tadhg Crowley and Matthew Kennedy (Cork) — all 20th-century makers — can also be found.

The other type of uilleann pipes played in Chicago is modeled after those made by William and Charles Taylor. Natives of Drogheda, County Louth, they emigrated to Philadelphia in 1873 and turned out perhaps as many as fifty sets of pipes before their deaths in 1892 and 1893.

The Taylor style of pipe-making evolved in direct response to the new performance conditions encountered by Irish pipers who had emigrated to the United States in the 1800s. Taylor sets were larger, heavier, louder, more durable and more extravagantly ornamented than the prevailing style in Ireland.

This was because the Irish piper in America was, until the 20th century, a popular performer in frequent demand among non-Irish audiences as well as Irish ones. Though professional pipers in America were itinerant like their counterparts in Ireland, they enjoyed a higher public image and status and required a more elegant instrument to match their rise in station. The Taylor style of pipe-making was a product of America's Gilded Age, and the tradition once established was continued in Chicago during the early 1900s by James Cahill and James Early. Since 1930, Patrick Hennelly has been the only pipe-maker in Chicago to work in the Taylor tradition.

There is one set made by James Early in the early 1900s that has been discovered recently in Milwaukee. James Cahill was reputed to be a good pipe repairman and chantermaker, but no complete set of his remains. Patrick Hennelly followed the basic Taylor pattern but instituted several innovations of his own inspiration. Taylor sets can be seen in photos 6, 8, 9, 10, 13 and 23 in Appendix E.

Hennelly has experimented persistently in form and design such that every one of his sets is slightly, and sometimes radically, different from its predecessors. His masterpiece was made for James Watson in the early 1950s (see photo 22, Appendix E).

The drones do not come out the end of the stock as usual but receive air from the top of the stock to which they are attached. Instead of having the drones extending horizontally, they are compressed and piled up vertically above the stock, exhibiting what might be termed the "skyscraper principle"; this makes them easier to reach for tuning purposes.

The stock itself is not the traditional round type but is round at the bag-end, merges into an elliptical shape in the center, and finally terminates as a rectangle from which the small and middle regulators emanate.

The two big regulators (identical in pitch) are attached to the front and the back of the stock to conform with the positions of the small and middle regulators. The bag-stock, or wooden cup that is inserted in the bag and holds the stock, is also unique in that it is slanted at an angle of forty degrees downward so that it holds the stock, drones and regulators without putting a strain on the bag.

The chanter's face is flattened instead of being left round as is generally done. This way, the player's fingers lie across the holes more naturally.

The pipes are trimmed exquisitely in nickel silver and bronze, with decorative patterns on the chanter and end ferrules of the regulators. The drones are covered with celluloid, a formica-derivative substance that simulates mother-of-pearl inlay.

The bellows are wedge-shaped instead of following the traditional curved shape, and they are also covered with celluloid to protect the wood. The keywork on the chanter and the regulators follows the basic flat slab style of the Taylors, but Hennelly revised the mounts and made the touchpieces of the chanter keys to resemble both the G# key of the modern Boehm flute and the flat, square shape of his own design. Slight innovations in the bottom hinge of the chanter were also introduced.

All things considered, the pipe-making of Patrick Hennelly represents an important link between the late 19th-century and present-day styles. Hennelly produced about a dozen sets, three of which are known to remain in Chicago (c.f. McCullough 1975). Had there been a sizeable demand for uilleann pipes in the United States during the peak period of Hennelly's pipe-making career, he might have gained a reputation as high as that held by the Taylor brothers.

However, the 1930s, '40s, '50s and early '60s were years in which interest in the uilleann pipes was at its lowest point in America, and Hennelly's work was done largely as a hobby for his own pleasure. There appears to be no one now living in Chicago who will succeed Patrick Hennelly as a resident pipe-maker of that city.

Two types of concert flutes are in use. One is the same Boehm-system metal flute used by orchestras and bands throughout the U.S. But by far the most common type is the wooden flute of 19th-century vintage. These wooden flutes appear in two basic varieties: the pre-Boehm types and those that are influenced by Boehm's innovations.

The pre-Boehm types are conically-bored and have from four to fourteen keys, reflecting the numerous styles and conceptions of flute-making then current. Some are equipped with tuning slides. After Boehm, many makers of wooden flutes adapted portions of his fingering system and key mechanisms; the cylindrical bore was also introduced, and the heads were occasionally made of ivory and silver or fitted with a Boehm lip-piece.

The English firms of Rudall and Rose; Rudall, Rose, and Carte; and Rudall, Carte, and Company were the most prolific makers of these hybrid wooden flutes in the British Isles during the late 1800s, and many of their instruments are still seen in the hands of Irish musicians. German-made wooden flutes of the late 19th and early 20th centuries are also common among Irish musicians, and at least one flute player, Paddy Cronin of Boston, is making his own wooden flutes. Wooden flutes have been difficult to obtain, but in recent years several small firms have started to manufacture new ones for the growing Irish market.

Although the typical wooden flute used by Irish musicians is sometimes criticized as being the less perfect specimen in terms of acoustics, correct intonation, tone color and range, it is still considered by most performers and aficionados of Irish music as representing the ideal kind of flute timbre for Irish music.

The reason typically given is that the wooden flute has a more aesthetically pleasing tone than the metal flute, a more "earthy" quality that is in character with the overall musical tradition. The fact that most wooden flutes employ the same fingering system as the tinwhistle (upon which flute players generally begin learning Irish music) is another point in their favor. Perhaps also the metal instrument is regarded as foreign to the idiom, though this would be by virtue of its appearance and not its pedigree, since the uilleann pipes and bodhrán are the only instruments used by Irish folk musicians that are not found in other musics.

Many parents today start their child on the Boehm flute because of its greater availability and ease of tone-production with the intention that, after having become proficient on the metal flute, the child will he able to switch to a wooden flute and find any problems presented by this type easier to handle.

In music competitions both types of flutes are judged in the same division, though in many instances, adjudicators partial to the wooden flute have expressed their dislike of the metal flute in no uncertain terms. Many older players in Chicago have switched over to the Boehm flute since it is easier to blow than most wooden flutes; as long as wooden flutes are available, however, the Boehm flute will not completely supersede the older type.

Piccolos and fifes were commonly used in marching bands of the late 19th and early 20th centuries, but in Chicago today only one traditional Irish piccolo player is active. Possibly the shrillness of these instruments is a factor working against their acceptance among traditional players, as the major melody instruments used by Irish folk musicians are within the same written range and tend to complement each other in consort.

The tinwhistle is still very popular and is now starting to be thought of as a valuable solo instrument in its own right. As tinwhistle styles have grown more sophisticated and complex during the last few years, the instrument has lost its former stigma as merely a novice's instrument. Most flute players and uilleann pipers still retain the ability to knock out tunes on the tinwhistle, and there are some tinwhistle players who have devoted themselves to the tinwhistle alone in an attempt to develop the previously unexplored expressive capabilities of the instrument.

There are two types of tinwhistles used by Irish musicians. The Clarke brand of tinwhistle, first manufactured in England in 1843, is conically-tapered with the wide end at the top; it is made by folding a single thin metal sheet over on top of itself to form the closure. The six holes in front give a diatonic scale based on the lowest note of the instrument that is obtained when all the holes are covered. A small block of wood set in the mouthpiece forms the fipple.

The Clarke is pitched a whole tone below concert pitch, with the bottom note giving a middle C. The Clarke appears to have originated in a period when it was still common practice for Irish musicians to play below concert pitch. Its breathy, soft flute-like tone is considered by some to represent the most desirable sound for the playing of Irish folk music.

The Generation brand of tinwhistle comes in six sizes, designated by their lowest note: Bb, C, D, Eb, F and G. The key of D whistle is the one most favored by musicians since it is in concert pitch and can be played with other concert-pitch instruments. Generation tinwhistles are cylindrical in shape, six-holed and topped with a plastic mouthpiece that incorporates the fipple, duct and lip. This device gives the Generation type of tinwhistle a tonal brilliance lacking in the Clarke and allows for a much more distinct articulation and a clearer, cleaner sound.

The Generation, like the Clarke, is manufactured in England. Though the Generation is most commonly seen at the present time, the Clarke has not yet totally vanished and is a favorite of older players and, indeed, many younger ones as well.

- **Free Reeds**

The two-row button accordion is the most common member of this instrument class found among Chicago's Irish musicians. Three-row models are also appearing with more frequency, though the piano accordion holds second position as far as numbers. Most of the two-row accordions are manufactured by Paolo Soprani of Italy, though Hohner has recently brought out a model that has taken some of the Irish accordion market.

The B/C type is the standard now, with the inner row of buttons in the key of B major, the outer in the key of C major. Other tunings, such as C/C# and C#/D were formerly popular but began to lose appeal after the Second World War and the emergence of a new button accordion style greatly facilitated by the B/C type of instrument.

The two-row button accordion is often referred to by its exponents as "the Irish accordion" to distinguish it from "the Continental" (three-row) and piano accordions. Three-row and piano accordions have been gaining favor in recent years among Irish accordionists since they are capable of being used to play many other different types of music.

Each type of accordion is judged within its own separate division in music competitions; among accordion players, there is no controversy such as exists between proponents of wooden and metal flutes. Accordion players constitute at least a quarter of Chicago's active Irish musicians, making this instrument type the most numerically popular at present.

Since its introduction into Ireland during the second half of the 19th century, the concertina has always been very strong in County Clare and the border areas of two of Clare's neighboring counties, Limerick and Tipperary. Cork, Kerry and Galway have also provided several concertina players, and there is currently a revival throughout Ireland. The concertina does not seem to have been widespread among Irish musicians in the United States, however; of the thousands of 78 rpm records of Irish-American musicians made from 1900 to 1950, only one was of a concertina player — William J. Mullaly (Columbia 33086).

Although the first concertina invented by Sir Charles Wheatstone in 1844 was octagonal in shape, the modern instrument is hexagonal with keys on both sides of the bellows (Howarth 1971:322-323). The Wheatstone type of concertina is double-action (the same note sounds whether the bellows is pressed or drawn) with three rows of buttons. The more recently developed and more commonly seen type in the hands of Irish musicians is the Anglo-German variety that has three rows but a single-action mechanism (a different note on the press from that sounded on the draw). There is also the German concertina that is single-action with two rows (Ó Duibhir 1972:19). The concertina does not seem to be either gaining or losing popularity among Irish musicians in Chicago. There are currently two players of the instrument, both of whom also play another instrument.

The mouth organ is not now being played publicly by any Irish musician in Chicago. This instrument, like the tinwhistle, traditionally has been considered a beginner instrument, or, at least, not a "serious" musical instrument. However, two record albums made in 1976 that feature Dublin mouth organ virtuoso Eddie Clarke demonstrate the capabilities of the instrument as a vehicle for serious musical expression in the hands of a skillful traditional player. It is possible that the mouth organ, like the tinwhistle, may soon enjoy a period of renewed popularity.

- **Keyboards**

The piano is the only keyboard now used by Irish musicians in Chicago, though a decade ago there were two players of Irish music who used an organ. Generally, an acoustic upright piano is employed, but one pianist who travels frequently to different performance occasions around the city brings along her own portable electric piano. There are no more than four active, accomplished piano players in the Chicago Irish music community at present, though many of the city's school children who were taught music lessons by Irish Catholic nuns often had their first exposure to Irish music via this instrument.

- **Percussion**

The bodhrán is an ancient Irish frame drum from fifteen to twenty-four inches in diameter with a head made of animal skin: goat, horse, deer, ass or greyhound. It is held upright when played and may be struck with the hand or with a stick approximately eight inches long that is knobbed at both ends (Ó Súilleabháin 1974:4). The bodhrán was traditionally used in a ritual context as part of the festivities surrounding the hunting of the wren on St. Stephen's Day.

John B. Keane's 1959 play, *Sive*, used the bodhrán in its incidental music, and the composer Seán Ó Riada added it to his stage and concert works beginning in 1960 during the Abbey Theatre production of Bryan McMahon's play, *Song of the Anvil*. While the bodhrán is still used for St. Stephen's Day activities, it is also found in other performance contexts where dance music is played. The bodhrán is used to accompany any number of melodic instruments.

The modern drum set with snares, bass, cymbals and woodblock came into prominence in Irish music during the 1930s as céilí bands of the period wanted to add a stronger rhythmic drive and greater metrical precision to their sound. Occasionally, drums accompany soloists, duets, trios and quartets, but, during the last decade, they have been replaced in many of these performance contexts by the bodhrán.

There are no more than four accomplished players of full drum sets in the Irish music community of Chicago, and only two are active. The bodhrán has yet to assume the same role in formal performances as is held by the drums, though there are many persons who own a bodhrán and, presumably, play it in private if not in public.

A pair of spoons, either metal or wooden, represent the most easily obtainable of the percussion instruments used in Irish folk music. Spoons are the modern equivalent of bones — formerly made from animal jaw bones but now constructed of ebony, pine, maple, hickory, walnut and other woods. Spoons and bones are used to accompany dance tunes. At times, one finds coins, bottles, pens, ashtrays and other common household, tavern or personal items used to beat time on a hard surface. Pizza boxes and metal trays have also served as bodhráns when the real thing was not available.

The use of percussion instruments in informal performance situations occurs as a response by the player to the rhythm of the dance tune. There is no premeditation; the response is immediate once the urge to beat time along with the tune is felt. Thus, a session of music might contain a great deal of impromptu percussion activity by the audience or players, or it might contain little or none depending upon the mood of the participants and their inclination to add a percussive dimension to the performance.

The uilleann pipes and the bodhrán are the only instruments used by Irish musicians in Chicago that are not mass-manufactured. Patrick Hennelly has been making uilleann pipes in Chicago for the last fifty years, and Tom McMahon has been making bodhráns for the last few years. All other instruments are either bought in Ireland by the musicians or friends and relatives and brought back to Chicago, purchased in local Irish import stores, found in second-hand stores or obtained from normal music retail stores. Other than the uilleann pipes and the bodhrán, there does not seen to have been any tradition of "home-made" instruments among the Irish music community of Chicago during the 20th century.

- **Performance Practice**

Traditional Irish music is essentially a tradition of solo performance. However, performances by more than one musician are common. Musicians may play in duets, trios, quartets, quintets, sextets and so on up to any number of players. When five or more musicians play together in a formal performance context, the ensemble is generally considered to be a "band", though competition rules for the Chicago Fleadh Cheoil state that a band must consist of "at least six and not more than ten" members (Chicago Irish Musicians' Association 1976:4).

Outside of the competitive sphere, however, many bands exist with fewer than six and more than ten musicians. In a photograph taken at a concert of local Chicago musicians in 1965, thirty-four musicians appear onstage playing at once.

Duets and trios are most common in both public and private performance contexts. "Compatible" combinations of instruments that complement each other in timbre are used; fiddle and flute, fiddle and pipes, fiddle and accordion, fiddle and tinwhistle, mandolin and tinwhistle, accordion and banjo, flute and banjo, accordion and flute, piano and fiddle are a few types of duet combinations found in Chicago. A pair of fiddles or two flutes or accordions together are found less often.

The possible instrumentation of trios is similarly varied: flute, accordion, fiddle; fiddle, flute, pipes; accordion, fiddle, banjo; tinwhistle, flute, fiddle; piano, accordion, fiddle. In truth, any mixture of instruments might be seen as a duet or trio, since they are formed on the basis of personal and stylistic affinities between or among the players. In duets and trios, each instrument plays melody.

In public performance, duets and trios are often characterized by a considerable degree of stylistic diversity and spontaneity, the idea being to complement rather than to duplicate each other. Lead and second parts or melodic or harmonic counterpoint are not found, although when two fiddlers are playing, one might play the melody an octave lower or possibly provide an elementary drone accompaniment during part of the tune. Accordion, concertina, and plectrum players will often insert chords for emphasizing particular points of a tune, especially at cadences.

Duets and trios that are professional and perform frequently in public will, of course, take more care to rehearse and arrange their performance. In these contexts, more effort will be made to synchronize versions of a tune so that the performance achieves a note-for-note closeness. Duets and trios that do play a great deal publicly and professionally have of late begun to experiment with counterpoint, harmony and with one or two instruments dropping out temporarily during the course of a tune to attain varied texture and more dramatic effects.

Ensemble performance of Irish music occurs at informal sessions, at céilí dances, at concerts when musicians gather onstage for a few tunes and at the céilí band competition at the Fleadh Cheoil. At a céilí dance or music session, any number and type of instruments may play, and one generally finds fiddles, accordions, flutes and tinwhistles, with possibly a plectrum or two, a piano and maybe a concertina or a bodhrán (spoons are likely to appear at a session but not at a céilí).

Musically-speaking, a céilí is simply an informal session where the tune genres are chosen by the dancers; the individual tunes are for the most part selected by the musicians unless a special tune is required for a particular dance. Except for the piano and percussion instruments, all the instruments play the melody in unison. In the céilí context, the more instruments there are playing is considered to be ideal, and in neither the céilí nor the session is there any effort made to control the number of instruments that participate. Thus, one may find a general distribution of several instrument types in these contexts, or there may be sessions or céilís that have mostly fiddles, flutes, or accordions.

The music at a céilí consists of tunes drawn from the common stock of dance tunes that all Irish musicians in Chicago possess, whereas sessions sometimes feature airs and unusual dance tunes in addition to the regular diet of standard dance music.

A **céilí band** is a more formally organized ensemble than a session group. A piano and a modern drum set are all but mandatory as a supporting rhythm section, though the drums have been falling out of favor recently due to a scarcity of capable drummers in Chicago and to a change in taste among musicians and audiences for bodhrán accompaniment or no percussive accompaniment at all. Fiddles, accordions and flutes are the main melodic instruments in a typical céilí band, though tinwhistles, uilleann pipes and banjos are also used when present. Céilí bands that have opted for more contemporary non-Irish material frequently employ a vocalist and a tenor or alto saxophonist.

The céilí band is essentially a band that plays Irish dance music. It was developed as an ensemble form in the early 20th century in Ireland. The present form of instrumentation and the roles of each instrument were standardized by the 1930s. The efforts of individual musicians in the céilí band are oriented toward the achievement of a musical performance that is rhythmically regular and melodically uniform. There is no attempt at harmony, counterpoint or polyrhythm among the melody instruments. The piano plays the chord progressions with no syncopation, and the drums lay down the regular strong-weak accent patterns required by the meter of the tunes.

By the time the céilí band had become popular in Ireland, Irish folk dances had already fallen out of favor with many Irish-Americans. The assimilation into mainstream Anglo-American entertainment tastes had made Irish dancing old-fashioned among the "lace-curtain" element of the Irish-American community. For this reason, few American céilí bands were ever organized, and fewer still were those that were able to last more than a short while.

Bowen's Irish Orchestra and Pat Roche's Harp and Shamrock Orchestra were two Chicago céilí bands of the 1930s, with Roche's group representing the newer type complete with two accordions, a set of drums and a piano added to fiddle, flute and uilleann pipes. Bowen's Irish Orchestra (two fiddles, two uilleann pipes, one flute) featured instrumentation similar to the first céilí bands of rural Ireland in the early 1900s. The Cooley brothers had a band that played in a number of taverns where dancing was held during the late 1950s and early 1960s, but since then there have been no stable, year-round adult céilí bands in Chicago.

Temporary céilí bands are pulled together about two weeks before each Fleadh Cheoil in the spring and then disbanded as soon as the céilí band competition has ended. Young musicians in Irish music schools are frequently organized by their teachers into "junior" and "minor" céilí bands and play at exhibitions and at competitions.

At Irish Northern Aid benefit concerts, the assemblage of musicians may be dubbed "The Provisional Céilí Band", yet the group is not an organized céilí band but simply an impromptu ensemble of available musicians put together to provide entertainment or "continuity music" for the event. This also occurs at concerts of local musicians in Chicago, where as many musicians as can be mustered are gathered onstage to play a few tunes as part of the program.

The **consort** is a term used by this writer to describe a new type of ensemble that appeared in Irish folk music beginning in the early 1960s. The consort is a new departure within the idiom and differs strikingly from previous ensembles. Since 1970 nearly a dozen consorts have arisen and made public performances in Ireland, tours in Europe, America, Britain and Australia and album recordings that have had a profound impact on the other areas of solo and ensemble performance of Irish folk music.

The consort is professional, tightly organized, meticulously rehearsed, and is created specifically for public performance. The consort is not, like the céilí band, a dance band, despite the fact that a large portion of its repertoire is made up of dance music. A consort performance requires a discerning, attentive audience; consequently, its natural habitat is the concert hall, the coffeehouse, the folk festival stage or the television studio. It is usually not found at dances, weddings or other occasions where the musical performance is of secondary importance to other activities such as dancing, drinking or conversation.

The audience at a consort performance is, unlike the majority of non-performers at a session or a céilí, involved exclusively with the musical performance, and the typical concert-hall behavioral norms of silence and attention throughout the performance are strikingly evident.

The instrumentation of the consort is carefully selected in order to express a certain sound ideal formulated by the organizers. Eclecticism has become a noticeable feature of consorts, and virtually every instrument used in Irish folk music, in addition to imports from other musical idioms, may be heard.

Consort repertoire encompasses several categories of instrumental and vocal music, including dance music and airs (especially those airs from the Gaelic sean-nós tradition), ancient clan marches, descriptive pieces, tunes of the 17th- and 18th-century harpers and folk songs from Scots, English, Anglo-American and Irish sources in both Irish and English. At least one consort has experimented with Breton folk music.

Depending upon the particular emphasis of a consort, dance music may make up from fifty to seventy per-cent of the total repertoire, while airs and songs may account for roughly twenty to thirty per-cent of the total. The effort by consorts to achieve diversity and novelty in repertoire has resulted in the rediscovery of many dance tunes and airs that were either unknown outside a limited geographic area or were seldom played anymore, having dropped out of general circulation. In addition, several airs and harp tunes have been resurrected from manuscript collections dating back to the 18th century in an attempt to bring these older representatives of the tradition to the attention of modern musicians.

The most distinctive feature of a consort is its arrangement and presentation of the musical material. Unlike previous ensembles in the idiom, the melodic instruments do not always confine themselves to playing in unison. The instruments in a consort are carefully orchestrated to blend in a number of different combinations designed to achieve various textural and timbrel effects. Instruments appear, vanish and reappear throughout the course of a tune or a tune medley in an attempt to heighten interest and dramatic impact.

The dichotomous structure of most Irish dance tunes (two eight-bar parts each of which can be subdivided into four-bar and two-bar phrase units) and the symmetrical structure of many songs and airs serve as perfect grounds for creating a musical dialogue in which successive parts or phrase units are alternately stated by various instrumental combinations.

Counterpoint is an essential element of the consort approach to Irish folk music and is created in a number of ways. Sometimes the two parts of a tune are played simultaneously against each other, or perhaps two different versions of the same tune might be played in opposition to each other. Increasingly, consorts are beginning to devise original contrapuntal figures, usually nothing more than short ostinato patterns or simple countermelodies that supplement or embellish the main melody. Occasionally, the counterpoint can become quite elaborate with as many as four separate lines of more or less equal interest present at once.

Simple harmonies produced by the left-hand bass of accordions, the droned open strings of fiddles, banjos, bouzoukis and other strings and the regulators of the uilleann pipes have also become characteristic of the consort approach. A controlled, abbreviated form of improvisation also occurs in some consort arrangements, generally in a context in which some form of counterpoint is also used.

There is often a considerable amount of freedom for individual musicians in a consort. Though the overall form of the consort's performance is highly structured and precisely ordered, there are frequent opportunities within a piece for a soloist to assert his or her individuality. The necessity for melodic uniformity that exists in other ensemble contexts in Irish folk music is less crucial to the consort that has as its major goal the presentation of its individual components in such a way that a sense of variety and virtuosity is continuously maintained. Thus, variation in melody, rhythm, phrasing and articulation is permissible and, in fact, desirable at certain times during a consort performance. Solo passages occur often within consort arrangements, and, especially on recordings, performers will play an entire tune or medley solo.

This change in the presentation and structure of Irish folk music has caused an alteration in the previously defined concepts of certain instrumental roles. Melodic instruments are often used to provide harmonic support, while all instruments (including percussion) can be employed to establish a contrapuntal background to the main melody. This is an inevitable result of the implementation of orchestration techniques to realize the concept of varied presentation, texture, and tone color.

The freedom as to possible contexts in which an instrument can be used has undoubtedly contributed to the development of the consort as an experimental medium that stretches the limits of allowable deviation from the idiom's norms to the utmost. Along with the use of counterpoint, harmony and improvisation, the extension of instrumental roles portends the potential emergence of a separate idiom that would transcend the realm of traditional Irish music while continuing to receive basic inspiration and repertoire from traditional sources.

The consort idea was pioneered in 1960 by the Irish composer Seán Ó Riada (1931-1971) when commissioned to create incidental music for Bryan McMahon's play, *Song of the Anvil*, set to premiere at the Abbey Theatre in Dublin that fall. Ó Riada decided to create a score more closely reflecting the music suggested by the play's rural setting and "conceived the idea of using a group of traditional musicians for this purpose" (Ó Riada 1965:5). A button accordion, two fiddles, a tinwhistle, uilleann pipes, flute and bodhrán made up the original ensemble.

Ó Riada later added himself on harpsichord, brought in another fiddler and began using a vocalist who sang in Irish and English. In addition, one fiddler also played concertina, the piper played the tinwhistle, the flute player played both tinwhistle and concertina, the bodhrán player sometimes switched to bones and the accordionist was capable of handling the bodhrán. Thus, Ó Riada's ensemble (named Ceoltóirí Chualann) had vast musical resources upon which to draw.

Ó Riada disbanded Ceoltóirí Chualann shortly before his death in 1971, but the impact of his experiment had been enormous. It gave rise to an entirely new concept of presenting Irish traditional music in public performance and stimulated intense interest in the music among persons who had previously been uninterested in traditional music in its solo or céilí band manner of performance.

Ó Riada sought to create a synthesis of Irish music with techniques adapted from art music. While he himself never quite achieved this goal, the consorts that have been spawned in the wake of Ceoltóirí Chualann have come very close to developing a new idiom within the larger tradition.

In the process, this has strengthened the tradition by providing new repertoire, new personalities and new methods of realizing heretofore unexplored resources of a rich and diverse folk music tradition.

In America, the consort idea has found approval mostly among young Irish musicians, yet, at the present writing, there is no consort in the United States or Canada that has come close to the Irish consorts in terms of innovativeness, musicianship or stability. No consorts have emerged in Chicago. Economically, such a group is unfeasible at present, and only the younger musicians who are free to practice full time have displayed any real interest in emulating the consort type of musical presentation.

The practical difficulties of finding the right combination of musicians free to devote large amounts of time toward creating a consort sound is one factor that has stymied the development of a permanent or even semi-permanent ensemble such as a consort or a céilí band, and the dismal economic situation for such a group is another relevant factor. Since there are few musical occasions in Chicago that spend much money to hire Irish musicians, there is no monetary incentive to organize a group and keep it together.

Pat Roche's Harp and Shamrock Orchestra of the mid-1930s dissolved fairly quickly after its engagement at the World's Fair and recording sessions in 1934. Pat Roche claims that the musicians all wanted to strike out on their own and make more money for themselves; while this might be true, it is also a fact that after the prestigious World's Fair performances and recording dates with Decca, the band was simply not needed to perform the functions required of Irish folk musicians in the Chicago Irish community of the day.

Then as now, the music for céilís was provided by a number of musicians gathering, informally and performing a selection of tunes chosen on the soot by dancers and musicians. Bar owners wish to hire as much entertainment for as little expense as possible and tend to favor duets and trios for this reason, especially in small establishments such as those that make up the majority of Irish taverns in Chicago. Bands are not needed on radio with the numerous recordings now available, nor are they required for television. Step-dancers at exhibitions and competitions prefer the accompaniment to be played by one musician in a clear and definite manner rather than risk the confusion that often occurs when two or more musicians play different versions of a tune.

Within the next few years, however, were the financial prospects for such ensembles to improve, it is possible that a consort or céilí band of a permanent nature could arise from among Chicago's young Irish musicians, but none is presently in the works.

CHAPTER THREE: Repertoire and Styles

IN THE AREA of repertoire, Irish music in America has remained distinct from other native and imported musical traditions. Anglo-American instrumental music (particularly as found in New England, the Middle Atlantic States and the Appalachian Mountains) is the only tradition with which Irish music has interacted and exchanged repertoire. This exchange appears to have been largely unilateral, with numerous tunes of identifiable Irish origin (primarily reels, jigs and hornpipes) being incorporated into the Anglo-American repertoire, but relatively few Anglo-American tunes being adopted by Irish musicians.

A possible explanation for this is that the nucleus of the Irish repertoire had crystallized by the middle of the 19th century when most of the interaction between the idioms appears to have taken place. The Anglo-American repertoire, on the other hand, was still in a formative stage and relied upon input from other musical traditions similar in structure, instrumentation and tonality.

The phenomenon might also be seen as a demonstration of the strength of the processes by which innovation from outside the tradition is reworked into a form that is in accordance with the tradition's standards. It is possible that the filtering process of Irish music during this period of musical and cultural contact was so powerful that whatever tunes were borrowed from the Anglo-American tradition were refashioned to such an extent that their distinctive Anglo-American features were obliterated and the tunes transformed beyond recognition.

It seems more likely, however, that the music of the rural hills and hollows rarely reached the ears of the Irish musicians of the Bronx, Boston, Philadelphia, Chicago and the other large Irish-American communities of the 19th century. There is also no evidence that if such music was heard it would be appreciated or emulated. Irish music played in America still derives its repertoire from the tradition as performed in Ireland.

The genres of the current repertoire of Irish folk music are given in Figure 2. The two major divisions are dance music and airs. Dance music is subdivided according to the type of dance it accompanies. Most of the dance music currently performed was created in the late 18th and early 19th centuries to accompany the solo dances devised by dancing masters in rural Ireland (Breathnach 1971:61).

Some tunes, such as reels, were borrowed from the 18th-century repertoire of Lowland Scots fiddle player-composers such as Daniel Dow, William Marshall and Niel Gow and his sons. Although the hornpipe, double jig and slip jig have parallels in the dance forms of England and Scotland, most of the music for these dances originated in Ireland, with only a few tunes appropriated from English and Scottish sources.

Irish folk music scholars have frequently maintained that many jigs were adapted from older clan marches, song airs or pre-18th-century dance tunes but, aside from some of the older pieces, it seems more plausible that they were brought into existence simultaneously with the development of the solo jig dance in the late 18th century (Breathnach 1971:60). However, French and Italian antecedents for the jig form have also been postulated and discussed, particularly in view of the Continental influences upon the music of the 18th-century Irish harpers (Townsend 1971, Breathnach 1973)

The **reel** has become the most popular of the dance tune genres, though 18th- and 19th-century collections suggest that the double jig was the favorite tune type of that era. Like the **hornpipe**, the reel is in 4/4 meter, though hornpipes are played with more deliberate emphasis on the strong beats of each measure such that the first and third beats are played as if they were dotted eighth notes; usually they are notated as eighth notes, however.

The **single jig**, like the **double jig**, is in 6/8 time, though it is sometimes notated in 12/8. It differs from the double jig in its rhythmic emphasis and in the steps danced to it. In the province of Munster, particularly in parts of Cork and Kerry, single jig tunes called **slides** have remained very popular and are generally in 12/8 time. The **slip or hop jig** may have once been two separate dances but now refers to one class of tunes in 9/8, the only one of the solo dances performed in triple meter that has survived.

Dance Music

Accompaniment for solo dances:
- reel
- single jig (slide)
- double jig
- hornpipe
- slip jig (hop jig)
- set dance (long dance)

Airs
- slow air
- song air
- harp tune
- march
- piece
- descriptive piece

Accompaniment for ensemble dances:
- set, half-set
- céilí dance: 3-4-8-12-16-hand reel and/or jig
- figure dance (country dance)
- barn dance
- polka
- highland fling
- schottische
- waltz
- mazurka
- quickstep
- varsovienne
- choreographic composition

Figure 2: Tune Genres in the Irish Folk Music Repertoire.

Set dances, also called long dances, were devised by the dancing masters as the ultimate showcase for their terpsichorean skills, and each dance is performed to its own special tune. These tunes are either in 6/8 or 4/4 time (jig or hornpipe rhythm) and have extended second parts twelve or more measures long. The majority of dance tunes consist of two eight-measure sections, though some tunes have three or more parts and may vary in the order and number of times each part is repeated.

The musical accompaniment for ensemble dances has been adapted from the already extant reservoir of dance tunes for solo dances. **Céilí dances**, such as the 3-4-6-8-12-16-hand reels and jigs, are danced to reel and jig tunes that also accompany solo reels and jigs. During the early 19th century, the dancing masters introduced group dances fashioned from the quadrilles then popular in France. Known as "sets" (or "half-sets" if two instead of four couples dance), these dances are in 6/8 and 2/4 time and make use of simple jigs and reels.

Several of these tunes that accompanied the 19th-century sets survive today in the guise of slides and polkas. Figure dances, such as "The Walls of Limerick", "The Bridge of Athlone" and "The Siege of Ennis" (dances that have been absorbed into the repertoire of international folk dancing as representing Irish dances) also annexed tunes in 6/8 and 2/4 time or reworked old pieces into new ones.

Although **barn dances, polkas, schottisches, waltzes, mazurkas, quicksteps, varsoviennes** and **highland flings** were 19th-century emigrants to Ireland from European ballrooms, the music for these dances when performed in Ireland was subjected to the filtering process whereby "foreign" elements were transmuted into a form compatible with the native Irish idiom. Thus, the music for these dances conforms to the eight-bar, two-section structure characteristic of most Irish dance music.

In the last decade at Irish step-dancing competitions in Ireland and North America, a new event called the "teacher's choreography" competition has appeared. The accompanying music is a **choreographic composition** for a specific ensemble dance invented by a teacher and involving from six to sixteen male and female dancers.

Traditional solo dance steps and ensemble dance figures are blended and juxtaposed to form a series of consecutive, interlocking patterns that are intended to embody and communicate some theme, event or concept of Irish or Irish-American culture history, such as "The Meeting of the Waters", "The Gates of Erin", "The Fox Chase", "The Men behind the Wire", "A Nation Once Again", "The Mullingar Races" and so forth.

The musical accompaniment is generally performed by a solo musician and is designed by this musician to fit the meter of each section of the dance composition. Tunes from the existing stock of dance music are used and organized into a medley that parallels the various changes in the course of the dance.

The other major classification, **airs**, encompasses a number of musical forms diverse in type and origin. There has been some dispute among scholars regarding airs. In most instances airs are wedded (or were at one time wedded) to lyrics in Irish and/or English. In some cases, only the airs have survived and have assumed a new identity of their own. To complicate the issue further, many Irish folk songs are often sung to dance tunes, especially double jigs.

Currently, the most frequently played airs derive from the sean-nós tradition of Gaelic singing. These airs are often called **slow airs** because of the slow performance tempo and the rubato method of interpretation in which the basic rhythmic structure of the air is varied according to the demands of the text and the mood and creativity of the singer. Pieces of music designated simply as **song airs** are drawn from Irish-Gaelic, Anglo-Irish and Scottish and English folk song and are used for a variety of purposes: lullabies, humorous, satirical, love, political and drinking songs.

Very little of the **music of the Irish harpers** of pre-conquest Ireland has survived; most of the airs attributed to Irish harpers were composed in the late 17th and early 18th centuries. The harper Turlough O'Carolan (1670-1738) was the most renowned and prolific of these post-conquest harpers; over two hundred of his compositions have come down to the present, largely through printed sources (O'Sullivan 1958).

Scholars have disputed whether or not O'Carolan's compositions can be considered as belonging to the native Irish tradition since many of them were created by O'Carolan's own admission in imitation of Corelli, Vivaldi, Gemimiani and other Italian composers of the Baroque period. O'Carolan's works are also often denied admittance to traditional status on the basis of the non-aural means of transmission through which his music has been perpetuated.

However, the music of O'Carolan and his harping contemporaries is currently enjoying a renaissance in Ireland and also among Irish musicians in America. Today, O'Carolan's music is being learned primarily through aural transmission via recordings.

There are only a few clan **marches** that have survived intact, although scarcely more than half a dozen are commonly known and performed. There are numerous other marches dating back to the 19th and 20th centuries that are usually associated with patriotic, nationalistic "rebel" songs of the Anglo-Irish tradition. These marches have little affinity musically speaking with the old Gaelic clan marches but seem to derive instead from the idiom of modern martial music.

A number of double jigs were played the **"piece way"** in the 19th century; that is, they were played in a slow, highly embellished and elaborated form, sort of a *tour de force* of variation in waltz tempo (Breathnach 1972:22-23). The art of playing tunes the piece way is now practiced only by uilleann pipers and has generally fallen out of favor.

There are also a few **descriptive pieces** of music, such as "The Battle of Aughrim", "The Old Man Rocking the Cradle" and "The Fox Chase", in which the sounds of battles, the rocking of a cradle and a fox hunt are imitated. Unusual sound effects are introduced, and the piece combines various dance tunes and song airs. These are considered virtuoso pieces, and they are not commonly heard except on formal, concert performance occasions.

It is the dance music that has dominated the repertoires of most Irish musicians during this century, despite the fact that Irish music and dance have followed separate paths of development since the 19th century. Surprisingly, the decline of traditional dancing as a community-wide social activity in Ireland did not also entail the demise of the dance music. Instead, the playing of Irish dance music has become an art form in its own right and is generally not performed as accompaniment to dancing. Similarly, the separation of instrumental airs from their lyrics has resulted in the loss of the lyrics rather than the airs.

Irish musicians in Ireland and America favor playing dance music in preference to airs, and, of the dance music, it is the reel that is paramount. Airs are very seldom played, publicly at least; those that are performed represent only a very small portion of the total corpus of airs in the tradition.

Of the dance music, double jigs run a near second to reels; hornpipes place barely ahead of slip jigs, single jigs and set dances. Other dance tune types, such as barn dances, highland flings, schottisches, mazurkas, etc. are rarely played unless dancers are present and request them.

It is not uncommon, in fact, for musicians participating in an informal session to play reel after reel, one tune generating another, in succession for an hour or longer. At some point, however, someone usually realizes what has been happening, and the group will proceed to play a few token jigs or even a hornpipe or two before resuming another onslaught of reels. Sessions are often evaluated and described in terms of the quantity and quality of reels performed.

This situation is in part due to the emergence of the dance music as an autonomous musical system within Irish music. As the performance of dance music became a self-fulfilling, activity for performer and audience both, a re-orientation of evaluative standards regarding the musical performance took place. Aesthetic criteria that formerly granted high status to a musician who excelled in accompanying dancers now yielded to a set of values that emphasized the musician as a musician, i.e. the player's mastery of the musical instrument and a select part of the idiom chosen for public presentation.

The development of technique assumed a new importance as it became the major means of evaluating a performer. The statement of an early 19th-century piper, Ned Gaynor of County Louth, that "my music isn't for the feet or the floor, but for the ear and the heart" (O'Neill 1913:202) aptly expresses this concept.

When the Irish musicians of the 19th century arrived in America, they found audiences who did not dance Irish solo or ensemble dances, and in these kinds of performance contexts the musician as instrumentalist gradually replaced the musician as dance accompanist.

Reel-playing functions as a sort of *rite de passage* among Irish traditional musicians. It is one of the chief criteria by which a musician aspiring to full acceptance within the tradition is judged. Some hornpipes have also become recognized as "show pieces" specially suited for the exhibition of skill, and there are many players who believe that until a musician has learned how to correctly interpret slow airs, complete understanding of the idiom is lacking.

In theory, any genre of Irish instrumental music could be capable of fulfilling this threshold function. It is the reel, however, that has evolved most generally as the focal point of the tradition.

When asked why they prefer playing reels over other types of dance music, Irish musicians invariably make a reply to the effect that a reel offers more of a challenge to one's musicianship by providing increased opportunity for displaying finesse and ingenuity within the structural confines of the tune. It is felt that "more can be done with a reel", and that it is, therefore, better suited to serve as a vehicle for personal interpretation and expression. Again, it is theoretically possible that any dance tune genre could act as a proper ground for the exhibition of musicianship, and a slow air, when interpreted by a knowledgeable and skillful performer, is similarly malleable.

Audience preference may also have been responsible to some extent for the change in repertoire emphasis. Musical occasions, such as concerts, radio and television broadcasts, sessions in private homes or bars, are attended by audiences whose ostensible primary intention is to listen to the musical performance. In those situations where the performance is directed toward creating and sustaining audience interest, the reel has become omnipresent.

In listening to tapes and recordings of Irish musicians performing in a live audience context (or witnessing it oneself), one is struck by the considerable amount of immediate vocal response the first few bars of a "slashing" reel elicit from the listeners as compared to the relative silence that greets the opening strains of an air or other dance tune genres.

Due to recordings, tours of concert groups and frequent communication between musicians in Ireland and America, little substantial difference in repertoire exists. That is, the same tune genres are found, and musicians from America have no trouble finding common ground when meeting with Irish musicians for a session. Local or individual settings and tunes exist, but the common repertoire is large enough that a large body of tunes is always in general circulation and known to the majority of musicians.

- **The Chicago Repertoire**

It is possible to speak of a Chicago repertoire — that is, tunes played commonly in Chicago but not heard much elsewhere. It is more accurate perhaps to state that certain tunes have become associated with certain individuals or groups of musicians in Chicago. This becomes evident when musicians from Chicago meet musicians from other cities in the United States; tunes are played by Chicago musicians that are totally strange to the others, and vice versa.

Until quite recently, musicians in Chicago rarely travelled to other cities. The last great national Irish music convention held by the Irish Musicians' Association of America took place in 1964, and no similar meeting of Irish-American musicians has taken place on a national scale since, except for twenty select musicians from New York, Chicago and Washington chosen to perform at the Smithsonian Institution's Festival of American Folklife in July, 1976. This relative insularity has no doubt contributed to many tunes that are played in Chicago being unknown in other areas of the country.

This state of affairs is not static, however, for new repertoire is constantly being introduced from outside sources into the community of Chicago Irish musicians. The increase in recordings of Irish musicians in Britain, Ireland and America over the last few years has been one major source, and records of ensembles have been especially influential. Particularly among younger musicians, one will notice the tunes from a new album of a consort or a céilí band being learned and performed in the same sequence and grouping as presented on the album, as if new additions to the repertoire were absorbed as blocks rather than as individual items.

The reiteration of medleys is not a new phenomenon, however; the medleys on early 78s were also digested whole by many musicians in the 1920s, '30s and '40s, and many of these medleys still are heard in the same arrangement as they were recorded several decades ago.

Individual musicians who have visited Chicago for short periods or who have lived there are also an important source of repertoire. Fiddlers Paddy Cronin, Ed Reavy and Paddy Killoran, accordionists Joe Cooley and Kevin Keegan and flute player Seamus Cooley are remembered by many in Chicago for the tunes they brought with them in the 1950s on visits or during short residencies, tunes that had up to then not been heard in Chicago.

Céilí bands, such as the Tulla Céilí Band, the Coleman Country Band and the Countryside Céilí Band have also passed through Chicago and left a substantial imprint on the local repertoire. The concerts of Irish music presented by Comhaltas Ceoltóirí Éireann have injected new repertoire through performance and recordings every year since 1972.

In the Chicago Irish music milieu, dance tunes predominate, especially in public performance contexts. As elsewhere, reels are the most common, with double jigs in second place, hornpipes in third and tunes such as single jigs, slip jigs and so forth rarely heard except at dances where requests are made for them by the dancers.

Certain musicians, however, are noted for specializing in genres other than reels. Musicians from Counties Kerry, Cork and Limerick have a large stock of slides and polkas in their repertoires, whereas these tune types are infrequently found in the repertoires of musicians from other parts of Ireland. Other musicians, particularly those from the northwestern and north central parts of Ireland often have an abundance of tune genres such as mazurkas, schottisches, highland flings and barn dances. Although most musicians have one or two tunes in every genre at their command so that they can always fill a request when performing publicly, it is not every musician who specializes in a particular genre other than reels, double jigs or hornpipes.

Musicians who perform frequently for Irish-American dances are well-equipped with waltzes, quicksteps, varsoviennes, highlands flings and tunes used to accompany ensemble dances like "The Stack of Barley", "The Siege of Ennis", "Shoe the Donkey" and "The Keelrow". Musicians who accompany step-dancers at exhibitions must become conversant with the thirty-odd set dances required in the championship competitions and, in addition, concentrate on tunes in other genres that are the special favorites of the dancers.

Not many musicians have a large repertoire of slow airs, and those that do are rarely heard performing them in public. The airs most often played are any of a half dozen that are standard and common: "An Coulin", "Boulevogue", "The Dear Irish Boy", "The Blackbird", "Roisín Dubh", "Sliabh na mBan", "An Raibh Tú Ag An gCarraig?". Some musicians do not play any slow airs from the sean-nós tradition but know a few simple airs to popular Irish songs.

- **Composition of New Tunes**

Chicago Irish musicians have also composed tunes that, while not yet in general circulation, are played by some musicians. It is difficult to ascertain exactly how many musicians compose tunes or how many tunes are newly-composed, since the practice in Irish folk music, unlike that of Scottish folk music, is to not publish new compositions or, in some cases, to play them for anyone except those belonging to a small circle of friends.

Many musicians admit to composing tunes on the spur-of-the-moment in the manner of an improvisation; they generally do not write them down or record them for later perusal or performance. Still other musicians who compose tunes refuse to acknowledge this fact, as they do not wish to be thought of as meddling with the tradition or trying to improve upon it.

Historically, the role of individual composition has been downplayed in Irish folk music and is only now beginning to receive the critical attention it deserves. Individual compositions have not been considered important among Irish folk musicians, quite possibly because there is so great a fund of tunes already in existence. Yet, in creative and talented musicians, it seems that the urge to contribute something of their own to the tradition eventually surfaces, and a new tune is composed.

Perhaps the tune was inspired by another tune that was prominent in the musician's mind as the new tune was developed; indeed, many scholars of Irish folk music have speculated that much of the repertoire came into existence this way — variant spawning variant *ad infinitum*. Or possibly the new tune is truly distinctive and represents a genuinely original entity.

With the exception of *Where the Shannon Rises*, a 1971 collection of seventy-seven dance tunes and one air composed by Cavan-born fiddler Ed Reavy (now a resident of Philadelphia), new compositions by contemporary Irish musicians have not been published and publicly offered for sale since the 18th-century, when editions containing compositions — real and purported — of the harper O'Carolan (Neale 1726, Wright 1728) and Walter "Piper" Jackson (E. Lee 1774) were produced (c.f. Breathnach 1974 for a discussion of the authenticity of Jackson's compositions and O'Sullivan 1958 for a discussion of tunes attributed to but not composed by O'Carolan).

Although Reavy's reputation as a composer had been growing for many years, it was not until the publication of his book that he became duly recognized as a composer of Irish traditional music. It is no exaggeration to impute the sudden rise in compositional activity among Irish-American musicians to the efforts of Ed Reavy in this area (c.f. McCullough 1978 for a more detailed analysis of Reavy's work).

Both young and old musicians compose tunes. Among Chicago musicians under age thirty, fiddler Liz Carroll, pianist/button accordionist Marty Fahey, piano accordionist James Keane, Jr. and tinwhistle player Johnny Harling have composed at least one tune. Flute player Noel Rice, button accordionist Jim Thornton and button accordionist Tom Maguire are musicians in the thirty-to-forty-five age bracket who have composed at least one tune and possibly more. Among senior musicians, fiddler John McGreevy and concertina/button accordionist Terry Teahan are the only publicly acknowledged composers of new tunes.

Terry Teahan has composed, as of December, 1977, thirty tunes that he remembers and can perform. He claims to have composed others but forgot them before he started to recently write them down and/or record them on cassette tape. Ten of the tunes are reels, six are polkas, four are hornpipes, four are double jigs, two are waltzes, two are slides and one is a highland fling.

This is a well-diversified assortment and is indicative of Teahan's breadth of repertoire in general. It might be noted that, despite Terry's renowned reputation as a storehouse of rare slides and polkas from his native County Kerry, reels predominate and constitute one-third of his compositions.

Terry says he starts composing a tune with "one or two notes; if I haven't heard it before, I keep adding." This method of establishing a basic melodic motif and then building upon it appears to be the general method used by Irish traditional musicians in creating new compositions. Depending upon how seriously the composer treats the subject, the tune might be finished in five minutes or perhaps worked on again and refined for another hour or two.

Anything might spark the desire to compose; many musicians state that they begin composing a tune when they are "fooling" or "goofing around", "warming up" or playing melodic progressions on their instrument that are not parts of actual tunes. Ed Reavy, for instance, would be struck by a "mood", and when the mood asserted itself:

> He would practice "exercises" on the fiddle in various tempos and rhythms, using a variety of loosely structured improvisations. He would do this until he hit upon a "good measure" that appealed to him. Then he would "build up" the tune by adding more "suitable parts" to it until the tune was complete. This was done through "pure inspiration" (Moloney 1975:21).

An occasional new composition may find its way into a magazine or onto a record, but the vast majority are circulated orally and briefly among a limited number of musicians. "John McGreevy's Reel", composed by McGreevy, is on his long-playing record on the Philo label; Liz Carroll will feature a couple of her compositions on her two upcoming Shanachie albums; Terry Teahan's tunes have been recorded on his Topic LP; one composition each by Tom Maguire and Jim Thornton have been recorded by Irish fiddler Seán Ryan on an Outlet album.

People and incidents drawn from daily life form a partial inspiration for composition, and this is reflected most strikingly in many of the tune titles. While some tunes, especially a first effort or a composition by a player who does not regularly compose, may be called simply "McGreevy's" or "Seán Ryan's Number Two", composers who have made many tunes inevitably create distinctive names for each one.

Ed Reavy's tunes were named later than when they were actually composed, and this is the case with many other compositions. Reavy's tunes were nostalgic and evocative of past persons and places he had known in Ireland during his youth, and in naming the tunes he chose titles that commemorated these things. A few, such as "Love at the Endings", "Never Was Piping So Gay" and "The Ireland We Knew", expressed a more broadly reflective "mood" (Moloney 1975:23).

Terry Teahan's tunes are unanimously commemorative of his family, friends or current events and feature such titles as "The Day I Spent with Mick", "Dayhill's Fiddle", "The Gannon Boys", "McCullough's Whiskers", "Maida's Mistake", "Chuck's Wedding", "Mickey Chewing Bubble Gum" and so forth. Other than a very vague and subjective connection with the prevailing "mood" at the time of composition, tunes do not musically reflect their titles in any specific way.

To what extent this new upsurge in composition will influence the general repertoire of Chicago's Irish musicians remains to be seen. Publication and widescale distribution in printed or aural form give a definite assist to new compositions.

This renaissance of composers of Irish traditional music in the United States and in Chicago can be viewed as an attempt on the part of these musicians to expand their role as preservers and transmitters of the tradition to include that of active contributors to the future development of the idiom.

By their efforts to define the shape and content of the traditional repertoire, they have sought to demonstrate that it is possible to participate more fully in the growth of a tradition regardless of one's distance from that tradition's original source. Most importantly, they belie the veracity of the belief that a folk music tradition does not create new material; in this instance, it would appear that only a living, thriving tradition has performers creative enough to replenish and stimulate itself with new compositions based upon traditional forms.

- **Style in Traditional Irish Music**

The term **style** as used by Irish musicians denotes the composite form of the distinctive features that identify an individual's musical performance. The elements of style can be translated into four main variables: *ornamentation, variation in melodic and rhythmic patterns, phrasing* and *articulation.*

These variables can be viewed as stylistic universals for this idiom in that their occurrence or non-occurrence characterizes every performance and serves as the basic evaluative standard by which an individual's performance is judged by other musicians.

The styles of Irish traditional music are continually undergoing change and have coalesced from a number of diverse sources. Some styles are representative of a particular locality, region, county or province; others are associated with individual musicians whose playing greatly influenced their contemporaries and left a substantial imprint upon the tradition's subsequent development. Some styles have adopted techniques used in the sean-nós style of Gaelic singing, while a few have borrowed heavily from other instrumental traditions. Still others have been generated by the development of new technology in instrument construction.

The evolution of a style is a cumulative process. A style is a combination of elements absorbed unconsciously or appropriated outright from other styles and then reshaped and refined into a "new" style that is distinct yet never entirely divorced from its predecessors or contemporaries.

This process is not exclusively eclectic, however, for elements derived from the personal creativity of individual musicians frequently forms the basis of a new style. Nevertheless, these innovations are always conceived and channelled within an established, accepted framework such that even the most seemingly idiosyncratic traits will, upon closer inspection, be seen to reflect the shaping influences of stylistic norms found elsewhere in the larger tradition.

Styles fluctuate greatly in popularity among traditional Irish musicians. The aural media of the 20th century have had a profound influence on stylistic development, from the early 78 rpm recordings of Irish and Irish-American performers to current recordings of contemporary musicians.

Since the 1920s numerous recordings have been issued that proved subsequently to be responsible for the stimulation of new styles or the spread of styles formerly restricted to certain areas. Radio and television have also been powerful shaping forces in the growth of styles, as the traditional music programs broadcast by Radió Telefís Éireann have been a major channel by which new and locally restricted styles have been disseminated throughout Ireland.

The role played by organizations involved in the revival of Irish folk music, such as Comhaltas Ceoltóirí Éireann, must also be taken into account, as "official" standards of styles and ideals of proper traditional performance are formulated and dispersed through the various organizational media that include schools of Irish music instruction, printed tutors and the annual All-Ireland competitions in vocal and instrumental music.

Style in Irish music, though guided by certain conventions, is not perceived by traditional musicians as a rigid, static set of rules that must be dogmatically or slavishly followed. It is, instead, a flexible, context-sensitive medium through which an individual's musical expression can be given a form and substance that will invest his performance with the desired communicative values.

- **Irish Music Styles in Chicago: The Past**

Attempting to trace the roots of Irish music styles in Chicago past the turn of the century is difficult clue to the extreme lack of documentation. Francis O'Neill was the only contemporary commentator writing about Irish music in Chicago during the late 19th and early 20th centuries; unfortunately, O'Neill's skills as a musical analyst do not approach his abilities as a biographer and historian.

One might hope to find assistance in the O'Neill music collections, particularly the *Music of Ireland* (1903) and *Waifs and Strays of Gaelic Melody* (1922). These two works give the name of the contributor from each tune was obtained; it might be possible, therefore, that by analyzing the tunes of each informant, some clues as to individual styles could be gleaned.

However, these collections were compiled before reliable recording machines were widely available, and one has only to compare the settings of tunes in O'Neill's collections with versions of the same tunes as played by present-day players to realize that O'Neill was putting down only a bare skeleton of the melody.

There is, in fact, no other sensible way to present a work containing a thousand and more tunes; to put down the tunes as they were played would have been next to impossible at the time, and the task would have perhaps never been completed.

An earlier collector, George Petrie (1789-1866) of Dublin, had discussed his experience with obtaining tunes "from pipers, fiddlers, and such other corrupting and uncertain mediums" (Petrie 1855:xvii-xviii). What distressed Petrie was the propensity his informants had for varying the melody each time they played it.

> For our vocal melodies, even when in the hands of those players whose instruments will permit a true rendering of their peculiar tonalities and features of expression, assume a new and unfixed character, varying with the caprices of each unskilled performer, who, unshackled by any of the restraints imposed upon the singer by the rhythm and metre of the words connected with these airs, thinks only of exhibiting, and gaining applause for his own powers of invention and execution, by the absurd indulgence of barbarous licenses and conventionalities, destructive not only of their simpler and finer song qualities, but often rendering even their essential features undeterminable with any degree of certainty (Petrie 1855:xvi).

Variation of rhythm and melody, however, is the life-force of Irish folk music and is one of the chief criteria for determining a truly competent, knowledgeable performer. Petrie, of course, came to the music as an outsider and was concerned with editing and archiving the music he collected; the problem of accurately notating tunes from Irish musicians who engaged in melodic and rhythmic variation as a matter of habit was still present in O'Neill's era, and the task of the collector was no easier. O'Neill relates this incident concerning John McFadden, a fiddler particularly prone to variations:

> While visiting Sergeant Early during a theatrical engagement in Chicago in 1911, Patsy Tuohey, on the writer's suggestion, tried to learn "Hawks' Hornpipe" from McFadden. Phrase by phrase they progressed, Tuohey submitting patiently to many minor changes according to Mac's fancy, until he thought he had the tune noted correctly. Then he played it, apparently in good style, but not to his preceptor's satisfaction evidently. "Let me show you, Patsy," says Mac, in a kindly tone, and swinging his bow again ran the tune over once or twice. "Why, man alive, that's not how you gave it to me at all! You've changed the tune again; I guess we'll let it go this time," exclaimed Tuohey, as he started to play something else on his pipes (O'Neill 1913: 396).

Thus, when O'Neill began to assemble his collection, he was immediately faced with the problem of dealing with variants. An "Inquest Committee" consisting of several local Irish musicians, Francis O'Neill and his chief aide in the work, Officer James O'Neill, supervised the editorial proceedings that included the reconstruction of tune fragments, the selection of variant settings and the exclusion of those versions that were "least desirable" (O'Neill 1910:55).

The reconstruction process was described in a *Chicago Tribune* article of March 2, 1902:

> A striking example of this [the reconstruction process] is in the air "The Woods of Kilmurry". This was one of the old elusive and ever fugitive airs which Captain O'Neill had tried to call back from the time when, at the spinning wheel, his mother wound up the old song with the words "the flourishing state of Kilmurry". Only the last bars to which these words were sung were remembered sufficiently to recall. Officer O'Neill put these bars on paper and then went to work to write backwards to a logical Irish beginning. This he has done and the Chief [Captain O'Neill] and Inquest Committee are satisfied that the world's judges of Irish music will find it so (Anonymous 1902:53).

This is a far cry from the usual selection process by which Irish music has been winnowed and threshed throughout the centuries. One cannot help but wonder how many other tunes were similarly provided with "logical Irish beginnings", middle parts and endings by O'Neill and his associates.

The same method was practiced upon tunes found in other printed sources, particularly those which had been subjected to the effacement of an arrangement or harmonization intended to please polite, drawing-room tastes. It was frequently declared in these instances that "the music as sung or whistled by Patrolman O'Neill has been pronounced by the Committee as better Irish and better music than were embodied in the print" (O'Neill 1910: 55).

The merits of O'Neill's editing practices are not at issue here. What must be realized is that because of these methods and the absence of sound recordings of the tunes chosen for inclusion in the books, no informed stylistic assessment of the musicians who contributed the tunes is possible. The tune as published in the O'Neill collections may or may not have been an accurate transcription of what was actually played by the informant. For insight into the styles extant in Chicago at the time, the occasional comments of O'Neill about the players themselves are the only available source.

A single grace note   B double grace note   C triple grace note
D quadruple grace note   E short roll   F long roll
G double-cut roll   H long cran   I short cran
J bowed triplet   K legato triplet   L staccato triplet
                                                                                                   M trill

Figure 3: Vocabulary of Embellishments Used by Irish Musicians.

Piper Bernard Delaney of Offaly was described as favoring "the free and rolling style with a liberal sprinkling of graces and trills" (O'Neill 1913:310). The style of Leitrim-born piper James Quinn, one of Chicago's earliest musicians who came to the city in the 1840s, featured the "close staccato of the classic Connacht school of piping, and like most old-time players, he was inordinately addicted to embellishing his tunes with a surprising number of variations" (*ibid*.:224). Jimmy O'Brien of Mayo was another "neat, tasty piper of the Connacht school of close players" (*ibid*. 1910:21).

James Kennedy of Leitrim was a "sweet, expressive fiddler, and, as far as time and tone are concerned, he left nothing to be desired" (*ibid*. 1913:368); "his tones were remarkably even and full", and he "was the smoothest jig and reel-player encountered in Chicago" (*ibid*. 1910: 34). Fiddler Edward Cronin of Tipperary was "adept in his peculiar style of free-hand bowing and slurring" (*ibid*. 1913:394) that "gave marked individuality to his style, which was both airy and graceful" (*ibid*. 1910:45).

Kerry-born fiddler Timothy Dillon was noted for his "plaintive, pleading, haunting tones ... indescribably weird and wailing even in his reveling reels ... notwithstanding the luxuriance of his turns, trills, and triplets we noticed that his finger tips slid slightly, from the stops with much frequency, thereby shading his tones in a most expressive way" (*ibid*. 1913 :395). Chicago-born George West, already an outstanding fiddler at age seventeen, had "facility in graces, trills, and triplets" (*ibid*. 1910:41).

Fiddler John McFadden of Mayo was so noted for his extraordinary variations that it became "a matter of no little difficulty to reduce his playing to musical notation" (*ibid*. 1913:396); "the airy style of his playing, the clear crispness of his tones, and the rhythmic swing of his tunes, left nothing to be desired, yet in the manipulation of his instrument he violated all the laws of professional ethics. His bow hand seemed almost wooden in its stiffness, and the bow itself appeared to be superfluously long, for he seldom used more than half of it" (*ibid*.:395).

Teenager Selena O'Neill was a Chicago native and a student at the Chicago Musical College who had great drive in her fiddling: "She goes at it so wicked — so vicious, that she'd lift you off the floor" (*ibid*.:406).

As for flute players, only two are mentioned with regard to style. Kilkenny-born Father James Fielding was a flute player who "brought out the notes with a round, full tone" (*ibid*.1910:47). Clareman Patrick O'Mahony was also apparently notable for the same quality: "unlike many performers on the flute, whose 'puffing' was so distressing and unpleasant, Big Pat's tones were clear and full" (*ibid*.:19).

Though these descriptions are for the most part too general, there are some grounds for speculation. With regard to piping styles, there was both the "close" staccato style of piping popular in the western province of Connacht as well as the more "open" legato fingering method developed in the eastern counties of Ireland.

It may be surmised from the remarks about McFadden that the use of long bow strokes by fiddlers was prevalent; slides and slurring were also a part of the Irish fiddler's repertoire of expressive devices. Aside from the aesthetically desirable full tone quality produced by good flute players performing with well-made flutes, there is no indication of how flute players ornamented, phrased or articulated the tunes.

Graces, turns, trills and triplets refer to the types of embellishments used and would appear to be the same as those embellishments used today — graces translating as single and double grace notes; turns indicating long, short and possibly double-cut rolls,; trills meaning exactly that; triplets referring to either bowed staccato triplets or triplets fingered legato (see the vocabulary of embellishments below).

Melodic and rhythmic variation seems to have been an important aspect of superior players' performances, though occasionally distracting when several musicians were playing in consort.

What seems certain is that during this period, Irish music in Chicago was marked by a wide diversity of stylistic traits that reflected the variety of provincial, regional and local styles existing concurrently in Ireland. Even as late as the 1940s, the style and repertoire of one parish in rural Ireland might be radically different from that of the neighboring parish a few miles distant.

Despite the phenomena of musicians from different sectional and stylistic backgrounds suddenly coming into close contact in 19th-century American cities, no pan-American style of Irish music emerged. Stylistic sovereignty was maintained, although some styles gained a large number of adherents for short periods of time.

Of the thirty-four Irish-born musicians in Chicago who provided the bulk of music for O'Neill's first two collections (*Music of Ireland*, 1903, and *The Dance Music of Ireland*, 1907), fourteen were from the province of Munster, eight from Connacht, seven from Leinster and five from Ulster (O'Neill 1907:3).

It might be possible to conjecture that, since these were the most prominent musicians of Chicago's Irish music community, their styles might have been influential as well. However, aside from the original counties and provinces of the musicians, there is next to nothing known about how they actually played, or whether or not they abandoned or modified the style of their native area when they came to Chicago.

A similar dearth of information about styles in Ireland at this time compounds the difficulty of making accurate judgments about styles. All that can really be determined is that musicians from the Munster counties of Cork and Kerry and the Connacht counties of Leitrim and Mayo were most numerous during the late 1800s in Chicago and quite possibly exerted a commensurate influence in the area of style.

The emergence of the commercial recording industry occurred during the 1920s, when scores of new companies joined the few established labels that had controlled the business up until then. Along with the "race" and "hillbilly" series, the more diverse labels also maintained a sizeable "Irish" series that featured a variety of Irish-American performers and included several of the finest Irish traditional musicians of the day.

The recordings made during the 1920s and '30s (as well as the few privately-made cylinders made by O'Neill and other Chicago musicians from 1900 to 1940) reveal an interesting assortment of instrumental styles that reflect older styles brought over from Ireland after the mid-19th century, styles subsequently introduced by musicians who arrived in the last great wave of Irish emigration to America in the 1910s and '20s and styles developed in the United States.

As with the recording of other American folk and ethnic musics of the period, the recording of Irish folk music facilitated a wider dissemination and more extensive cross-fertilization of styles and repertoire formerly unknown outside a particular locality or circle of musicians.

Although syncretic processes had already taken place to a limited extent in the repertoire of American Irish musicians, the diffusion of style was a much slower process wholly dependent upon personal interaction among musicians. Recordings rendered this method of style transmission obsolete by providing access to style on a mass, impersonal level that made it no longer necessary to personally know or to have ever heard of the musicians whose styles one wished to copy or incorporate.

This acceleration and extension of the process of style acquisition exerted a profound influence on the future development of the tradition. Despite the fact that many of the styles in circulation among present-day Irish-American musicians are reflections of those currently popular in Ireland, the influence of these early recordings in shaping the norms of modern style in both Ireland and America has been substantial.

Several of the players recorded in the 1920s and '30s are still revered as paragons of excellence against which the efforts of modern musicians are measured, and many of their tunes are played by present-day musicians in the same grouping, order and setting as they were recorded forty and fifty years ago.

Other tunes and tune-settings recorded during this period have since attained the status of "classics" or "standards" in the traditional repertoire and serve as test pieces by which musicians aspiring to notoriety are judged.

- **Irish Music Styles in Chicago: The Present**

The Chicago Irish music community of the 1970s still exhibits strong links in the area of style that extend back to the 1920s and, in some cases, even further beyond. The rise of new styles has not resulted in the abolition of the older ones, and the varied stylistic elements that exist in Chicago today make this local tradition of Irish music a vibrant and colorful entity.

- **Uilleann Pipes**

The premier uilleann piper in Chicago is Joe Shannon. Joe was born in 1919 near Kiltimagh, Mayo, which was then, as in the poet Raftery's time a century before, a district where one could hear Irish music "from the cradle to the grave". All of Joe's seven older brothers played Irish music, and one of his earliest memories is of his cousins and neighbors gathering in the family home for a long night's session with flutes, fiddles, tinwhistles and melodeons.

The first uilleann piper Joe heard was his cousin, Eddie Mullaney, shortly after the Shannons moved to Chicago in 1929. With encouragement from Mullaney and the loan of a practice set from flute player Paddy Doran, Joe took up the instrument while still in grammar school. "I was so small," he said, "I had to stuff books around my waist to keep the pipes from falling off me." Pipe-maker Patrick Hennelly later provided him with a full set, and, in 1934, Joe was invited to play with the céilí band organized by step-dancer Pat Roche for the Chicago World's Fair.

After the band broke up, Joe continued playing at Irish functions throughout the Chicago area until the responsibilities of his job with the city fire department and his growing family forced him to retire from public performance. In 1967, Eddie Mullaney gave Joe his set of pipes that had been made by the Taylors of Philadelphia around 1880 for John Beatty of Chicago. This set was described by Francis O'Neill as the "triumph" of those pipe-makers' genius (O'Neill 1913:281). It was the acquisition of this aurally powerful, visually dazzling, instrument that inspired Joe to take up the pipes with renewed fervor; indeed, he claims that he plays with greater agility and spirit now than at any other time in his life.

Though there were several expert pipers living in Chicago during the 1930s, it was the recordings of Patsy Tuohey and Chicago-born Tom Ennis that served as Joe's early stylistic models. A vaudeville piper named Charlie McNurney had often seen Tuohey play, and he told Joe a great deal about Tuohey's technique. The recordings of Tuohey and Ennis provided the opportunity to study the nuances of these musicians in careful detail. Though Joe feels a strong affinity with Tuohey's piping and can recreate Tuohey's medleys note-for-note and chord-for-chord, he is closest in overall style to Tom Ennis, who was influenced by Tuohey yet preserved his own uniqueness.

Joe has great respect for modern Irish pipers, particularly the late Leo Rowsome (1903-1970), but his piping is distinct from the styles that have been popular in Ireland during the last few decades. Joe represents an extension of what has been termed the "American style" of piping as exhibited in the recordings of Tuohey, Ennis, Michael Carney and Eddie Mullaney.

Frequent staccato triplets are interspersed with single rolls, double-cut rolls, trills, crans and single and double grace notes in a melodic setting rendered with generally legato phrasing. The articulation of jigs is more staccato than is the case with reels or hornpipes.

The first note of a note group (four eighths in a reel or hornpipe, three eighths in a jig) is often emphasized to contribute to the rhythmic drive either by gracing it or by holding it slightly longer than the normal eighth-note duration. The regulators of the pipes are used occasionally to heighten the contrast between sections of the melody, but the main emphasis is on bringing the full range of ornamentation to bear in the performance of the melody. Each tune is approached as if it were a stunning showpiece of epic proportions.

There is evidence that a number of different styles were developed by American uilleann pipers in the 19th century. The only one that has survived intact is the style first brought to large-scale public attention by Patrick J. Tuohey (1865-1923). Starting around 1890, Tuohey became a professional piper and was hailed by his contemporaries as having "no equal anywhere" (O'Neill 1913:313).

He was the third generation of his family to play the uilleann pipes and came to Boston from Loughrea, Galway at the age of three. After the death of his father in 1875, Tuohey began tuition on the pipes with Bartley Murphy of Mayo, one of his father's former pupils. He received "what might be regarded as a post-graduate course" in the finer points of piping from John Egan (c.1840-1897), a native of Dunmore, Galway who had emigrated to New York City (*ibid.*). It has been suggested that Tuohey's renowned expertise on the regulators was derived from Egan (*ibid.*:236); for about a year in the early 1890s, Egan and Tuohey played together throughout the Eastern United States.

William Taylor (c. 1830-1893), the famous Philadelphia uilleann pipe-maker, was also an outstanding performer of the uilleann pipes who may well have influenced Tuohey (O'Neill 1913:160-161). Another influential player was Thomas Kerrigan (1841-1901), a native of Granard, Longford, and, like Tuohey, a child emigrant to America; Kerrigan who owned the first set of pipes made by the Taylors after they came to the U.S (*ibid.*:261).

Eddie Joyce (1861-1897) was a Boston-born piper and a pupil of William Taylor (*ibid.*:263). Joyce was a professional piper like Tuohey and was matched in 1885 in a piping duel against John Murphy (1865-1887), another Boston native and the son of Bartley Murphy, Patrick Tuohey's first instructor. The stake was for five hundred dollars and was promoted by sportsman Richard K. Fox and boxer John L. Sullivan; for some reason, the contest was never held (*ibid.*: 244).

These were a few of the East Coast pipers who were Tuohey's contemporaries and who may well have had an impact on the formulation of his style. By 1901, all except Tuohey had died; unfortunately, their deaths occurred before the advent of wide-scale recording, and their exact relation to Tuohey's piping will never be known.

Tuohey began making cylinders for public sale in the early 1900s (Ennis 1902:37); almost all of these have vanished, with about a dozen now preserved in the archives of the Irish Folk Music Division in Dublin, Ireland, and some cassette copies that have been circulated among avid collectors in the U.S. Tuohey also recorded three sides for Victor Records in 1923 shortly before his death; these commercial sides and the scattered copies of the few cylinders are all that remain of Tuohey's recorded oeuvre.

Tuohey may be regarded as a seminal figure in the development and spread of the American piping style. In attempting to explain the growth of this style, one commentator has hypothesized that the abrupt transplantation of a music of rural, peasant origins to an urban, multi-cultural environment gave impetus to the development of a repertoire and style of performance that "evolved for use on the stage of the variety hall and in vaudeville, and was designed to catch the attention of listeners of any ethnic origin, not relax them in an entertainment lasting for hours" (O'Neill 1973:vii).

To be sure, Tuohey's ability to arouse audiences to a fever pitch of excitement is legendary, and it is highly probable that this dynamic new style of piping appealed to Irish-American audiences as well as audiences of mixed nationality. Tuohey was hired to play for the Donegal Village exhibit at the 1893 Chicago World's Fair where his performance attracted great attention (Ennis 1893:5). Ten years later at the Irish Village section of the Louisiana Purchase Exposition in St. Louis, he again generated tremendous enthusiasm (O'Neill 1913:313); as late as 1913, he was still regularly employed as a stage performer (*ibid.*:315). Clearly, his career as a professional musician had a significant role in the shaping of his style.

Tom Ennis (1889-1931) and Eddie Mullaney (1885-1971) of Chicago were two pipers who grew up during Tuohey's heyday and were very much influenced by him. Neither Ennis nor Mullaney attempted to elaborate or extend the style they inherited, but both did manage to create a modicum of individuality in their performances.

Both played and recorded with fiddle players, and it was this merger of the highly-evolved American piping tradition with the newly-developing American Irish fiddle style fashioned by County Sligo emigrants that marked the transition from the uilleann pipes to the fiddle as the dominating instrumental tradition in American Irish music for the next several decades.

After the deaths of Tuohey in 1923 and Ennis in 1931, the uilleann piping tradition in America entered a decline that has only just begun to be reversed in the 1970s. By the 1950s, uilleann pipes had become the exception rather than the rule at Irish music performance occasions in the United States.

The inclusion of several tracks by Joe Shannon on a Rounder Records anthology of Irish music in Chicago (scheduled for release in 1978) will represent the first recordings by an American uilleann piper since the mid-1930s. American pipers taking up the instrument today have had to turn to Ireland for their sole inspiration, and it is interesting to recognize in the piping of Joe Shannon an earlier style preserved in a complete form. His piping provides a link to the Chicago pipers of the late 19th century, yet his playing maintains that earlier tradition in a vigorous and colorful form.

The example of Joe Shannon's piping shown in Figure 4 illustrates the salient features of the American piping style as expounded by Tuohey and Ennis.

The tune is studded with a profusion of ornaments, including single grace notes (bars 4, 6, 12, 14, 26), double grace notes (bars 2, 9, 10, 19, 27) and triple grace notes (bars 6, 14); short rolls (bars 3, 5, 7, 11, 13, 15, 17, 19, 20, 21, 23, 25, 27, 28, 29, 31) and double-cut rolls (bars 18, 23, 26, 31); legato triplets (bars 6, 14, 19, 27), staccato triplets (bars 4, 8, 12, 16, 20, 24, 28, 32) and crans (bars 1, 8, 9, 16, 24, 32).

Short rolls and crans are used to delineate phrases within each eight-bar section; single, double and triple race notes are used in addition to legato triplets to give drive and fluidity to the melody.

The volume of the chanter is constant and invariable, and, because the air that sounds the pipe chanter is bellows-blown, the articulation and accentuation of notes must be accomplished with the fingers. This is done by alternately employing staccato and legato fingering.

This is precisely the purpose of the staccato triplet figures, crans, grace notes, and rolls that appear in accented positions of the tune. The melody moves in bursts rather than in one steady rhythmic flow, and it is clear that this style of piping is not intended for the feet or the floor but for the ear and the heart.

The use of staccato triplets at the beginning of a measure (bars 4, 8, 12, 16, 20, 24, 28, 32) introduces an element of syncopation, as do the double-cut rolls in measures 13, 23, 26 and 31.

While the overall effect upon the listener is of a highly emphatic rhythmic pulse throughout the tune, the performance with its syncopation and changing accentuation pattern would indeed be a dancer's despair.

- **Fiddle**

Two distinctive, though related, fiddle styles are dominant in Chicago today. One is known as the **Sligo style** and was brought to the United States in the 1910s by fiddlers emigrating from County Sligo. The other style might well be called the **All-Ireland style**, since it is found among fiddle players in every region of Ireland, and, to some extent, was brought to fruition in the competitive arena of Irish fiddle competitions in the 1960s. These styles are represented most clearly in Chicago in the playing of John McGreevy (Sligo style) and Liz Carroll (All-Ireland style).

John McGreevy was born of Irish parents in Chicago in 1919 and did not set foot on Irish soil until 1959. Yet, his reputation as one of the world's most accomplished Irish fiddle players had already preceded him. The occasion of John's first visit to Ireland was the tour of Chicago-born Irish musicians, singers and dancers organized by Frank Thornton as a means of demonstrating the strength of these traditions among the Irish of Chicago.

Figure 4: "The Broken Pledge" (reel) by Joe Shannon, uilleann pipes. Recorded December 19, 1975 by L.E. McCullough and Miles Krassen.

According to Frank Thornton, "Johnny McGreevy played like a house-a-fire. Why, some nights, they'd get him started playing, and they couldn't stop him for hours. People over there couldn't believe he was born in America." That enthusiasm and intensity has always characterized the fiddling of John McGreevy; today, when Irish musicians visit Chicago, John is the one local musician most frequently and eagerly sought for a session.

John grew up at a period when some of the most influential Irish fiddlers of the 20th century were in their crime. He listened avidly to the 78 rpm recordings of Michael Coleman, James Morrison, Paddy Killoran and Paddy Sweeney and successfully mastered the complexities of the demanding Sligo fiddle style. Personal tuition during his late teens from fiddlers James Neary, James Giblin and Tom Fitzmaurice further honed his technical abilities and expanded his repertoire.

Throughout most of John's life, however, opportunities for playing Irish music on a professional level have been virtually non-existent. He recorded a few sides with Pat Roche's Harp and Shamrock Orchestra for Decca and a few sides with Eleanor Neary in 1938, also with Decca. He did not record again commercially until 1974, when he and flute player Seamus Cooley made an album for Philo Records.

During those lean years for Irish music in Chicago, John McGreevy was a stalwart member of a small circle of musicians who kept the tradition alive at the annual feis, an occasional tavern session and, most frequently, in the private homes of other musicians and aficionados. When Irish traditional music came to be discovered by larger audiences in the 1970s, John McGreevy was in the forefront of the revival and has been a well-received performer at several college concerts and folk festivals. He also served as president of the Chicago Irish Musicians' Association during 1974 and 1975, was voted Chicago Irishman of the Year in 1975 and has won first place in the local Fleadh Cheoil numerous times.

The fiddle style McGreevy took up received its genesis in an area of southern County Sligo late in the 19th century. The area bounded by Collooney, Sligo to the north, Boyle, Roscommon to the east, Ballaghadreen, Roscommon to the south and Charlestown, Mayo to the west has produced scores of outstanding flute and fiddle players in this century. In the 1910s and 1920s, several fiddle players from this area emigrated to America and eventually ended up making records for commercial companies.

The Sligo style was well represented on the commercial discs of the 1920s and '30s; the three major Sligo players of the period were Michael Coleman (1891-1945), James Morrison (1890-1947) and Paddy Killoran (1904-1965), who together accounted for over two hundred sides on Columbia, Victor, Decca, Brunswick, New Republic, Gennett, Varsity, Perfect, Montgomery Ward, Vocalion, Okeh and Regal.

There were other important Sligo-style fiddlers in America at this time who were for various reasons rarely recorded or not recorded at all: James "Lad" O'Beirne, Tom Cawley, Paddy Sweeney, Larry Redican, James Neary and James Giblin. The style quickly bred a succeeding generation of noted fiddlers who came to maturity in the 1950s and carried the tradition through to the 1970s, including John Vesey of Philadelphia, Paddy Cronin of Boston, Andy McGann, Paddy Reynolds, Martin Wynne, Joey Flynn, Vincent Harrison and Jackie Roche of New York and John McGreevy of Chicago.

Two sources believed to have served as models for the Sligo fiddle style are (1) the fiddling of Cipín Scanlon and (2) the piping of John O'Gorman, both of them itinerant musicians who traveled throughout the northwestern counties of Sligo, Leitrim, Roscommon and Mayo during the late 1800s.

Scanlon was said to have been an expert in bow control and was also well-versed in Scottish fiddling, having journeyed there several times during his travels. He was known primarily as a teacher and apparently had a significant influence on the generation of Sligo fiddlers who went to America early in the 1900s. The use of the bowed staccato triplet so characteristic of Sligo players like Coleman, Morrison and Killoran may well have originated with Scanlon.

Reporting the observations of a contemporary Sligo correspondent of the early 1900s, Francis O'Neill said of John O'Gorman that "in close fingering and 'peppering' he was an expert" (O'Neill 1913:296). Sligo-born fiddler Martin Wynne of New York also mentioned to this writer O'Gorman's propensity for flavoring his tunes with staccato triplets, i.e. "peppering". This element is still very much present in Sligo-style fiddling; the staccato bowed triplet as shown in the example of John McGreevy's playing on page 56 (bars 7, 9, 13) is a staple device.

Rolls are present in quantity as well, and the bow is used in a varied manner, with long and short strokes interspersed with the staccato triplets. Drones and double-stops are absent, for they would interfere with the development and decoration of the melodic line. As with the example of American-style piping in Figure 4, staccato triplets introduce syncopation (bar 7) as well as demarcate phrasing (bars 9 and 13).

Though it might be expected that the records of Coleman and his contemporaries would have had the greatest effect on younger musicians learning the music rather than on older players already firmly rooted in their stylistic ways, the impact of the recordings by the Sligo fiddlers of the 1920s and '30s on the Irish music community in Ireland and America was extensive and remarkable considering the number and variety of styles that existed at the time.

The large contingent of Sligo fiddlers in the United States at this time and the extraordinary quantity of their recordings can only partially account for this phenomenon. More than either of these factors, the rapid spread of the Sligo style from a small area in northwestern Ireland was due to its utilization and extension of instrumental techniques and stylistic traits that already existed in the idiom of Irish music but had not yet been fully developed by fiddle players. The Sligo style as expounded by Coleman, Morrison and their peers presented a synthesis that was novel yet wholly steeped in the tradition, a synthesis that has served as the basis for subsequent developments in traditional Irish flute, tinwhistle and accordion styles.

Liz Carroll was born in Chicago of Irish parents in 1957. Her grandfather played the fiddle in County Limerick, and her father plays the button accordion; as long as she can remember, there has never been any scarcity of Irish music in the Carroll home. Liz received early tuition from nuns at her grammar school and began playing Irish tunes in her early teens. Much encouragement came at this time from the late Joe Shanley; later, John McGreevy provided her with a large stock of tunes.

In 1973 Liz won second in the All-Ireland 16-18 Fiddle Competition and won first place in the same division the next year. In 1975 she won the coveted All-Ireland Senior Fiddle Competition and also took first place that year in a duet with piano accordionist James Keane, Jr. of Chicago. Liz plays the tinwhistle and button accordion and is a talented step-dancer as well.

Though only twenty-two years old, she is undoubtedly one of the finest Irish fiddlers playing today and has managed to create a style that is distinctive as well as eclectic, mature though highlighted by a strong streak of youthful excitement. She has two records forthcoming on the Shanachie label and will also appear on two anthology albums from Rounder Records.

Liz has absorbed virtually every stylistic influence extant in Irish traditional music today. Though she received a basic orientation to the Sligo style via John McGreevy, she soon became a competent exponent of the newer fiddle styles now emerging among younger fiddle players in Ireland. Clare, Galway, Kerry and Donegal are counties that possess distinctive fiddle styles but which did not receive wide attention via recordings until the last decade.

Regional styles that were formerly restricted in their circulation have in the last decade become much more widely known; while some observers fear this breakdown of regional styles will lead to a bland mixture, such has not been the case thus far. Instead, the sudden infusion of various styles has given Irish fiddling a lift and a multi-faceted character. The rise of new accordion styles and the rise in status of the button and piano accordions in Irish traditional music during the 1950s have also had an impact upon fiddling.

Figure 5: "The Widow's Daughter" (reel) by John McGreevy, fiddle. Recorded December 3, 1975 by Miles Krassen.

The example of Liz Carroll's fiddling shown in Figure 6 is a typical Sligo-style approach in its melodic treatment of the tune. A good deal of the bowing, however, is the single-stroke type that characterizes the Donegal fiddle style. The sliding movement into the note D in bars 22 and 30 and the sustained dotted quarter note E in bar 5 are frequent devices used by Kerry and Clare fiddle players.

Another non-Sligo technique is the way in which the melodic line is syncopated in bars 1, 5 and 13. Normally the measure would begin with the long roll on the E, and a D would be used as the fourth member of the eighth-note group (see Figure 7).

Instead, the measure begins with a D and changes the accentuation pattern that would have existed had the long roll been on the strong beat instead of a weakened position. This is a device often used by young Irish fiddlers, though its point of origin is not known. The influence of the uilleann pipes has also been acknowledged by many young Irish fiddlers, and the staccato triplets used in bars 3, 7, 11, 15, 20 and 28 are examples of typical piping triplets.

Figure 6: "The Green Mountain" (reel) by Liz Carroll, fiddle. Recorded January 24, 1976 by L.E. McCullough and Miles Krassen.

Figure 7: an alternative, non-syncopated rendition of the opening figure in bars 1, 5, and 13 of "The Green Mountain".

- **Flute**

Two styles of flute playing have pre-dominated in Chicago during the last few years. One is a staccato style, while the other is considerably more legato and more ornamented. It is difficult to place regional labels on flute styles, since one style will appear in various places throughout Ireland. It should be mentioned, though, that the staccato style has come to be associated with the area around Counties Sligo, Leitrim and Roscommon, while the legato style has come to be known as characteristic of the East Galway region.

Kevin Henry was born in 1929 in Doocastle, Mayo, very close to the Sligo border. There were four fife-and-drum bands in his townland. These ensembles had arisen in many areas of rural Ireland during the political agitation of the post-Famine years and continued through the 1940s. In times of political unrest they were rallying points for community solidarity and marched at political rallies. In times of more relaxed feeling they were an interesting diversion for the people.

Kevin became interested in the tinwhistle from listening to Paddy Marin, Michael Ryan and Peter Horan when he was a young lad of around seven. He soon took up the flute and was influenced by several flute players who lived around the nearby village of Cloontia. He emigrated to England in 1947 and came to New York City in 1953. During these years he played for Irish dances, and in Duncaster, England, he joined a warpipe band.

Kevin arrived in Chicago in 1956 and immediately became immersed in the Chicago Irish music milieu. He was a steady performer on the dance hall and music bar circuit for a number of years and took up the uilleann pipes in the early 1960s. It was at this time also that Kevin became acquainted with members of Chicago's larger folk music community, as represented by organizations like The Old Town School of Folk Music. "I figured it was time that other people should hear about the music, " says Kevin, and by the mid-1960s Kevin Henry was a frequent performer in Chicago folk music clubs and the University of Chicago Folk Festival. Indeed, he was the first live Irish musician many folk music devotees in Chicago had ever seen, though, currently, Irish music in Chicago is now heard much more frequently outside the Irish community.

The example of Kevin's flute playing in Figure 8 shows his staccato style at its highest intensity. Few embellishments are used — perhaps an occasional single or double grace note and almost never any triplets or rolls. Instead, accent, phrasing, articulation and rhythmic lift are accomplished by staccato tonguing and by using breathing pauses to delineate the phrases of the melody.

Tom Morrison, a flute player from Riverstown, Sligo, who made many 78 rpm records in the 1920s and '30s, was a famous exponent of this style, and it is believed that he was typical of many flute players around the region. John McKenna, a Leitrim flute player from the same period who also recorded numerous 78s in New York City, was similar in style to Morrison.

Today, flute players from the Leitrim-Sligo-Mayo-Roscommon region have become less staccato and much more ornamented, though a clear continuity in phrasing ideas can be observed in flute players of Morrison's and McKenna's day as well as modern flute players like Seamus Tansey, Matt Molloy, Patsy Hanley, Roger Sherlock and Josie McDermott.

The legato style of Irish flute playing is best exemplified in the playing of Seamus Cooley, a native of Peterswell, Galway. Seamus began with the tinwhistle as a young boy and eventually graduated to the flute. Much of Seamus' early repertoire and stylistic ideas came from Jim Fahey of nearby Derrawee, Galway. Seamus would meet Fahey at local fairs and particularly admired Fahey's smooth, lyrical playing.

Figure 8: "The Flowers of Redhill" (reel) by Kevin Henry, flute. Recorded December 10, 1975 by Miles Krassen.

Seamus' brother, accordionist Joe Cooley, was another important influence. The Cooley brothers played together often as duets and in several renowned céilí bands, including the legendary Tulla Céilí Band of the early 1950s. In 1949, at the age of twenty, Seamus emigrated to London, England, and met a number of outstanding Irish musicians including piper Willie Clancy, fiddlers Martin Byrnes, Michael Gorman and Bobby Casey, flute player Roger Sherlock and accordionists Raymond Roland and Eddie Bolger (Krassen 1974).

Seamus arrived in Chicago in 1958 and has been a mainstay of the city's Irish music community ever since. Today, he plays mainly in sessions and at concerts of local musicians. Along with fiddler John McGreevy, he recorded an album for Philo Records in 1974 and has been invited to appear at several folk festivals around the Midwest.

Figure 9 shows an example of Seamus Cooley's legato style. Contrasted with the previous musical example, the phrases are longer, much more ornamentation is present and the legato phrasing and articulation endows the tune with a very different rhythmic pulse than the previous example. Long rolls assist in maintaining the legato movement, and single and double grace notes are used to articulate more precisely when required (bars 2, 4, 6, 8, 12, 14, and 16). It should also be mentioned that both flute players in these examples were using wooden flutes, though the type of flute has no bearing on style.

Figure 9: "Michael Preston's" (reel) by Seamus Cooley, flute. Recorded January, 1974 for Philo Records, Philo 2005.

- **Accordion**

Accordion styles in Irish music have changed most radically during the last few decades. As late as the 1940s, the accordion was entirely derivative in style; accordion players were limited to a diatonic scale and attempted simply to adapt as best as they could to the tunes as played by other instruments. It was not until the introduction into Irish music of the two-row chromatic accordion around 1950 that the accordion began to cast off its subservient role and emerge as a potent stylistic force.

Paddy O'Brien of Tipperary was one of the first B/C button accordion players to record commercially. He made several records for English companies in the early 1950s, and his music had an immediate impact upon Irish accordionists. O'Brien emigrated to New York City in 1954 and spent eight years there before returning to Ireland. His residence in the United States further established the primacy of his style on American accordion players.

Joe Cooley, Sonny Brogan and Bill Harte were three Irish accordion players who were transitional figures between the old style of the single-row accordions and the newer style devised by two-row players. While they played two-row accordions, they attempted to retain as much of the older style's rhythm, articulation and gracing as possible. Today, there are several players of the two-row accordion who have continued the transitional style refined by Cooley, Brogan and Harte, most Irish traditional accordionists (both button or piano accordions) have taken up the Paddy O'Brien-inspired style.

In Chicago both the older and newer accordion styles exist, although there is little evidence that young players are acquiring any but the most modern style. Piano accordion players unanimously have adopted the new style of button accordion playing.

Terry Teahan is Chicago's oldest active Irish musician. Born in 1905 near Castleisland, Kerry, he remembers there being around two dozen fiddle, flute and concertina players in the immediate neighborhood when he was growing up. He recalls only one accordion player living in the district at the time. Irish music and dance were an integral part of the familial and social milieu at the time, with musical performance occurring largely at dances that were held frequently in private homes, dance halls in the nearby towns, or quite often on cement platforms built by a wide spot in the road. Terry took up the concertina at age eight and studied for two years under the legendary Patrick O'Keeffe, a music teacher proficient on fiddle, flute, tinwhistle and concertina.

After he stopped taking lessons from O'Keeffe, Terry did not play music again until nearly thirty years later. Yet, a large part of his current repertoire consists of tunes he acquired during this brief period of early tutelage under O'Keeffe. Terry explains this extraordinary tenacity of memory as resulting from the nature of the physical environment itself: "There was no radio or television or even records to distract you then; when you heard a tune at a dance, there was nothing in the world to knock it out of your head, unless maybe the birds or the wind. Once you had a tune, you had it."

Though he arrived in Chicago in 1928 and frequented the Irish dances held throughout the city, he did not take up playing again until 1942 when he was persuaded to enter an amateur talent contest on the Morris B. Sachs Radio Hour on station WENR. He borrowed a one-row Globe accordion from fellow Kerryman Tim Gehene, played "Miss McLeod's Reel" and was judged the winner hands-down.

By this time his own children had begun step-dancing lessons with Pat Roche, and, to accompany them and keep up their interest, he bought a one-row Baldoni accordion from New York. Within five weeks he was playing regularly for the Sarsfield Limerickmen's Club for five dollars a night, and from 1943 through 1966 he played throughout Chicago for dances, taverns and dancing schools.

Terry has always been a source of primary instruction for many musicians in the Chicago area and is still willing to give advice and assistance to beginners. Unlike many musicians, he has never allowed his interest in acquiring new tunes to stagnate; in addition to constantly discovering unusual tunes in manuscripts and old books, he is a prolific composer of polkas, slides, jigs, reels, hornpipes and highland flings, with thirty tunes to his credit. About three years ago he became actively involved again in Irish musical affairs and is frequently called upon to perform for workshops, concerts and weddings.

Terry Teahan's style is displayed prominently in his rendition of a Kerry slide from his native area (Figure 10). It is a clear example of the old style of one-row accordion playing. It employs a limited amount of ornamentation, primarily double grace notes in this ease (bars 1, 3, 9, 11). These are achieved by the technique known as "splitting the note", where the note to be graced is struck and then followed by the next button higher on the accordion. Syncopation is absent, and the melody and rhythm are very clearly phrased and articulated. The left-hand bass is occasionally used at certain points to accent a part of the melody that the player feels should be emphasized. The actual chord produced by the bass buttons is irrelevant, since the primary function of the left-hand bass is rhythmic and not harmonic. Usually, the tonic chord is used, with the fourth or fifth occurring now and then. Some older style one-row accordionists do not use the bass button at all.

The newer style of button accordion playing is exhibited by Jimmy Thornton of Chicago. He was born in 1945 in Oak Park, Illinois, a western suburb of Chicago. He was introduced to Irish music through his father, flute player Frank Thornton, and Jimmy and his two brothers played in his father's flute band as youngsters. There were very few other young Chicagoans interested in Irish music during the 1950s, and Jimmy found himself dropping away from the music while obtaining B.S. and M.S. degrees in mathematics at Loyola, DePaul and Northeastern universities. It was not until 1969 that he took up Irish music again in earnest, this time on the two-row button accordion. It was accordionist John Lavelle, a native of Chicago now living in San Diego, who provided the basic instruction, and Jimmy quickly achieved a proficiency that enabled him to win several medals at Fleadhanna Cheoil in the United States and Ireland. He still retains a high degree of competency on the flute and is much in demand as a performer as numerous Irish music occasions in Chicago.

Figure 10: "Katie Scollard's" (slide) by Terry Teahan, accordion. Recorded June 3, 1976 by L.E. McCullough.

Figure 11 illustrates Jimmy Thornton's accordion style. An immediately noticeable point of contrast with the previous example is the number of triplets Thornton uses. These triplets are created simply by inserting a passing tone between two notes a third apart, i.e. putting a G between an F# and an A, inserting an E between a D and an F# or slipping in an A between a G and a B (bars 4, 6, 11).

Figure 11: "The Green Fields of Kerry" (jig) by Jimmy Thornton, accordion. Recorded June 2, 1976 by L.E. McCullough.

Figure 11, cont.

The use of these triplets is a hallmark of the new accordion style pioneered in the 1950s by Paddy O'Brien. With the addition of a second row of buttons to the accordion, the inner row functioned as the main row, and the outer row was used as a source of embellishments. Using the instrument in this way, triplets are very easily achieved, and the entire rhythmic movement of the melodic line can be made much more legato.

An occasional double grace note (bars 17, 20, 25 28) is used, and this is achieved in a slightly different manner than when a one-row accordion is used, since the two-row player has the outer row at his or her command. Single grace notes (bar 23) are also much easier to obtain with the two-row instrument. Rolls on the fiddle can be simulated by a two-row accordion player, although there are none in this example.

Bars 1, 9, 20 and 28 reveal another interesting embellishment developed by two-row button accordionists. The three eighth-note triplets are reorganized into a group of two eighth notes and two sixteenth notes. This particular rhythmic configuration does not occur on other instruments used in Irish music. Sometimes the two sixteenths occur in place of the second eighth note, as in the first measure, or they may be found in the position of the third eighth note, as in bar 20. Again, this is related to the technique of "splitting the note" as used by one-row accordionists, but the options allowed by the second row vastly increases the ornamentation possibilities for the two-row button accordionist.

Two-row players influenced by the new style of accordion playing are generally more concerned with the left-hand bass. A constant bass accompaniment is kept up; syncopation is not generally employed except by the most accomplished and adventuresome players. Again, while correct harmonic progressions are of secondary importance to the rhythmic function of the bass accompaniment, new-style accordionists usually are more concerned with playing chords that are more or less harmonically correct in terms of the melody.

Paddy O'Brien once stated in an interview that he tried to achieve the same variations on the accordion as could be played on the fiddle (Finian 1970:10). While O'Brien and the early new-style accordionists may have received inspiration from fiddle players, there is evidence that fiddle players are now listening quite closely to the performances of accordionists. In two short decades, the accordion has risen to a status equivalent to the uilleann pipes, fiddle and flute.

- **Other Instrumental Styles**

The instrumental styles discussed in the preceding pages have constituted the most influential styles in the Chicago Irish music community over the course of the last several decades. Other instruments played by Irish musicians in Chicago are patterned after the prevailing styles on uilleann pipes, fiddle, flute and accordion.

Tinwhistle players derive stylistic inspiration from pipers and flute players; concertina players often follow accordion players closely; plectrum players tune their instruments like the fiddle and use that instrument as a stylistic model. It is possible that other instruments besides the pipes, fiddle, flute and accordion might some day become more prominent and take a more decisive role in shaping style.

With the exception of the uilleann pipes, each of the current instrumental styles now in favor in Chicago have been created in Ireland and then disseminated in the United States. Local styles peculiar to Chicago do not exist, as the tradition has retained such close links with Ireland that new styles native to Chicago have not developed during the 20th century. This might possibly change, as new styles could emerge from the young players now arising in Chicago.

Styles in Irish music do not arise in a vacuum, however. A flourishing community of musicians is a necessary prerequisite for the development of a style; otherwise, outside models will be sought and imitated

CHAPTER FOUR: Song Repertoire and Vocal Styles

SINCE CHICAGO IS a huge cosmopolitan city with a vast diversity of ethnic groups and thriving emigrant cultures, it is somewhat surprising to realize that there is still a large amount of cultural leavening that takes place. Those aspects of foreign traditions that are adaptable to public performance or exhibition in the American urban environment tend to flourish, though admittedly undergoing some degree of change through culture contact.

There are some art forms, however, that retreat within an ever-shrinking, non-public milieu, shunning (and often shunned by) outsiders and gradually becoming inaccessible to many members of the emigrant group itself.

This is the situation in which Irish folk song in the Irish language finds itself in Chicago. The city is the home of several fine singers in the Irish language, yet only rarely have these singers had the opportunity to perform outside their own circles of Irish-speaking friends and relatives. Performed almost exclusively at private gatherings, the *sean-nós* tradition of Irish folk song is an art form that has not proven suitable for the tavern, the dance hall or other public venues where instrumental music has found an appropriate niche. Indeed, many of these singers are unknown as performers except to a few friends and relations who might hear them in their homes.

Irish folk song in English is more frequently heard, yet even so, it is thin on the ground. The type of song most often heard belongs to a song tradition that derives from the Irish folk song idiom, the "stage-Irish" song tradition that evolved during the 19th century in English, Irish and American music halls and vaudeville troupes. There has been a good deal of interchange between the stage song idiom and the folk tradition over the years with the result that songs found in the folk tradition are occasionally traceable to known stage composers. Thus, the folk tradition provided the inspiration for the stage tradition, yet was itself influenced by stage creations later absorbed into the folk tradition.

Defining the two idioms, folk and stage, presents special difficulties because the stage idiom developed originally as a mimicry or parody of the folk tradition. Stage-Irish songs embodied many of the characteristics of folk songs and dealt with similar themes and subjects. While it might appear at first glance that stage-Irish songs are either comical or mawkishly sentimental, it is also quite true to state that the folk tradition has its share of comical songs as well as songs filled with pathos.

Both traditions use the theme of emigration and the emigrant's nostalgia for Ireland, and songs concerning relations between lovers are also found in both idioms. There are considerably more songs in the folk tradition that relate to historical events of the past and present; in these instances, the song is not created for entertainment purposes but for educational or partisan political purposes.

The Irish folk song tradition has always been eclectic with regard to songs in the English language. Some of the oldest English and Scottish ballads have been recovered from singers in Ireland; in some cases, these songs are no longer sung in their countries of origin (Corcoran 1969: 59).

Broadsides published by English and Irish urban printers in the 18th and 19th centuries were adapted into the Irish rural song tradition, and the songbooks of Irish songs published by American companies in the middle and late 19th-centuries also found their way back to Ireland and into the repertoires of many Irish folk singers.

This eclecticism has not occurred in Irish-language songs, as the language barrier has proven effective against outside influences. The isolation, both geographical and cultural, that often separates speakers of English and Irish in Ireland undoubtedly contributed to the relative "purity" of the Irish-language song tradition.

Ultimately, it is performance style that is the most crucial distinction between the folk and the stage idioms. Repertoire is the most elastic criterion, since a successful performer of folk songs, when faced with new audiences in a new performance context, will inevitably make alterations in his or her repertoire to satisfy the demands of listeners. Yet the performance style will continue to be maintained as long as the performer wishes to be identified as a folk performer.

Ornamentation, tone-quality, dynamics and melodic and rhythmic variation are the important variables in assessing the traditional style of Irish folk song performance in both English and Irish. (Bodley 1972:44-53). Ornamentation may be in the form of a single grace note before a main melody note, but it may also constitute a portion of the melodic line itself (*ibid.*:51).

The tone-quality of traditional Irish singing is markedly different from the trained or stage singer. Vibrato is absent. Female voices are "light, flexible, and agile" (*ibid.*:46), and male voices try to achieve a tone-quality similar to that of the female; even male voices in the lower ranges do not strive for the resonance characteristic of trained voices.

Dynamic variation does not occur; as with instrumental music, it is not an important affective or expressive device (*ibid.*:47). Variation in melody and rhythm is dictated by the ability and creativity of the singer as well as the words of the song. With most singers variations occur to fit the changes in text from verse to verse (*ibid.*:50-51).

Two examples of Irish folk song from Chicago singers will illustrate the traits mentioned above. Figure 12 is a song in English entitled "The Rocks of Bawn" sung by James Keane, Sr. Keane was born in the Gaelic-speaking area of Connemara in western Galway in 1935 but moved to the transplanted Gaeltacht community in County Meath at age two.

Figure 12: "The Rocks of Bawn" by James Keane, Sr., vocal. Recorded January 28, 1976 by L.E. McCullough and Miles Krassen.

This settlement was an attempt by the Irish government to assist Irish-speaking farmers in the West of Ireland to maintain the language and its associated cultural traditions by giving them more economically-viable acreage than existed in Connemara. The community in County Meath was a microcosm of the larger Gaelic community in the West, and the song tradition in Irish continued unabated.

Most of James Keane's repertoire dates from his youth in Meath, though it was undoubtedly enlarged when he met singers from other parts of Ireland upon his emigration to England in the early 1950s. James arrived in Chicago in 1958 and has since become a well-known exponent of Irish folk song in the local community. Still, he has retained his original style and has not sacrificed an iota of tradition to achieve his popularity as a performer. In 1975 he was runner-up in the All-Ireland Senior Men's Irish Singing Competition in Buncrana, Donegal, and has consistently won first prizes in both English and Irish Men's Singing at the Fleadhanna Cheoil in Chicago over the years.

The example of James Keane's singing is notated by text phrases rather than by bars and has not been put in strict meter because of the rubato style of performance. Even when performing songs that are quite clearly in a meter like 6/8, 9/8 or 4/4, Irish folk singers will often employ extensive rubato. Triplets and grace notes ornamenting a sustained note are the embellishments used.

Figure 13 is an example of a song in Irish, "An Sceilpín Draighneach", as sung by Mary Cooley of Chicago. Mary was born in Lettermore, Galway in 1932, in the heart of Connemara. She was a monoglot Irish speaker until she came to Pittsburgh, Pennsylvania in 1957 to work as a maid for a Squirrel Hill family. She moved to Chicago in 1959 and married flute player Seamus Cooley. She did not start singing publicly until the early 1970s and was somewhat surprised at the acclaim that greeted her performances. She is now a frequent performer at local Irish functions in Chicago and won the All-Ireland Senior Women's Singing competition in Ennis, Clare in 1977.

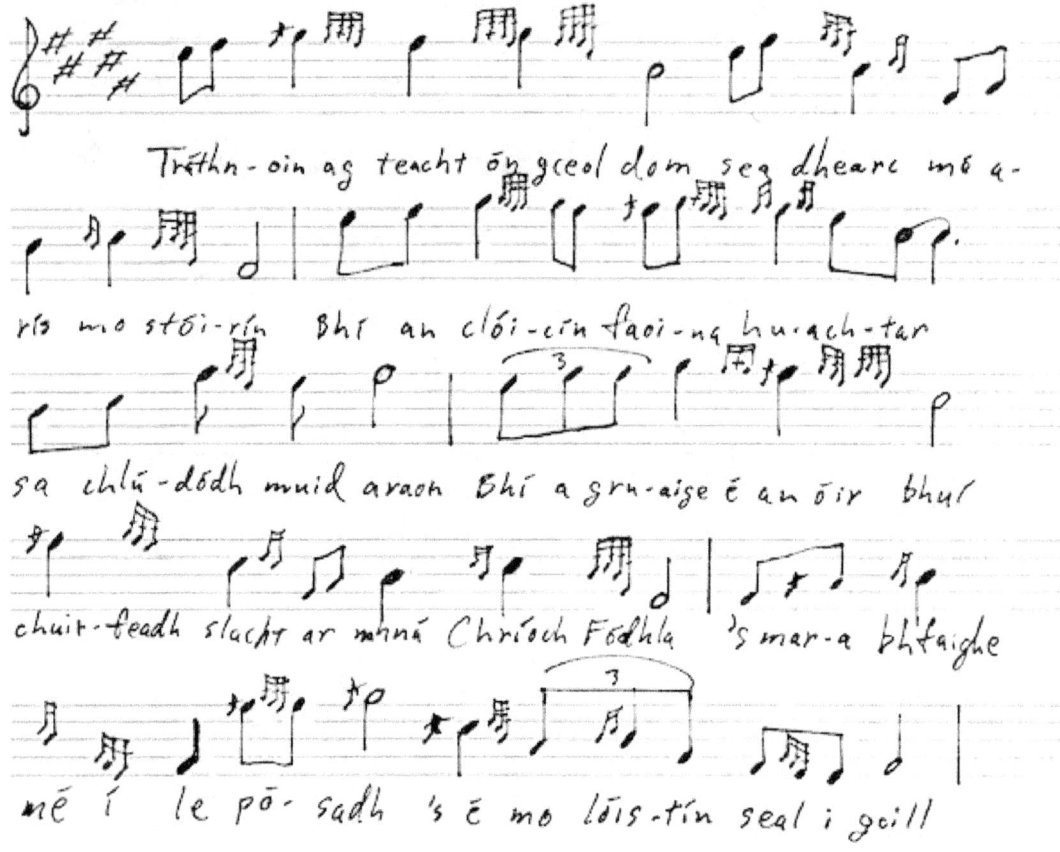

Figure 13: "An Sceilpín Draighneach" by Mary Cooley, vocal. Recorded December 14, 1975 by Miles Krassen.

translation:

One evening coming from a music session then I saw my love again.
Her cloak was under her bosom and would cover us both.
Her hair the color of yellow gold would put adornment on the women of Ireland.
And if I don't get her to marry me, then my lodging will be in the graveyard for a while.

In 1903 there were ten to fifteen thousand Irish speakers in Chicago (Buck 1903:109). The author of a book on foreign languages of Chicago noted that "immigration is especially strong from those counties in which Irish is most spoken" (*ibid.*). Currently, native Irish speakers in the Chicago metropolitan area make up six per-cent of the locality's Irish population, or roughly 5,600 people (City of Chicago 1976b:8).

No singers of Irish folk song are mentioned in Francis O'Neill's works, and the vocalists who performed at public concerts of Irish music (see Chapter One) seem to have been conscious of themselves as trained singers, i.e. sopranos, contraltos, tenors, baritones, basses. Possibly traditional Irish song was so commonplace as to not merit special mention. Very likely, the position of Irish folk song in Chicago during the 19th and early 20th centuries was similar to the position it now occupies, with singers performing at informal occasions in private homes and taverns, or at weddings, wakes and christenings.

There has been a strong effort on the part of the Irish music clubs in Chicago to foster a greater interest in Irish folk song by encouraging performers to come forth at céilís and sessions. Concerts put on by the music clubs have begun to include more singers, and a special emphasis is placed on songs in Irish. The Chicago Gaelic Society attempts to get its pupils involved in singing in Irish. Maureen Creighan, a singer from Carraroe, Galway, has organized a group of four or five singers. The group, called the Shamrock Gaels, performs at concerts and miscellaneous Irish organizational events around Chicago.

With the exception of James Keane, Sr., Mary Cooley, Maureen Creighan, Maida Sugrue, Nora McDonough and a handful of others, Irish folk singers in Chicago do not perform publicly. They do not perform publicly perhaps because of shyness, or perhaps because there is no performance environment genuinely conducive to unaccompanied traditional singing. There is evidence that there are singers of Irish folk songs in Chicago who possess very rare and interesting songs and unusual versions of standard songs, both in Irish and in English. Unfortunately, the social climate is not right for these singers to make public appearances.

All of the singers of Irish folk songs in Chicago are over forty years of age and are emigrants from Ireland. Young American-born persons do not seem inclined to seriously take up the art. Although a group such as the Shamrock Gaels may succeed in encouraging young people to become interested in Irish folk song, singing is not as easy to orchestrate and administer on a group basis as is the performance of instrumental music or step-dancing.

The Irish folk song tradition, in both Irish and English, has always been a tradition of solo performance; a glance at the transcriptions of Figures 12 and 13 will readily indicate the difficulty of organizing Irish folk song into ensemble performance. Even more than Irish instrumental music, Irish folk song is thoroughly an art form oriented toward the individual performer, and this may be the most significant factor that has colored its American experience.

Irish folk song is also an art form that developed in small, private performance contexts where the function of the song was very definitely to communicate a story, a message, a worldview expressed by events drawn from daily life. In American cities like Chicago, the function of song has become increasingly oriented toward entertaining rather than informing the audience. The current scarcity of Irish folk song in Chicago suggests that the Irish community's entertainment tastes have changed radically over the last century.

The Irish folk songs heard in Chicago today are the standard ones. Love songs, songs of emigration and songs dealing with political events in Irish history comprise the subject matter. *Macaronic songs* (songs with Irish and English lines interspersed) are not heard, and there is no likelihood that a new influx of songs will occur unless a renowned singer emigrates from Ireland.

Thus, while the performance style of Irish folk song has been successfully transplanted to American cities like Chicago, the tradition as a living, thriving entity has suffered tremendous diminution. Songs in Irish have had the greater difficulty in achieving a secure position, particularly since the Irish language has not been transmitted from Irish-speaking emigrants to their American-born children with any high degree of success. Thus, despite the current revival of interest in Irish instrumental music in Chicago, the idiom of Irish folk song will remain in the shadows as a tradition appreciated by and accessible to a small minority.

CHAPTER FIVE: Performance Occasions

CHAPTER ONE mentioned a number of musical occasions at which Irish folk music has been featured in Chicago over the last century, and this chapter examines them in detail. The performance occasions discussed here are those where Irish folk music is found in Chicago in 1978. Ten types of occasions are distinguished according to three interrelated criteria, with each type representing a certain kind of performance domain. The context of the occasion, the role of the performer and the primary orientation or purpose of the performance itself are factors that distinguish one domain from another.

For instance, the **domain of dance classes** consists of a number of individual occasions that all feature musicians performing for dancers who are receiving instruction in dance; the primary orientation of the musical performance is to provide a service, that of musical accompaniment, for persons involved in a learning situation.

The **domain of dance competitions**, however, is made up of occasions that feature musicians performing for dancers involved not in a learning situation but a competitive one; the context is different, as is the orientation of the performance, but the basic role of the musicians in providing dance accompaniment is the same. These, then, are two different but closely related domains of musical activity.

The **concert domain** is a set of musical occasions in which the musician orients his or her performance toward an audience whose primary motivation (nominally, at least) is to listen to a prepared, formal musical presentation. The **domain of commercial entertainment**, however, consists of occasions in which the musical performance is secondary to other activities. The performer is oriented toward providing a set performance routine for the entertainment of an audience that is there for reasons other than simply hearing music.

Within the **domain of commercial entertainment**, Irish music may be found in several diverse contexts related by virtue of their use of musical performance. The performance of an Irish musician in a bar is similar in purpose to Irish musicians playing at a suburban shopping mall during St. Patrick's Week; in both instances the musical performance is secondary to other activities — drinking, dart-playing, billiard-playing in the bar and shopping, sight-seeing, participating in raffles for trips to Ireland in the shopping mall context.

By contrast, a musician may be hired to provide entertainment for private parties by families, friends or neighbors. Here, the performance takes place in a **non-commercial domain** where the entertainment of the hosts and guests is the chief reason for hiring the musician; the profit motive and the related pressures it brings to bear on performances in commercial contexts are absent.

A **session** is a domain of musical occasions that often shares the same environment as other occasions belonging to different domains. Although a session may occur in a tavern, it does not belong to the domain of commercial entertainment since the orientation of the performance is not toward a general audience. Instead, performers at a session are primarily interested in the effect of the performance upon themselves and their fellow session players. Since they are not paid for performing and since their performance is not formal nor prepared in advance, session performers do not need to shape their performance to the desires of anyone but themselves. The context may be the same as performances intended to serve as commercial entertainment (and, indeed, the tavern may do better business because of the session), yet the orientation and motivation of the performance and its format are different.

Different domains of musical occasions can exist simultaneously in the same environment. The Fleadh Cheoil is chiefly organized by its promoters as a forum for musicians to compete for prizes and medals, and the events of the Fleadh Cheoil are scheduled with this central idea in mind.

There are, however, at every Fleadh, numerous musicians who do not choose to compete but, instead, spend the entire time playing in impromptu sessions around the Fleadh venue. At the same time, many non-musicians attend the event as spectators. They pay a fee at the door and view the competitions as they would any other concert presentation of Irish music.

These preliminary remarks on the nature of performance occasions are meant simply as an explanation for the format in which they are presented in the pages that follow. For a more detailed discussion of methods designed to analyze the contexts of performance occasions, the reader should consult Fishman (1970:37-56), where the major concepts of domain analysis are outlined.

There are undoubtedly instances where the data does not fit snugly within the rigorous categories established for it; what, for example, is the domain when a traditional Irish musician is playing at a formal concert broadcast over the radio and played in a bar where customers are dancing to the music? That is a particularly slippery Gordian Knot the reader is invited to entangle at leisure.

- **Commercial Entertainment**

Irish musicians were formerly very much in evidence as commercial entertainers in the United States and were employed by proprietors of hotels, taverns, restaurants and pleasure cruises in the 19th century, as can be inferred from the biographies of Irish-American musicians in Francis O'Neill's *Irish Folk Music: A Fascinating Hobby* (1910) and *Irish Minstrels and Musicians* (1913).

The Irish musician has vanished from most of these contexts as the tastes and preferences of American audiences have asserted themselves in other directions. The only context in which Irish musicians in American cities like Chicago are currently found on a regular basis as commercial entertainers is that of the Irish-owned or Irish-oriented bars, although some musicians sporadically are used to promote various business enterprises such as travel agencies during St. Patrick's Week in mid-March.

In the era when bars were known as saloons, Irish musicians were frequently hired to entertain the patrons of such establishments. Some Irish musicians in 19th-century America owned or managed saloons, and many more found steady work in the numerous Irish-owned taverns that flourished in urban centers.

In the 20th century, Prohibition significantly reduced the number of tavern jobs for Irish musicians; of even greater and more lasting significance were the changes that occurred in the musical entertainment tastes of tavern-goers as the 20th century progressed. Irish-owned bars were also gradually losing their Irish clientele, and radical changes in the popular music idiom eventually succeeded in forcing the Irish musician from all but a few Irish-oriented bars.

Jukeboxes, muzak systems, radio and television have replaced much live music in taverns, and proprietors do not generally consider Irish music to be a particularly "hot" item in commercial terms. Even in bars that take immense pains to style themselves as "genuine Irish pubs", Irish folk music is only inadvertently heard.

Changes in the demographic composition of tavern-goers is also an important factor. Though many Irish-oriented bars have a regular clientele of largely male persons over forty years of age who have recent familial ties with Ireland, there has been a much greater number of persons of both sexes and under thirty years of age entering these sanctums formerly inhabited only by "old-timers". In bars such as these that still remain nominally Irish-oriented, one is likely to find virtually any type of American popular music of the last twenty years, from vintage Elvis Presley and Frank Sinatra to modern country-western to current top-forty rock and disco hits.

Only Ireland's 32, a tavern on the city's Northwestside, hires any Irish folk musicians, and that is not a regular commitment by the tavern. There are a score of bars in the Chicago area that advertise themselves as Irish bars with "the best in Irish musical entertainment". The music encountered in these places is not Irish traditional music but an interesting hybrid form of Irish-derived music.

This hybrid form has many faces; primarily it is vocal music accompanied by electric guitars, basses, and organs. The song lyrics are usually from the stage-Irish tradition, although popular Top 40 hits are often performed. When Irish folk songs are performed, they are either "rebel" songs, humorous songs from the stage-Irish repertoire or sentimental emigrant songs. If there is a competent instrumentalist in the group, some Irish dance tunes might be played.

Traditional Irish musicians are not hired to play at these hybrid taverns, though they might occasionally appear and be invited up for a tune or two by a friend in one of the bands that have been hired. Numerous Irish-oriented bars in Chicago do not even bother with engaging a hybrid musical group but hire bands that play bluegrass, country-western or rock and roll from the 1950s and early 1960s. Bar owners not surprisingly have discovered that the best musical entertainment for their purposes is that which encourages customers to consume greater amounts of drink. Whether or not they originated with this idea in mind, hybrid Irish musical forms have become synonymous in the minds of bar owners and many bar patrons with "drinking music", "good time music" and music with which one can sing and shout and spend money. Traditional Irish music in its normal performance format does not usually have the same impact upon the clientele's spirits and pocketbooks.

To be successful in a tavern performance context, a musical performer or group of performers must literally have their act together. They must be highly polished, well-rehearsed and thoroughly and continually oriented to the needs and desires of the audience. Traditional Irish musicians in Chicago are entirely the opposite. They are unceasingly individualistic, spontaneous and self-absorbed. It is not the Irish traditional musician who has changed over the years, rather, it is the audiences of the Irish-oriented taverns who have revamped their expectations of what a musical performance should accomplish.

There were a number of bars up to the mid-1960s that employed Irish traditional musicians as regular performers. Those bars have disappeared or changed their employment policies; presently, there is no tavern in the Chicago area that employs Irish folk musicians on a steady, regular basis.

The revival of interest in Irish folk music has not escaped other entrepreneurs, however. Irish music is beginning to become a more valuable commodity for promotional purposes. Shopping centers around Chicago, in particular, have used Irish musicians and step-dancers to assist in the promotion of books, Irish-made products and travel agency-sponsored raffles for trips to Ireland.

Irish musicians performing in these contexts do not mind the commercial use being made of their art; instead, they welcome the opportunity to perform in front of an audience that might contain interested, appreciative people who may never before have had the opportunity to hear Irish traditional music or see Irish folk dancing. Since the performers are less limited by audience demands in choosing their repertoire for performance, and since the audience in most cases is not spending large sums of money to hear the performers, the pressures on the performers are considerably less than would be encountered in a tavern context. The performers are part of the spectacle; they are special and perhaps exotic to much of the audience in exhibition contexts of this kind, whereas, in a tavern, their function as strictly service workers is more apparent.

The future of traditional Irish music in commercial entertainment contexts in Chicago will probably continue to develop along the lines of the last few years. Fewer employment opportunities in taverns will exist, but more engagements will be secured as performers at exhibitions and promotional events.

- **Non-Commercial Entertainment**

Francis O'Neill, in discussing some of the Irish musicians he met during his first years in Chicago, mentions a fiddle player named O'Malley, who lived with his wife and children in a tenement in the Stockyards district. Though missing one finger from his left hand, O'Malley was a fine fiddler and "eked out a living by playing at house dances" (O'Neill 1910:41-42). O'Neill's choice of words is most interesting here, as the dictionary definition of "eke" is "to make or supplement with great effort or strain" (Davies 1970:229). From all indications, this is exactly the occupational hazard of the professional Irish musician who attempted to make a living of playing at private, non-commercial entertainments in Chicago during the 19th and early 20th centuries; the money to be made from this livelihood was too little and too infrequently obtained.

While the opportunities for playing at house dances, rent parties, weddings, wakes, christenings and other occasions were in abundance, the persons hosting the function not uncommonly shared the same economic stratum as the musicians they hired. Payment was not always in the coin of the realm, either; food and drink were often the only remuneration hosts were willing or able to offer in exchange for musical entertainment.

The Irish community of Chicago still employs musicians to provide entertainment for affairs such as weddings, anniversary celebrations, banquets, parties and so on, but it is not always performers of Irish music who are hired. "Modern music" or "American music" is preferred by many Irish-Americans, and Irish music — when it is brought in — is regarded as a curiosity.

The month of March features a sharp increase in the number of private, non-commercial functions that hire Irish musicians, as many party-givers like to obtain some sort of Irish music for their soirees around St. Patrick's Day.

The economic situation of Irish musicians who play for private parties has not markedly improved since the days of O'Malley and his fellow house-dance players. There are no Irish musicians in Chicago who make an exclusive, full-time living from playing at private, non-commercial entertainment occasions. Since many of the occasions are hosted by friends, relatives or neighbors of the musicians, the degree of familiarity tends to inhibit the freedom of the musicians in asking for large sums of money as payment for their services.

Due to the informal, non-commercial nature of the occasion, the musician's role as a specialist is not as clear as it would be were the performance occurring in a formal, commercial context. Consequently, there is no set standard of payment for the musician in these circumstances. As in the earlier years of the 20th century, recompense may be with "hospitality" (food and drink) or with a small sum of money (from five to twenty-five dollars).

The type of musical performance given by a musician in an informal, non-commercial context depends on the audience. The audience may take a very active part in the performance with requests for tunes, songs and dance accompaniment. The musician does not perform a prepared program but either decides what to play on the spot or allows the audience to determine the structure and content of the performance.

Any type of instrument may be seen at occasions of this kind, although in the Chicago Irish community at present, the accordion is the instrument most commonly encountered at non-commercial entertainment contexts due to its versatility in playing various types of music to satisfy different audience preferences. For, even at nominally Irish affairs, there is not infrequently a demand for music that is not Irish, and the most popular and most often employed musicians are those prepared to accommodate diverse tastes.

- **Radio and Television Broadcasts**

When the first Irish radio programs began in Chicago in the late 1920s, live performances by local Irish musicians were the norm, as recordings were not that plentiful. The programs of that period were also somewhat different in nature than their counterparts of the present day. They were much less of a media event performed for the benefit of a communications enterprise or commercial sponsors; instead, they were in many respects simply an informal gathering of individuals from the Irish community who passed on news and gossip of interest to the community and varied the talk with music, song and dance. Records might be played as a novelty, but live musical performance was crucial to the ambiance of these programs.

There were some great musical moments on the early Irish radio shows in Chicago. Pipers Tom Ennis and Eddie Mullaney played for years on Maurice Lynch's program on WCFL, and John McGreevy and the Nearys often brought in visitors from out of town, such as James Giblin, Martin Wynne, Paddy Cronin, Louis Quinn and Ed Reavy, to play for a Saturday or Sunday morning radio show. Some shows even had regular ensembles of musicians who played on their show each week, such as Jack Hagerty's Irish Hour during the 1950s that featured an ensemble of nine musicians comprising fiddles, flute, accordions, piano and drums.

Today, the situation is altered. Irish radio programs in Chicago have clearly become channels for the promotion of the business enterprises that sponsor the air time. Recordings are used almost exclusively as filler between commercials. Only one or two programs have a policy whereby a visiting musician from out of town can be brought in for an impromptu performance.

Although there is still one live remote broadcast (from the Abbey Tavern on the city's Northwestside), the music featured is hybrid Irish music, generally the performers booked to play at the bar for that week; Irish folk musicians are rarely heard.

In the early 1960s, Chicago Irishman Eamonn O'Malley hosted a half-hour television program on Channel 26 every Sunday evening. Many Chicago step-dancing schools were seen on this program, and several Irish musicians from the city also appeared as accompanists for the dancers.

There is currently no regular television program devoted to the Irish community of Chicago, and Irish musicians do not appear with any frequency on local television.

When Irish musicians do appear on local media outlets, they are not paid. It is as if they were receiving a great gift for which they are placed in debt. The fact that they were granted a few minutes on the air is considered appropriate recompense for their performance. Instead of a featured attraction of great interest to the community, Irish musicians performing on radio and television in Chicago have become supplicants at the door of the residence that was formerly their own.

- **Concerts**

The programs of concerts given by Chicago Irish social and political organizations in the late 19th and early 20th centuries have revealed that Irish folk music was not in high demand for these occasions (see Chapter One). When Irish musicians did appear onstage at those concerts, they were already at this time beginning to be regarded as a novelty by Irish-American concert-goers. An irritated Francis O'Neill wrote these words to William Halpin, an Irish friend, in a letter dated November 28, 1911:

> Few of our people care a snap for even Irish music. The poor scrub who graduated from the pick and shovel and the mother who for many years toiled in some Yankee kitchen will have nothing less for Katie and Gladis or Jimmy or Raymond but the latest agony, if you please. Time and again have I been disgusted by the tittering and mockery of Irish audiences when a piper strikes up a merry tune, and this disconcerting conduct comes not from the American-born but from the Irish-born mainly.

The concert concept itself gradually lost favor with Irish-American organizations that discovered their members would apparently much rather attend a dance there they could be up on their feet dancing and socializing and not be bound by the concert decorum of maintaining silence and motionlessness. This general disinterest in the concert as a form of community entertainment also implied that there was nothing worth listening to, anyway, and traditional Irish music sank even deeper into the status of an oddity or an anachronism associated with the days of poverty and discrimination most Irish-Americans preferred to forget about whenever possible.

When the traditional Irish musician began appearing as a featured concert performer in the late 1960s, it mainly occurred outside the Irish community. The urban folk music revival of the '60s had uncovered a number of outstanding performers in various folk traditions languishing in obscurity for want of a sympathetic, appreciative audience.

Blues performers and hillbilly musicians who had spent the last thirty or forty years away from public performance were now rediscovered by a new audience and elevated to a new high status within the revivalist community, if not always within their own cultural group.

By the 1970s, the momentum of the revival had carried it into other traditions besides those of the African- and Anglo-American, and traditional Irish musicians and singers started turning up at folk festivals, university concerts and coffeehouses and bars run by folk music clubs. Articles on Irish folk music and musicians occasionally graced the pages of general folk music magazines, and there were now more reviews of Irish folk music records in these same journals.

The result of this sudden focusing of attention on what had a decade before been a relatively unknown musical tradition outside its own ethnic community was that Irish traditional music reasserted its claim to the concert venue, a claim it had been denied for decades.

Frank Thornton's Chicago group that toured Ireland in 1959 put on two concerts to raise funds for their trip. These were concerts organized entirely by the musicians, singers and dancers themselves; since the event was for the benefit of the performers and not held under the auspices of a social or political organization, the form and content of the concert was a radical departure from concerts of Irish music held in Chicago previously (c.f. pages 155-56).

During the 1960s, the Chicago Irish Musicians' Association sponsored an occasional concert of local musicians. In 1969, several musicians from Ireland gave three concerts in Chicago; this tour was organized by Frank Thornton as a way of thanking the persons in Ireland who had assisted in his tour a decade before. Funds from the performances were used to provide relief for victims of violence in Northern Ireland.

In 1972, Comhaltas Ceoltóirí Éireann started its annual tours to North America with Irish musicians, singers, and dancers. These concerts were convened in halls, with male performers dressed in black-tie-and-tuxedo attire and ladies in formal evening gowns. Irish folk musicians presented in a dignified, respectable manner (the five-dollar ticket price was a further reminder that this was not an event for those seeking cheap diversion). For many Irish-Americans, the CCE concerts were the first real contact with actual Irish traditional music they had ever had, and the sober, professional, formal concert presentation undoubtedly gave many persons in the local Irish community cause to appraise their local Irish musicians with a bit more esteem.

Other factors have assisted the re-entry of Irish folk music into American concert venues. One is the emergence of new ensemble forms for presenting the music. Irish folk music is now intended for listening, it is no longer merely music for dancers or music to which audiences can sing or shout along. Large halls and auditoriums rather than small private clubs or taverns serve as the contexts for these concert performances.

When the Irish ensemble, The Chieftains, came to Chicago in July, 1976, it was no real surprise that they performed in the Civic Opera House for a minimum eight-dollar ticket charge. What did come as a small surprise to some was that, after their sold-out concert, the group was whisked away in black limousines to the rooms of the Irish Fellowship Club of Chicago, an organization of the local Irish-American elite that had largely ignored local Irish musicians throughout its seven decades of existence.

Many of the money-raising activities sponsored by groups providing aid to persons in Northern Ireland were concerts that brought Irish folk musicians to the stage. By 1973, Chicago's Irish music associations had begun to follow the example set by Frank Thornton years earlier and put on their own benefit concerts to obtain funds for carrying out their programs of furthering the tradition.

Increasingly, traditional Irish musicians in Chicago, as well as throughout the United States, were regaining their place as concert artists. The Chicago Irish music clubs feature four or five concerts of local performers each year, and it has now become customary for Irish entertainers, even hybrid, stage performers, to include some local Irish folk musicians as "continuity music", or entr'acte entertainment.

Most Irish folk music activity in Chicago still takes place away from the concert stage, and one is still able to detect the tittering and mockery that infuriated O'Neill in the early years of this century.

Nevertheless, the return of the Irish traditional musician to the concert stage has been an important step in the revival of the tradition in Chicago over the last decade. With Irish musicians able to assume the role of concert performers worthy of public attention, a new and welcome sense of pride and value in the practice of Irish music has also appeared.

The format of Irish folk music concerts devoted exclusively to the music are varied. Solos, duets, trios, quartets and ensembles ranging from five to two dozen musicians take part in these concerts. There are also singers occasionally and several appearances by step-dancers performing solo and group numbers. A wide range of music is heard, encompassing nearly all the genres of dance music and airs. Sometimes, comedy skits or short plays about Irish rural life thirty years ago and more are given by some of the musicians; these inevitably incorporate music, song, and dance.

Performers are not paid for these concert appearances, and, indeed, few ever concern themselves with this aspect of the occasion, as they are happy to be onstage in front of an appreciative audience. For those musicians who do perform as "continuity music" for out-of-town artists, there is money available depending upon whether the musician is able to negotiate skillfully with the event promoter. Concerts put on by Chicago Irish music clubs always use the proceeds to strengthen their treasury, and these concerts are viewed by the performers as co-operative enterprises for the good of the tradition.

The most significant aspect of the return of Irish folk music to concert performance contexts in Chicago is that it is one of the most efficient means of spreading the music to persons not familiar with the tradition. The variety of the concert format is useful in showing the full spectrum of the tradition to newcomers; in addition, the concert venue is a neutral site where persons from outside the Irish-American community can feel comfortable and non-obtrusive.

Other performance contexts that feature Irish music generally are restricted to a limited part of the tradition's repertoire, especially dances, dance and music competitions and dance exhibitions. Many of these performances also take place in environments that are somewhat xenophobic and closed to the casual outsider, particularly private homes, musicians' associations meetings and taverns inhabited by an overwhelmingly Irish clientele. Thus, concerts of Irish folk music provide a showcase for the tradition and have undoubtedly sparked the interest of many new converts to Irish traditional music.

- **Dances and Céilís**

The role of the Irish folk musician in providing accompaniment for the dances held by members of the Irish community in Chicago has decreased steadily throughout the 20th century. Once Irish dancing was synonymous with and inseparable from Irish music; the two were inextricably intertwined, such that when it was mentioned that an Irish dance was held, it was taken for granted that Irish music would be performed to accompany it.

Such is no longer the case. The reason for the change is not to be found solely in the fact that Irish-Americans have adopted alien dances, for many of the "traditional" dances of Ireland were fashioned from dance forms introduced from Europe and Britain (Breathnach 1970:117; Roche 1927:v). The jig, reel and hornpipe were among these dances created from imported 18th-century dance forms, and the "sets" that are today taken by Irish traditional dancing authorities as the high point of Irish folk dancing were revised versions of French quadrilles from the early 19th century.

These imported dances, however, were not merely accepted by Irish dancers; they were completely reshaped in accordance with the already-established steps and meters so that they became, in effect, fully naturalized Irish dances, native rather than foreign.

The music used to accompany these dances in Ireland was different than the music created for it in the original place of formulation. Later in the 19th century, a new wave of foreign dances entered Ireland from European and English ballrooms.

These included the polka, the schottische, the mazurka, the waltz, the barn dance, the varsovienne and others that lasted only temporarily. The Famine of the late 1840s had wiped out the class of professional dancing masters that had flourished before the mid-19th century, and these new imports were not as successfully or as ingeniously adapted to the native Irish dancing idiom.

In America, the contact with other dance forms was frequent. Yet, seemingly, there existed no filtering process as had previously operated in Ireland. Dances emanating from the mainstream of American popular culture were adopted in whole, and the result was not a blend or a syncretism of two different dance traditions but a complete supplanting of one tradition by another. The distinction is best comprehended by the realization that, in the past, the dancing at a 19th-century Irish crossroads in the countryside would not have been referred to by its participants as "Irish-French dancing" or ''Irish-Bohemian dancing'' or "Irish-English dancing" or "Irish-Scots dancing", despite the fact that many of these dances being performed were originally inspired by dance forms popular in France, England, Scotland, and Central Europe.

Yet, the dancing that takes place at the vast majority of Irish dances in Chicago are invariably described in advertisements and by the dancers themselves as "Irish-American". Often the hyphenated term is dropped, and "American dancing" is used. The widespread currency of these terms, particularly in contrast to what is called "Irish dancing", indicate that a process of annihilation rather than acculturation has occurred.

When discussing the subject of Irish dancing in America with persons involved in the promotion of Irish culture, it becomes immediately apparent that "Irish-American dancing" is much more American in character than it is Irish. An Irish-language instructor and Irish ensernble dance leader in Chicago commented that at dances sponsored by Irish organizations in the city, the participants begin with an Irish folk dance "to establish nationality; then they start jitterbugging."

A former leader of a New York-based Irish cultural revival group stated that "there are numerous Irish organizations in the New York area which have sponsored public dances. While they call their dances Irish, it's a rare occasion that they may dance a Walls of Limerick or Siege of Ennis, which are rather simple folk dances."

In Chicago, there are numerous dances held by Irish social and political organizations. They are attended almost exclusively by the members of these organizations, who are Irish emigrants or first-generation Irish-Americans. "Irish-American" or "American" dances are those that are in greatest demand. For most dancers this means fast or slow dances, i.e. waltzes or foxtrots. Occasionally, an Irish folk dance like the "Siege of Ennis" or "Stack of Barley" will be played by the band; not unsurprisingly, these dances attract the least number of dancers onto the floor.

It would appear that the dances held by groups of this kind are primarily social in their function; that is, they are convened as an organizational activity where the members can meet and pursue conversational or business interaction. Careful observation of the participants at dances of this sort reveals that, not only does a small percentage of the total crowd engage in dancing at any one time, but there are many individuals who do no dancing at all throughout the course of the evening. In view of those facts, it is easier to understand why the type of dancing is of less relevance to a large portion of the participants.

Traditional Irish musicians do not perform at these dances, or, rather, if they do play, they do not perform traditional Irish music. As will be seen in Chapter Six in the discussion of various types of performers, some Irish folk musicians supplement their income by performing for dances held by Irish groups where "American" and "Irish-American" dancing is practiced.

The musical accompaniment found at these occasions is provided most often by three to six musicians (although there is a one-man band who sings and plays an electric organ with a rhythm unit, and there is also another local musician who plays piano accordion, sings and keeps time with a bass drum and cymbals).

An accordion (usually a piano accordion but sometimes a two- or three-row button accordion) is the lead instrument; sometimes, a cordovox is used. A standup acoustic bass is often used, though an electric guitar-type bass might also be seen in some ensembles. There is always a set of modern drums, one or two electric guitars and very possibly an electric organ and a tenor or alto saxophone.

There is a vocalist (often doubling as an instrumentalist) who sings between the dances (though often singing during dances as well). The only member of the group with any rudimentary knowledge of Irish folk music is the accordion player, who in many cases began his or her career playing Irish folk music but discovered that greater income was to be derived by playing hybrid or non-Irish music. On the rare occasions when these ensembles play Irish folk music, the performance style is completely alien to the normal traditional performance styles.

It has been necessary to describe in some detail the hybrid form of dance occasion that is popularly thought of as constituting genuine Irish folk dancing. This trend in dance preference among the Chicago Irish was already visible in the late 1800s, and Chicago musicians today who were playing in the 1930s remember that "Irish" and "American" dances were interspersed at Irish dances. Different musicians would perform for the various dance idioms, or, in some venues, different rooms in the hall or different platforms in the park would he used for the two types of dancing.

It was not until the 1970s that a conscious effort to revive Irish traditional dancing was made in Chicago. This type of dancing has been designated as "céilí dancing" and is also known as "Rincí Gaelacha". This dancing corresponds to the general concept of "folk dancing" as practiced by international folk dance groups in the United States, and it is céilí dancing that American folk dance groups perform when they turn to the folk dances of Ireland. Céilí dancing in its present form was a product of the Gaelic League revival of Irish culture that began in the 1890s in Ireland and in Irish communities in England and America.

The term "céilí" is a Gaelic word that denotes in common parlance "an evening visit, a friendly call" (Dinneen 1970:184), or simply an informal social gathering of neighbors in rural Ireland; gossip, storytelling, music and dancing might occur throughout the course of the visit (Morton 1973:179).

It was not until the 20th century that the word was used to signify a formal occasion of Irish music and dance. This newly-attached meaning resulted from the efforts of the London branch of the Gaelic League that held the first occasion formally and officially designated as a "céilí" on October 30, 1897 at Bloomsbury Hall, London. The occasion consisted of Irish folk music, song and solo and ensemble dancing. It was intended to provide an informal, sociable atmosphere of Irishness for Irish emigrants in London.

By calling the event a céilí, the organizers hoped to convey a general feeling of neighborliness and nostalgia reminiscent of the nocturnal assemblies in Irish country houses (Breathnach 1971:50). Today, the céilí has become the refuge for those irritated by the absence of Irish music and dance at most Irish-American dances; the céilí also serves as a focal point for the scattered remnants of the Irish communities in cities like Chicago and is a major means of fostering Irish cultural activity.

Céilí dances such as "The Walls of Limerick", "The Bridge of Athlone", "Paddy O'Rafferty", "Haste to the Wedding" and "The Siege of Ennis" were the result of the Gaelic League's unceasing efforts to create an "Irish Ireland". In the area of dance, this entailed the purging of "foreign" dances from the céilí venue, as new dances believed to be truly Irish in origin were devised. The efforts of the revivalists, though inspired by laudable intentions, seem to have actually done more harm than good, for they succeeded in banning a considerable number of excellent and unique dances and replacing them with dances that, ironically, were based on adaptations of foreign quadrilles created earlier in the 19th century (Breathnach 1971:49).

In any event, many connoisseurs of traditional Irish dancing believed that "these simple contra dances proved inadequate as substitutes for all those that had been prohibited" (Roche 1927:v). Indeed, it is entirely possible that this cultural revolution in ensemble dance forms may have, by virtue of its random, sweeping reforms, actually assisted in the process whereby foreign dances entered Irish dancing with no native filtering process to modify them, as had occurred in the past.

Whether it was judged inadequate or not, céilí dancing continued to thrive, and the céilí is one of the only public musical occasions where the balanced, reciprocal relationship between traditional Irish music and dance is still in evidence. Céilí dances are danced to Irish dance music, and the musicians performing are knowledgeable Irish folk musicians. The format of the céilí is organized by a dance leader or director who leads the dances and teaches the dances when necessary; the director also acts as liaison between the musicians and dancers, makes general announcements and serves as the master-of-ceremonies.

Céilís are often proceeded and concluded by a good deal of spontaneous music-making by the players; between dances, musicians are apt to strike up a brief session and play a few tunes of their own choice until they are asked again to provide the accompaniment for the next dance. Occasionally, musicians are called out for solos while the dancers rest, and other participants are often called on to sing a song or do a solo step dance.

Leadership among the musicians is provided by one or two musicians who are usually experienced céilí performers and high in seniority; there is no formal acknowledgement of their leadership role at this event, but they are inevitably the final arbiter in deciding what tunes to play for the dances, what the initial tempo will be and when to switch from one tune into another during a medley of tunes.

Céilís draw a crowd varying widely in age and comprising roughly equal numbers of males and females. University students, teenagers, families with small children and single adults of all ages are present. Though attended primarily by persons who are of Irish birth or ancestry, many persons attend who are not at all connected with Ireland in any familial way. These individuals come to hear Irish music and dance Irish folk dances; the céilí is also an excellent opportunity for young musicians learning Irish music to pick up new tunes and to play over the tunes they have already learned. Interaction with experienced musicians is easily attained at a céilí.

The céilí has been a safe haven for Irish folk musicians in Chicago during the last decade, as the last of the Irish dance halls closed down. As their services were rejected with increasing frequency by the sponsors and participants of dances held under the auspices of Irish-American social and political groups, it became clear that only a group that insisted on Irish dancing and Irish music at a dance event could stem the tide of changing tastes (MacColla 1972:6).

Only Irish folk dances are performed at céilís in Chicago, and, since the first céilí held in 1972 by the Irish Language Association, the concept has spread throughout the city. The three Chicago Irish music clubs sponsor céilís, with two of the clubs holding céilís once a month. There are the céilís held by the Chicago Gaelic Society (formerly the Irish Language Association) every month, and there are also special céilís held for various reasons. Musicians and dance leaders are not paid for performing at a céilí, but the event is not perceived in economic terms. Instead, Irish musicians are glad of the comfortable atmosphere where they can play the music they enjoy playing the best, while at the same time helping foster traditional Irish music in a traditional performance context.

It is doubtful whether Irish folk musicians will actively participate in Irish-American dances to the same degree as they did a century or even half century ago. The turnover in dance traditions has been too complete. As long as the céilí exists as an alternative, Irish folk musicians in Chicago will leave the Irish-American dances to those who desire them. While the majority of adult Irish-Americans in Chicago do not seem inclined to forsake the foxtrot for "The High Caul Cap", it is even more unlikely that very many of their children will exchange the dances of the disco for those of the céilí.

- **Dance Classes**

A half century ago, it was not uncommon to find teachers of Irish step-dancing in Chicago who were musicians as well. Those teachers who did not play Irish dance music engaged the services of an individual who did, as the technological equipment that would make it possible for pre-recorded music to be played in any private and public context had not yet been refined. Lacking the presence of a musician, the teacher could always lilt the tune; yet, as his pupils progressed to more intricate dances and steps, musical accompaniment became imperative.

Currently, Irish musicians do not play for dance classes of the more than thirty Irish step-dancing schools in the Chicago area, except when rehearsing an especially elaborate choreography routine that changes meter, tempo, and tune. Otherwise, dance teachers (who today arc nearly always non-musicians) find it much cheaper and easier to teach their pupils by means of a few records and cassette tapes. Although technological improvements rendered the musician obsolete in this performance domain, dance teachers are quick to point out that pre-recorded music is more efficient tor their purposes since, barring battery failure or surges in the line current, a record or tape is always the same every time it is played.

Occasionally before a dance competition, a live musician will be brought in by a dance teacher so that the pupils can get some experience hearing what the expected dance music accompaniment will sound like during their competition. Most teachers, however, do not take this precaution, and the Irish traditional musician has all but totally disappeared from this performance domain in Chicago.

- **Dance Competitions**

The Irish word *feis* (plural, *feiseanna*) means a "feast, festival a parliament, session, convention" (Dinneen 1970:445). In 1897, the Gaelic League inaugurated an annual gathering of musicians, dancers and poets in the spirit of the thrice-yearly gathering of the brehons, bards and poets convened during the pre-Christian era in Ireland when the kingdom of Tara was at its zenith (Flood 1905:323).

The Gaelic League called its event a *Feis Cheoil* (Irish for Music Convention), and held competitions in Irish music, song, and poetry in the Irish language in the hope of rejuvenating what was felt to be a moribund culture. When competitions of Irish step-dancers were organized later in the early 1900s, the general term *feis* was used to describe the occasion.

Currently, there are over forty annual feiseanna held in the United States and Canada each year. Most of the feiseanna are in the Northeastern and Middle Atlantic States, although there are several important feiseanna held in the Midwest also. The first Chicago Feis held along modern guidelines took place in Pilsen Park in 1945. The Chicago Feis has been held each year since, though the location has moved several times over the decades.

The Chicago Feis is similar in most respects to other feiseanna around the country. It attracts between thirteen and fourteen hundred step dancers from the Northeastern, Middle Atlantic and Midwestern states, and there are always close to a hundred competitors from Canada as well. Competitions are held at stages, and a stage may be located in a classroom of a school building, on a wooden platform in a field or parking lot or on the concrete of a park pavilion.

Dancers are assigned to various stages where the *adjudicator* or panel of adjudicators judges their efforts in each competition. Depending upon the number of stages that need to be filled and the number of available musicians, there may be from one to three musicians playing at a stage.

The musicians choose their own selections within the genre of the particular competition. The musical selections depend upon the age and experience of the dancers. If a group of children under age eight is dancing reels, a melodically simple, easy-to-follow polka or reel will be played. As the competitors increase in age and skill, tunes that are more complex and more interesting to the musicians can be played without causing the dancers to make mistakes because of confusion from the music.

However, it is not an uncommon occurrence for a player stationed at a stage where dancers in the novice grades are competing to play the same tune for well over an hour, lest the wrath of parents and teachers be incurred for showing "favoritism" by playing different tunes for different dancers.

Musicians are paid for performing at a feis; the standard rate at the Chicago Feis is now sixty dollars for a day's (and often night's) work. Competitions begin at nine o'clock in the morning and often continue until nine, ten or eleven o'clock in the evening.

Often, musicians from out of town are brought in. This is not simply because there are not enough local musicians to perform for all the stages. The championship events are hotly contested, and for these competitions outside performers are often used (non-local adjudicators are used in every competition). This is done both as an attempt to maintain the appearance of absolute impartiality as well as for the comfort of the musicians and adjudicators, who may well become the target of abuse from the more vehement and embittered supporters of the losers.

Most musicians do not relish the idea of playing for a feis, since they work very hard and very long, particularly in a large feis like that in Chicago. They do so partially out of a sense of duty and also for the extra income and status that accrues from being at the center of an important event like the feis.

Although they may complain occasionally about the heat, the humidity, the dust, the rain, the endless lines of dancers, the heckling from irate parents and the innuendoes from suspicious teachers and adjudicators, most musicians are pleased that their talents are sought. For the Irish folk musician plays an indispensable role in this public manifestation of a major element of contemporary Irish-American culture.

The feis is a day-long pageant replete with the color, excitement and communality that vividly recall the rollicking fairs, pattern days and other large-scale social gatherings that have held such a vital place in Irish society since its earliest, pre-Christian beginnings. Were the Irish musician to vanish from this domain, something more significant than a musical tradition would have passed from the scene.

- **Dance Exhibitions**

Occasionally, teachers of Irish step-dancing schools are invited to have their pupils, or a select group of pupils, give a performance for some institution or institutionally-sponsored event. Dance exhibitions of this kind take place throughout the year, especially during the month of March, but around other national holidays like Christmas, Easter and Memorial Day that feature public gatherings.

The contexts for the exhibitions may be at senior citizen homes, Rotary Club luncheons, church festivals, Irish-American organization meetings, shopping malls, television studios and local, national and international folk festivals. Teachers regard these performances as an important means of not only advertising their own teaching operation but as a means of creating a greater awareness of the art of traditional Irish dancing. Exhibitions are also seen as a way, in addition to competitions, of eliciting approval for the pupils by securing public recognition for the skill they have painstakingly acquired over the years.

The musician's role in all of this is comparatively minor, and he or she is engaged to provide exactly what music is required —no more and no less. Exhibitions of this sort usually do not exceed more than a half hour, and the musician need only play a few simple reels, double jigs, hornpipes, slip jigs and perhaps a set dance. Most of these can be chosen at the event, though for some of the more complicated choreography pieces, advance rehearsal is necessary.

Many dance teachers record accompaniment music on cassette tape recorders and carry this with them in case of an emergency; indeed, some dance teachers use pre-recorded music in preference to live musicians, whether musicians are available or not. Teachers who do use live musicians usually rely on one or two experienced players.

Not all musicians are well-suited to accompanying dancers. The styles of step-dancing have become much more complex than was the case two decades ago, and many musicians are not highly sensitive to this fact. A few musicians are in great demand for step-dancing accompaniment because of their overall competency and flexibility in adjusting to the requirements of a dance exhibition.

Musicians are generally paid for playing for a dance exhibition, though the amount rarely exceeds twenty-five dollars. Because of the prevalence of records and tapes, musicians are not in a good bargaining position, as they can be replaced by pre-recorded music if their demands exceed the available funds. And many of the audiences that witness these dance exhibitions would not appreciate the difference between live and recorded music in this performance context, anyway.

- **Music Competitions**

There is only one occasion in Chicago where Irish musicians perform in competition, and that is the Fleadh Cheoil. The Chicago Fleadh Cheoil is based on the model of the Fleadh Cheoil competitions that originated in Ireland during the 1950s. Competitions are organized for each instrument for different age groups. Only the singing is divided by separate gender categories. There are one hundred and thirty-nine competitions in all, and prizes are awarded to the first, second and third place contestants.

The Fleadh Cheoil in Chicago is open to all competitors; there is no discrimination in regard to residence, race, creed, gender, age or even instrument, as there even exists a "miscellaneous instrument" category. The Fleadh Cheoil is chiefly intended by its organizers as an occasion where players of Irish folk music and singers of Irish folk songs can gather and perform among their peers and an audience of appreciative aficianados.

The competition categories are divided into three main groups: solo playing, group playing (any more than one instrument) and singing. The solo competitions are further divided into a category in which the competitors play a mixture of dance tunes and airs and a category in which the contestants play only airs.

Instrumental competitions include those for fiddle, flute, tinwhistle, two-row accordion, three-row accordion, piano accordion, concertina, uilleann pipes, harp, mouth organ, banjo, piano, drums, war pipes and "any other instrument". Only the fiddle, flute, uilleann pipes and tinwhistle are allowed in the slow air category. Group playing comprises duets, trios, céilí bands and marching war pipe bands.

Singing is divided into English and Irish and further divided by gender. There is also a competition for newly-composed songs in Irish and in English, a collection of previously unpublished dance tunes and a collection of previously unpublished songs in English or Irish. There are competitions for whistling and lilting. Age categories are delineated along the following lines: Under 11, 11 to 14, 14 to 16, 16 to 18, Over-18.

The Fleadhanna Cheoil in Chicago during the early 1960s used local musicians to adjudicate competitions, and there were so many personal feuds that erupted because of the disagreements concerning adjudication that the Fleadh was not held again until 1974. During 1974, 1975 and 1976, the adjudicators were from Ireland; in 1977, Irish musicians from New York were flown in. Plans for 1978 have not as yet not been finalized, but everyone concerned with the Fleadh planning is agreed that local adjudicators run a greater risk of being accused of partiality. Local individuals also have to live year round with the controversies stirred up by their decisions.

The problem of impartial adjudicators points up the seriousness with which the Fleadh Cheoil is taken by some persons. To many musicians and listeners, the Fleadh is simply a musical occasion, an event where Irish music can be heard from noon to eight or nine o'clock in the evening. Many musicians do not compete at all, especially the older ones who have no intense desire to win medals or trophies and have no interest in establishing or defending a reputation.

The majority of contestants in the Chicago Fleadh Cheoil (indeed, any Fleadh Cheoil) are under age twenty-five. The Fleadh has evolved away from its original objective of being just a large-scale session or festival; its competitive aspects have assumed great importance to some musicians and aficionados, as it functions as a kind of proving ground upon which individual musical reputations are gained and enhanced.

The Fleadh Cheoil is a means of vaulting an unknown young performer into the spotlight of local, national and even international renown. Older players who have already established reputations are less interested in the gun-fighter mentality that sometimes infuses the Fleadh Cheoil competitions. Many older players refuse to perform, pleading nervousness; other senior musicians enter competitions to give the audiences a good show, to provide some drama and interest in the event, or because they genuinely enjoy the competitive aspect of the occasion.

It is the younger players, however, who comprise the bulk of Fleadh Cheoil contestants. First- and second-place winners are entitled to go to Ireland and compete in the All-Ireland Fleadh Cheoil held each August. American performers have been lucky in this regard, since in Ireland, there are fleadhanna held for each of the thirty-two counties. These first- and second-place winners go on to the provincial fleadhanna, of which there are four. The first- and second-place provincial victors are then entitled to compete in the national All-Ireland Fleadh Cheoil. Thus, an American contestant has one less round of competition.

Competitors from Chicago have done well in the All-Ireland. In the four All-Irelands since 1974, Chicago musicians and singers have won thirty-four prizes, fourteen of them firsts. Seven of the firsts were won in the highly competitive over-18 categories in fiddle, piano accordion and women's Irish singing.

The Fleadh Cheoil in Chicago is held in the spring of each year, and virtually all the city's Irish musicians appear, though all do not compete. During the competitions (usually held in the classrooms and main auditorium of a high school), small groups of musicians begin sessions in the hallways or outside the building. The high point of the event is the céilí band competition, for this is the one event in which nearly all the senior musicians participate. There are always two, sometimes three céilí bands, and excitement is always high among the audience for this competition.

The Fleadh Cheoil, like concerts and céilís, is an occasion where the general public can see Irish traditional music in a comfortable, neutral milieu. The crowds attending the Chicago Fleadh Cheoil usually number in the hundreds, and, though there is not an extensive advertising campaign, many persons from outside the Irish community do attend. While the Fleadh Cheoil has not figured as an essential element of Chicago's Irish music scene over the years, its existence is an indication that the tradition is alive and flourishing.

- **Sessions**

The performance domain discussed in the preceding pages have all possessed one thing in common: they are occasions where the musical performer directs his or her performance to an audience made up largely of non-musicians.

The session, however, is an occasion where the musician plays primarily for self-satisfaction in the company of fellow musicians. The musicians playing in a session are not attempting to entertain, although there may be a number of bystanders who are thoroughly entertained by the performance. The chief motivation of a performer in a session is to express his or her musical individuality by engaging in a communal performance occasion with other musicians; if members of an audience are pleased with the musical performance, the musicians are also pleased, but their priority is toward making the musical performance fulfilling to themselves, not the audience.

The session may occur as a derivative event on the periphery of another musical occasion, such as a Fleadh Cheoil, or in the backstage area during a concert, or between dances at a céilí. Theoretically, whenever two musicians meet, a session can take place; usually three or four is the standard number of musicians starting up a session.

A session may be deliberately called. A meeting place — such as a home, a tavern, a music club — may be arranged, and several musicians will converge. Some of these venues may become habitual and develop a reputation as a place where good sessions can be found.

Any number of musicians may participate in a session, although most musicians feel that when the number exceeds six or seven, the performance situation becomes too chaotic, and the impact of the music is weakened and dissipated.

Virtually any instrument may be found at a session. It is the musicians participating in a session who determine who else shall participate; these decisions are made on the basis of personal likes or dislikes, not on abstract grounds of number or type of instruments or stylistic traits.

Sessions are loosely organized and usually leaderless and democratic in nature, depending upon the personalities of the performers. Some sessions are strongly dominated by an assertive player who attempts to set the pace of the session and select the tunes that will be played, but such behavior is not looked upon with favor by most musicians.

There are unwritten and largely unspoken points of etiquette that session participants observe. Overly aggressive behavior is not tolerated, nor is the performer who insists on playing too fast or too loud.

An important part of the session code of conduct is concerned with the selection of which tunes to play. Visitors or young musicians are often invited to choose a few tunes for the group. Often a musician will "suggest" a tune by playing softly the first few bars of it; if no one responds, he will cease and either attempt another tune the others might know or allow someone else to make a choice. If the performer's suggestion is taken up by the other players, there is a sense of satisfaction that, despite whatever differences might exist among them, they are on the same wave length in at least some respect.

For although the session is an occasion where an individual can be free of the restraints that bind in other domains, there is also a strong desire to achieve a measure of solidarity with other persons who possess the same commitment to an esoteric, specialized body of knowledge.

Sessions are spontaneous in format and repertoire, and virtually any tune in the Irish folk music repertoire may be performed. Dance music predominates in sessions, and most of the dance tunes are reels. Sometimes a slow air or a song is heard if specially requested by a musician or audience member. During a really exciting, fast-paced session, the music pours forth in an unrestricted flow, each tune suggesting another, as long as the musicians can muster enough energy and enough new tunes to continue. Once a tune has been played, it is generally not played again unless the musicians have a special liking for it or it is requested by a bystander.

In explaining the dynamic of the Irish music session, one immediately thinks of the jam sessions of jazz musicians, and comparison between the two idioms is not without interest.

Cameron's definition of a jazz jam session as "an informal but traditionally-structured association of a small number of self-selected musicians who come together for the primary purpose of playing music which they choose purely in accordance with their own esthetic standards" (1954:177) is an adequate encapsulation of the Irish music session as well.

Cameron, however, goes on to describe how jazz musicians make strenuous attempts to hold their sessions away from the interference of public scrutiny and unwelcome musicians; Irish musicians, while they do not enjoy being incessantly harassed by obnoxious bystanders devoid of intelligent interest in the music, do not make a concerted effort to hold their sessions in obscure, out-of-the-way places. Indeed, most Irish musicians feel a session should be in public so the tradition does not become hidden away in small circles of musicians playing only in private homes.

Some environments are more conducive to a good session than others, of course, and the primary consideration in selecting a public session venue is the good will of the management. A relaxed atmosphere is also important. Public attendance is welcomed, as it is felt that a session is made more lively. Though musicians do not deliberately recruit an audience, they seldom make objections when one materializes.

The Irish music session also functions, like its jazz counterpart, as a means of enculturating the novice (Becker 1951:136). Aspiring musicians are exposed to the lore of the idiom, as well as to the aesthetic attitudes of other performers. They also learn a good deal about the technical performance of the music by watching mature musicians and, above all, by listening to them.

While one might agree that the Irish music session is "a proving ground for upwardly mobile individuals within the musical community" (Stebbins 1968:322), there is not the same degree of tension or conflict that many commentators have attributed to the jazz session. The Irish music session is not a "cutting session" in which the newcomer must challenge and conquer the established performers or be demolished and humiliated.

Possibly because the Irish music session has such a flexible structure that allows performers to play all the time if they wish without deferring to others, and because Irish musicians are not competing with other musicians for jobs, the tension and conflict that might be present in a situation where musicians in the same economic market might be required to "prove" themselves are not present.

The Irish music session does offer a young player the chance to display his or her command of the idiom and ability to perform competently in an accepted traditional style. New musicians at an Irish music session are viewed with interest until their abilities can be discerned; if they are still in the learning stages, they receive encouragement and supportive comments with some occasional mildly-expressed constructive criticism.

If the newcomer is a fully accomplished performer, he or she may expect to be asked to play a solo or two that will be listened to with great interest, and the newcomer will be plied eagerly for new and unusual tunes the others may not have heard.

As long as the newcomer is not personally offensive, he or she will not be regarded as a threat or interloper but as a welcome member of the musical community.

In Chicago today, impromptu sessions might occur at any musical occasion where two or more Irish musicians are playing. Regularly scheduled sessions are held in the headquarters of the Francis O'Neill Music Club on the city's Northwestside every Thursday night, although this generally attracts only the young players who are enrolled in the club's music classes. Sessions are guaranteed to occur after the formal meetings of any one of Chicago's three music clubs, but regular weekly sessions of adult musicians are not currently organized in Chicago.

The only sites where sessions of adult Irish musicians consistently take place are in taverns. There were a number of these venues in the 1950s, though in 1978, only one tavern can be counted on to have a session of this kind, the 6511 Club located at 6511 S. Kedzie. It was formerly named Flanagan's and was also known to some musicians as Tom's or Frank's, having seen a succession of owners. It is small, austere in furnishings and equipped only with a billiard table and jukebox for diversion.

Its beige brick exterior is cast in the typical Chicago post-World War II architectural mold of a simple two-story rectangle squatting inconspicuously in the middle of the block alongside other similarly nondescript buildings. Aside from the metal shamrock above the small square window next to the front door, there is no other sign or announcement of the establishment's title or type of business other than an occasionally lighted Tuborg Beer sign above the door.

The 6511 Club started having Irish music sessions about three years ago, and when Hoban's Tavern a few blocks north on 63rd Street closed in the fall of 1975, the 6511 Club was the only tavern on the Southside of Chicago where Irish musicians could gather for a session. The bar has never had commercial entertainment, as it is too small; musicians who play there receive some free drinks from the bartender and possibly a few dollars from an enthusiastic patron (though the customers are much more likely to show their appreciation by buying the musicians drinks).

The customers are mostly male. They are generally between the ages of forty and sixty, though the last two years have seen many men in their twenties and thirties frequenting the bar. Music sessions tend to draw younger patrons, particularly females. Friday and Saturday night crowds are more heterogeneous in terms of gender and age. While the majority of customers are from Ireland, there are several persons from the predominantly Polish and Lithuanian neighborhood that also stop in on occasion. There are several other bars along the street, and sometimes patrons from other taverns make a brief appearance.

Sessions of Irish music occur primarily on Friday, Saturday or Sunday nights, although a handful of musicians may decide to stop into the club on a weekday night, or visiting musicians from out of town may be brought in whenever they are in the area. The sessions begin after the musicians have had a few drinks to relax and they proceed at a leisurely pace from anywhere from one-to-six hours.

When the bar is unusually crowded, a back store-room is opened, and the music session can be moved in there, if the noise of the bar is too distracting to the musicians. Some of the patrons are attentive to the session, while others continue their various activities of billiard-playing, conversing, drinking or staring silently into space. Occasionally, some impromptu dancing may be seen.

Ireland's 32, a tavern on the Northwestside, is a larger establishment that offers commercial entertainment and sometimes hires Irish folk musicians. Only the 6511 Club, however, makes an effort to encourage open sessions, and it is the only Chicago tavern that has retained such a policy toward the holding of sessions. The 6511 Club's owner and bartenders are enthusiasts of the music, and this is the chief reason that the sessions are allowed to occur.

In assessing the importance of the session in the musical culture of Irish folk music in Chicago, it should be realized that the session is the one musical occasion that has remained firmly within the control of the musicians themselves. It is the nucleus of the living tradition and is the chief means of transmitting the values and knowledge possessed by the idiom's experienced elders to younger, emerging players.

The session serves as a forum for the exchange of new ideas and new repertoire and is, at the same time, a solid reaffirmation of the existing musical order, as the old tunes are resurrected and given another airing. It is cathartic and thoroughly revitalizing.

The session has been the chief vehicle for keeping the tradition alive in Chicago during the excessively lean years suffered over the last half century. Though Irish traditional music vanished from the mainstream American popular entertainment world and even receded into the backwaters of its own ethnic community, it continued to thrive in sessions both in private homes and at small taverns among musicians and aficionados fired by an insatiable enthusiasm for "a good crack".

The last decade may have witnessed an increase in céilís, concerts and Fleadhanna Cheoil featuring Irish folk music, but, without the existence of the session, it is difficult to see how the revival of the last few years could ever have been possible.

CHAPTER SIX: Performers and Audiences

- **General Characteristics**

WHEN CONSIDERED AS a group, performers of Irish folk music in America exhibit a great deal of heterogeneity, defying the analyst who would rashly attempt to draw a clear composite portrait of the typical representative of this population. Indeed, it is this tremendous variation in musical and geographic features that renders the Irish folk musician in America such an absorbing subject of study.

It is possible, however, to obtain a general view of the persons involved in the performance of Irish folk music in Chicago and of the personal and musical relationships that exist among them. This chapter also discusses the relationship of the musician to the non-musical community and examines the importance of the musician within the changing value system of the Irish community in Chicago.

The chief demographic characteristics that define the performer of Irish folk music in Chicago are **national origin**, **age**, **gender**, **religion**, **socio-economic status**, **residency** and **education level**. These parameters are not static, however, but are subject to shifts both sudden and gradual that increase or diminish their importance as accurate profile indices.

As far as national origin, the majority of performers of Irish traditional music in Chicago are natives of Ireland, with nearly every county of Ireland represented among the Chicago Irish music community. First-generation Irish-Americans whose parents came from Ireland comprise the next sizeable group, although the last decade has witnessed the hitherto nearly unknown phenomenon of many persons with no Irish ancestry whatever becoming active, proficient performers of Irish folk music. This group with origins outside the Irish community now rivals the first-generation group in number.

Second-generation performers whose grandparents came from Ireland are rare unless their parents played the music; it is only in the last decade that persons who are three or more generations removed from Irish-born forebears have become involved with Irish folk music. Continuity of the tradition in Chicago seems to have been limited to only two generations in a family; that is, second-generation performers did not have grandparents who played the music, nor do first-generation performers whose parents played succeed in transmitting the tradition to their offspring.

The revival of Irish-American ethnic cultural consciousness has taken place during the last few years may manage to extend the link through three generations, particularly since new methods of transmission are able to reach more young people than was previously the case (see Chapter Seven). Among the younger players coming to Irish music today are several whose Irish ancestors came to America three and more generations ago and who, culturally speaking, have as little familiarity with Ireland as individuals whose lineage is wholly non-Irish.

Still, it is true to state that Irish folk music in Chicago, as in the other American cities where it exists today, remains an activity predominantly performed by Irish emigrants or persons with very immediate familial ties to Ireland. This close bond to the tradition's source has pertained throughout the history of Irish folk music in America and has contributed significantly to the preservation of the idiom in America in the same form as it exists in Ireland.

If one were to chart an age profile of traditional Irish musicians in Chicago, one could not help but notice the preponderance of performers born before 1930 and the comparatively miniscule number of performers born between 1930 and 1950.

The reasons for this disparity were discussed in Chapter One and can be seen as a indication of the breakdown in the continuity of the transmission process that began in the 1930s and continued through the 1950s and into the early 1960s. Coupled with the marked decline in Irish emigration to America after 1930, the inability to pass the music on to the generation of Irish-Americans growing up in the 1930s, '40s and '50s has had serious consequences for the general strength of the tradition.

Within the last ten years, however, many performers have been drawn from the generation born after 1950, and the continuity of transmission has to some extent been partially restored. This resurgence of interest following a lapse of one complete generation can best be explained by the increased public accessibility of the music that has been paralleled and, in some cases inspired by, the growth of festivals, musicians' associations and schools offering instruction in Irish music.

The one hundred to one hundred twenty-five pupils currently enrolled in Chicago's schools of Irish music are a potentially rich source of adult musicians who could totally reverse the declining trends of the tradition and reshape the character of Irish folk music in Chicago in the 1980s and 1990s.

The increased participation of Irish-Americans born after 1950 has occurred alongside a growth in the number of female performers of Irish music in Chicago. In the first three decades of the 20th century, fiddle players Selena O'Neill and Theresa Geary were two of Chicago's most renowned Irish musicians. Since the mid-1930s, pianist Eleanor Neary and accordionists Nell O'Hara and Mrs. McLaughlin, fiddlers Ann Scully, Anna McGoldrick and Eileen Fitzgerald and concertina player Mrs. Tangney were also stalwarts of the Chicago Irish folk music scene during the 1930s, '40s and '50s.

In addition to Eleanor Neary, pianist Nancy Harling, fiddlers Maida Sugrue, Una McGlew and fiddler/pianist Mary McDonagh are currently active in Chicago Irish music circles. Among female Irish musicians under age twenty-five, fiddler Liz Carroll is the most accomplished and the most widely known, having won the All-Ireland Senior Fiddle Championship on her first attempt in 1975 at age eighteen.

However, in examining documentary evidence from sources that describe Irish musical occasions throughout the late 19th and early 20th centuries, the paucity of women performers is immediately apparent. While newspaper accounts of Irish music concerts given in the late 1800s indicate that women were frequent participants, women invariably performed operatic versions of highly-arranged Irish airs from *Moore's Melodies* or presented pseudo-classical settings on harp and piano of *Moore's Melodies* or Irish nationalist songs written by Anglo-Irish poets of the middle and late 19th century.

Women's activity in the Irish traditional music milieu of the day is difficult to accurately reconstruct. The 1903 photo of the Chicago Irish Music Club has no women among its twenty-six members, nor are any women aside from Theresa Geary, Selena O'Neill and pianist Nellie Gillan mentioned by O'Neill as being known for their musicianship during that period. Since O'Neill spoke quite enthusiastically about these three women, it cannot be assumed that other women players of Irish folk music in Chicago were not mentioned by him for any other reason than that they very likely did not exist.

Of the nearly two dozen Chicago Irish musicians who appeared on 78 rpm records between the First and Second World Wars, there were four women: pianists Frances Malone, Kathleen Kearney and Eleanor Neary and fiddler Selena O'Neill. The 1957 membership list of the newly-formed Chicago Irish Musicians Association shows only seven female members of the sixty-member body, and, of those seven, only four were actually performing musicians. A photograph taken at a 1965 concert of Chicago Irish musicians reveals three women among the thirty-four performers onstage.

Currently, males continue to make up the majority of active performers, but the proportion of male-to-female musicians is substantially lower in the under-twenty-five age bracket than in the twenty-five-to-fifty age group or among Irish musicians over fifty years of age.

Participation by females is not limited to any particular instrument, nor are there separate male-female categories in instrumental competitions. This trend of increasing public performance by young female Irish folk musicians is occurring in Britain, Ireland, Australia, Europe and North America. It is reflected in several magazine and newspaper photographs of Irish music ensembles consisting of persons under age eighteen, ensembles in which there is often a majority of females.

Out of the one hundred and five mixed solo competition categories in the 1977 All-Ireland Fleadh Cheoil, thirty-five (one-third of the total) were won by women (Treoir 1977:3-7). Also of interest in this regard is the fact that the uilleann piper chosen for the Comhaltas Ceoltóirí Éireann North American tour in 1977 was a female, Máire Ní Ghráda of Cork. The uilleann pipes have traditionally been thought of as a male instrument, especially in terms of public, professional performance.

The greater public activity of women in Irish folk music in recent years has not been responsible for any changes within the tradition, as far as musical performance is concerned. That is, an identifiably "feminine" dimension has not emerged in the performance of Irish traditional music.

Most Irish-born and first-generation performers of Irish music in Chicago are of the Roman Catholic faith or, if not active practitioners, are from Roman Catholic backgrounds. Of the comparatively smaller number of non-Catholic Irish emigrants to the United States over the last two centuries, few have associated themselves with the mainly Catholic Irish-American community that sponsors Irish folk music activities. The scarcity of non-Catholic performers of Irish traditional music from among the Irish-born group seems to result from the lack of exposure to the music in Ireland arising from cultural or social class differences rather than from any type of abstention founded upon blatantly sectarian grounds. In areas of Ireland where Catholics and Protestants share similar socio-economic traits and have not had a long tradition of overt religious animosity, Irish traditional music is just as likely to be found among both groups.

The newly-emerging group of Irish musicians in Chicago who have existent or non-existent ancestral ties with Ireland reveals a wide diversity of religious backgrounds, ranging through most of the Protestant faiths and including Jews, atheists, lapsed Roman Catholics and Eastern Orthodox Catholics, Mormons and some recently-created revivalistic religious groups. This suggests that the role of religion as an important variable in the determination of a composite portrait of the Irish musician in Chicago is becoming less significant.

In terms of socio-economic traits most Irish musicians in Chicago belong to the various sub-categories ranked under the heading of "middle-class". In this they mirror the socio-economic experience of the overall Chicago Irish population in which the 1969 median family income was $13,400 ($14,500 for families in the suburbs) and $3,400 for unrelated individuals in both Chicago and its suburban areas (City of Chicago 1976b:23).

Occupations of performers are varied, encompassing blue-collar jobs (maintenance employees, workers in the building trades, plumbers, electricians, truck mechanics, elevator operators, factory workers, railroad employees) and white-collar positions (civil servants, employment service contractors, travel agents, primary- and secondary-school teachers, bank clerks, salesmen, biological laboratory workers).

Despite the high regard for education that exists among the American Irish, most Irish folk musicians have achieved their present station without recourse to post-secondary level education. American-born performers of Irish folk music are more likely to have attended college, and this is particularly true of those musicians under age twenty-five.

Residency patterns are equally as diverse as occupational choice among Irish musicians in Chicago, with performers spread throughout the city limits and suburbs of the Chicago metropolitan area, living in one- and two-bedroom apartments and small duplexes in the city as well as spacious split-level and ranch-style homes in the suburbs. Many musicians moved to different sections of the city or out of the city and into suburban areas during the 1960s and '70s as part of the general urban drift that characterized Chicago's population during this period — a period in which seventy-two per-cent of the city's inhabitants changed address at least once between 1960 and 1970 (City of Chicago 1976b:21).

It was noted in Chapter One that the American Irish have tended to lose their cultural distinctiveness as they have risen in the American socio-economic pyramid, casting off old traditions and attitudes like worn, out-of-fashion clothes. Though the dichotomy of the "lace curtain Irish" versus "shanty Irish" is less acute now than it was a few decades ago, it becomes quickly apparent to any observer of Irish-American social functions featuring Irish folk music that the "lace curtain element" (i.e. those of the upper class or aspiring to upper-class status) is noticeably absent at these occasions.

Despite the improvement in socio-economic status achieved by many performers of traditional Irish music (both emigrants and American-born), there is a strong feeling among them that Irish folk music in America is a "grassroots" music that has been in the past, is presently and will be in the future supported and sustained primarily by persons of non-elite, humble social and economic backgrounds. The Irish-American social clubs and social occasions attended primarily by American-born lawyers, doctors, high-level corporation executives, university professors and administrators, politicians and wealthy businessmen are typically no more sympathetic toward nor supportive of Irish folk music than are the members of a Masonic Lodge, B'Nai B'rith Society or Bulgarian-Macedonian Beneficial Association.

- **Specialists and Professionals**

Among the larger community of Irish musicians in Chicago, there exist several sub-groups delineated according to the degree of **specialization** and **professionalism** characterizing their performances. These two terms have been discussed in detail by other authors, most notably Alan Merriam, who set forth the basic definitions that will be used in this discussion (1964:124-125).

A **specialist** is an individual who performs a particular service utilizing a set of skills or a body of knowledge not possessed by all members of the society. A **professional** is a specialist who receives some form of economic compensation for the performance of his or her specialized activity.

By these definitions, all performers of Irish music in Chicago could be considered specialists in that they have acquired a unique set of musical skills and possess a restricted body of musical knowledge; however, as will be seen, some performers are more specialized than others within the idiom.

Similarly, most traditional Irish musicians in Chicago have been the recipient of some kind of economic compensation, ranging from free food and drink to monetary payment. The degree of professionalism, however, varies considerably among musicians.

Very few performers of Irish folk music in the United States or in Ireland are fully professional, i.e. able to live entirely by their earnings from musical performance of music teaching. This was not always the case, as has been mentioned in Chapter One, but the current value of traditional Irish music as a commodity in the entertainment market of the Irish-American and mainstream American communities is not too high, though it is rising in Ireland. Thus, in this paper, the term "professional" is used to refer to musicians who are fully professional and economically self-sufficient via their musical activity.

A great deal of respect is given to these professionals by their non-professional fellow musicians, as it is generally held that professional performers are able to practice music more intensively and perfect their technique and their command of the idiom by frequent public performance. However, since the professional Irish musician is most often hired to play in taverns, his or her reputation not uncommonly becomes tinged with the unsavouriness generally attached to persons working regularly in a tavern environment. Thus, while the status of a professional is high in musical terms, it may be considerably lower when the individual is viewed in an overall social perspective.

Traditional Irish musicians have often been the chief musical specialists of their communities, but specialization within the musical community itself has also been known in the past. Many musicians who performed with vaudeville companies during the last century oriented their repertoire and performance style for a specific stage performance situation. It was not uncommon for such performers to limit their repertoire to a few tunes carefully selected and rehearsed for frequent public performance; some performers, in fact, possessed only a small tune repertoire — mostly popular song airs and simple dance tunes — but played for audiences generally unacquainted with the tradition and likely to be uncritical concerning the performer's repertoire choice.

Since comedy monologues and sketches, songs and dances were also featured in many stage acts of professional 19th-century Irish musicians, a small stock of tunes was all that was necessary. Francis O'Neill relates one amusing incident illustrating this type of musical specialist, Chicago-born uilleann piper Charles McNurney:

> A very capable performer on the Union pipes of the few tunes comprising his theatrical repertory, was "Charley" McNurney, the musical member of the "Callahan and Mack" vaudeville combination, which toured Australia very early in the twentieth century.
>
> Some four or five days after their first performance at Sydney, Mack was approached on the street by a man whom he recognized as the occupant of a seat in the front row at every performance.
>
> "Excuse me, sir," said the man, "but would you mind telling me what might be the tail of your name?"
>
> "The tail of my name! What do you mean?" answered the piper, in surprise.
>
> "Oh, I mane no offense at all, sir; only surely there must be something afther Mack."
>
> "So there is, indeed," replied the man of music, good-naturedly. "My name is McNurney."
>
> "For God's sake, Mr. McNurney," exclaimed the fascinated exile, "is there only three 'chunes' in the pipes? Night after night I've been going to hear you play, but never a 'chune' comes out of your chanter but the same three."
>
> Of course the disappointed lover of the music of his motherland was not aware that "Charley" McNurney was but following the custom of musicians and vocalists in the theatrical profession, who seldom vary the favorite numbers in their program (O'Neill 1913:344).

Most non-professional performers, on the other hand, play at a variety of musical occasions and, consequently, have developed a diverse repertoire to meet the various demands placed upon them at these occasions. Many musicians, however, concentrate in certain areas of the tradition in consonance with their own personal preferences and capabilities. Some play only dance music and have but one or two airs; others know mostly song airs and only a few dance tunes besides a plethora of waltzes; fewer musicians have an evenly-balanced repertoire encompassing the full spectrum of Irish folk music.

In the last decade a new class of specialists has come into being whose repertoire is tailored especially for accompanying Irish dance competitions. Along with the increase during the 1960s of Irish step-dancing schools, pupils and feiseanna came an entirely new style of solo step-dancing introduced into the United States and Canada by teachers who had been visiting Ireland for several years and began returning with new steps based on changing aesthetic conceptions of traditional Irish solo dancing.

The new dancing style is marked by a growth in complexity of step patterns, and the relationship between the steps and the musical accompaniment has in many cases been drastically altered, most noticeably in the area of tempo.

Reels are danced to extremely rapid accompaniment, while the increased complexity of step patterns for hornpipes and figure dances has necessitated a great decrease in the accompaniment tempo for these dances. The treble jig (a new genre fashioned from the double jig solo dance) requires the playing of a double jig slowed down to less than half the normal speed.

It is a common complaint of many Irish folk musicians that dancers are now trained in such a way that they are unable to dance to music as it is normally played outside of formal dance competition and exhibition contexts (Breathnach 1965:3 and 1970:118). These criticisms ignore the fact that Irish dance music and Irish solo dancing have long been separate artistic entities that have developed apart from each other, though they originally were inextricably intertwined.

The distance between the two traditions was never before so obvious as it became in the last decade with the revolution in step-dancing technique and style. Since the majority of Irish folk musicians were unwilling or unable to adjust their accompaniment methods in accordance with the change in dancing, a new class of musical specialists came to the fore.

Set or figure dances are extremely important in the competitive Irish step-dancing hierarchy, as they are used to determine the "champions" of various age groups and represent the most rigorous test of a step-dancer's skill. They are not generally played by most musicians, since few set dance tunes are held to be particularly interesting as musical compositions. However, musicians playing for the championship events must know the specific set dance tune that accompanies each of the thirty-odd set dances, as a competitor may request or be requested by the adjudicator to perform any of the dances in the set dance repertoire.

Fiddler Liz Carroll and piano accordionist James Keane, Jr. of Chicago have been in great demand for feiseanna throughout the U.S. and Canada for the last four years because of their ability to play the set dances required for the championships and because of their solidly consistent performances on the dancing competition stage. Their technical competence is augmented by their flexibility in adapting to the particular requirements placed upon them in different circumstances.

Liz and Jim are also eagerly sought by Irish dance teachers in Chicago to play for exhibitions put on by the dancing schools, especially for the choreographed compositions created by the teachers. These compositions are complex juxtapositions of several airs and dance tunes encompassing various genres, tempos, keys and meters, and there are few active Chicago Irish musicians skilled enough to perform them in all their subtleties

When Irish ensemble dancing was more commonly found in the Chicago Irish community fifteen and more years ago, there were musicians who specialized in providing the dance music to accompany dances along the order of "The Stack of Barley", "the Kerry Set", "The Clare Set", "The Siege of Ennis" and other miscellaneous highland flings, barn dances and polkas. These musicians were in constant demand to play at the dances of organizations and at dances sponsored by individual entrepreneurs held in parks, ballrooms and taverns.

Accordion and concertina player Terry Teahan played the Irish dance circuit in Chicago for 23 years (1943-1966) for at least three nights a week. While he loved the music and the dancing, the performing also supplemented his modest income as an Illinois Central Railroad employee. Terry and the other musicians that occasionally performed with him did not rehearse or arrange their repertoire; they each possessed a common stock of Irish dance tunes in the required genres and "belted them out", according to Terry.

Before the recent change in Irish solo dancing, these musicians were also engaged to play at feiseanna, but they have now had to yield this context to other specialists as the requirements for feis musicians have become more complex and demanding in terms of repertoire specialization. "Most of the music in those days was geared to dancing," says Teahan, speaking of the decades before 1970. "I'm out on a limb today unless I have a dancer. They're part of you. A dancer to me is more essential than having another musician with me."

A typical playing night for Terry Teahan during the 1940s, '50s and '60s might include playing for a dance held by a club such as the Sarsfield Limerickmen's Club for five dollars a night; after finishing up there, he would go to fiddler Tommy Ryan's loft at Jackson and Cicero on the Westside and play for more dancing. Later, John Scott (button accordion) and Pat Richardson (drums) would stop over and join him after their engagement playing for dancers at Connolly's Tavern a half block away.

For playing at Mayoman Tony Morrally's dance at 47th and Halsted on the Southside, Terry would receive twelve dollars. Terry stresses this was very good pay at the time, but he would leave his home at Springfield and Polk on the Westside around eight o'clock in the evening, travel by bus and streetcar to the dance, and arrive home Sunday morning "just in time to go to eight o'clock Mass."

Terry Teahan and his musical colleagues have been replaced at the majority of Chicago Irish dances by the hybrid ensembles described in the preceding chapter. These ensembles that provide "Irish-American music" play very little traditional Irish music, but very often the lead instrumentalist is a musician formerly involved in playing traditional music. Such a musician is Jimmy Thornton, a native of Oak Park, Illinois, now living on Chicago's Southwestside and teaching at a Chicago public high school.

Beginning at an early age on the tinwhistle, Jimmy advanced quickly to the flute and in 1969 took up the button accordion. He is a solid traditional player and has won several prizes in Irish traditional music competitions; he plays mainly with a hybrid band called Ted Healy and the Bachelors that performs exclusively for paid occasions: dinner dances, benefit dances and weddings.

Jimmy rarely discusses his activities with the band except to comment that it dulls his traditional playing skills somewhat. He makes it clear that he plays with the group strictly for the money and not for any aesthetic reasons. He feels fortunate that his traditional style has not significantly suffered from his involvement with another musical idiom; this is a fate that frequently befalls traditional players who become immersed in performing in a hybrid ensemble. When Jimmy teaches the tinwhistle, flute or accordion, it is Irish folk music that he transmits and not the hybrid "Irish-American" repertoire of Ted Healy and the Bachelors.

Uilleann piper Joe Shannon represents another type of performer who almost never plays in public and, on the rare occasions he does so, does not request or receive monetary compensation. This reticence is not due to lack of ability, for Joe has been acknowledged as the most accomplished uilleann piper in the U.S. by pipers and piping connoisseurs in Ireland, England, Scotland and America.

In the 1930s and '40s, Joe often played in public, beginning with Pat Roche's Harp and Shamrock Orchestra at the 1934 Chicago World's Fair. After the Fair ended, Joe teamed up with accordionists Tom Tracy and Tony Lowe and played in taverns throughout the Southside, notably Erin's Isle at 56th and Halsted and the Celtic Club at 76th and Halsted. Joe also played the city's Irish dance circuit during this period.

Today, however, he is a father of twelve children (most of them grown and living away from home) and a City of Chicago fireman. Joe no longer drinks alcoholic beverages, and this, too, is a possible reason for his wishing to avoid performing in taverns, or at venues where the chief and sometimes only payment is in drink. His only public appearances in recent years have been at the informal music sessions held when touring groups of Irish musicians, singers and dancers visit Chicago or when there is a concert of local Irish musicians organized by a Chicago Irish musicians' club.

The only public performance Joe has ever made outside the city was when he flew to Washington, D.C. in July, 1976 to take part in the Irish cultural events at the Smithsonian Institution's Festival of American Folklife. Since then there have been numerous offers made to Joe by festival and tour promoters, but he has turned all of them down.

All pipers or aspiring pipers are welcome to Joe's home, and Joe will gladly host a small informal session in his house. Yet, in spite of the urgings of his friends and many admirers, Joe Shannon possesses no desire to become involved again with professional, regular public performance, although he feels that he has never played the uilleann pipes better than he does at present. Instead, he is content to remain a parlor piper, an amateur virtuoso who plays simply for the enjoyment of himself and a few devotees and fellow musicians.

None of the five specialists mentioned here are fully professional nor have they ever been so at any time during their musical careers. this is due in part to the limited market for their services in the Chicago area. Were they to move to an area such as New York that has more opportunities for the performance of Irish folk music, they could possibly attain full professional status much more quickly and easily, should they wish.

A greater demand for Irish folk music in Chicago might come about were there to be a sudden, drastic change in the entertainment tastes of the patrons of Chicago's Irish taverns and of the individuals who attend the dances sponsored by local Irish social and political organizations. Until that occurs, anyone attempting to make a full-time living from playing or teaching Irish music in Chicago will find the going rather precarious.

Since its earliest existence in Chicago, Irish folk music has been primarily the province of non-professional, non-specialized musicians and teachers. While opportunities for professionals and specialists have arisen from time to time, the musical occasions of the Irish community have been staffed largely by average "musicianers" who play the dance tunes and airs they learned as youths.

Most musicians hired for performances are engaged by promoters who have the idea it is necessary to pay money to ensure that some musical entertainment will be provided as scheduled for the particular occasion. The quality of the music, its authenticity as a genuine expression of Irish culture, the appropriateness of various instruments to certain performance contexts are rarely considered by the organizers of these events. In many instances, it becomes clear that if the music was recorded rather than live, neither the organizers nor the audience would be distressed or perhaps even aware of the difference.

Though it might be possible to gauge a tradition's health according to the number of full-time professional performers and instructors it can support, it should be remembered that the bedrock of Irish traditional music in Ireland as well as in America has always been its non-professional performers, its talented amateurs, its parlor players who play solely for the "crack".

Professional performers may well provide an ideal role model and may have an effect on the surface consciousness of their audiences and non-professional colleagues, but it has been the largely unpaid and unrecognized amateur performers who have maintained the tradition through the fat and the lean periods and who have truly shaped the tradition's form and character.

- **Interactional Patterns**

The model giving the clearest insight into the patterns of interaction among performers of Irish folk music in Chicago is that of a large constellation of small clusters comprised of individuals sharing a number of personal and musical affinities. These clusters are not based on a hierarchy of musical competence, as their members span a wide range of ability levels.

Instead, extramusical factors are the chief determinants of the composition of these small groups, with individual performers, geographic areas and aesthetic attitudes toward public performance serving as the main organizational foci.

While some clusters are almost wholly isolated and self-contained, most are linked with some other groups by musicians whose activities are not restricted to one group.

Interactional patterns are to some extent shaped by the frequency of an individual's participation in public performance. Some players are almost total recluses, having retired from active musical performance years previously. Others may shun public performance but perform occasionally in the company of a few select friends who are also musicians.

Among musicians who perform in public regularly and mix freely with other musicians at public events, there are still numerous cliques of musicians who feel musical and personal ties with each other and who, at a céilí or session or feis, will be seen performing together most of the time.

Factional strife and personal rivalries appear occasionally, and instances of a particular musician refusing to attend or participate in a musical occasion where a rival performer will be present are not unknown. An event such as a céilí or concert sponsored by one group may be boycotted by musicians belonging to another organization or clique in the aftermath of a dispute.

These differences stem from personal disagreements and personality conflicts among the musicians and are generally concealed under a veneer of cool formality and superficial cordiality. Individual performers sometimes complain of receiving the "cold shoulder" treatment from musicians in another clique, but such incidents are less common now than in former years.

The relatively few performers active in Irish musical occasions and the Irish music clubs of Chicago constitute a small but significant interactional network. News of events, rumors and gossip about personalities and occurrences circulate quickly and freely within this network, although its members belong to several different clusters. These individuals are the ones most intensively involved in the decision-making processes of the Irish music clubs, and they are most often visible at public musical occasions.

Since 1964, there have been no national conventions or national organizations that draw together dispersed groups of Irish musicians living in various parts of the United States, and there is very little contact among musicians living in different cities, aside from occasional visits by individuals. Even the regional fleadhanna cheoil in New York and Chicago are attended almost exclusively by performers from the local metropolitan area. Communication between musicians in different cities is, understandably, by personal means — via letter, telephone and personal visits; no national network or channel exists among performers of Irish traditional music in America.

This fragmentation of the musical community has had deleterious consequences for the tradition, as the decline in interaction among performers has led to a weakening of the process by which new members are initiated into the tradition. The reduced visibility and accessibility of Irish folk musicians in Chicago, as they retreated into private homes and private or restricted gatherings, has made it difficult to attract many new performers.

The disappearance of musical occasions brought about a diminution of performance standards. Performers once highly accomplished have, through lack of performance opportunities with other musicians on a regular basis, lost a considerable amount of technique, repertoire, and interest.

Initiation into the idiom of Irish traditional music is not difficult to achieve once the novice has become proficient in performance. Until recently, most performers were introduced to the music through a member of their family or by a neighbor or family friend who played.

This pattern still holds for many musicians, but increasing numbers of new musicians have entered the tradition after hearing Irish folk music on records or in concert rather than by experiencing it from a member of their family or local community.

No special ceremonies or elaborate, formal rites of passage regulate or confirm the novice's musical maturity; graduation into the ranks of the fully-initiated is conferred by a hearty handshake, a few concise words of sincere praise and some simple acts of hospitality.

It would seem that a process of entropy has steadily been atomizing the interactional networks of Irish folk musicians in Chicago and, indeed, throughout the United States. Many musicians are aware of this trend and, as will be seen in the next chapter, are beginning to take active steps to reverse it while there is still time.

It is interesting to note that in the case of a rural music like traditional Irish music, the transition to an urban environment in America did not uproot its basic interactional patterns but, if anything, intensified them. Whereas in a desolate, emigration-ridden country parish in Ireland in the 19th and early 20th centuries there might be very few musicians and even fewer musical occasions, a thriving Irish community in a city like Chicago could boast a flourishing musical culture stimulated and shaped by performers from all areas of Ireland, their former local loyalties transferred intact to another highly localized situation in the Irishtowns of America.

Urbanization has not been the cause of the dissolution of the community of Irish musicians in American cities like Chicago; rather, it has been the process of suburbanization that has resulted in a tenuously-linked network of musicians scattered throughout a huge metropolitan area.

The diaspora to the far-flung suburban areas of Chicago that has marked the rise of the Irish community to unprecedented heights on the socio-economic ladder has engendered in its place the dispersion and isolation of Irish traditional musicians into small clusters of performers fragilely-bound in a steadily contracting network of vastly reduced interaction.

- **status and role**

This discussion centers around two types of status distinctions: **musical status** and **personal status**. Any attempt to characterize the status of musicians must inevitably view the performer from the perspective of both his or her performing peers and from the viewpoint of the larger community of which he or she is a part. To put it another way, the status of a musician can be defined in terms of musical traits and in terms of the personal traits that derive or are believed to derive from the fact of being a musician.

Within the community of Irish folk musicians and knowledgeable aficionados, a performer's musical status is dependent upon a number of variables. Technical excellence is an obvious criteria for high musical status, and virtuosity is recognized and enthusiastically commended. Although there are no vote polls like those conducted in the jazz and pop idioms, the relative strengths and weaknesses of outstanding performers of the past and present constitute a frequent topic of discussion among Irish musicians.

Professionalism is a related status determinant, as professional players are often judged to be highly polished, "gold-medal" performers, although this is not always borne out in reality. In some instances, full-time professional public performance has resulted in wearing down and coarsening a player's abilities and sensitivities.

Many musicians who are not exceptionally talented in the technical execution of the music often achieve a high status by virtue of their inventiveness and their ability to instill a large amount of individuality and distinctiveness into their playing. Stability and dependability are other traits that draw praise; musicians often state that a certain player is "solid" or "steady", meaning that the performer maintains an even, competent level of musicianship and is not subject to erratic spells or loss of control. "Steady" players are especially valued for céilí bands or dance accompaniment because of their consistent, predictable (though rarely spectacular) level of performance.

The ability to adapt to an unfamiliar style or tune setting is another praiseworthy characteristic that implies a flexibility and a sensitivity to other musicians. Having a large repertoire also increases an individual's musical status, as does having a repertoire of rare and unusual tunes and tune settings. If a musician does not possess any of the above-mentioned attributes but has lived long enough, he or she may attain some measure of status by virtue of seniority.

Musical status is generally achieved, though the offspring of a distinguished performer often absorbs some of the high status reflected from the parent. However, the son or daughter of a famous musician must eventually prove the legitimacy of his or her claim to high musical status on the basis of musical performance. Dynasties of traditional Irish musicians, with performers occurring in three or more generations are not uncommon in Ireland. There are, in fact, popular sayings in Irish that indicate the respect given to those whose musical abilities can be traced through their forebears and are rooted in a family heritage. For instance, "ní ón ngaoth a thóg sé é", or, "it wasn't from the wind that he got it" — the "it" referring to the individual's musical skill.

Status ranking among traditional Irish musicians is fluid, and status hierarchies fluctuate according to the relative strength with which the determining factors are held by individual musicians. A performer might have a high musical status due to brilliant technical ability, but this might be offset by arrogance and insensitivity to other players. Conversely, mediocre performers might have a high status among their colleagues as a result of their seniority, occupying a revered position as an "old-timer".

Stability and consistency of performance, technical ability, and seniority are the most significant traits that define a performer's leadership role in a session or at a céilí. These are the factors that command the greatest amount of respect among musicians, and they are the ones most frequently mentioned by Irish musicians when evaluating their peers.

The status of musicians in the eyes of non-musicians in the larger community is shaped by a different set of standards. Musical status among persons outside the musical tradition is most often the result of the performer's visibility in the public eye. Performers who have been commercially recorded or who play often in public are the first mentioned by persons whose knowledge of the music is minimal and superficial or whose contact with the music is infrequent. Occasionally, the opinions of other musicians may help mold the status hierarchy of a non-performer.

A performer who is accorded a high musical status may frequently not be the recipient of an equivalently exalted personal status. To some extent, the nature of the musical occasion has a certain effect on determining what a musician's personal status will be in the estimation of the larger community; a musician who performs habitually in bars would be accorded a lower status than a musician who plays only at dances sponsored by social and cultural groups and attended by families.

The professional musician also suffers from this ambivalence; he or she is respected for the musical proficiency that enables a living to be made from musical skill alone, yet the professional player is simultaneously denigrated because if he or she entertains in bars the work environment is often populated by persons of ill repute, or if he or she operates a school of Irish music this profession is considered to he nothing more than a hobby of slight value in the "real world".

The fundamental determinant, however, is that the traditional Irish musician is not viewed by Irish-Americans as being indispensable nor as possessing a unique body of skills and knowledge. The role of the Irish musician in most of the musical occasions in which he or she participates is that of an adjunct; the musician provides a simple service — musical entertainment or accompaniment to dancing — for which some form of compensation may or may not be received.

The necessity for the services of the Irish folk musician in American cities like Chicago has been decreasing over the years. Irish dance classes use records and tapes in preference to live performers held to be too "erratic" and "unreliable". Irish-oriented taverns use any type of musical entertainment the owners believe will be satisfied with minimum payment while bringing in a large crowd and selling a huge amount of drink.

Curiously, the only occasions where a traditional Irish musician in the United States is certain of receiving recognition and status as an artist rather than a hireling are at concerts or festivals outside the Irish community that are attended predominantly by persons who have in many cases never before heard Irish folk music before. Persons who regularly frequent musical occasions sponsored by Irish cultural revival organizations, such as Irish-language instruction groups or Irish music clubs, are generally more aware of the musicians as preservers of an important aspect of the Irish cultural heritage.

After the fall of the Gaelic aristocracy in 17th-century Ireland, there were still some members of the old Irish lords and some few landowners of the Anglo-Irish Ascendancy who acted as patrons to the harpers and uilleann pipers of the 18th century. These musicians did not achieve a status or importance beyond that of house entertainers, however, and their tenure in the Big Houses of the Ascendancy was always marked by uncertainty. More often, they were itinerant and dependent upon the support of the more humble orders of society.

Still, the itinerant musician was considered a tradesman's equal in status; indeed, the following vignette from the 18th century suggests that the itinerant musician may have enjoyed even higher status:

> Mr. Derrick, in his Letters, tells a story to our purpose. He and his fellow traveller being driven by a shower of rain into a hut near Killarney, entered into conversation with their hosts, a poor old couple. "We asked the woman (says he) how she intended to support her family. Some of them, she answered, as they grow up, shall go out to service, and one or two help me, in and about my rounds at home; as for Donough, my eldest boy, who was blinded by the small pox, we have got a man to teach him the bagpipes, with which and begging, there is no fear, under God, but he may get an honest livelihood, and live very comfortably; at any rate, it is better than being a sorry tradesman." (Walker 1786:110)

As the 19th century progressed, professional folk musicians in Ireland found it more difficult to eke out a living from public performance in Ireland. The segment of society that had latterly provided them with the bulk of their livelihood had been economically and psychologically ravaged by the Great Famine of 1845-1849. The Act of Union in 1800 that had brought Ireland closer into the United Kingdom by stripping her of an independent, sovereign legislative body had the concomitant effect of driving out the majority of large Ascendancy landowners who had also occasionally supported the professional musicians.

The Famine accelerated this process of decline and instigated among its survivors an all-consuming land hunger that combined with a severely puritanical worldview toward the pursuit of pleasure to force the professional musicians and dancing masters into the poorhouse or onto the steampacket bound for America.

The performer of traditional Irish music was reduced to a level of insignificance never before encountered in Ireland; the grimness of the situation was reflected in these comments, made around 1880 by a woman from Donegal who had survived the Famine:

> It didn't matter who was related to you, your friend was whoever would give you a bite to put in your mouth. Sport and pastimes disappeared. Poetry, music, and dancing stopped. They lost and forgot them all and when the times improved in other respects, these things never returned as they had been. *Marbh an gorta achan rud* [The Famine killed everything] (Dunleavy 1974:23).

The Irish musicians who emigrated to America in the wake of the Famine were greeted by a much greater range of opportunities. However, the boom did not last all that long; by 1900, changes in the tastes of popular entertainment-going audiences were already evident and had forced many Irish-American musicians to abandon an entertainment medium that no longer had any use for their talents.

Other musicians who had comedy routines in their acts were harassed into an early retirement by zealous protectors of Irish national honor who asserted that the comedy sketches of the Irish vaudeville performers represented scandalous calumnies upon the Irish character while providing free ammunition for anti-Irish bigots. The *Chicago Citizen* frequently blasted professional Irish theatrical and musical performers it felt were giving an unbecoming picture of the ethnic group to outsiders, as in this editorial titled "So-Called Irish Dramas":

> The traditional and conventional stage Irishman must be driven from the stage, if it takes murder to do it ... Of Harrigan and Hart, *The Citizen* can have nothing to say. The men are evidently from the slums and not the product of any race or decent order of Intelligence, but from the abortive condition of civilization which surrounded them. They and their "plays" are for the vulgar and inane ... If others will not, let the Irish people demand that, if they are to be pictured and analyzed on the stage, then real impulses and aspirations, and their native politeness, courtesy, and manhood shall be the theme and subject. The kipeen and the bottle, the tattered coat, the caubeen and the dudeen must be banished from the stage as national characteristics. Hiss the actor that vulgarly and ignorantly presents either. (*Chicago Citizen* 3/8/1884:4).

In addition to changing tastes among the Irish-American audiences that attended musical occasions, the irreversible workings of the American assimilation process was undermining the position of the traditional Irish musician within the ethnic enclave. Writing in 1913, Francis O'Neill discussed the reasons behind the decline of the traditional musicians in the Irish-American communities of the early 1900s:

> A score of years ago pipers, fiddlers, and singers, filled a large part of every Irish programme, and they were invariably treated with due consideration; and it is more than likely they would be at least as much in evidence on Irish platforms in more recent times were they satisfied with conventional compliments for their services. Irish music has come to be regarded as merely an accessory to the success of some money-making entertainment, independent of all consideration of its ethical value ...

> In new and growing communities, church extension absorbs not a little of the energies of the Irish race, and the majority of their organizations also have religious affiliations. Consequently their entertainments, with few exceptions, are gotten up in the interest of charity or church building, hence paid talent is not in favor. Pleasure clubs engage bands or orchestras to play at their balls because nothing but the latest in steps and music will satisfy the members, and if an Irish tune is played at all, it is a hackneyed one included in a set of quadrilles.
>
> Where then is the Irish musician to obtain patronage? If neglected by our own people, what can he reasonably expect from others?
>
> The most accomplished Irish musician must inevitably drop out of sight, unless willing to respond to calls in every part of the city to "play a few tunes" without expectation of fee or reward, other than applause and good wishes.
>
> Under such circumstances, of which we have many instances in mind, what motive except pure love of it can those musically inclined have, to spend time and money in learning to play Irish music from which they can seldom hope to derive any pecuniary advantage ...
>
> Commercialism of the day has apparently stunted the nobler impulses of our natures, as far as music is concerned. Instead of securing the best talent available for Irish gatherings, committees on entertainments not infrequently engage the lowest bidder (which of course means the poorest performer) if free service can not be obtained. Quite obviously the result is not calculated to advance the interest of Irish music ...
>
> If Irish music is to regain its lost prestige — and its fruition is not beyond the range of possibilities — the attitude of chronic apathy must come speedily to an end ... Difficulties will disappear, and the problem will solve itself when we make the study of Irish music worth while, and that will be when we show our appreciation by paying for it liberally on all occasions. The demand will create the supply as with other commodities (O'Neill 1913: 480, 482).

Unfortunately, the dynamic of demand-and-supply advocated by O'Neill was overwhelmed by the dynamic of acculturation that had already made substantial inroads into the cultural life of the American Irish. O'Neill's assessment of the social factors contributing to the decline of traditional Irish music in the United States was keenly incisive; sixty-five years later, it remains an accurate description of the music's current status in Chicago.

O'Neill perceived the problem in fundamentally economic terms. The Irish folk musician was a skilled craftsperson who deserved to be paid on the basis of technical accomplishment, the store of unique musical knowledge and the important role of serving as cultural conservator. Above all, the Irish musician was to be treated with the dignity accruing to this singular role.

Low personal status for musical specialists is often found in cultures throughout the world, yet, in many of these cultures, the musician — despite the taint of social ignominy — is recognized as an essential member of society who performs tasks that are important, even crucial, to the society's well-being. The value of the Irish musician to the Irish-American community is open to serious speculation, as the role of Irish music is less clearly defined even, in many eases, to the musicians themselves.

The Gaelic Revival of the 1890s and early 1900s had an impact in America as well as in Ireland, as organizations and small informal groups were formed in American cities to promote the growth of the Irish language and related aspects of Irish culture, such as music, song, dance, history and literature. The movement attempted to increase public awareness of Irish music by holding competitions and festivals offering cash prizes for the winners. However, the revival efforts were chiefly concerned with the abstract concept of displaying the tradition and not with supporting the flesh-and-blood performers of that tradition.

No program for reviving Irish music could have any realistic hope of success if it ignored the basic social conditions that had brought the musical tradition into disrepute and deterioration. Trotting out musicians onto competition and concert stages was a measure that, while helping arouse public knowledge, did nothing to strike at the primary socio-economic reasons for the music's diminished status.

O'Neill again presents the dilemma with clarity in his reflections upon the fate of an itinerant Irish fiddler, Mrs. Bridget Kenny:

> The Gaelic Revival brought Mrs. Kenny into the limelight, and after she had outclassed all competitors as a traditional violinist at the annual Feiseanna, winning first prize year after year, she was proclaimed "The Queen of Irish Fiddlers".
>
> This remarkable woman's talents ought to have been regarded as a national asset. Yet it does not appear that any effort was made to take advantage of the opportunities presented by her discovery, by the establishment of a school in which the much vaunted traditional style of rendering Irish music would be taught and perpetuated.
>
> No. "The Queen of Irish Fiddlers", amid salvos of applause was handed her first prize with monotonous regularity and allowed to pass out and resume her daily perambulations as before, along the streets of the Irish capital, to woo the reluctant coin from purses often no less slender than her own (O'Neill 1913:387).

In the six decades that have passed since O'Neill was writing, the situation has changed little for Irish folk musicians in Ireland and America. While Irish music is currently enjoying a popularity boom in Ireland, Britain, Europe and North America, the "reluctant coin" is no more easily obtained, though the purses are generally more hefty than in former times.

The role of the Irish musician in Ireland is clearly defined in terms of the national culture of the island, whereas in the United States, the Irish musician is in a much more ambiguous position. The Irish musician in America is in the curious predicament of actively preserving a cultural element that the majority of his ethnic group do not even recognize as a part of what they conceive their ethnic heritage to be.

Desirable role models have also changed for the Irish-American community. It is no longer necessary for an Irish-American youth to rise in the socio-economic ranks by becoming a boxer, stage artist, priest, politician, policeman, gangster, baseball player or musician. Other avenues are now open, and young Irish-Americans, who might a half century ago have sought admission to the occupation of entertainers, may now enter virtually any profession or career (McCaffrey 1976:157-158).

Parents who have made special efforts and monetary sacrifices to obtain tuition for their children from schools of Irish music do not view this activity as an apprenticeship or training for an adult career in music. Irish music is a nice pastime, a pleasant hobby for youngsters and adults; competitions add a bit of spice to the normal daily run of events, and exhibition performances are seen as being important for their value in presenting a small slice of Irish culture for the edification and entertainment of the general public. For most parents, however, the pursuit of Irish music as a career is not perceived as desirable for their children.

One important reason for this elimination of Irish music as a prestige career choice is that the chances of achieving a stable, comfortable income level as a full-time professional performer of Irish folk music are presently very low. Although Irish folk music is now experiencing a revival of interest, the amount of money spent by American consumers of Irish folk music records, concerts and festivals is miniscule when compared to other sectors of the modern popular entertainment industry. Irish traditional music in the United States is definitely a minority musical tradition cherished and supported by a small though growing segment of the population.

The intensity of musical involvement is another decisive factor in the formulation of the personal status of a traditional Irish musician by non-musicians. Over-indulgence in or excessive seriousness about musical activity contributes to a lowering of status in the eyes of those not "addicted" to such a pastime. Performers who are zealous enthusiasts of Irish music are said to be "mad for the music" or "cracked about the music".

These terms, though usually delivered good-naturedly, imply a lack of control on the part of the "cracked" or "stone-mad" performer when in the presence of music; the performer is rendered helpless by the inability to contain his or her fondness for music to the extent of becoming so involved as to lose track of time, forget or ignore necessary obligations and generally relinquish contact with the reality of the nonmusical world.

With a popular mythology of this type widespread among the people who Francis O'Neill hoped would undertake a cultural renaissance, it is not difficult to understand why a performer of Irish music is not viewed as a valuable repository of a unique tradition but simply as a crank who can liven up a social gathering with an "old tune or two".

Irish musicians may count themselves lucky, however, that they have escaped the yoke of social deviance that has often been placed upon musicians in other American idioms, such as rock, jazz, blues and country-western, and in several other societies throughout the world (c.f. Merriam 1964:123-144 for a number of studies relating to the status and role of musical specialists cross-culturally). Irish musicians are not considered to be degenerate or reprehensible, nor are they shunned or ostracized; they are simply not accorded the high personal status that they might expect to receive as performers of a venerable, complex musical tradition.

Unlike American jazz and rock musicians, who have sometimes been at ideological and aesthetic loggerheads with their audiences and with mainstream society in general, Irish musicians in America have not had to maintain a special role-distance by cultivating special role-behavior patterns, argot, dress or gestures (Coffman 1971:20-32; Stebbins 1969:406-415).

Performers of Irish folk music in the U.S. live conventional, normal lives. They generally hold steady jobs (except for the professional musicians), dress and groom conservatively, raise typical nuclear families when married and are not noticeably in the vanguard of movements agitating for radical social, economic or political change.

It is this unrelenting diet of normalcy, however, that might offer the best explanation as to why these people continue to spend inordinate amounts of their leisure time playing a music very few people, even from their own ethnic community, are interested in hearing. When a bricklayer, janitor, warehouse worker, lawyer or office employee has emerged from the blue- or white-collar workaday world he or she inhabits forty or more hours a week, the search for a means of unlocking the door to the part of oneself that lies fitfully sublimated beneath the outward semblance of orthodoxy becomes paramount and urgent. For most people that door is never unlocked, and the years are spent in attempting to forget it ever existed at all. For a few fortunate ones, however, that barrier is dissolved in the heat of the sublime passion fired by a "great rake of reels".

- **Audiences**

Audiences attending Irish music occasions in the United States are, like the community of Irish musicians, becoming much more heterogeneous in composition. Occasions that were formerly almost exclusively attended by Irish emigrants and Irish-Americans — céilís, feiseanna, fleadhanna, concerts and sessions — are now engaging the interest of persons from outside the ethnic group.

In addition, Irish folk musicians in cities like Chicago are playing at occasions sponsored by non-Irish groups more than perhaps ever before. While professional Irish-American musicians had during the 19th century played before audiences that were widely varied in terms of their ethnic makeup, it is now the amateur performers who are emerging into the public consciousness as Irish traditional music continues to gain new adherents and admirers among the non-Irish community.

The formality of the performance context determines to a large extent the nature of the audience's interaction with the performers. In less formal situations, such as céilís, sessions, feiseanna or performances in taverns, the audience is continually active, and the hum of innumerable conversations provides a steady drone-like accompaniment to the music. Though the musicians may perform on a stage or platform or in a corner, the physical separation is never a barrier to audience involvement that may take the form of greeting the players by name, requesting tunes, shouting encouragement, conversing with the players or simply emitting loud, sharp whoops.

There are, of course, persons who listen quite attentively in these contexts and who spend much time in the immediate performance area talking to the performers between sets, buying them drinks, encouraging them and often asking for favorite tunes. It is this hard-core group of devotees who are the last ones to leave a session or a céilí and who may, in fact, do their utmost to prolong a good session by supplying drinks or prodding the performers to keep playing. In the absence of regular patronage, the occasional beneficence of these individuals is greatly appreciated by performers.

Formal occasions, such as concerts, fleadh cheoil competitions and step-dancing exhibitions, call into effect a more reserved behavioral mode from the audience. Sustained verbal interaction with the performers is limited to intermission or breaks in the performance, although clapping and foot-tapping to the rhythm of the music often occurs during the performance. At these more formal occasions, the physical separation of audience and performers is more marked in terms of distance as well as by barriers such as a high stage at the end of the room with chairs in well-defined rows facing the stage.

While traditional Irish musicians do not have any exaggerated respect for the musical knowledge and perception of the majority of their audiences, neither do they express any overt hostility with regard to those who attend the musical occasions at which they play. They may privately subscribe to the feelings of one Irish-American fiddle player who stated that "the American Irish have no more respect for tradition than a dead dog", but they are not specifically critical of the persons who surround them at céilís, feiseanna, concerts or sessions, unless there is noticeable apathy or antagonism on the part of the audience. Otherwise, the Irish folk musician in an American city like Chicago continues to coexist with the audience in a state of amicable detente.

CHAPTER SEVEN: Performers' Associations

THE FIRST MUSICIANS' associations organized by Irish musicians in America appeared around the start of the 20th century. They were outgrowths of informal gatherings and sessions that took place in private homes and were begun originally with the intention of transferring the sessions from a private to a public venue so that greater participation involving more players and listeners would be possible.

The Irish Music Club of Chicago was one of the earliest known of these associations, and its rise and fall was chronicled by one of its founding members, Chief Francis O'Neill.

Irish musicians in Chicago had been accustomed to performing at weekly gatherings held in private homes, such as flute player James Kerwin's home at 2954 S. Wabash, fiddler James O'Neill's residence at 3522 S. Washtenaw and piper Barney Delaney's house at 3746 Forest Avenue on the Northside. Yet, somehow, these private sessions did not meet the growing public demand for Irish music, and "in an evil moment an aggressive enthusiast conceived the idea of forming a permanent (?) organization, with monthly meetings in a rented hall, etc. Picnics and balls were to vary the anticipated pleasures and provide a revenue which was to be disbursed among the musicians" (O'Neill 1910:58).

The fledgling organization nearly foundered at the outset when the election of officers sparked latent rivalries among the musicians:

> It would appear that the officers of the new organization had already been selected in private caucus, the wheels ran so smoothly and the election therefore was a mere formality. One prominent piper who had conspicuously flung his initiation fee to the treasurer, left the hall in high dudgeon, when he had not even been nominated for any office, and never returned (*ibid.*).

This initial crisis passed without seriously endangering the club, however. "Many citizens with Irish sympathies, though not of Irish ancestry, attended the monthly meetings and the free midsummer picnics at 'Leafy Grove', and everything went along swimmingly for a time" (*ibid.*:58-59). However, disputes arose concerning the distribution of the proceeds from the club's grand ball, and other personality clashes festered in the wake of this incident. "The musicians began to drop away from that forth," wrote O'Neill; "a few excellent ones maintained their membership with great tenacity for a year or two, but there came a time when tactless and undiplomatic outbursts could no longer be endured, and the 'Irish Music Club' was left without musicians worthy of the name ... After less than eight years of inharmonious existence, the most enjoyable, companionable, and representative association of Irish musicians, singers, and dancers ever organized in America degenerated into a mere shadow of its former prominence, until its disruption in 1909, following a clash of mercenary interests" (*ibid.*:59).

Still, the dissolution of the club did not greatly affect the practice of Irish folk music in Chicago, and musical occasions featuring Irish music continued to take place. The club was briefly reorganized a couple of years after the first disruption, "but the absence of a staff of competent musicians from its membership, renders the Club's name an anomaly, and its potency for good not all that could be desired" (*ibid.*:59-60).

The formation of the Irish Music Club of Chicago had been an experiment, an attempt to extend the conviviality of a private music session to a larger performance context. Although there were hopes that money could be raised by such a venture, there was no imperative need for its organization, nor was there any real hardship wrought upon the tradition by the club's demise.

The next attempt to launch an Irish music association in Chicago was undertaken in response to a vastly different situation than had existed a half century earlier. The impulse to organize a formal association was no longer felt to be the product of capriciousness or mercenary interests or grandiose schemes; instead, the formation of the Chicago Irish Musicians Association in 1956 was viewed by its founders as an absolutely necessary measure to insure the continued survival of Irish music in Chicago.

Frank Thornton, a flute player and native of County Kerry who had arrived in Chicago in 1929, was deeply distressed by the precarious state of Irish music in America. A visit to Ireland in the early 1950s had shown him that more modern forms of music — mainly American and British popular music — were replacing traditional Irish music in many parts of Ireland. When Frank had left home in 1929, there had been sixteen musicians from the surrounding townland (a half-dozen square miles) at the farewell party in his honor. Seven years later on his first return visit, only two of those musicians remained, the rest having died or emigrated. Worse yet, it was apparent, particularly by the 1950s, that the young people following Frank's generation had not taken up the music with anywhere near the same fervor as had his generation.

In 1951, a small group of Dublin musicians formed An Comhaltas Ceoltóirí Éireann (The Musicians' Association of Ireland). By 1955, CCE had grown considerably to where there were one hundred twenty branches or local music clubs in the thirty-two counties of Ireland. CCE was beginning to prove itself as a viable institutional mechanism for creating greater public awareness of Irish folk music, and it was the success of Comhaltas that provided the model for Frank Thornton's decision to form a similar body in America. He wrote letters to the most prominent and active Irish musicians in the United States and asked them to assist him in an effort to organize a national association "to promote, teach, and keep alive the beautiful traditional music of Ireland in America."

On August 19, 1956, at four o'clock in the afternoon, the first meeting of the Irish Musicians' Association of America was convened in the Walnut Room of the Midland Hotel, 172 W. Adams Street in Chicago. Twenty-one musicians were in attendance, with representatives from New York, Boston, Cleveland, Philadelphia, Kansas City, Detroit, Houston, and Chicago present.

In his opening speech, Frank Thornton clearly set forth the convention's purpose: "To prevent the decay of our Irish traditional music, we must here and now consolidate our entire efforts to form an Irish Musicians' Commission or Association of America to promote, teach, and forever keep alive our Irish Traditional Music" (Irish Musicians' Association of America 1956:1).

The convention heard speeches by several delegates in support of the proposed association, officers were elected, a constitution and by-laws were considered, territories were delineated, dues and finances were discussed, and a closing prayer concluded the meeting at 7:05 p.m. Articles of Incorporation were filed with the State of Illinois January 13, 1958, and the Irish Musicians' Association of America, Inc. was already immersed in its task of propagating Irish folk music in the United States.

Twenty-two branches were eventually formed, and annual conventions were held in various cities: New York (1957, 1959, 1962), Philadelphia (1958), Boston (1963), Providence (1964), Cleveland (1960), and Chicago (1961). Delegates were sent from each branch to the convention, and such matters as a constitution, by-laws, officer elections, financial reports and other items pertaining to the conduct of a national association were discussed. Most memorable, however, were the music sessions that lasted throughout the weekend; these conventions are still fondly remembered by many musicians for the great sessions that took place.

Factionalism and petty disputes over leadership, finances, and the running of the organization's business affairs eventually caused the disintegration of the national association. The national conventions were discontinued, and several local associations collapsed or entered into a period of inactivity.

Participants in the early days of the Irish Musicians' Association of America are reluctant to talk about the exact events that led to the disruption, but the most oft-stated theory is that the trouble occurred among musicians in New York.

However, this failure to create a successful institutional framework that could assist in the rejuvenation of Irish traditional music in the United States only increased the sense of desperation felt by many individuals concerned with the retreat of the tradition into an ever-shrinking number of isolated circles of performers.

The Chicago branch continued to function throughout the turmoil in the Eastern territories. Meetings were held at McDermott's Tavern at 5445 S. Ashland Avenue, and concerts and dances were held to obtain funds for the treasury. A local Fleadh Cheoil was held for three consecutive years, 1964-1966, but the event was dropped after serving as an occasion for the eruption of feuds and controversies among musicians upset by the quality of adjudication. After a period of relative dormancy in the late 1960s, the Chicago Irish Musicians' Association began a new surge of activity in 1972. A concert tour of musicians, singers and dancers from Ireland was brought to Chicago and other American cities by Comhaltas Ceoltóirí Éireann in October of that year, and a new spirit of enterprise was evident among local musicians.

A Chicago Fleadh Cheoil was again held annually beginning in 1974. Adjudicators from Ireland were used this time and for the next two fleadhanna; musicians from New York were brought in to adjudicate the 1977 Fleadh. Concerts by Comhaltas Ceoltóirí Éireann continued to be sponsored by the Chicago Irish Musicians' Association, as the Association sought to continue a close relationship with CCE.

The Emerald Music Club was formed in 1973 and began holding monthly céilís and Irish music classes for children. This group was an outgrowth of a weekly informal music session that had been held for the past couple years at the park house in Mayfair Park, 4550 W. Sunnyside Avenue on Chicago's Northwestside. With the formation of the Emerald Music Club, the group moved the céilís and most of the club's activities to the Swiss Club at 2634 N. Laramie Avenue, also on the city's Northwestside.

Although neither the Irish Musicians' Association nor the Emerald Music Club were restricted geographically in terms of membership requirements, the two organizations have taken on a sectional cast. The Irish Musicians' Association is identified with the Southside and the Emerald Music Club with the Northside, though members of both organizations do not always come from the particular area associated with the clubs. However, each organization tend to orient nearly all of its activities toward those members living in the same general vicinity.

Considering the enormous size of Chicago and its suburbs (two hundred twenty-seven square miles), it is not surprising that more than one musicians' association has arisen to serve the many Irish musicians scattered throughout the metropolitan area. The rise of new clubs has not been welcomed by all, however; some musicians believe that the creation of new associations weakens the overall tradition by spreading the energies of the city's few active musicians too thinly.

Supporters of diversification counter this argument by stating that more clubs can serve more people in previously remote areas. Personality conflicts and disagreements concerning internal club matters have also been a significant factor in the formation of new music clubs.

In 1976, the Francis O'Neill Music Club was begun by several former members of the Emerald Music Club, most notably flute player Noel Rice. This club, along with the Irish Musicians' Association, is affiliated officially with Comhaltas Ceoltóirí Éireann. Like the Emerald Music Club, the Francis O'Neill Music Club focuses its efforts in the city's Northwestside and has its headquarters in suburban Park Ridge.

The club sponsors classes in Irish music, weekly music sessions for pupils, monthly sessions and céilís for adults and frequent concerts for the public by visiting and local musicians. The club also undertook the organization of the two concerts by CCE in October, 1977, a function formerly filled by the Irish Musicians' Association. The Francis O'Neill Music Club may very well run the 1978 Chicago Fleadh Cheoil also, as the division of responsibilities and obligations between the two CCE branches has yet to be completely clarified.

The Irish Musicians' Association has suffered some setbacks and lost its meeting place in the upstairs room of Hibernian Hall at 3350 W. 63rd Street when that building was sold by the Ancient Order of Hibernians in 1976. The Association has also become less active in promoting céilís and does not have a teaching program. Still, the association presents concerts of local and visiting musicians and provides musicians for various functions operated by other Irish organizations.

The Chicago Gaelic Society is a group dedicated to teaching the Irish language. Formed originally in 1972, the society has since its inception sponsored monthly céilís on Chicago's Southwestside. Currently, céilís are held at Highlander's Hall, 3035 W. 51st Street, and the society has linked up with the Francis O'Neill Music Club for several events.

While there is no cohesive national organization of Irish musicians' associations in the United States like the Irish Musicians' Association of America, Inc. that flourished in the 1950s and early 1960s, those clubs that have affiliated themselves with Comhaltas Ceoltóirí Éireann have formed a loose connection on a regional, territorial basis. The U.S. and Canada are considered as one province equivalent to one of the four provinces of Ireland and the one province that takes in the whole of Britain; this North American region is sub-divided into four territories: U.S. Eastern, U.S. Midwestern, U.S. Western, Canada.

The U.S. Midwestern region comprises the two branches in Chicago — the Irish Musicians Association and the Francis O'Neill Music Club — and branches in Detroit, St. Louis and Minneapolis. An Irish Music club in Cleveland has chosen to remain unaligned with CCE for the present. Currently, Daniel O'Kennedy of Detroit is the Midwestern Region Co-ordinator, with new elections to be held in the summer of 1978. Owing to its greater number of musicians, Chicago is the natural center of the Midwestern region, and several musicians from Chicago have undertaken concerts and céilís for other branches in Minneapolis, St. Louis and Detroit.

It is interesting to note that many members of the Irish music clubs of Chicago are not musicians. In some cases, these non-performing members are the parents of children involved in the music classes offered by the clubs, but often they are simply Irish music enthusiasts interested in supporting this aspect of Irish culture.

One recalls Francis O'Neill's remark concerning the turn-of-the-century Chicago Irish Music Club: "Many citizens with Irish sympathies, though not of Irish ancestry attended the monthly meetings and the free mid-summer picnics at 'Leafy Grove'" (O'Neill 1910:58-59); it could well be surmised that these individuals were, more than likely, not players of Irish music.

Of the sixty persons listed as members of the Chicago Irish Musicians' Association in 1957, one-third (twenty members) did not play an instrument, sing or dance. They were, instead, aficianados of Irish music who joined the association in an effort to help promote these arts in any way they could. There are many such individuals in the Irish music clubs of Chicago today, and they are recognized by the performing members as being invaluable to the success of the club's activities by providing technical, advisory and monetary assistance. They also comprise the necessary community, without which the tradition becomes meaningless.

Not all Irish musicians in Chicago belonging to the clubs are active members of the clubs, nor are all Irish musicians in the city necessarily members of any club. Some musicians are averse to joining organized group functions, while others prefer to play solely with a few close friends and eschew large public gatherings. Occasionally, a musician might become embittered about some aspect of the club's policies or internal politics and many withdraw out of protest. Often these musicians return to the club after the crisis is over or a change in officers or policies has taken place.

Irish musicians' clubs in Chicago have taken the leading role in fostering the revival of interest in Irish music and have become a necessity rather than a superfluity. The capability of such associations to channel and utilize the available resources more efficiently and to undertake activities that involve a high degree of co-ordination among different groups have given musicians' associations a prominent position in the Irish music community of Chicago.

Associations have been able to spark the latent spirit of unity and solidarity among musicians who had previously been isolated within a small, closed interactional circuit. The personality clashes and petty feuds that often surface in the associations are more quickly resolved in the institutional setting where there is an attempt to preserve democratic, impartial procedures. The various separate networks of musicians dispersed throughout the expansive metropolitan area have been brought into more frequent contact with each other through participation in musical occasions organized under the auspices of a local musicians' association.

The increased visibility and accessibility of traditional Irish music brought about by these public occasions have not only stimulated the performers themselves but have aided greatly in the efforts to restore the continuity of the transmission process through the initiation of newcomers into the tradition. The mature exponents of the music are able to be seen and heard by young players, and an important element of the learning process is having the opportunity to observe the music in a live performance setting.

Furthermore, by performing in a public context among fellow musicians and a supportive audience, the connotations of inferiority, worthlessness and irrelevancy that have lain heavily upon Irish folk musicians in the United States in recent decades have been considerably dispelled. The musicians' associations, by reintroducing Irish folk music into the forefront of the Irish-American community's cultural consciousness, have done much to increase the status of the performer of Irish traditional music by bringing about a recognition of the performer as an active carrier of an important aspect of the Irish cultural heritage.

The attempts by musicians' associations in Chicago to reintegrate traditional Irish music into the cultural life of the Chicago Irish community have had a noticeable psychological impact upon performers and audiences alike. The fortunes of Irish folk music in Chicago would very likely be much the poorer without them.

CHAPTER EIGHT: Methods of Transmission

THE TRANSMISSION OF Irish folk music in Chicago takes place by both **formal** and **informal** means. Both types have co-existed alongside each other since the 1940s, although it is only within the last five years that formal methods have become more dominant and more organized. The increased use of formal transmission methods has occurred chiefly because of the inability of informal methods to adequately ensure the transmission of the tradition large enough numbers. Often, individuals learn by both formal and informal means.

Most of the Irish musicians in Chicago over age forty learned the tradition by informal means. As children they heard the music being played by older siblings, parents, relatives, friends and neighbors. In many parts of rural Ireland, Irish music was one of the few available leisure-time social activities, and participation in music was a normal endeavor for both male and female youngsters. Children would begin perhaps by attempting to play instruments lying around the house, often when no one was within hearing. Or they might obtain a tinwhistle from an adult or older child and begin playing with that. When their musical aptitude was discovered, they would receive rudimentary instruction from an older person who played the instrument in which they were interested.

This instruction generally consisted of the older person playing a simple tune and the learner trying to imitate as best as he or she could manage. Almost all of the musicians over age forty state that their first instruction in Irish music was obtained in such a manner. After being acquainted with the operation of the instrument, they received no formal instruction but observed older players closely whenever the chance presented itself. Playing with other novices on or near the same level as themselves was also a learning method.

Eventually, after gaining a modicum of proficiency on their instrument, novices could take part in informal sessions of music in their own home or the homes of a neighbor or relative. Contact with a greater number of musicians gave the aspirant a greater opportunity to pick up new tunes and learn new techniques.

Among Irish-born musicians in Chicago, the reasons for taking up the music or a particular instrument are considerably varied. Noel Rice of County Offaly had begun playing Irish music on the tinwhistle at an early age and was hoping to take up the uilleann pipes. His family was not able to afford even a practice set of pipes, however, and he was given a flute instead.

Kevin Henry of County Mayo and Frank Thornton of County Kerry became interested in the flute as children because of the flute bands that existed in their localities and frequently marched through the village. Pat Cloonan of County Galway started on the melodeon around age ten because it enabled him to excuse himself from farm chores.

Seamus Cooley of County Galway would experiment with his brother Joe's accordion while Joe was working in the fields; later, he saw flute player Jim Fahey playing at fairs and took up the flute. Maida Sugrue and Terry Teahan of County Kerry were "given" by their parents to Patrick O'Keeffe, a musician who travelled the Cork and Kerry countryside and taught fiddle, flute, tinwhistle, concertina and accordion. O'Keeffe was liable to appear at any time of the day or night when he was in the vicinity or in need of a meal or a bed.

Almost all of these musicians started before their early teens, and all appear to have been highly self-motivated. In nearly every case, one or more members of the immediate nuclear family unit played Irish music.

Musicians over age forty who were born in Chicago report similar experiences, with the difference that 78 rpm recordings of Irish-American musicians were significant influences in motivation, repertoire and style. Neither the parents or siblings of John McGreevy played Irish music, but the recordings he heard on the family gramophone of the great Irish-American fiddlers of the 1920s inspired him to take up the fiddle.

Many Chicago-born musicians received music lessons from Catholic nuns in flute, violin or piano; after learning the fundamentals of their instrument, they sought out older Irish musicians in the city. When John McGreevy was fifteen he met Mayo-born fiddler Jimmy Neary at a party and subsequently began coming to Neary's house to learn tunes and observe stylistic techniques. Eleanor Neary, Jimmy's wife, started to learn Irish tunes from O'Neill's printed collections after a year or two of piano lessons from the nuns.

Joe Shannon was given a practice set of uilleann pipes by flute player Paddy Doran and was able to watch his piping cousin, Eddie Mullaney, a few times. However, Shannon received his greatest insights as a beginner from 78 rpm records of Irish-American pipers and also learned a lot by playing frequently with fellow teenager John McGreevy.

These patterns still occur in the transmission of Irish music in Chicago today. Fiddler Liz Carroll (now age twenty-two) received violin lessons from nuns at her Catholic grade school and then proceeded to make the acquaintance of other local fiddle players. She learned a great deal of her initial repertoire from a tape of John McGreevy's playing. Her father also played the accordion, and her maternal grandfather in County Limerick was a fiddle player; these sources provided encouragement and inspiration if not actual direct tuition.

Jim Thornton (age thirty-three) was taught the flute and tinwhistle by his father, Frank; along with his two brothers, he played in his father's tinwhistle band. Later, in his mid-twenties, he acquired a two-row button accordion and learned how to play by watching other accordion players and listening to records and tapes.

Piano accordionist Jimmy Keane (age nineteen) was taken by his father to a local music store for lessons on the piano accordion beginning around age seven. When he was fifteen, Jimmy began attending Irish music sessions and concerts around Chicago; tapes, records and playing with other musicians in his age group augmented his repertoire and his grasp of the idiom.

- **Formal Methods**

Currently, the younger the individual interested in learning Irish music, the more likely formal methods of transmission will be employed. Formal schools of Irish music instruction have by and large replaced the Catholic grammar school lessons for most beginning students of Irish music in Chicago.

These schools are operated by organizations or by individuals. The roots of the present schools of Irish music lie in the flute and tinwhistle bands organized in the 1940s and 1950s by men such as Pat Roche, Bob Flately and Frank Thornton.

Some children were taught free-of-charge and learned to play simple Irish marches, song airs and a few dance tunes. The bands played at Gaelic football and hurling matches, parades, concerts and exhibitions throughout Chicago. Few of the pupils ever progressed past the basic level of musicianship on their instrument and did not continue in the band or with Irish music after their mid-teens. As a mechanism for transmitting the tradition in a permanent way, these bands were too limited in repertoire, instrumentation and pedagogical methods.

They did, however, serve as a public reminder to parents that opportunities for introducing their children to Irish music did exist in Chicago. The individual teachers of Irish traditional music now active include: Tommy Ryan (fiddle), Jim Thornton (tinwhistle, flute, button accordion), Pat Cloonan (button accordion), Michael Flatley (flute, tinwhistle), Liz Carroll (fiddle, tin whistle, button accordion).

Of the three Irish music clubs in Chicago, the Emerald Music Club taught Irish music lessons from 1975 through 1976, and the Francis O'Neill Music Club has taken over most of that constituency beginning in 1977.

The Chicago Irish Musicians' Association has not yet started any teaching program but has been giving the matter serious consideration for some time. The schools all charge fees, generally ranging from three to five dollars for a half hour lesson. Both group and individual lessons are given.

This format of Irish music instruction became popularized in the United States during the 1960s. The opening of a school of Irish music by Galway born fiddler Peter Kelly in 1964 was the first attempt in two decades to conduct a formally-organized, commercial school in the New York area. The success of this experiment was immediately apparent, and schools of Irish music based along similar lines proliferated in the New York metropolitan area over the next few years.

Presently there are over a dozen such schools, with several having over a hundred pupils. In at least two cases, the teachers make the school their full-time profession. New York is the only area of the United States that has so far been able to support so many schools of this magnitude; the large Irish and Irish-American population of the area is one important factor, as is the fact that a number of Irish music competitions are held within the area every year and provide public outlets for the demonstration of skills acquired in the school.

Chicago has considerably fewer Irish music schools, and none of them enable the teacher to earn a full-time living from the enterprise. There are only one hundred to one hundred and twenty-five pupils in the entire Chicago metropolitan area enrolled in these schools. In the opinion of Chicago's Irish music teachers, this represents an improvement over the previous decade, particularly since it appears that a number of these pupils will continue playing the music and possibly blossom into first-rate adult players.

The one institutionally-sponsored Irish music school in the Chicago area at present is operated by the Francis O'Neill Music Club. Classes in button accordion, piano, tinwhistle, flute and beginning and advanced fiddle are held in the basement hall of the Pickwick Theatre in Park Ridge, a northwestern suburb of Chicago. The beginning fiddle students receive instruction in the Suzuki Method by a violin teacher from Northwestern University.

Approximately fifty to sixty students are enrolled in the classes offered by the club. Like most other schools of Irish music, there is a more or less equal number of boys and girls with ages ranging from eight through sixteen. Most, but not all, of the pupils are of Irish ancestry.

Lessons at the club are given each Saturday and are both group and individual in format. On Thursday nights there are informal sessions for the students with as many as possible encouraged to attend. The club holds a monthly music session for adults and for those youngsters who are capable of and interested in participating. The idea, says the club's chairman Noel Rice, is to create an environment for the music with as many facilities and opportunities for learning and performing as can possibly be arranged. It is hoped that the pupils will integrate the practice of Irish music into their daily lives and perceive it not simply as a parentally-instigated/enforced adolescent activity but rather as a serious avocation that will continue through adulthood.

Students of formal music schools are taught to read music and are instructed in the basic operation of their instrument if they have not received such training before. Little effort at communicating music theory is made, and (except for the one teacher of Suzuki violin) students do not receive scales or exercises but are launched immediately into the task of learning simple dance tunes, marches and song airs. The settings of these tunes are skeletal; the techniques of ornamentation and melodic and rhythmic variation are not taught until the student has shown the ability to play the tunes at proper tempo with steady rhythm, correct intonation and coherent phrasing.

Printed tutors are rarely used, one chief reason being that there are very few competent, readily available Irish music tutors in existence. Music is either xeroxed from Irish music tune books or handwritten from the teacher's own playing. The teacher plays the tune through once or twice as an example of what the tune should sound like, and it then becomes the student's objective to master and memorize the tune. Since these tunes are later played by the pupils in group performances, efforts are made to present identical versions to all students.

This is especially important in that the more promising pupils are organized by age into ensembles that compete against other similarly organized ensembles from other schools at music competitions and also perform at exhibitions and concerts. Pedagogy is oriented toward ensemble performance of this kind, and standardized versions of tunes are learned for these occasions. A certain conformity is thereby encouraged, and is, perhaps, inevitable in view of the approach to instruction and the reliance upon printed materials as repertoire sources.

The chief purpose of these schools is to give students a basic acquaintance with the idiom of Irish music, an idiom that in its most developed aspects is highly sophisticated and complex. With one of the primary goals being to prepare students for cohesive ensemble performance, there is understandably less emphasis on imparting the more idiomatic elements and nuances of style. It is hoped by instructors that the more astute pupils will be able to develop an individual performance style of their own. "Learn to walk before you take swimming lessons" might best express this viewpoint.

There has been a good deal of criticism, however, directed at the "products" turned out by the standardized teaching utilized in these schools. While agreeing that Irish folk music should be taught to young people on a wider scale, it is felt that those who have been taught in this manner by institutionalized pedagogical procedures acquire only a superficial understanding of the idiom and perform in an undistinguished, mediocre manner. The stress on uniformity and group performance, it is alleged, induces a reliance on non-individual and uncreative musical thinking and performance.

Though it is true that a larger quantity of musicians does not necessarily ensure a rise in the quality of musical performance standards, the schools of Irish music have done much to disperse the tradition among a greater number of people than would have been possible if the individual, informal approach were exclusively followed.

One of the most critical problems Irish music in the United States has faced during the last few decades has been the drastic decline in the number of young Irish-Americans arising to replenish the ranks thinned by the deaths or retirement from active performance by older players. The vast reduction in the numbers of emigrants from Ireland since World War II has made the recruitment of performers from the succeeding generation of young Irish-American even more crucial.

With the geographic fragmentation of the Irish-American communities continuing to accelerate, the task of maintaining an adequate number of competent performers to keen the tradition alive and flourishing has been a formidable one that has had to make use of new methods designed to cope with the exigencies of a changing social and cultural context. The formerly used methods of informal transmission that entailed a one-to-one teacher-and-pupil learning relationship have not been able to work as effectively in the 20th-century American urban milieu as they did in the past, and have, therefore, been modified.

Whereas in the past the student or student's parents made the initial move to seek out an experienced musician, the modern schools of Irish music actively solicit pupils by advertising on local Irish radio programs, in Irish-American newspapers and in local Irish import shops.

Various reasons are given by teachers and parents of pupils when discussing the importance of giving children Irish music instruction. To some, Irish music is a pleasant pastime for the children, a wholesome, controlled activity by which the children (and parents) cultivate friendships among their peers. Many parents, particularly those who are not musicians, achieve vicariously through their children's participation in Irish music, especially when their youngsters win medals and trophies in Irish music competitions and mention in local newspapers.

The most common response offered by teachers and parents when asked to define the real value of Irish music is that involvement in Irish music stimulates and sustains an awareness of Ireland in the child. With the continued dissolution of homogeneous Irish neighborhoods, churches, parish schools, sporting clubs and political organizations, the Irish music school has assumed an institutional responsibility for effecting the socialization of young Irish-Americans into the contemporary Irish-American cultural environment.

For children whose home life is permeated with Irishness, and whose familial connections are Irish, the Irish music school is a means of extending that ethnic identity into a peer group situation. Most, if not all, of the other children will have Irish or Irish-American parents. The teacher will almost certainly be Irish or Irish-American. Most of the performance occasions at which the child performs will be organized by Irish associations and attended primarily by Irish and Irish-American audiences. The child will interact with children who may have been to Ireland or who may have even been born there. And, if the pupil is victorious in the Chicago Fleadh Cheoil, he or she will be entitled to go to Ireland and compete in the All-Ireland Fleadh Cheoil. Even the trophies and medals won by competitors embody some aspect of Irishness in terms of external symbols.

To Irish and Irish-American parents concerned that their offspring might reach maturity without being adequately exposed to and informed about Irish culture, the practice of Irish music acts as an enculturative mechanism where each week throughout the year an atmosphere of Irishness is maintained. Over a period of several years, this has a cumulative effect, or so it is hoped, of strengthening the child's identification with Ireland while incidentally inculcating the merits of self-discipline, peer-group competition and co-operation, and dedication toward the achievement of personal goals.

From the child's point of view, involvement in Irish music is not something submitted to intensive examination or soul-searching. If they are of Irish ancestry, the pupils' participation is a natural extension of their home life into a peer-group activity. The crucial point comes at the end of the pupil's full-time participation in the music school, when weekly lessons are discontinued and the student's active involvement with the school ceases. This point usually comes in middle or late adolescence, generally because the pupil becomes immersed in other activities having to do with school, athletics or work.

Some former Irish music school students that do not continue playing the music actively may, however, continue to read Irish-American newspapers, listen to Irish records and radio programs and attend events within the adult Irish community open to teens, such as picnics, festivals and dances. They might take lessons in the Irish language or courses in Irish literature and history. They might participate in Irish sports, such as hurling, camogie or Gaelic football. And, if their ties to the Irish community are sustained through early adulthood, they might eventually become an active member of an Irish social or political organization. Thus, even if they do not themselves continue to actively perform Irish folk music, they may very likely be instrumental in shaping the cultural and social environment necessary to support that music.

- **Informal Methods**

During the last decade there have been ever-increasing numbers of persons in their late teens, twenties, thirties and even forties who have become interested in playing Irish folk music. Often they have cultural or familial ties with Ireland and have suddenly become more interested in this aspect of their ethnic heritage. Often, though, these individuals are drawn to Irish music for a multitude of different reasons. Most have had experience in one or more musical idioms and are proficient on one or more instruments. For these initiates to Irish folk music, the formal schools are too basic and too limited in their goals and instructional approach. Most schools of Irish music are also intended primarily for children and young adolescents and are impractical for older persons becoming involved with the music.

The transmission of the tradition in these instances is accomplished by informal methods. The usual pattern is for an individual to become interested in Irish music after hearing it performed live or on a record or in a movie or television soundtrack. The next step is for the novice to seek out a performer living in the area who can point out the musical fundamentals of the idiom and of the particular instrument the novice performs or is interested in performing, especially if the instrument is an unusual one like the bodhrán, bones, or uilleann pipes.

Usually the novice listens to the experienced player perform and perhaps tape records some tunes or receives some music in manuscript form. At the same time, the individual attempts to locate other experienced performer and begins to attend musical occasions where Irish music occurs. As the novice builds a repertoire and stabilizes the basic technique, he or she can begin to participate in informal sessions where invaluable experience in playing with others can be gained while discovering a great deal of information about styles, techniques, repertoire and performance practice. Recordings and tapes continue to be utilized by the novice in an effort to increase repertoire and become familiar with the idiomatic features of the music.

Any actual teaching that does take place occurs at the teacher's or the pupil's home. The pedagogic methods employed in this situation are diverse and differ according to the amount of self-motivation possessed by the novice and the availability of learning resources. Contacts are always initiated and sustained by the learner, unless, perhaps, it is a parent who is the instructor.

The learning process itself is informal and highly personalized; the frequency of learning sessions is variable, there is no set curriculum or schedule of events, nor are there generally more than one or two individuals involved at a time. What is actually transmitted depends upon the abilities of the pupil to grasp the material and upon the resources of the experienced performer. Though the student may later selectively absorb certain elements of what has been observed, the first level of the learning process consists of the pupil's direct imitation of the teacher's example.

Another feature of this personalized, individual method of transmission is that there is no monetary remuneration paid to the teacher, though a gift of some use or meaning to the teacher might be offered, such as a record or a tape of Irish music. Many performers would refuse to accept money, believing that their knowledge and skill should be passed on freely to others who are genuinely interested.

Both the isolation of Irish-American musicians cut off from other players and the frustrations of novices learning the music have been greatly alleviated in recent years by the widespread adoption of the portable cassette tape recorder. This device has become the primary agent of repertoire transmission between Ireland and the United States and among musicians separated by great distance in America. Whenever an Irish-American musician goes to Ireland, or an Irish musician or ensemble visits the United States, the cassette recorder is certain to be present. The number of cassette tapes of private and public, solo and ensemble performances of Irish folk music possessed by Irish musicians in America is inestimable.

The cassette recorder is particularly helpful to students of Irish music struggling to master the crucial stylistic features of the idiom, features that are difficult to explain verbally and also not easily communicated via print. The cassette recorder is a highly efficient tool for gathering and storing repertoire and for comparing styles of different players, two elements that are very important when learning any musical idiom and particularly necessary in view of the chiefly aural nature of the Irish folk music tradition. Also, any player, not just those who are considered accomplished enough to be commercially recorded, can be taped by an individual, and a wider knowledge of the various sub-styles of the tradition can be gained.

As a means of communication among present-day Irish musicians in the United States, the cassette recorder is unparalleled. This is a rare instance, perhaps, in which a product of modern technology has proven immeasurably helpful to the preservation and perpetuation of a folk music tradition among its native practitioners.

Irish music instructor Noel Rice believes that at least three years are necessary for a youngster to fully comprehend the idiom of Irish folk music and achieve creditable fluency in it. Thus, it remains to be seen whether the current crop of pupils in Chicago's Irish music schools will produce enough competent performers who will take an active role in the Chicago Irish music community as adults and take charge of transmitting the tradition to the succeeding generations.

The utilization of both formal and informal methods of transmission has greatly assisted in the task of keeping the music alive and flourishing in Chicago by insuring that new blood is continually drawn into the tradition. While formal transmission methods seem to have received the greater emphasis of late (particularly among the younger novices), the older informal methods are still in existence and still are capable of producing competent, knowledgeable players. If the formation of musicians' associations has been one means of creating a greater enthusiasm for Irish folk music within the Chicago Irish community, the organization of Irish music schools has been the chief method of recycling that enthusiasm back into a self-generating process of renewal.

CHAPTER NINE: The Tradition and The Media

• Recordings

THE MASS COMMUNICATIONS medium that has had the most direct influence upon traditional Irish music in the United States has been that of commercial recording. The commercial recording industry has used various formats for issuing recordings of Irish music; these have included wire cylinders and 78 rpm discs from the 1890s to the 1950s, 45 rpm discs and long-playing albums since the 1950s and cassette tapes within the last decade.

The impact of the commercial recording industry upon the dissemination of styles and repertoire among Irish musicians during the first four decades of the 20th century was discussed in Chapter Three; when the heyday of Irish music recording was occurring in the 1920s and '30s, the commercial disc was the major channel by which Irish musicians in Chicago were made aware of developments in the Irish music communities of Boston, New York and Philadelphia.

Very little of the Irish folk music recorded in England or Ireland was reaching America at that time, and it was not until the late 1940s that American Irish musicians had access to recordings made by their counterparts overseas. However, recordings made by American Irish musicians who lived in or managed to travel to Chicago, New York or Philadelphia had as great a distribution in Ireland and England as they had in America.

After World War II the major commercial labels like Victor, Columbia, Decca and Gennett had virtually ceased to issue new recordings by Irish musicians in the United States, finalizing a trend that had begun as early as the mid-1930s. A few small, privately-owned, independent companies attempted to take up the slack, believing that a market for traditional Irish music still existed in America, though it was clearly not as large or as lucrative as a decade or two before.

Copley Records of Boston was the most prolific and long-lasting of these companies, as they concentrated on recording Irish musicians in Boston and New York and also released recordings made by Irish musicians in Ireland. Copley and its fellow small labels were hampered in their distribution, which was limited to a few Irish import stores in a handful of large cities in the East and Midwest.

In the early 1970s, Irish traditional music began to find adherents among the non-Irish community in America. Companies devoted to North American folk music began to record Irish-American musicians, and two companies (Shanachie Records of New York and Green Linnet Records of New Canaan, Connecticut) have devoted their efforts exclusively to producing albums of Irish and Irish-American musicians. Shanachie Records has instituted a mail-order service that can supply any Irish folk music record now in print within a few weeks after its release. This improved and extended distribution will be crucial to the success of these small companies in getting their records to the people who are interested in them.

The major focus of recording activity has shifted, however, from the United States to England and Ireland, and, consequently, fewer American Irish musicians are now being recorded. Irish companies like Gael-Linn, Claddagh, Outlet and Mulligan and English labels like Topic, Free Reed, Leader and Silverhill are now providing the majority of Irish traditional music records, although recordings of Irish musicians touring Germany have also begun to be commercially issued by Intercord.

While new tunes are received from personal contacts between musicians, a considerable amount of new repertoire is introduced via commercial recordings. Musicians who have ceased learning tunes years ago are obviously not affected as much by new developments, but among younger players, new releases of traditional Irish music receive careful attention and are often the main source of repertoire for musicians who learn tunes aurally and not by means of printed collections.

The relationship between the commercial recording industry and Irish folk music in America is interesting, since the growth of the medium paralleled precisely the overall decline of Irish folk music in the United States. Yet, without the development and expansion of the industry, the new styles that have proven so influential in shaping the tradition during the 20th century would never have had anywhere near the impact they did.

The American piping style of Patsy Tuohey in the early 1900s, the Sligo fiddle style in the 1920s and '30s, the two-row button accordion style in the 1950s and the various regional styles of Ireland that have gained wider currency in the 1960s and '70s were disseminated chiefly through commercial recordings, and their importance in the history of Irish folk music in the 20th century has been enormous.

However, at the same time the commercial recording industry was bringing these new developments in Irish folk music to wider public attention, it was also busily releasing a flood of recordings by stage-Irish performers. Items by traditional performers in the Irish catalogues of the major recording companies were always in the minority as compared to operatic or stage-Irish entertainers. After the mid-1940s, traditional Irish music disappeared altogether from the catalogues of the major labels, and only stage-Irish musical entertainment was released.

The stage-Irish musical idiom was developed in the United States during the late 19th and early 20th centuries; in essence, it took Irish folk song themes and provided them with lyrics based upon clichés and stereotypes of Irish history and Irish character. The lyrics were then yoked to musical compositions that bore little relationship to the Irish musical idiom upon which they were ostensibly based.

What is most interesting about this process is that in a short time, the derivative idiom came to be thought of as the original — as the "real old Irish music" — not only by uninformed Americans of non-Irish ancestry but by Irish-Americans themselves.

To a large extent, the derivative stage-Irish idiom has shaped the Irish-American community's concept of what their national musical heritage is, and it is obvious that the widespread dissemination of stage-Irish recordings by the commercial recording industry has played a significant role in this conceptualization process. Thus, while the industry assisted in the spread of new styles that helped invigorate the tradition of Irish folk music, it simultaneously played a prominent part in alienating the Irish-American community from that tradition.

The medium, of course, not only reflected changing popular tastes but formed them. The radically different social and cultural environment that Irish emigrants found in America undoubtedly was a factor in the shifting musical entertainment preferences of the Irish-American community.

Nevertheless, after World War II, the consumers of Irish music recordings were not left with much choice as to what type of Irish music they would be offered by the major recording companies.

- **Radio and Television**

The broadcasting media of radio and television have exerted a less profound impact upon the musical development of traditional Irish music in America. Instead, they have functioned primarily as purveyors of aesthetic attitudes and musical entertainment preferences that have evolved among the American Irish in this country.

Of the two, it is radio that is more heavily involved with Irish music; there are currently no regular television programs featuring Irish music in Chicago (or anywhere in the United States). The only time Irish musicians appear on television is around St. Patrick's Week in March; usually, these appearances are part of performance by a step-dancing troupe. Perhaps with the introduction of more localized cable programming in the future this situation will change.

Radio, however, is a more locally-oriented medium in many respects. Currently, there are eleven Irish radio programs on Chicago radio. Total weekly programming time for these shows encompasses eleven hours and twenty minutes. Some of the programs have been running for two decades, though on different stations and at different days and times.

Pat Roche, Tom McNamara, Jack Hagerty and Eamonn O'Malley are among the older program hosts, while Paddy Barry, Bobby Ryan, Mike O'Connor, Declan Moran and Alex McGrath and Declan Sheedy are more recent additions. Tom Gibbons continues the program begun by his father in the 1950s.

Each Irish hour has a similar format consisting of news from Ireland, announcements of local events of interest to the Chicago Irish community, advertisements for local Irish-owned or Irish-oriented businesses, and prerecorded and live musical selections. Due to the economic strictures of the commercial radio medium, a large amount of program time is taken up with commercials for various sponsors, with the result that very little music is actually played on many Irish shows.

In some programs the ratio of speech-to-music is as high as three-to-one — three minutes of speech to one minute of music, with most of the speech not related to the particular musical selections.

Irish folk music is played much less than the stage-Irish and other derivative idioms on these Irish hours. When asked to discuss the basic criteria for choosing their musical selections, program producers (who are the same as the program hosts) consistently state that their aim is to please the largest number of listeners. In doing so, they also assuage sponsors who lend their financial support to the program in anticipation that a large number of people will be listening.

Producers also solicit requests and dedications from their listeners over the air in an attempt to stimulate listener participation and to demonstrate to sponsors that people actually are listening. Due to the fact that a substantial number of Americans of Irish ancestry are unaware of the existence of any but the derivative idioms of Irish folk music, program producers are not inclined to play recordings of a musical idiom many listeners would quite possibly not even recognize as being Irish.

The amount of Irish folk music played over the air is also determined by the attitudes of the producers themselves. Pat Roche is a step-dancer and a long-time supporter of Irish folk music in Chicago and, therefore, plays much more traditional Irish music than his peers. Other program hosts enjoy the traditional music and play it as often as they feel their audience will tolerate; others are either apathetic towards the music, or, in some cases, covertly hostile.

The Irish radio programs of Chicago differ in respect to the motivations of their producers as well. Seven of the shows are operated by businessmen who use the program as a vehicle for advertising their own enterprise; these include two Irish import stores, a funeral parlor, a travel agency, an insurance agency and a family of stage-Irish and American popular music entertainers. With regard to the other producers, it is difficult to ascertain to what extent the show functions as a genuine "community service" or simply as a means of enhancing the producer's status as a local celebrity.

In the 1920s, '30s, '40s and '50s, Irish radio programs in Chicago featured live performances of traditional Irish music to a much greater degree than is now the case. Many programs had regular performers who played each week; listener requests as well as pre-established tunes were played. Occasionally, visiting musicians from Ireland or from other American cities would stop in, and exciting, impromptu sessions would result.

Live musicians make rare appearances on Irish radio shows in Chicago today, chiefly when the host agrees to help promote a musical occasion coming up, such as a fleadh cheoil, a feis or a local concert. The show hosted by the Ryan Travel Agency on Sunday evenings is broadcast live from the Abbey Pub at Addison and Narragansett on the city's Northwestside. The Abbey features a variety of stage-Irish and hybrid Irish entertainment, and the radio show promotes these performers as well as other commercial sponsors. If there is a traditional musician in the audience, however, and there is a shortage of regular pub-promoted performers, the traditional player may be asked to perform a couple of tunes over the air.

The only other live radio broadcast of recent vintage that featured Irish music in Chicago was the Sunday Night Irish Hour from Hibernian Hall; this program ended in 1976, when the Hall was sold by its owners. The half-hour show was also sponsored by a travel agency specializing in flights to Ireland, but advertisements were brief and to the point. Local traditional musicians made up the "house band", and there was a good deal of solid Irish traditional music performed during the program. A different Irish dancing school was featured each week, and there were often visitors from out of town who dropped by to play, sing, or dance.

The Sunday Night Irish Hour's role as a showcase of Chicago's traditional music talent has not been replaced since its termination. Often, Irish musicians would sit at home and listen to the show with their cassette tape recorders at the ready, waiting for a new tune or a new performer to arrive over the airwaves.

Though Irish folk musicians in Chicago may listen to their local Irish programs for Irish news, upcoming local events, and information on charter flights to Ireland, the influence of radio as a medium capable of stimulating or disseminating new developments in the idiom of traditional Irish music has been nullified in the past few decades.

There are no shows dedicated totally to the presentation of Irish music in Chicago, and the music plays an incidental role as "continuity music" between commercials and announcements. Without exception, Irish radio programs in Chicago service to reinforce the existing status quo of musical entertainment taste and aesthetic values of a listening audience that remains largely uninformed about the older traditions of Irish music.

CHAPTER TEN: Continuity and Change:
The Dynamics of Acculturation and Irish Music in Chicago

NETTL HAS POSTULATED three avenues of possible development for a rural-based European folk music tradition once it arrives in the United States (1962: 59).

The first is **full-scale acculturation** in which the stylistic elements, instruments, repertoire and aesthetic ideals of the tradition merge with an American tradition or traditions to form a new synthesis. An example of this would be the blend of various British Isles idioms with African and colonial American elements that formed the basis of a new Anglo-American folk tradition of music, song and dance in the 18th and 19th centuries.

A second possibility is **partial acculturation** in which the European folk tradition might remain distinct yet manifest evidence of considerable borrowing from other traditions — the polka phenomenon, for instance, that represents an amalgamation of 19th-century East-Central European traditions with American pop music styles of the 20th century.

Or, it could happen that **no acculturation** occurs, and the emigrant tradition is not influenced at all but continues to be distinctive, separate and self-contained while still maintaining close links to its Old World source. This is the course followed by Irish folk music brought to America after the mid-19th century, though the path has been far from straight and narrow.

Irish folk music in the United States has staunchly resisted acculturative pressures, and the fundamental core of the tradition has remained virtually intact after well over a century and a quarter of residence in this country.

That is, the structural forms of the dance music and airs have not deviated from patterns established in Ireland during the 18th century. There has also been a strong continuity of performance styles during this period. While new tunes have entered the repertoire from within and without, there are still tunes played today that were played by Irish musicians one and two centuries ago. Although many new instruments have been adopted by Irish musicians in Ireland and America, these new additions have adapted to styles and repertoire already extant in the idiom.

The ability of this form of Irish music to resist the assimilative pressures that it faced in the United States was due in no small part to the large numbers of musicians who arrived with the more than four million Irish emigrants to America from the Famine to the Second World War.

American Irish musicians were able to retain a close relationship to the tradition in Ireland by means of a continuing stream of new emigrants and also by means of music collections published by individuals like Francis O'Neill. The issuance of commercial recordings in the first few decades of the 20th century also helped American Irish musicians keep in touch with new developments overseas.

Of course, little is known about the fate of Irish musicians who journeyed into the interior of rural America during the 1800s; it can only be assumed that their music was engulfed and assimilated by the traditions of the area in which they settled. In the urban areas where tightly-knit Irish neighborhoods and social networks existed, Irish music was able to thrive and take on new vigor.

In Chicago during the 19th century, the large community of Irish musicians who settled there insured that the city would be an important center for Irish music in America. In addition to local musicians, professional players who travelled throughout the U.S. inevitably passed through Chicago and contributed to the city's Irish music tradition. The work of Francis O'Neill in collecting and publishing Irish music gained worldwide attention, and the names of O'Neill's musical contemporaries were celebrated among Irish musicians across America and in Ireland.

Despite Chicago's important role in the history of Irish music in America, the city's Irish music tradition has remained conservative. The instruments in use among Chicago musicians today are the standard instruments that have been in the idiom of Irish music for the last half century. The new eclecticism in instruments that has become characteristic of ensembles and of younger players in Ireland has not greatly affected the tradition in Chicago. The uilleann pipes, fiddle, flute, tinwhistle, accordion, concertina, piano, drums and bodhrán are the major instruments seen in the hands of Irish musicians in Chicago; younger players there have not to date appeared particularly interested in playing instruments other than these standard ones.

In regard to performance practice, Irish music in Chicago has also remained conservative. Perhaps because of the current economic infeasibility of organizing a standing ensemble, no céilí bands or consorts exist in Chicago other than those assembled for a night's performance. In this respect, the situation is no different from what it was a century ago when Irish music was performed solo, in duets, trios and in loosely-organized informal ensembles playing in sessions and for dances.

Irish musicians in Chicago have been open to the acquisition of repertoire from Irish musicians living in other cities, and the Chicago repertoire has kept pace with the tradition in other American cities and in Ireland. The frequent visits of Irish musicians from Chicago to Ireland, and the appearances of musicians from other American cities and Ireland in Chicago during the last few years have given Chicago musicians many opportunities to hear new tunes.

The increase in recordings of traditional Irish musicians in Ireland and America has also been a repertoire source of Chicago musicians. The composition of new tunes by Chicago musicians has not been extensive, but it has occurred, showing that the tradition in Chicago is not wholly lacking in the creative capacity so important to a living music tradition.

Old and new styles co-exist in Chicago's Irish music community. Older players in their fifties, sixties and seventies, such as uilleann piper Joe Shannon, fiddler John McGreevy and accordionist Terry Teahan, have preserved intact the styles that they inherited during the 1910s, 1920s and 1930s. Younger musicians have drawn upon these older players as well as current performers in Ireland, with the result that the city exhibits an interesting diversity and chronology in style.

With the older musicians in Chicago receiving recognition for their abilities through recordings and an increasing number of public performances, it is possible that the older styles that date back to the early part of the 20th century and beyond may continue to thrive.

The tradition of Irish folk song has not fared as well as the folk music tradition in Chicago. There are a number of outstanding exponents of Irish folk song who live in Chicago, but with a few exceptions, these performers do not perform publicly. The folk song tradition in the Irish community of Chicago does not appear to be getting stronger, either, as there are no young people taking it up, nor do any of the older performers compose new songs.

The folk song tradition is even more conservative than the folk music tradition, but this may be due in part to the fact that it has had little opportunity to experiment with new repertoire or styles due to its precarious position. The derivative, hybrid idioms of Irish song have completely overwhelmed the Irish folk song tradition in Chicago, and the tradition does not play a significant role in the city's Irish musical affairs.

The performance occasions at which Irish music can be found in Chicago have changed over the last century, although there has been some continuity in this area. Irish folk music has been ousted from most Irish bars and Irish dances held by Irish social and political organizations. Céilís have increased since the early 1970s, however, to offset the disappearance of Irish folk music and dancing from public dances.

Irish music is still found in non-commercial performance contexts and at sessions. Irish music has become more prominent at formal concerts, both within the Irish community and outside of it. While the ordinary Irish musician has been replaced in dance competition and exhibition contexts by musicians with more specialized repertoires and performance styles tailored to the occasion, the teaching of Irish dancing in classes has become almost totally devoid of live musical performance. Live Irish music has also become much more infrequent on radio and television broadcasts in Chicago.

The performers of Irish music in Chicago have become more demographically diversified than a few decades ago, as the music has been taken up by many persons not of Irish ancestry. Female performers have increased also, and there are now many players under age twenty-five who have become interested in the music. Irish music in Chicago is no longer an "old-timers' music" played by male, blue-collar workers above age forty but is performed by a heterogeneous population reflecting the broadened sector of the populace that now makes up the audiences for the music.

The role of the Irish musician in the Irish community of Chicago as a cultural conservator has remained valid, yet it is not a role that is perceived by a large portion of that community. Since the number of professional Irish musicians in Chicago has declined, the music is looked upon by most Irish-Americans as little more than a hobby for amateurs.

Yet, a growing number of Irish parents in Chicago have begun to view Irish music as a means of reinforcing the ethnic identity of their children, and among these people, the Irish musician's role as an active bearer of a cherished element of the ethnic heritage is secure.

Performers' associations have recently become a much more potent force for creating greater public awareness of Irish traditional music in Chicago. They have also reintroduced Irish music to a greater number of people in the Irish-American community who had previously been uninterested in the tradition. By sponsoring events such as the Fleadh Cheoil and concerts of local and visiting Irish musicians, the musicians' associations have instigated a new enthusiasm among audiences and performers alike.

Schools of Irish music in Chicago have sought to institutionalize and formalize the transmission of the tradition to insure its survival in the generation. As of this writing, it appears that these attempts are having a noticeable impact on implanting Irish music in the consciousness of many young Irish-Americans. This is also the added result of drawing many of their parents into a closer involvement with the music.

Many Irish musicians from Chicago are now being recorded by commercial record companies, and this will likely have beneficial effects on the local tradition, as these players begin to rise in the estimation of their peers and the general public. Local media, such as radio and television, have been negligent in their support of Irish music; due to the commercial broadcasting system, this is not likely to change soon, unless a traditional Irish musician gains access to a media airspot. The radio programs devoted to the Chicago Irish community have consistently shown their preoccupation with the mainstream musical tastes of their audiences and have not been especially adventuresome in their promotion of Irish folk music.

All things considered, Irish music has not fared too badly in its transplantation to Chicago. In spite of a decline in emigration from Ireland, the diaspora of the Irish community throughout the metropolitan Chicago area and a diminishing of the music's importance in the lives of the ethnic group that created it, the tradition of Irish music in Chicago has produced several outstanding musicians who are known and respected in Ireland as well as America.

While there are more Irish musicians and musical occasions featuring Irish music in New York, Irish music in Chicago is still a vigorous idiom that has proven itself capable of resisting assimilative pressures while reproducing itself in succeeding generations. During the last three decades, only New York has been able to match the number of talented young American-born Irish musicians under age twenty-five. It will be remembered that the first tour of American-born Irish musicians to perform in Ireland came from Chicago in 1959.

The tremendous revival of Irish music in Ireland within the last decade has undoubtedly had an impact on the tradition in Chicago. Since Ireland is a much more culturally and demographically homogenous society than Chicago, the role of Irish music in Ireland is more clearly defined as part of the majority national culture. In Chicago, Irish music is simply one of a hundred traditions competing for the loyalty and support of its audiences. That it has remained as strong as it has for well over a century is indeed remarkable.

Speaking of the folk music of European ethnic groups in America, Nettl (1962:64) states that the group:

> ... does not usually trust to the usual channels of oral tradition to assure the survival of the songs. Instead, it organizes singing groups and clubs, it sponsors professional entertainers, it develops specialists. Folk music becomes the concern of the intellectual leaders of the ethnic groups ... and it is changed under the pressure of Americanization and urbanization.

In applying this general developmental pattern to Irish music in Chicago, some points of difference quickly emerge. Irish music was not initially affected adversely by its transferral to an urban environment in American cities; instead, the expanded opportunities for performing Irish music in America during the 19th century represented an improvement in employment conditions and social status for musicians emigrating from a psychologically and economically ravaged post-Famine Ireland. Rather, it is suburbanization and not urbanization that has been a significant factor in the music's late-20th-century development.

There have been professionals and specialists among Irish folk musicians since idiom's genesis in the 18th century, and it is the existence of professionals and specialists that has contributed a great deal to the tradition's health and well-being in Chicago. Professionals and specialists do not exist in communities where there is no need for their services.

Oral tradition has never been the exclusive means of transmitting Irish traditional music, although in the past there was considerably less emphasis on formal methods of pedagogy. The collections of Francis O'Neill have probably made a more significant and indelible impact on the living tradition of Irish music both in Ireland and in America than any single recording of Irish music ever issued. Six decades after their publication, O'Neill's *Music of Ireland* and *The Dance Music of Ireland* are regarded by traditional Irish musicians as "the Bible" of the idiom (Breathnach 1971:123).

However, the chief legacy of the American experience upon Irish music in Chicago has been the increasingly imperative need to organize a diminishing number of performers into some kind of centralized activity, be it céilís, music competitions, musicians' associations or schools of Irish music. This is not, perhaps, evidence of Americanization or urbanization as much as it is the result of modernization — the attempt of an 18th-century rural tradition to adjust to a 20th-century urban environment.

One interesting aspect of the transplantation of Irish music to American cities like Chicago has been the growth of hybrid, derivative traditions alongside the folk tradition. While the hybrid idioms have achieved a more prominent place in the consciousness of the general American public who might not be expected to know or care whether the music they hear is authentically Irish or of a hybrid form, the hybrid idioms have also become dominant within the Irish-American community's musical preferences.

As George Bernard Shaw commented, "the unsubstantial fancies of the novelists and music-hall songwriters of one generation are apt to become the unpleasant and mischievous realities of the next" (Wakin 1976:5).

In Chicago, the folk idiom has not been influenced in style, repertoire, instruments or performance practice by the hybrid idioms. After the hybrid idioms had been established long enough to acquire their own elements of tradition and their own distinctive structural and stylistic features, they ceased to borrow from the folk idiom.

One of the most curious aspects of Irish music in Chicago is its recent rise in popularity among persons who are not Irish. Instead of violating the integrity of the idiom or resulting in its assimilation into other American musical idioms, this focus of attention from outside the ethnic group has contributed to the affirmation of Irish music as an important and valuable musical expression. The tradition has not become ghettoized or restricted solely to members of the ethnic group, and this has increased its chances of survival in a non-native environment.

Of even greater significance is the growing number of Americans of non-Irish ancestry who have become highly proficient performers of Irish music in spite of having had no previous cultural or familial connections with the tradition. A <u>reverse process of assimilation</u> has occurred, whereby Irish music has gained adherents from outside the ethnic group, while declining in importance within its own ethnic community.

It is possible that, if this present trend continues, the emigrant tradition might eventually be transferred virtually intact to the trusteeship of musicians who play the music in the accepted, genuine manner but who are not ethnically related to the emigrant group. Thus, the emigrant tradition would continue to flourish in its adopted environment even as its ethnic audience and performer base alters and expands.

Or, as was said of the Norman invaders who settled in Ireland during the Middle Ages, "Hiberniores Hibernicis ipsis" — they became "more Irish than the Irish themselves".

APPENDIX A:

"Lines Written On The Most Dreadful Fire That Broke Out In Chicago In America"

composed by Jeramiah Cronan

published by P. Brereton, 56 Cooke Street, Dublin, 1871.

You sympathising Christians, I pray you listen unto me,
While I relate the dreadful state of thousands in America;
The fearful fire that has broke out, it leaves us all in grief and pain
For the loss of our dear Irish friends, alas, will never see their home again.

On the 7th of October we'll remember it now and for evermore,
The dreadful fire that has broke out which caused thousands for to deplore;
The raging flames with pains and screams for which we'll weep both night and day;
Most dreadful was their sufferings in Chicago in America.

It was a shocking sight to see those victims young and old
In frightful flames and tortuous pains enough to make your blood run cold;
Mothers, sons, and daughters in thousands they aloud did cry
For mercy and forgiveness unto the Lord that rules on high.

When they were leaving Ireland and parting the home they loved so dear,
Little did their relations think that this sad news they were doomed to hear;
Their neighbors, friends, and parents who of times for them did pray,
They are now consumed in fire in Chicago all in America.

Those who escaped this dreadful doom they claim our pity, too;
To see them running from the fire shouting, "Alas, what shall we do?"
The mothers with their children it was heart-rending for to hear;
The screams of them were terrifying; the hardest heart would shed a tear.

As they suffered this most awful death, we hope their souls in heaven may dwell;
The pains and torture they went through, I'm sure no mortal tongue will tell;
Their loving friends in Ireland will weep for them many a day,
With broken hearts lamenting their loss by fire in America.

Now there has been a noble call through the world everywhere
To raise up a subscription for the surviving sufferers there;
And in every part let each feeling heart come forward with their mite
For to assist those poor distressed, may God protect them day and night.

So now to end these feeling lines I hope you all will lend your aid
And freely extend your charity to those poor suffering people God has saved;
And may you receive the reward that has been promised upon the great accounting day,
And for those poor Christians that lost their lives, let young and old now for them pray.

APPENDIX B:

Discography of Commercial Recordings Made by Chicago Irish Musicians

SECTION A: 78 rpm discs made between 1921 and 1938.

TOM ENNIS, uilleann pipes
* Victor 18286
jigs: Three Little Drummers-Connachtman's Rambles-Joy of My Life-Nancy Hynes-Kerrigan's
airs: Believe Me If All Your Endearing Young Charms-Killarney-The Last Rose of Summer

* Victor 18366
reels: The Maid That Left the Country-Drowsy Maggie-Around the World for Sport
hornpipes: Murphy's-Derry-McNamara's

* Victor 21444 (w/ Ed Geoghegan, piano)
jig: Trip to the Cottage
reel: Dublin Reel

* Victor 21542 (w/ Ed Geoghegan, piano)
reel: Wexford Reel
reel: Miss Casey

* Parlophone E3023
jig: The Freize Breeches
hornpipes: The Kildare Fancy-Off to California

* Celtic 1001
jigs: Sarsfield's-The Rakes of Clonmel
jigs: Humours of Bandon-The Campbells Are Coming

* Odeon 20077 (w/ John Mueller, piano)
air: The Dear Irish Boy
air: The Coulin

* Cardinal 2028 (w/ John Mueller, piano)
reels: Little Judy
jigs: The Cook in the Kitchen

* Gennett 5003 (w/ John Garridy, fiddle)
polkas: untitled
reels: untitled

* Vocalion 14354 (w/ John Mueller, piano and James Morrison, fiddle)
jigs: Paddy in London-Butcher's March-Sligo Bay
reels: New Steampacket-The Bucks of Oranmore-The Gardner's Daughter

* Columbia 33021 (w/ John Mueller, piano and James Morrison, fiddle)
set dance: The Job of Journeywork
jigs: untitled

* Columbia 33042 (w/ John Mueller, piano and James Morrison, fiddle)
reels: The Bag of Potatoes-The Templehouse-The Pigeon on the Gate
set dance: The Blackbird

* Columbia 33043 (w/ John Mueller, piano and James Morrison, fiddle)
jigs: The Black Rogue-Saddle the Pony
hornpipe: Derry Hornpipe

* Columbia 33046 (w/ John Mueller, piano and James Morrison, fiddle)
set dance: The Humours of Bandon
reels: The Maid Behind the Bar-Trim the Velvet

* Columbia 33394
?: Roy's Wife
jigs: Ragan's-Nora Creena

* Columbia 33421
reel: Trim the Velvet
hornpipe: Rickett's-Dr. Carroll's

* Unknown
reels: Swallow's Tail-The Maid Behind the Bar-Fermoy Lasses

SELENA O'NEILL, fiddle and LEROY SHIELD, piano
* Victor 21526
hornpipe: The Bantry Hornpipe
slip jigs: The Swaggering Jig-Give Us A Drink of Water

* Victor 21718
air: Thanksgiving
hornpipes: Whitney's Fancy-Tom O'Neill's

JOE SULLIVAN, uilleann pipes and BILLY MCCORMICK, fiddle
* Columbia 33192
reels: The Merry Blacksmith-Fair Athenry
hornpipe: Tuohey's Favorite

PADDY DORAN, flute; JOE SULLIVAN, uilleann pipes; JOE OWENS, piano
* Columbia 33202
jigs: Follow Me Around the Garden-The Lark in the Meadow

PADDY DORAN, flute; JOE OWENS, fiddle; DENNY FLYNN, uilleann pines; ? HARTE, piano
* Columbia 33238
jigs: Off She Goes-The Valleys Are Blooming
reels: Tom Henry's Favorite-Pete Brown's Fancy

PADDY DORAN, flute and KATHLEEN KEARNEY, piano
* Gennett 5604
hornpipe: Captain Coughlan's
jig: Bowen's Favorite

MICHAEL J. CASHIN, fiddle and TOM DOYLE, flute
* Victor 21594
reels: The Kerry Reel-The Shannon Shores
jigs: Ginger's Favorite-The Bog of Allen

* Victor 21718
comedy sketch: Heather and Sedge (Trip to Erin)
reels: Drowsy Maggie-Scotch Mary

FRANCIS CASHIN, fiddle; TON CAWLEY, fiddle; ? FORD, guitar
* Columbia 33388
hornpipes: The Bashful Bachelor-The Sunshine Hornpipe
comedy sketch: Coming from Reilly's Party (vocal by Cashin)

* Columbia 33400
reels: The Mountain Lark-The Wheels of the World
jigs: The Silver Tip-The Frog in the Well

PADDY DORAN, flute; TOM CAWLEY, fiddle; FRANCES MALONE, piano
* Columbia 33110
reel: The Moving Bogs of Powelsboro
reel: Sweeney's Favorite

* Columbia 33144
reel: Miss Forkan's Fancy
jig: The Drumshambo Jig

* Columbia 33182
jig: The Castlebar Lasses
reel: The Gatehouse Maid

PAT ROCHE'S HARP AND SHAMROCK ORCHESTRA: Pat Roche, step-dancing; John McGreevy, fiddle; Paddy Durkin, accordion; Eleanor Neary, piano; Pat Richardson, drums
* Decca 12007
hornpipes: The Boys of Bluehill-The Stack of Wheat
polkas: Molly Durkin-Doran's Favorite

* Decca 12008
reels: The Green Mountain-The Longford Maid
set dance: The Blackbird

* Decca 12060
polkas: Babes in the Woods-Little Green Cottage
set dance: The Humours of Bandon

SECTION B: LP discs recorded in the 1970s.

McGreevy and Cooley. John McGreevy, fiddle and Seamus Cooley, flute. Philo 2005, 1974.

Sop'n Up the Gravy: The 1973 Battle Ground Old-Time Fiddlers' Gathering. Various artists, including John McGreevy, fiddle and Kevin Henry, tinwhistle and bodhrán, Log Cabin 8001, 1974.

Hollow Poplar: The 1974 Battle Ground Old-Time Fiddlers' Gathering. Various artists, including John McGreevy, fiddle; Seamus Cooley, flute; Mary Cooley, vocal; Liz Carroll, fiddle. Log Cabin 8003, 1975.

Ladies on the Flatboat: The 1975 Battle Ground Old-Time Fiddlers' Gathering. Various artists, including Frank Burke, fiddle; Albert Neary, tinwhistle; John Neary, spoons. Log Cabin 8004, 1976.

Fleadh Ceoil '75. Various Artists, including Michael Flatley, flute. Dolphin 5013, 1976.

Old Time Irish Music in America: Terry Teahan and Gene Kelly. Terry Teahan, accordion and concertina. Topic 12TS352, 1977.

Irish Traditional Music from Chicago. Joe Shannon, uilleann pipes; John McGreevy, fiddle; Eleanor Neary, piano; James Keane, Sr., vocal; James Keane, Jr., piano accordion; Terry Teahan, accordion and concertina; Maida Sugrue, fiddle and vocal; Frank Thornton, flute; Jim Thornton, accordion; Liz Carroll, fiddle. Rounder 6006, 1978.

> SECTION C: albums due to appear within the next year featuring Chicago Irish Musicians.

- An anthology of the compositions of Ed Reavy, featuring various artists, including Liz Carroll and Armin Barnett, fiddles. Rounder Records.

- An anthology of Irish tinwhistle and flute players in the United States, featuring various artists, including Noel Rice, Kevin Henry and Michael Flatley, flutes. Rounder Records.

- An album of solos and duets by John McGreevy, fiddle and Joe Shannon, uilleann pipes. Morning Star Records.

- An album of solos and duets by Liz Carroll, fiddle and Tom Maguire, accordion. Shanachie Records.

- An album of solos and duets by Liz Carroll, fiddle and Marty Fahey, piano. Shanachie Records.

APPENDIX C:

Minutes of the First Convention of the Irish Musicians' Association of America, Chicago, 1956

Be it known that an Irish Musicians Convention, at the request of Frank J. Thornton, Chairman of the Irish Music Festival, was held in the Walnut Room of the Midland Hotel, in the City of Chicago, on Sunday, August, 19, 1956, at 4 P.M. The opening address, as follows, was given by Frank J. Thornton:

Ladies and Gentlemen: On behalf of the Irish Musicians Committee of Chicago, I extend to each and everyone of you a million welcomes to this, our first Musicians Convention in this great city. It is gratifying for me indeed to be one among you and for our committee to be fortunate enough in having the good council and support of such a genuine group of Irish Musicians. God bless you all.

Having already corresponded with each one of you, you are well aware of the purpose of this convention, but I might reiterate, to prevent the decay of our Irish traditional music, we must here and now consolidate our entire efforts to form an Irish Musicians Commission or Association of America to promote, teach, and forever keep alive our Irish Traditional Music.

To bring this about, it is entirely up to this convention to decide. This today should be the American Association's foundation of purpose. There is already established in Ireland this very program I am presenting to you. As the Chicago Music Chairman, I am in complete agreement with the Irish Association. It is known in Ireland as "Comhaltas Ceoltóirí Éireann", meaning "Irish Musicians Association". Branches of this association have been formed throughout the country. I have received a copy of the Association's constitution from Mr. Padraig S. O'Moinseall, the Association's General Secretary in Dublin, which I shall now read to you.

Then I will call on each one of you to give your advice and comments on the subject and, if you should find it agreeable in all major aspects, then to express your opinion on how it could be best established in this country. For your kind attention, I am very grateful.

The letter from Mr. Padraig S. O'Moinseall was then read.

The following speech was then made by Mr. Edward Reavy of Philadelphia:

My Dear Friends: I am delighted to see such a wonderful gathering of Irish traditional music lovers, assembled here today. It gives one a warm feeling to be among one's own people, and this feeling is magnified by the fact that we have all come with one precious goal in mind, namely, to nationalize our Irish traditional music. For many of us this will be the realization of a lifelong dream.

Ladies and gentlemen, you know and I know that during the past twenty-five or thirty years the traditional music in Ireland has been sadly neglected so much so that it nearly reached the stage of being replaced by the modern music of other countries. I, of course, have my own opinions regarding certain types of this brand of music, but if one expects tolerance, one must be tolerant. I do feel, however, and strongly, that the beautiful music of Ireland should not and will not be pushed into the background, for this music is Ireland, and to try to replace it with any other would be, to say the least, foolish. I thank God that our brother musicians in our homeland saw what was happening and united their forces, establishing a National Traditional Music Organization which is now flourishing throughout Ireland.

We, in America, must unite with out brother musicians in Ireland, in order to make their efforts a complete success. It will not be an easy task, my friends, but with God's help we shall not fail. We may look for many obstacles and disappointments along the way to unification, but with tolerance and understanding we shall attain our goal.

Lovers of Irish music, it has been my experience throughout the years that the worst enemy of Irish traditional music is petty jealousy among many of our own musicians. That is a cold hard fact we must face. We have reduced it to a minimum in Philadelphia, but this music cancer, as I call it, is very prevalent in New York City and Boston, where we have so many fine Irish musicians and, no doubt, we may look for it in other parts of the country, too.

What is the cure for this disease? By tolerance, understanding, and the guidance of intelligent leaders, it is hoped that those who are at fault will realize that music is a gift from God to be used as He intended, and not abused, for He who gave it can snatch it away in a moment. We should all remember that we must account for our abuses to the gift of music, just as we must account for any abuse rendered the many other gifts of God. Unity means strength, and we must unite solidly on a strong foundation, thinking together, together, respecting whatever amount of talent God has given to each of us. We must practice this religiously if we are to be successful.

In Philadelphia, our organization is called The Irish Musicians' Union of Pennsylvania, Inc. and is under the Laws of the commonwealth. Our constitution and by-laws are rather flexible. This allows us to operate on a family-type basis. The dues are $12.00 per year. Most of our members play wedding engagements, cafes, and dances. Also, we have two radio programs every Sunday, on which are announced the various Irish activities in and around the City of Philadelphia.

We have a membership of 65 men and a band consisting of 35 musicians who march in the Barry Day parade and the St. Patrick's Day parade each year. Monthly meetings are conducted on the third Monday of every month. Our officers are as follows: President, Vice-President, Financial Secretary, Recording Secretary, Treasurer, and Sergeant-At-Arms. Our Board of Directors handles all disputes and grievances. We practice the "Do Unto Others" principle and render all possible assistance to our brothers in sickness, death, or other misfortune. After each meeting, social sessions are held, allowing our members to play solos, duets, or in groups.

From years of experience I have found our method of organization to be very successful. We conduct our meetings on a strictly business basis, limiting them to an hour-and-a-half. This promotes good attendance and helps create renewed interest in our music. Then, too, most of our members derive a financial gain for their services.

And so, ladies and gentlemen, that is my report to you concerning our efforts to advance Irish traditional music. I have told you about our successes. I must also admit to failures. We have failed as teachers, for many of our musicians play by ear and cannot read music. This presents a serious problem, which we are trying to rectify by seeking ways and means to establish a sound method of teaching our young people.

Speaking of our young people, we must have some inducement for them to learn Irish music. It isn't enough to offer to teach them. We must have something to offer them when they have reached an advanced stage. At this point, I would say that our dancers and musicians should cooperate to a great extent. Together with our Irish Societies, they must work hand-in-hand in a creative capacity, whereby our young musicians and dancers will be fairly compensated for their services. Some will teach, others will form orchestras, and others will play individually or in small groups. This will hold, also, for the dancers. In any event, everything in connection with Irish music must tie in together, if we are to be successful.

I thank you.

A copy of the constitution of "Comhaltas Ceoltóirí Éireann" and the Application For, which was received from the General Secretary of the Association in Ireland were read to the Convention by Frank J. Thornton, and they were then presented for adoption by him.

Mr. Edward Reavy of Philadelphia nominated Mr. Thornton of Chicago as Convention Chairman. Seconded by Mr. John McGreevy of Chicago. Passed.

Mr. John McGreevy of Chicago was nominated by James Neary of Chicago as Recording Secretary, and this was seconded by Mr. Tommy Caulfield of Philadelphia. Passed.

Mr. Edward Reavy of Philadelphia asked of the members if they would use the name of the organization in Eire, or use another name for the organization.

Mr. Caulfield inquired as to honorary chairmen, or just titled "Chairman". Also, he mentioned the definite instruments to be considered.

Mr. L. Quinn of New York City explained his association with the home organization in Ireland, and inquired of possible meetings in the future here in America. Mr. Quinn was told by Mr. Thornton that by reading the Constitution it would state that meetings would be held and results forwarded every three months to the "Home Organization" in Dublin. He also requested that, this organization here today be the Home Organization of America. Mr. E. Reavy named this organization as "IRISH MUSICIANS ASSOCIATION OF AMERICA" affiliated with the parent organization in Ireland. This was seconded by Dan Lynch of Chicago. Mr. Reavy put the motion to the members, and was approved by the members.

Canada was mentioned as being affiliated with us, and it was decided that they could join with us if they wished, if they were interested.

Mr. F. Thornton of Chicago wondered then if we should change any of the constitution and Ed Reavy said we may change it, as the conditions are different here than they are in Ireland. Mr. F. Thornton asked if we should name a National Secretary of this organization, and he suggested Mr. Ed Reavy. Mr. Reavy declined. Ed Reavy mentioned that dancing, singing, and other organizations be invited to join in and help promote this organization. He said that once we got started, many other organizations would organize with us here in Chicago. A suggestion was made by L. Quinn that other committees be appointed as National workers or representatives from each city to organize their own city.

Mr. Ed Reavy suggested Mr. Frank Thornton as National Chairman and Mr. John McGreevy as National Secretary of this organization. This was passed by the members. Mr. L. Quinn suggested that the National Secretary appoint representatives from other cities to direct activities from their area. Seconded by J. Neary of Chicago. Passed.

Mr. F. Thornton appointed E. Reavy and Tommy Caulfield of Philadelphia, Mr. L. Quinn from New York City, Tom Shine of Kansas City, Missouri, and Father Kennelly of Houston, Texas. Pat Roche then suggested Mr. Martin Hardiman be elected Honorary Chairman, and gave the following talk:

> The home of Mr. Martin Hardiman has always been a monument to Irish culture where dancers, musicians, and singers have always found an open door. His son, Msgr. Hardiman, who is now Secretary to Cardinal Samuel Stritch, Archbishop of Chicago, is only too glad to display his Irish music and dance at any Irish gathering he has time to attend.

Mr. Hardiman's nomination as Honorary Chairman was seconded by E. Reavy and passed. Mrs. Neary suggested Maurice O'Halloran from Detroit. Passed. J. Neary suggested J. Giblin of Cleveland. These were approved by Mr. Thornton. Jim Donnelly was suggested from Chicago, and this was approved by Mr. Lynch. Tom Senier of Boston was suggested, and this was approved by Pat Roche.

Ed Reavy suggested that representatives of other cities look for musicians in these other cities and forward heir names here to the National Chairman. Also, he suggested that we have a publicity man and have letterheads printed listing our officers and representatives, to be used in connection with publicity of other cities. This was seconded by E. Reavy. Pat Roche was appointed and passed by members.

Mr. J. Neary suggested a charter for our organization, and Pat Roche asked that a Secretary be empowered to look into this. Mr. L. Quinn suggested that all names of members present here today at the Convention be inserted on that Charter. Passed.

Mr. Bob Flately made an address and explained his love for Irish Music, etc. Pat Roche also mentioned his meeting of Bob Flately at the Chicago World's Fair, and he told of Bob Flately's organization of Irish Flute Bands. Pat Roche nominated Bob Flately as Treasurer, but he declined. Mr. Thornton named Mr. Neary as Treasurer, and this was seconded by Mr. D. Lynch. Passed.

Tom Caulfield suggested that meetings be held once a month, and that they be short and interesting, and that we have a social hour afterwards. Meetings could be held at intervals in each district whenever possible, and results be forwarded every three months.

Mr. Reavy read a letter pertaining to the starting of organizations and of why this organization was formed. Mr. Thornton suggested that we use this letter as a main editorial in adopting our Constitution.

T. Caulfield explained that too many orchestra leaders have tried to play both Irish and American music, but played too much American and started to drive Irish music out of the picture. He also mentioned that O'Neill's music was going to be published again, which is a help to us. Pat Roche then explained how the Dancing Teachers' Commission was organized, and the need that such an organization be started. He explained our Aroch Feis [Oireachtas] and suggested that out musicians try as the dancers did, and told us that there was going to be one in Philadelphia sometime in November. He suggested to us that various county's sets do not go over, unless we could start a nationalizing of a certain set, so that everyone could dance a set. T. Caulfield mentioned that this set should be made short. Ed Reavy suggested we include all instruments in our Constitution so as not to leave any player out.

FINANCE — Mr. Ed Reavy suggested a per-capita tax from each territory and suggested some form of getting some money to help our organization get started and keep going. Mr. F. Thornton read that each branch can make their own rules, as long as they do not conflict with the original Constitution. Each branch would send through the Main Office in Chicago one pound to be sent to Dublin.

Mr. L. Quinn suggested each branch pay an affiliation fee of $10.00, and as things go it could be reduced or raised. Seconded by Ed Reavy. Passed. Mr. L. Quinn donated $10.00 for our organization. Ed Reavy gave $15.00 as a donation from the Musicians Association of Philadelphia. Other members gave a total of $41.00, to make a grand total of $66.00.

A national Charter was requested by Mr. Reavy. All literature to be on white with green ink was suggested by T. Caulfield. E. Reavy suggested we have a Convention once a year under the direction of the parent body. Seconded by Pat Roche. Passed. F. Thornton suggested that we insert the main purpose of our organization — to promote, teach, and forever keep alive the traditional music of Ireland. Mr. Ed Reavy suggested we have this Charter mimeographed. Mr. L. Quinn suggested not only musicians, but anyone who loves Irish music may apply for membership. E. Reavy suggested every publicity possible in this country and all Irish papers and Irish radio Programs, and that we be sure to send to all daily papers if possible, especially in Chicago. Ed Reavy suggested a Financial Report. It was $66.00 from members present. Ed Reavy suggested we all give a vote of thanks to our officers and members. Seconded and passed. Pat Roche suggested a vote of thanks to our out-of-town members.

A closing talk was then given by Mr. Frank J. Thornton, as follows:

> It is a matter of great joy to know the volume of work that can be accomplished when serious-minded men and women convene with high ideals, firm convictions, and an unanimous love for the purpose of their meeting. This convention has made history here today, and all those present will have their names inscribed in that history as the Founders of the Association. Let us go forward from here with the traditional music of Ireland. I thank you.

A closing prayer was led by Ed Reavy. Mr. Donnelly called our attention to the need of a spiritual director. Rt. Rev. Msgr. William J. Gorman has accepted this responsibility. The meeting was adjourned at 7:05 P.M. on a motion by Ed Reavy, which was seconded by J. Neary and passed.

APPENDIX D:

Showing the Principal Venues for Irish Music in Chicago since the 1930s

MAP #1: The 1930s and 1940s

- A. Madison and Sacramento (dance hall)
- B. Madison and California (dance hall)
- C. Root and Wentworth (dance hall)
- D. 47th and California, Gaelic Park (open-air dancing)
- E. 74th and Ashland, Celtic Field (open-air dancing)
- F. 69th and Wentworth (dance hall)
- G. 69th and Emerald (dance hall)
- H. 50th and Halsted, John Breen's (tavern)
- I. 56th and Halsted, Erin's Isle (tavern)
- J. 76th and Halsted, Celtic Club (tavern)
- K. 7425 S. Cottage Grove, McGinty's (tavern)
- L. Pulaski and Jackson, Naughton's (tavern)
- M. Cicero and Madison, Concannon's (tavern)
- N. Fullerton and Lincoln, McDermott's Tavern)
- O. 44th and Emerald (tavern)
- P. 26th and Albany, Pilsen Park (open-air dancing)
- Q. 4600 W. Lake, Mill Stadium (open-air dancing)

MAP #2: The 1950s and 1960s

- A. 47th and Halsted, Tony Morrally's (dance hall)
- B. 51st and Halsted, Mrs. Feely's Grove (open-air dancing)
- C. 2409 N. Halsted, Margaret O'Malley (dance hall)
- D. 63rd and Kedzie, Flynn's Hall (dance hall)
- E. Jackson and Cicero, Connolly's (tavern/dance hall)
- F. 4721 W. Madison, Keyman's Club (tavern/dance hall)
- G. 1423 W. 79th, Hanley's House of Happiness (tavern/dance hall)
- H. 69th and Halsted, The Regent (tavern/dance hall)
- I. 121 N. Cicero, West End Ballroom (dance hall)
- J. 4039 W. Madison, McEnery Hall (dance hall)
- K. Jackson and Cicero, Tommy Ryan's (dance hall)
- L. 3257 N. Sheffield, The Viking Ballroom North (dance hall)
- M. 6855 S. Emerald, The Viking Ballroom South (dance hall)
- N. 79th and Halsted, Blarney Club (tavern/dance hall)
- O. 54th and Halsted, Harp and Shamrock (tavern)
- P. 5545 S. Ashland, McDermott's (tavern)
- Q. Milwaukee and Montrose, Ireland's 32 (tavern)
- R. 63rd and Kedzie, Hoban's (tavern)
- S. 800 N. Cicero, Club Cabana (tavern/dance hall)

MAP #3: The 1970s

- A. 63rd and Kedzie, Hoban's (tavern)
- B. Milwaukee and Montrose, Ireland's 32 (tavern)
- C. 6511 S. Kedzie, Flanagan's (tavern)
- D. 3350 W. 63rd, Hibernian Hall (dance hall)
- E. 3326 W. 63rd, VFW Post (dance hall)
- F. 3035 W. 51st, Highlander's Hall (dance hall)
- G. 3711 W. 55th, Polish Eagles' Hall (dance hall)
- H. 2634 N. Laramie, Swiss Club (dance hall)
- I. 4550 W. Sunnyside, Mayfair Park (music club)

MAP #4: Present-day 1978

- A. 3035 W. 51st, Highlander's Hall (dance hall)
- B. 2634 N. Laramie, Swiss Club (dance hall)
- C. 6511 S. Kedzie, 6511 Club (tavern)
- D. Tuohey and Northwest Highway, Francis O'Neill Music Club (dance hall)
- E. Milwaukee and Montrose, Ireland's 32 (tavern)

MAP #5: Irish foreign-stock populations in 1920 and 1970

Each dot represents 100 foreign-stock Irish in 1970. Each encircled area represents the location of predominantly Irish communities in 1920.

Sources:

Historic City: The Settlement of Chicago. Chicago: Department of Development and Planning, 1976. Map of community settlement in 1920, pages 79-80.

Chicago's Irish Population: Selected Statistics. Chicago: Department of Development and Planning, 1976. Map showing distribution of foreign-stock Irish in 1970, page 5.

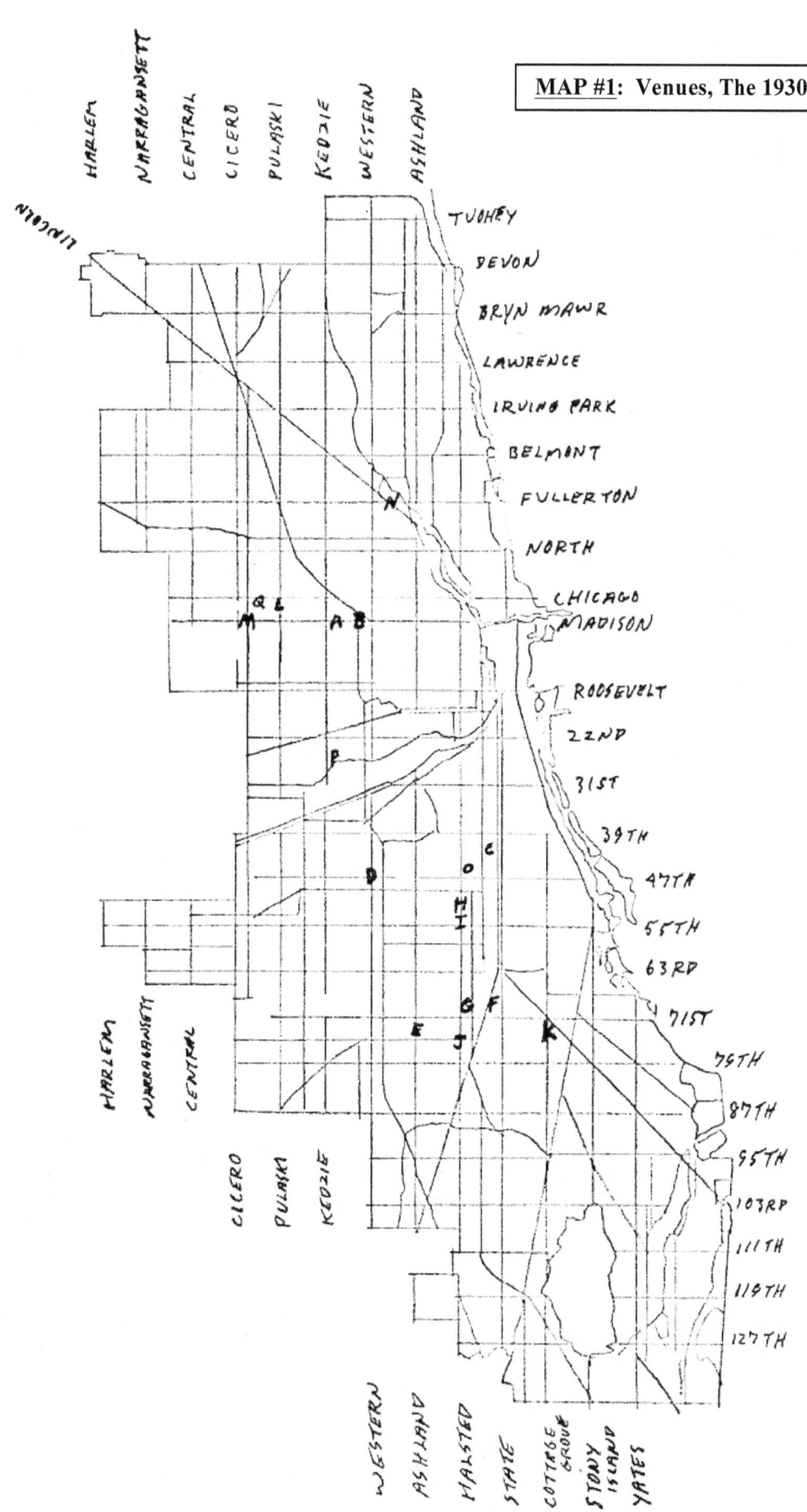

MAP #1: Venues, The 1930s and 1940s

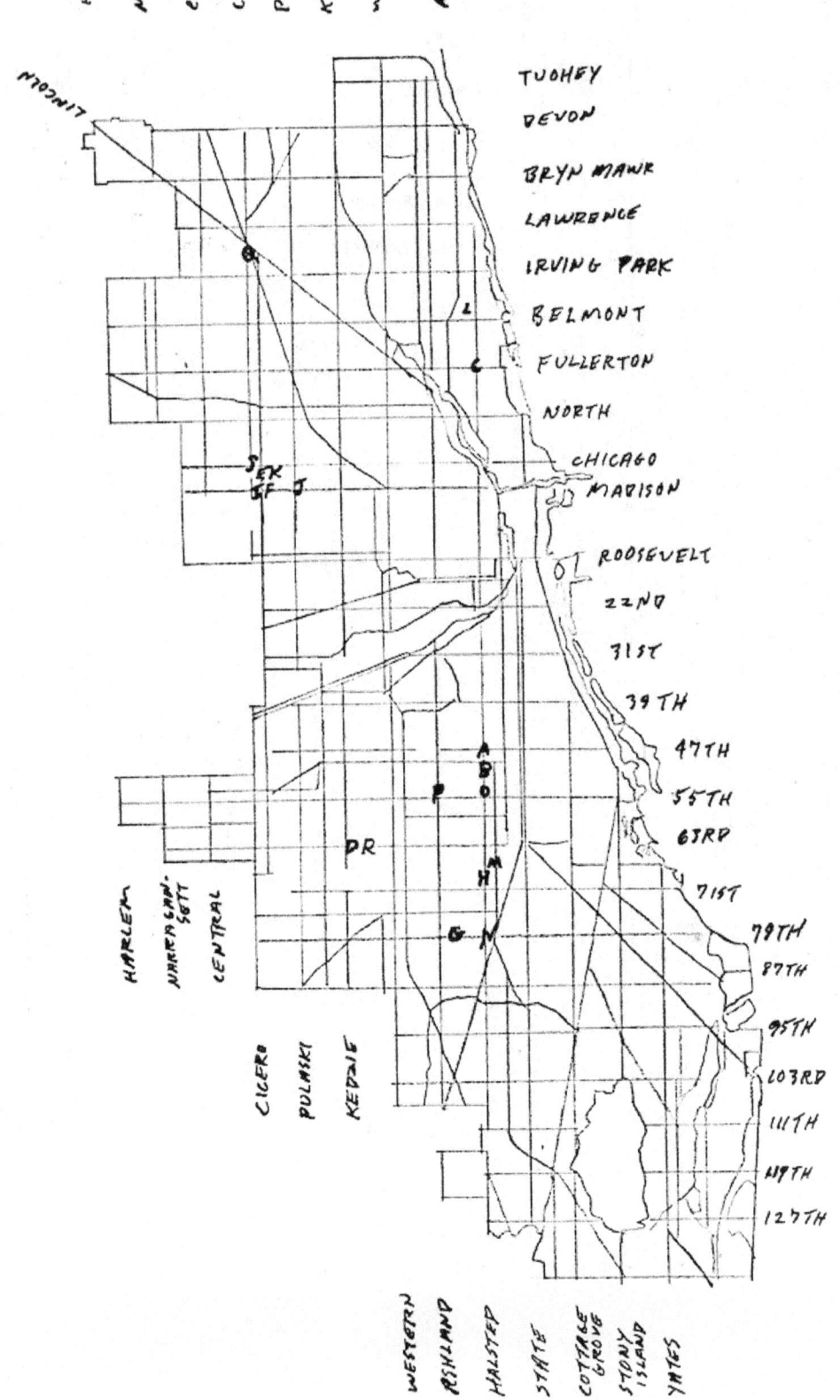

MAP #2: Venues, The 1950s and 1960s

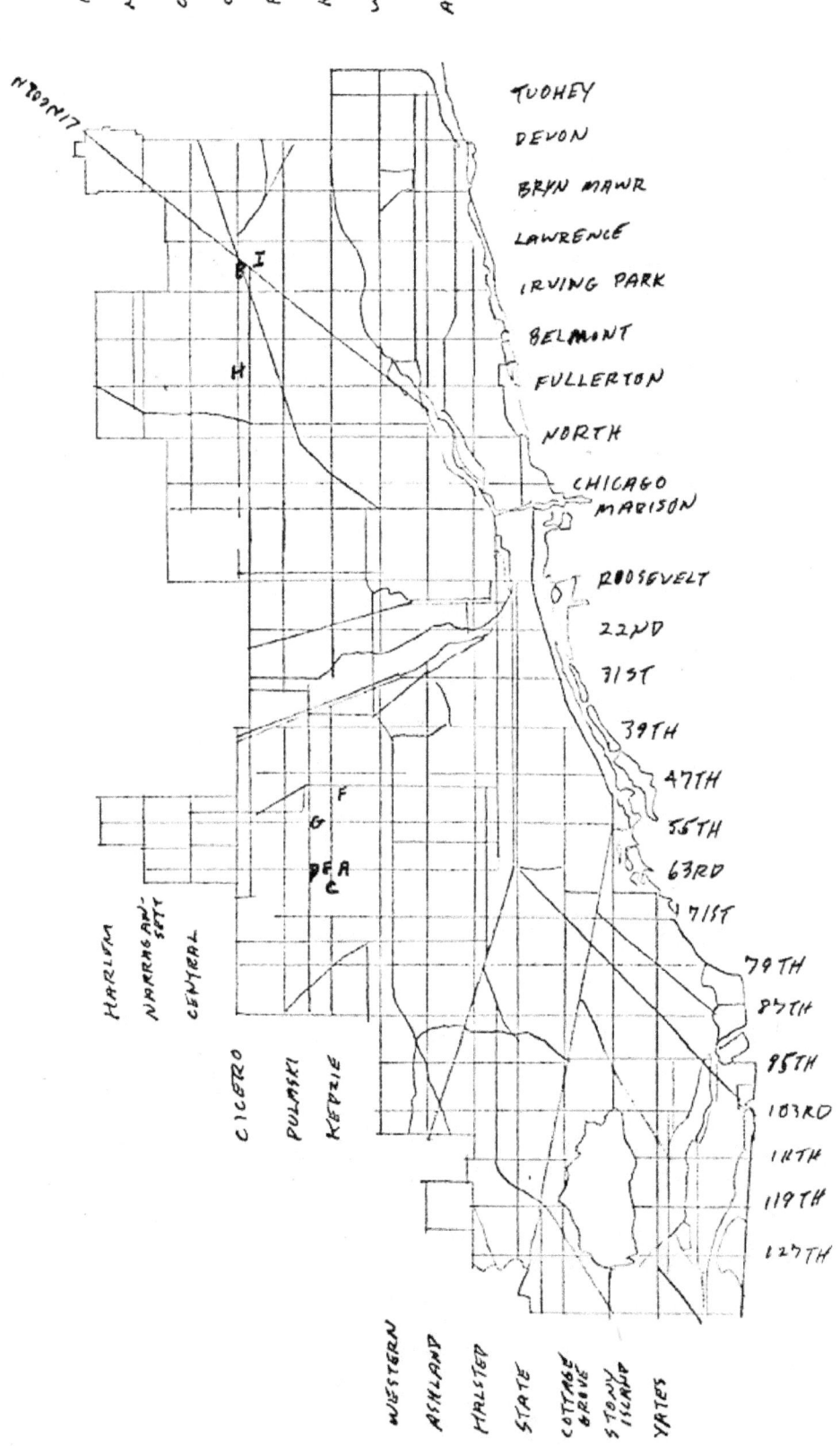

MAP #3: Venues, The 1970s

MAP #4: Venues, Present-day 1978

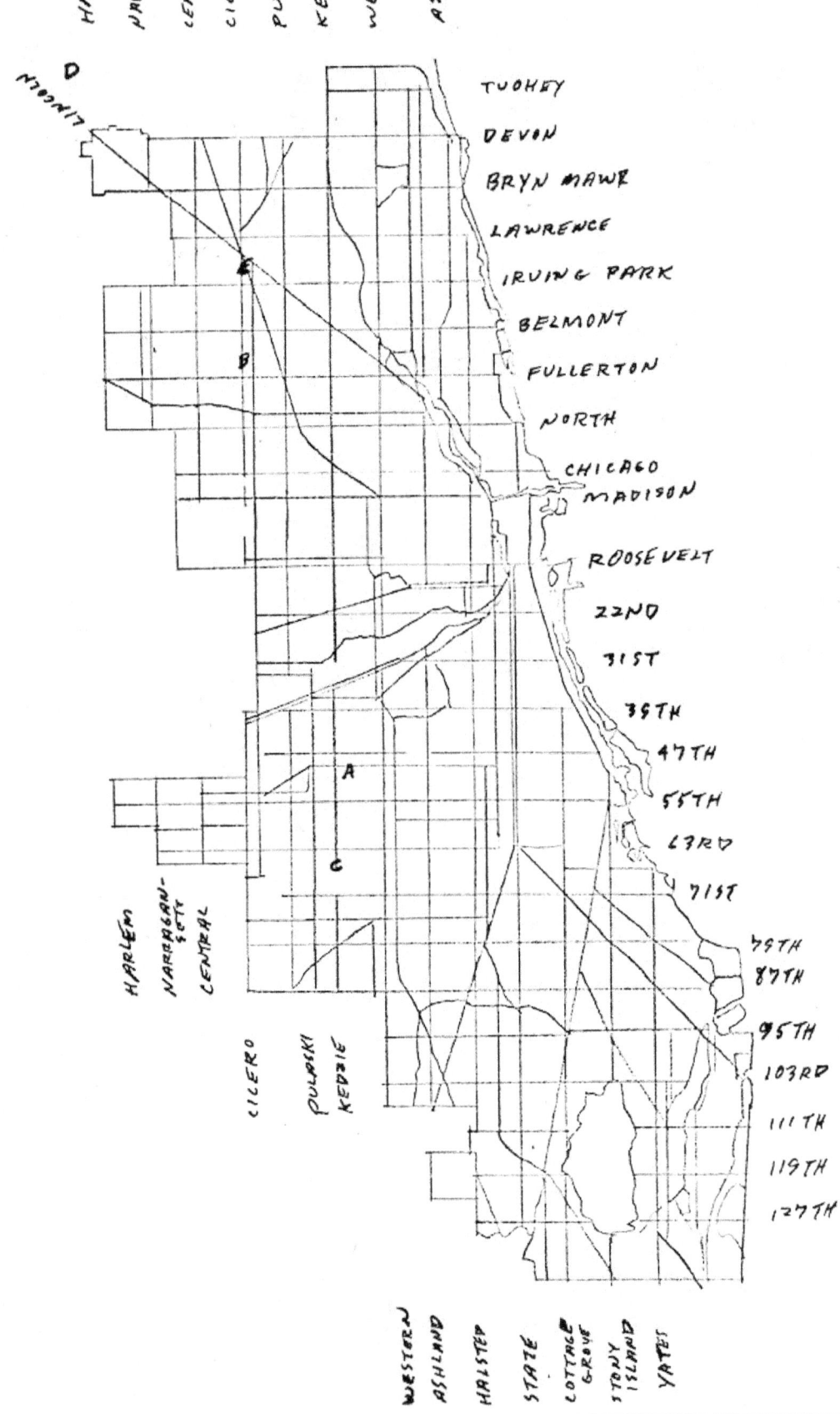

274

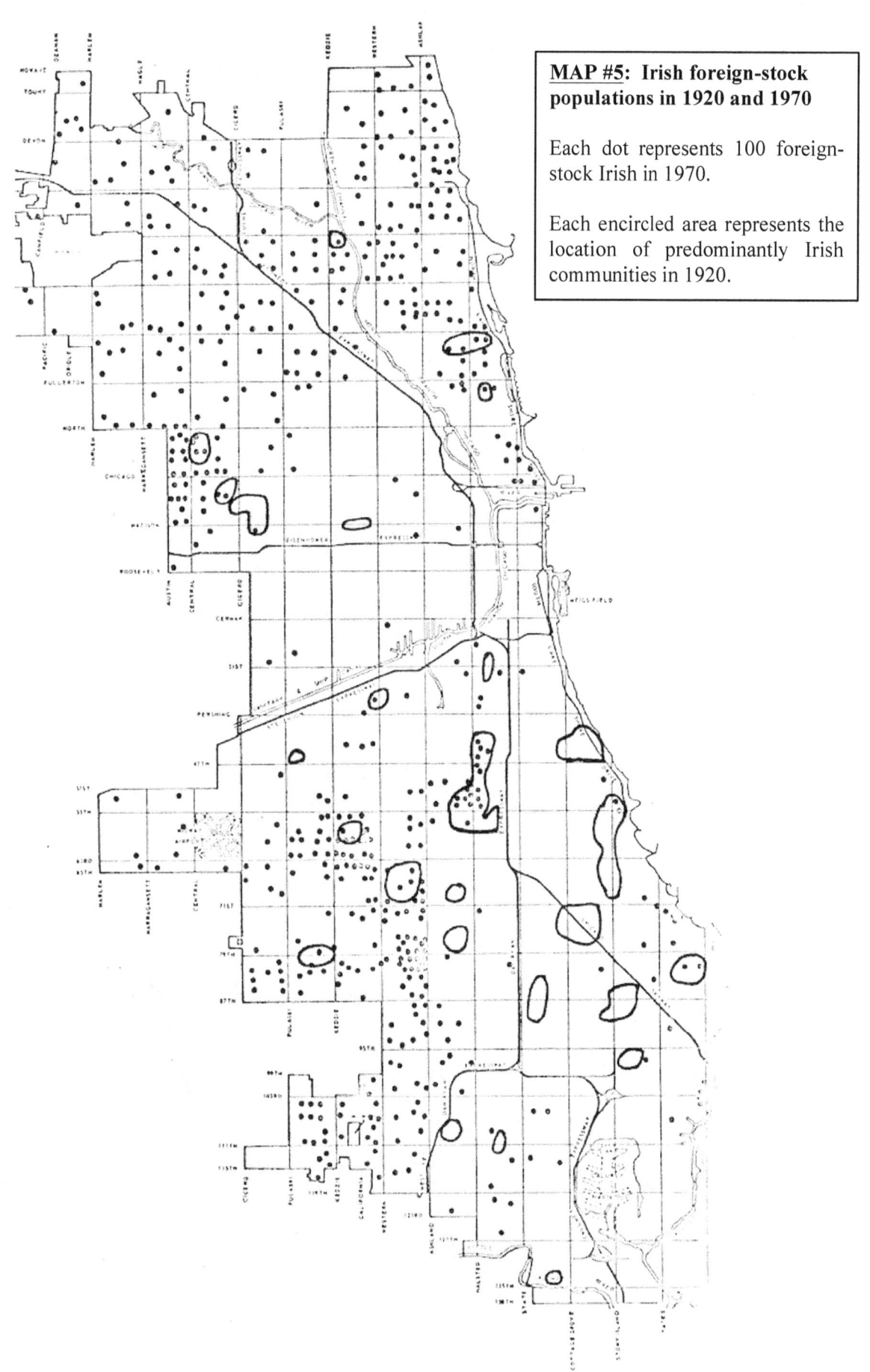

MAP #5: Irish foreign-stock populations in 1920 and 1970

Each dot represents 100 foreign-stock Irish in 1970.

Each encircled area represents the location of predominantly Irish communities in 1920.

APPENDIX E: Photographs of Various Chicago Irish Musicians

1. Francis O'Neill, early 1900s
2. James O'Neill, early 1900s
3. Chicago Irish Music Club, c. 1903
4. John McFadden (fiddle) and James Edward Cronin, early 1900s
5. Barney Delaney, early 1900s
6. Selena O'Neill, early 1900s
7. Thomas Kerrigan, late 1890s
8. Edward Joyce, mid-1890s
9. Patrick Tuohey, early 1900s
10. Joe Sullivan, Billy McCormick, Paul McNamara, Edward Cronin at a Chicago Feis, c. 1915
11. James Early (pipes), early 1900s
12. Bowen's Irish Orchestra, c. 1930: Joe Owens (fiddle), Denny Flynn (pipes), Paddy Doran (flute), Joe Sullivan (pipes), Billy McCormick (fiddle)
13. Eddie Mullaney, from a 1920s Victor Record Catalogue
14. P.J. Concannon (fiddle), Terry Teahan (accordion), Paddy Kenny (accordion) performing live over WOPA radio, early 1950s
15. Terry Teahan (accordion), Mrs. Tangney (concertina), Tom Sheahan (accordion), 1950
16. Paddy Sweeney, Eleanor Neary, Paddy Killoran at a New York Feis, 1954
17. Frank Thornton's Flute Band, late 1950s
18. The Chicago Céilí Band, 1959. Jimmy Thornton (flute), John Lavelle (accordion), Pat Gilhooly (drums), Beatrice Garrity (vocal), Eleanor Neary (piano), John McGreevy (fiddle), Margie Friel (vocal); Mary McDonagh (fiddle), Eileen Fitzgerald (fiddle)
19. Mike Scanlon (pipes), John McGreevy (fiddle), James Giblin (fiddle) performing live over radio, c. 1950
20. Céilí Band performing at the Chicago Fleadh Cheoil, 1965. Mike Madden (accordion), John McGreevy (fiddle), Kevin Keegan (accordion), James Neary (fiddle), Kevin Henry (pipes), Billy Soden (drums)
21. Liz Carroll (fiddle) and James Keane, Jr. (accordion) performing at a céilí, 1976
22. Patrick Hennelly with his masterpiece set of uilleann pipes, early 1950s
23. Joe Shannon, 1976
24. Jimmy Thornton, 1976
25. Seamus Cooley, 1976
26. Mary Cooley, 1976
27. James Keane, Sr., 1976

APPENDIX F: The Published Works of Francis O'Neill

The Music of Ireland, 1903.

The Dance Music of Ireland, 1001 Gems, 1907.

O'Neill's Irish Music, 250 Choice Selections for Piano or Violin, 1908.

Irish Folk Music: A Fascinating Hobby, 1910.

Irish Minstrels and Musicians, 1913.

O'Neill's Irish Music, 400 Choice Selections for Piano or Violin, 1915.

Waifs and Strays of Gaelic Melody, 250 Selections, 1916.

Waifs and Strays of Gaelic Melody, 400 Choice Selections, 1922.

Popular Selections from the Dance Music of Ireland, n.d.

REFERENCES CITED

Anonymous
    1902   "Chicago Leads Ireland as Storehouse of Irish Music", *Chicago Tribune*, Mar. 2, page 53.

    1970   "A Memorable Occasion", *Treoir* (Dublin) 2 (1):12-13.

    1976   "Music of the Old Masters", *Treoir* (Dublin) 8(4):10-13.

Becker, Howard
    1951   "The Professional Dance Musician and His Audience", *American Journal of Sociology* 57(2):136-144.

Bodley, Seóirse
    1973   "Technique and Structure in 'Sean-nós' Singing", *Irish Folk Music Studies* (Dublin)1:44-53.

Bray, Jim
    1973   "Joe O'Dowd: In a Class of His Own," *Treoir* (Dublin) 5(5):6.

Breathnach, Breandán
    1965   "As We See It", *Ceol* (Dublin) 2(1):3-4.

    1970   "The Dancing Master", *Ceol* (Dublin) 3(4):116-118.

    1971   *Folkmusic and Dances of Ireland*. Dublin: Talbot Press.

    1972   "The Humours of Glin: The Piece Way", *Ceol* (Dublin) 4(1):22-23.

    1973   "Tús an Phoirt in Éirinn", *Irish Folk Music Studies* (Dublin) 1:37-43.

    1974   "Piper Jackson," *Irish Folk Music Studies* (Dublin) 2:41-57.

Buck, Carl Darling
    1903   *A Sketch of the Linguistic Condition of Chicago*. Chicago: University of Chicago Press.

Bunting, Edward
    1796   *A General Collection of the Ancient Irish Music*. London: Preston and Son.

    1809   *A General Collection of the Ancient Music of Ireland*. London: Clementi and Company.

    1840   *The Ancient Music of Ireland, Arranged for the Piano Forte*. Dublin: Hodges and Smith.

Byrne, Francis John
    1969   "Latin Poetry in Ireland", in *Early Irish Poetry*. ed. James Carney. Cork: Mercier Press, 29-44.

Campbell, J.B.
    1894   *Campbell's Illustrated History of the World's Columbian Exposition*. Chicago: J.D. Campbell.

Cameron, Vl.B.
    1954   "Sociological Notes on the Jam Session", *Social Forces* 33(2):177-182.

Carney, James
    1967   *The Irish Bardic Poet*. Dublin: Dolmen Press.

Chicago Historical Society
    1930   *History of the Bridgeport Community, Chicago.* Chicago: Chicago Historical Society.

Chicago Irish Musicians' Association
    1976   "Competition Rules," in *United States Fleadh Ceoil.* Chicago: Chicago Irish Musicians Association.

City of Chicago
    1976a   *The People of Chicago: Who We Are and Who We Have Been.* Chicago: Department of Development and Planning.

    1976b   *Chicago's Irish Population: Selected Statistics.* Chicago: Department of Development and Planning.

Coffman, James T.
    1971   "'Everybody Knows This Is Nowhere': Role Conflict and the Rock Musician", *Popular Music and Society* 1(1):30-32.

Corcoran, Seán
    1969   "Two Songs", *Ceol* (Dublin) 3(3):66-70.

Corkery, Daniel
    1970   *The Hidden Ireland.* Dublin: Gill and MacMillan.

Corrigan, John
    1977a   "World's Fair of 1893 Opened New Vistas for Anxious Chicago Irish", *Chicago Irish-American News* 1(4):6.

    1977b   "Chicago Celebrates 'Irish Day' 150,000 Strong at 1893 Fair", *Chicago Irish-American News* 1(5):12, 22, 24.

Cotter, Geraldine
    1973   "Survey of Traditional Music", *Treoir* (Dublin) 5(4):8.

Cromie, Robert
    1958   *The Great Chicago Fire.* New York: McGraw-Hill.

Davies, Peter
    1970   *The American Heritage Dictionary of the English Language.* New York: Dell Publishing.

De Brún, Seamus
    1973   "A Memorable Tour", *Treoir* (Dublin) 5(1):1-4.

Dinneen, Patrick S.
    1970   *An Irish-English Dictionary.* Dublin: Educational Company of Ireland.

Dunleavy, Gareth J.
    1974   *Douglas Hyde.* Cranbury, N.J.: Associated University Presses.

Ennis, John
    1893   "The Irish Bagpipes", *Chicago Citizen*, Oct. 21, page 5.

    1902   "The Revival of Erin's Language and Music in Chicago", *The Gael* (New York) February:34-38.

Ffrench, Charles
    1897   *Biographical History of the American Irish in Chicago.* Chicago: American Biographical Publishing.

Finian
    1970   "The Legend of Paddy O'Brien", *Treoir* (Dublin) 2(4):10.

Fishman, Joshua A.
    1970   *Sociolinguistics: A Brief Introduction.* Rowley, Mass.: Newbury House.

Fleischmann, Aloys
    1952   *Music in Ireland.* Cork: Cork University Press.

Flood, W.R. Grattan
    1905   *A History of Irish Music.* Dublin: Browne and Nolan.

Fox, Charlotte Milligan
    1911   Annals of the Irish Harpers. New York: E.P. Dutton.

Howarth, James
    1971   "Free-Reed Instruments", in *Musical Instruments through the Ages.* ed., Anthony Baines. Harmondsworth, Middlesex, U.K.: Penguin Books, 318-326.

Jeffries, Elizabeth
    1973   "The Traditions of Bargy", *Treoir* (Dublin) 5(3): 13-1L1.

Krassen, Miles
    1974   "Seamus Cooley", album notes to *McGreevy and Cooley*, Philo Records 2005.

Landers, Mary
    1974   "Phil Moloughney", *Treoir* (Dublin) 6(5):20-21.

Lecky, W.E.H.
    1972   *A History of Ireland in the Eighteenth Century.* Chicago: University of Chicago Press.

Lee, Edmund
    1774   *Celebrated Irish Tunes.* Dublin: Edmund Lee.

Linnane, Kitty
    1973   "Kilfenora Céilí Band", *Treoir* (Dublin) 5(1):6.

MacColla, Eoin
    1972   Céilí Dancing in Chicago", *Treoir* (Dublin) 4(4):6.

MacMathúna, Seamus
    1974   "Patrick Kelly of Cree", *Treoir* (Dublin) 6(5):12-13.

McCaffrey, Lawrence
    1976   *The Irish Diaspora in America.* Bloomington, Ind.: Indiana University Press.

McCullough, Lawrence
    1975   "An American Maker of Uilleann Pipes", *Éire-Ireland* (St. Paul, Minn.), 10(4):109-115.

    1978   "Some Brief Analytical Remarks about Ed Reavy's Compositional Style in *Where the Shannon Rises*", album notes to forthcoming album on Rounder Records.

McGivern, John
    1959   "Visit of Chicago Concert Group to Drumshambo", *The Irish World and American Industrial Liberator and Gaelic American* (New York) Aug. 22, page 2.

McIlvaine, Mabel
    1915   *Reminiscences of Chicago during the Great Fire.* Chicago: Lakeside Press.

Merriam, Alan
    1964   *The Anthropology of Music.* Evanston, Ill.: Northwestern University Press.

Mills, Joe
    1976   "Aughrim Slopes Céilí Band", *Treoir* (Dublin) 8(5)16-17.

Moloney, Michael
    1975   "Medicine for Life: A Study of a Folk Composer and His Music", *Keystone Folklore* (Philadelphia) 20(1-2):5-37.

Morton, Robin
    1973   *Come Day, God Day, God Send Sunday.* London: Routledge and Kegan Paul.

Murphy, M.J.
    1893   "Irish Character Actors", *Chicago Citizen*, Sept. 30, page 1.

Neale, John and William
    1726   *A Collection of the Most Celebrated Irish Tunes for the Violin, German Flute, or Hautboy.* Dublin: J. and W. Neale.

Nettl, Bruno
    1962   *An Introduction to Folk Music in the United States.* Detroit: Wayne State University Press.

Niehaus, Earl F.
    1964   "Paddy on the Local Stage and in Humour: The Image of the Irish in New Orleans, 1830-1852", *Louisiana History* 5(1):117-134.

Ó Ceallaigh, Proinsias
    1963   "The Tunes of the Munster Poets", *Ceol* (Dublin) 1(1):11-12.

O'Daly, Máirín
    1969   "The Metrical Dindshenchas", in *Early Irish Poetry.* ed. James Carney. Cork: Mercier Press, 59-72.

Ó Duibhir, Seán
    1972   "The Concertina", *Treoir* (Dublin) 4(4):16-19.

Ó hEidhin, P.
    1977   "Paddy Slattery (1887-1977)", *Treoir* (Dublin) 9(4):25.

Ó Murchu, Luai
    1977   "Then Here's Their Memory", *Treoir* (Dublin) 9(1):20-21.

O'Neill, Barry
    1973   "Introduction", in *Irish Minstrels and Musicians*, by Francis O'Neill. Reprint. Darby, Pa.: Norwood Editions.

O'Neill, Francis
    1903   *The Music of Ireland.* Chicago: Lyon and Healy.

    1907   *The Dance Music of Ireland, 1001 Gems.* Chicago: Lyon and Healy.

    1910   *Irish Folk Music: A Fascinating Hobby.* Chicago: Lyon and Healy.

    1913   *Irish Minstrels and Musicians.* Chicago: Lyon and Healy.

    1922   *Waifs and Strays of Gaelic Melody.* Chicago: Lyon and Healy.

Ó Riada, Seán
    1965   "In Memoriam: Sonny Brogan", *Ceol* (Dublin) 2(1):5.

Ó Súilleabháin, Micheál
    1974   "The Bodhrán", *Treoir* (Dublin) 6(2):4-7.

O'Sullivan, Donal
    1927   *The Bunting Collection or Irish Folk Music and Songs.* London: Irish Folk Song Society.

    1952   *Irish Folk Music, Song, and Dance.* Cork: Mercier Press.

    1958   *Carolan: The Life, Times, and Music of an Irish Harper.* London: Routledge and Kegan Paul.

O'Sullivan, John
    1976   "A Kilkenny Minstrel", *Treoir* (Dublin) 8(5):5.

Petrie, George
    1855   *Ancient Music of Ireland.* Dublin: H.H. Gill.

Pierce, Bessie
    1937a   *A History of Chicago, Volume 1.* New York: Alfred Knopf.

    1937b   *A History of Chicago, Volume 3.* New York: Alfred Knopf.

Reavy, Edward
    1971   *Where the Shannon Rises.* Philadelphia: Joseph Reavy.

Richardson, Philip J.S.
    1960   *The Social Dances of the Nineteenth Century in England.* London: Herbert Jenkins.

Rimmer, Joan
    1969   *The Irish Harp.* Cork: Mercier Press.

Roche, Francis
    1927   *The Roche Collection of Irish Music, Volume 3.* Dublin: Piggott and Company.

Ross, Anne
    1970   *Everyday Life of the Pagan Celts.* London: B.T. Batsford.

Ryan, Paddy
    1975   "Jim Moran of Kilberry", *Treoir* (Dublin) 7(1):20-21.

Sears, Roebuck, and Company
    1902   *Catalogue.* Chicago: Sears, Roebuck, and Company.

Stebbins, Robert
    1968   "A Theory of the Jazz Community", *Sociological Quarterly* 9(3):318-331.

    1969   "Role Distance, Role Distance Behavior, and Jazz Musicians", *British Journal of Sociology* 20(4):406-415.

Townsend, Declan
    1971   "The Origin and Early History of the Irish Jig," *Éire-Ireland* (St. Paul, Minn.), 6(2):59-65.

Treoir
    1977   "Fleadh Winners," *Treoir* (Dublin) 9(4):3-7.

Ui Sheathruin, Éilis
    1976   "The Maestro from Ballyseskin", *Treoir* (Dublin) 8(3):22-23.

Unton, George P. and James W. Sheahan
    1871   *The Great Conflagration.* Chicago: Union Press.

Wakin, Edward
    1976   *Enter the Irish-American.* New York: Thomas Y. Crowell.

Walker, Joseph
    1786   *Historical Memoirs of the Irish Bards.* Dublin: J. Christie.

Wittke, Carl
    1952   "The Immigrant Theme on the American Stage", *Mississippi Valley Historical Review* 39:211-232.

Wright, Daniel
    1728   *Aria Di Camera.* London: D. Wright.

~ ABOUT THE AUTHOR ~

L.E. McCullough, Ph.D. has been an active organizer of Arts and non-profit community ventures since 1973, helping thousands of other Artists achieve their dreams and market their artistry to the world.

* More information about What he's done for Who, Where, When and Why:

    www.lemccullough.com

    www.lemccullough.weebly.com

    www.educationalclassroomplays.com

    www.lawrencemccullough.blogspot.com

    www.lemcculloughswhistleblog.wordpress.com

    www.linkedin.com/in/l-e-mccullough-3812a1127

Currently, Dr. McCullough lives in Woodbridge, New Jersey, and is married to the actress and Interfaith minister **Rev. Lisa Bansavage**, with whom he operates an educational film and theatre organization, Pages of History, Inc. (**www.pagesofhistory.org**).

www.ingramcontent.com/pod-product-compliance
Lightning Source LLC
Chambersburg PA
CBHW081454040426

42446CB00016B/3235